Historians in Public

Historians
in Public

The Practice of American History, 1890–1970

Ian Tyrrell

The University of Chicago Press
Chicago & London

Ian Tyrrell is professor in the School of History at the University of New South Wales in Sydney, Australia. He is the author of five previous books, including *Sobering Up: From Temperance to Prohibition in Antebellum America*.

The University of Chicago Press, Chicago, 60637
The University of Chicago Press, Ltd., London
© 2005 by The University of Chicago
All rights reserved. Published 2005
Printed in the United States of America
14 13 12 11 10 09 08 07   5 4 3 2

ISBN (cloth): 0-226-82193-5
ISBN (paper): 0-226-82194-3

Library of Congress Cataloging-in-Publication Data

Tyrrell, Ian R.
  Historians in public : the practice of American history, 1890–1970 / Ian Tyrrell.
      p.   cm.
  Includes bibliographical references and index.
  ISBN 0-226-82193-5 (cloth : alk. paper) — ISBN 0-226-82194-3 (alk. paper)
    1. Historiography—United States—History—20th century. 2. United States—Historiography. 3. Historians—United States—History—20th century. 4. Historians—United States—Political activity—History—20th century. 5. Historiography—Social aspects—United States—History—20th century. 6. Historiography—Political aspects—United States—History—20th century. 7. Public history—United States—History— 20th century. 8. Popular culture—United States—History—20th century.
  I. Title.
  E175.T975   2005
  973'.072'073—dc22

                                                              2005003459

♾ The paper used in this publication meets the minimum requirements of the American National Standard for Information Sciences—Permanence of Paper for Printed Library Materials, ANSI Z39.48-1992

To Dear Clio,
A Muse
My Muse

CONTENTS

ACKNOWLEDGMENTS

The writer of any academic work, especially one in gestation for as long as this book, incurs many debts. Roy Rosenzweig read the entire manuscript and made many helpful suggestions, as did David Thelen; the late Paul Bourke read parts of the manuscript in draft; Tom Bender provided vital feedback at key points in the writing; Michael Birkner, of Gettysburg College, generously shared his own notes, some copies of papers of Richard Hofstadter, and his views on Allan Nevins. William Rorabaugh hosted my visit to Seattle and provided his typically perceptive views on American historiography.

Thanks go to the participants in the Organization of American Historians—New York University Conference on Internationalizing American History (La Pietra conference, 2000), especially Marilyn Young, Colleen Dunlavy, David Hollinger, Dirk Hoerder, Molly Nolan, and François Weil. The seminar organized at the Institute for Social History in Amsterdam in 1998 by David Thelen for a special issue of the *Journal of American History* allowed me to air some of my views on American historians, and I benefited there from comments by Robin Kelley, Richard White, and others. The one-day conference hosted by Tony Badger at Cambridge University that followed soon after was equally helpful.

Advice, help, or encouragement was given at one time or another by many people, including David Kennedy, Ellen DuBois, Jim Gilbert, the late Martin Ridge, Peter Novick, Thomas Pressly,

Robert Skotheim, and David Engerman. Conversations with many others, especially Carl Guarneri, were invaluable. Bill Chafe and Richard Searle aided my visit to Durham, North Carolina. Cheers to all those who listened to and/or commented on my papers at the Johns Hopkins University Department of History seminar, March 2001. For that occasion, I thank especially Dorothy Ross for her encouragement and Ronald Walters for his perceptive and encouraging critique. Equally valuable were audiences at the Australian and New Zealand American Studies Association biennial conferences in 1992, 1998, 2000, and 2004; and at the 2003 Staff Seminar, School of History, University of New South Wales. A special debt of gratitude goes to Michael Henderson, who served for nearly two years as a research assistant of uncommon ability; and to the Australian Research Council for an indispensable Large Grant, 1999–2001, to fund the research and travel.

As usual, librarians provided vital aid at the Bancroft Library, University of California, Berkeley; Library of Congress; William R. Perkins Library, Duke University; John F. Kennedy Library, Boston; Harvard University Archives; Manuscripts and Archives, Yale University Library; Department of Special Collections, Stanford University Libraries; Department of Special Collections, University of Washington Libraries; Indiana University–Purdue University Library, Indianapolis; Columbia University Archives; Rare Books and Manuscripts, Butler Library, Columbia University; Huntington Library, San Marino, California; Northwestern University Library; National Library of Australia; University of New South Wales Library; State Library of New South Wales; Fisher Library, Sydney University; and the British Library, London. For research I also heartily thank the Alderman Library, Rare Book and Manuscript Collection, University of Virginia; the State Historical Society of Wisconsin; and the Library of the American Philosophical Society. Arthur Schlesinger Jr. kindly gave permission to consult his father's manuscripts.

An earlier version of chapter 2 first appeared as "The Great Historical Jeremiad: The Problem of Specialization in American Historiography," in *History Teacher* 33 (May 2000), 371–93, © Society for History Education. Used with permission.

Many thanks also go to my editor, Doug Mitchell, and his assistant, Tim McGovern, and to my meticulous copy editor, Pamela Bruton. Lyn Stump, School of History, University of New South Wales, gave valuable administrative aid in the final stage of preparing the manuscript. My family have had to endure another book, but I hope they will all be as pleased with the results as I am with their support over these many years. I have also greatly benefited from membership in that remarkable community of scholars in the Australian and New Zealand American Studies Association. Viva ANZASA! And to Clio, eternally.

ABBREVIATIONS

AASLH	American Association for State and Local History
AHA	American Historical Association
AHR	*American Historical Review*
ASNLH	Association for the Study of Negro Life and History
BBC	British Broadcasting Corporation
CAHSC	Committee on American History in the Schools and Colleges
CBS	Columbia Broadcasting System
CEEB	College Entrance Examination Board
CNN	Cable News Network
CPI	Committee on Public Information
CWA	Civil Works Administration
DAS	*Directory of American Scholars*
FWP	Federal Writers' Project
GPO	Government Printing Office, Washington, DC
HBC	History Book Club
HO	*The Historical Outlook*
HRS	Historical Records Survey
JAH	*Journal of American History*
LC	Library of Congress, Manuscripts Department
MVHA	Mississippi Valley Historical Association
MVHR	*Mississippi Valley Historical Review*
NAACP	National Association for the Advancement of Colored People

NAM	National Association of Manufacturers
NAW	*Notable American Women*
NBC	National Broadcasting Company
NBHS	National Board for Historical Service
NCPH	National Council on Public History
NCSS	National Council for the Social Studies
NEA	National Education Association
NEH	National Endowment for the Humanities
NHMC	National Historical Manuscripts Commission
NPS	National Park Service
NR	*New Republic*
NYHT	*New York Herald Tribune*
NYT	*New York Times*
NYTBR	*New York Times Book Review*
OSS	Office of Strategic Services
OWI	Office of War Information
PEA	Progressive Education Association
PW	*Publishers Weekly*
PWA	Public Works Administration
SAH	Society of American Historians
SAT	Scholastic Aptitude Test
SE	*Social Education*
SHSW	State Historical Society of Wisconsin
SHSW-COS	State Historical Society of Wisconsin—Correspondence with Other Societies
SHSW-NOC	State Historical Society of Wisconsin—National Organization Correspondence
SRL	*Saturday Review of Literature*
SS	*The Social Studies*
UDC	United Daughters of the Confederacy
USDA	United States Department of Agriculture
WPA	Works Progress/Projects Administration

Finding History in a Queue

I am standing in a line at San Francisco International Airport wait-
ing to go through security. In my baggage I carry a computer with
notes taken upon the topic of American historians and their public
audiences. I have been researching, among other things, the impact of Thomas Bailey and Edgar E. Robinson, both professors at
Stanford in the 1930s to 1950s. I strike up a conversation with an elderly man. I tell him a little bit about my topic, in response to his
questions about who I am and what I do. In a remarkable coinci-
dence, he turns out to be a former undergraduate student of both
Robinson's and Bailey's and remembered Robinson fondly as a
good teacher. In view of my interest in American historians' public audiences, he asks me what I think of Stephen Ambrose, one of
America's best-selling historians. In my briefcase I carry reports on
an accusation of plagiarism that had been leveled against Ambrose.[1] My new acquaintance finds this accusation "petty" and
launches into an attack on the narrowness of academic life. Just as
quickly as we meet, our paths diverge. He heads off toward his
plane, and I toward mine. I feel gratified by this encounter and the
lively debate we have had. As I endure the long flight back to Australia, I am able to reflect upon other encounters I have had with
American history's audiences and public discourse.

Conversing in an airport queue was not the main way that I
had experienced history during this trip. Rather, the mass media
defined my encounters. One story on PBS's *NewsHour with Jim*

1

Lehrer stressed the muse of historical writing in the work of William Manchester. Roger Rosenblatt saluted the career of Manchester, a nonacademic with a formidable reputation and a life history made poignant by the incapacitation of a stroke. That was not all. From the considerable dross emanating from the History Channel and its accounts of past crimes, scandals (with tales of Jackie Kennedy jostling with those on the Hatfields and the McCoys), and other weird and wonderful human-interest stories, I turned to a CNN piece about George W. Bush and the historians that he allegedly read. CNN was interviewing Jay Winik, author of *April 1865*, and Edmund Morris, author of *Theodore Rex*. Winik opined that the events of April 1865 represented another great crisis in American history comparable to 9/11 and that President Bush would take sustenance from the way these events were handled. Morris drew parallels between TR and President Bush. Both faced the challenges of power galvanized by the arbitrary events of terrorism: one in the form of an assassin's bullet in 1901 that claimed the life of Roosevelt's predecessor, the other by the most terrible single terrorist attack in American history.[2] History was alive and well in the American media.

The common thread among these (and many other) fragments I observed is the way history remains a critical part of American public discourse, and one on which many people have opinions. By their own repeated admission, academic historians claim to be marginalized in this discourse. In his presidential address to the Organization of American Historians in 2001, Kenneth T. Jackson reaffirmed the popular belief in "the weakness of a profession," claiming: "Over the past thirty years, historians have seen their job prospects shrink and their job security erode. Both the sales of scholarly history books and the number of undergraduate history majors have fallen."[3]

Yet these are jeremiads. In this book I will argue that the threat to history is a recurrent, exaggerated, and often misunderstood one and that history has adapted to and influenced its changing publics more than the profession is given credit for, though not evenly and not always in ways that are readily apparent. Evidence of historical scholarship's declining influence cannot be easily confirmed, for example, by claims of falling book sales. As will be shown, historians have been exaggerating their irrelevance to reading audiences for generations. Even for the contemporary period the facts are more complicated than a simple story of decline. Scholarly publishing of history has grown, not diminished, in the last decade, and although average sales of monographs have fallen due to decreasing library orders, university press history books still have a wider appeal than books in many other disciplines. Robert Townsend, who has studied these matters more intensively than anybody else, concludes that "the large proportion of titles being produced in his-

tory has a good financial rationale, as the field enjoys unusual success in
to a wider audience."[4]

Lest I be accused of adopting the role of Dr. Pangloss, let me make clear
that there is a vast territory of historical consciousness that academic works
neither tap nor address. This territory is indicated in the History Channel's
success, whatever the quality or scope of its programming. Launched in 1995,
the channel has over 83 million American subscribers.[5] It is also true that for
knowledge of the past, the public and the media often turn to nonacademic
sources. Neither Morris nor Winik are professional historians, and Ambrose
(who died later in 2002) was a former professor whose work stressed positive,
noble, and heroic stories, often of individuals, and was far removed in pace and
style from most academic history. Rosenblatt interestingly harked back to
Arthur Schlesinger Jr.'s *The Age of Jackson* for evidence that historians had hit
the heights displayed in the prose of Manchester before. Though Schlesinger
had long stints as an academic historian, he is remembered more as the presidential assistant to John F. Kennedy and as a popular interpreter of the president and his legacy. All these figures are well known, and recognition of Ambrose extended into the queue at San Francisco airport.

Yet it was interesting to me that my informant in that queue remembered
his teachers of the 1940s and their influence even though their work had long
been superseded or forgotten by the profession. This fragment backed my
hunch that there was more substance to the public role of professional historians than is apparent from contemporary discourse on the state of American
history, with its jeremiad of declining student knowledge and professional influence. At least some contemporary evidence supports my contention. Such
academic historians as Alan Brinkley, Douglas Brinkley, Patricia Nelson Lim-
erick, Simon Schama, and James McPherson commonly figure in the mass media as writers, commentators, consultants, and newspaper columnists at the
turn of the twenty-first century.

The conflicting evidence on the role of history in the American present is
difficult to evaluate without the deeper perspective that the discipline of history rightly favors. With this book I ask historians—and the interested public
and pressure groups—to take a step back and examine the earlier history of
these debates. This study will look at the cycles of public involvement of academics, charting their ups and downs; it will provide the context missing from
contemporary debates and seek explanations for historians' influence, or lack
thereof, over long periods of time. The subjects of my study are chiefly Americans writing on their own history, not those who specialize in other histories.
Yet cross-fertilization between American historians of the United States and
those of Europe, for example, was frequent until after World War II. Though

different groups of regional and national specialists have distinctive relationships to the topics under discussion, they also share common patterns of training, historical practice, and wider institutional and political influences—especially in the American Historical Association and through the important topic of history education in the schools. These circumstances make it neither possible nor desirable to avoid the case of non-Americanists entirely.

I had long ago decided to write a study on American academic historians and their audiences and cannot claim that my recent encounters with the public or its mass media have spurred dramatic new insights. Despite current harangues over history's failings, after completing this study I am even more certain that American academic historians have developed strong traditions of intervention in public debate and have long exerted influence, both direct and indirect, over American historical thinking and memory. These traditions took shape from the turn of the century to the 1950s. Over that period, historians did not in any uniform way argue that they could or should remain in an ivory tower, study history for its own sake, or pursue the dream of objectivity above all else. Rather, they much more persistently pursued the aim of making "use" of history—of showing the utility of history, academically speaking, for American public life and discourse. They were what I call "history makers," making history in both senses of the term.

This record of engagement has always been uneven and subject to ebbs and flows; yet despite changes, the historical profession established important elements of continuity in professional practice that have come down to our own time and bequeathed resources and traditions on which we still draw. The aspiration to write for a wider audience was never lost, though from the 1960s on, this ambitious project to reach out to public audiences became more complicated. Part of this complex story involves the legacy of the New Left. Though in some ways breaking with liberal history and Progressivism and criticizing the historians of the 1950s as elitist supporters of the state, the New Left displayed continuity by drawing on a legacy of concern for public relevance. Historiography continued to engage key social and political issues. Although desires to create a "useful" history had to compete with the growing possibilities of purely academic activity in the 1970s and 1980s, concern for the public usefulness of history had reemerged by the 1990s. This underlying pattern was not simply the product of individual will or high-mindedness. Useful history has stronger and deeper roots.

Professional demands, institutional changes within universities, and outside political pressures have tended to make American historians acutely aware of wider publics. These conditions first coalesced in the early years of

the twentieth century. Then, Progressive historiography found a congenial social and political climate for its efforts. Competition between state and private
universities, the geographical decentralization of the university system, and
the development of powerful pressures within and upon the state universities
made historians responsive to diverse publics and facilitated considerable innovation in history making. At the same time, this institutional pattern favored moderate reform rather than radicalism and revolutionary breaks in historical practice or political positions.[6] The larger political circumstances of
depression, war, and the growth of the American state also contributed to
pragmatic and often populist and utilitarian patterns of history making. Professional expertise could be put to work in government programs to further
democratic aims congruent with Progressive scholarship.

* * *

In writing this book I was able to build upon the work of historians who have
written impressively upon aspects of this topic. Michael Kammen, in *Mystic
Chords of Memory*, charted public and popular meanings of history principally
since the 1870s.[7] My study differs from Kammen's in focusing on academic initiatives rather than a broader consciousness. Within that context, I give greater
emphasis to historians' connections with government. I show in the pages that
follow that American historians became increasingly attached to "the state"
and often saw the state as a way of expanding the influence of history, but the
American federal state's practices differed from state manipulation in many
other countries. Insofar as historical memory has been depoliticized in the
United States, I emphasize that depoliticization itself is a political process, the
product of ideology and power. The study will highlight, for example, political
and ideological influences on school curricula and document how academic
historians both criticized and complied with the broader political pressures
upon them in teaching and in the emerging subdiscipline of public history devoted to such work as museums, archives, and government service.

A work of equal significance is Peter Novick's *That Noble Dream*.[8] Novick
complements Kammen nicely by focusing on the discourse of academic history. He argues that historians have pursued their professionalizing and Scientific History since the 1880s. Over that time, their debates have come to have
less and less to do with popular history, though this is not a central subject of
his narrative. In making his imposing case, Novick concentrates heavily on the
professional elite. He has less to say about activities where historians were
most likely to connect with wider audiences and where we might see history

not as a remote professional discourse but rather as involved with everyday history making. Novick gives relatively little attention to the attempts of academic historians to work with local and state history groups and institutions, efforts to influence the content of mass media, or early initiatives before the 1960s to develop public history expertise in government. While Novick no more than Kammen directly tackles the questions I am posing, these two broad syntheses of academic history and vernacular historical consciousness together provide an excellent starting point for connecting professional concerns with popular audiences and public memory.

Since Novick and Kammen wrote, American historians have begun to take the study of historical practice more seriously than before. Works by John Bodnar and David Blight have emphasized the importance of public memory and the role of interest groups and governments in the processes of remembering and forgetting.[9] Further studies of popular historical consciousness by David Thelen and Roy Rosenzweig, among others, reveal the richness of that field as a context for academic historians' outreach.[10] Gary Nash and others have explored the historical roots of the contemporary crisis over historical knowledge in the schools in illuminating detail.[11] Ellen Fitzpatrick has shown that academic history was, at least on the understudied margins of the profession, diverse and, by implication, more serious in its efforts to reach wider publics.[12] Several works have begun to reveal, though mostly for the contemporary period, the efforts of historians to connect with new media. Others are giving attention to the lineages of public history.[13] Yet these works supplant neither Kammen nor Novick in their scope.

As part of the attack on the alleged aloofness of the ivory tower academics, the whole question of the role of intellectuals in politics and of academic intellectuals as public and political figures has also received greater attention in recent years. The broad categories of narrow expert versus public critic of the social order have been canvassed; and the decline of advocacy in favor of professional neutrality has been explored and deplored. Yet for the period in question, these terms seem misplaced polarities. American historians tried to work as both scholarly experts and as advocates, linking these types together. The position was not quite the same as Antonio Gramsci's dream of a hegemonic alliance of new "organic" intellectuals with emerging social classes and elements of the "traditional" intellectual functionaries but operated along similar lines through the social practice of academics and their ties to institutions reflecting and promoting a Progressive reform ideology. Historians' attempts to juggle these shifting and contradictory roles came under pressure in the 1950s and 1960s along with the social institutions and political ideas that sustained the earlier work. In those decades the recognizably modern American practice of history was born.[14]

* * *

I have approached this book as a set of essays that can be read as separate narratives of American historians' engagement with audiences. I have done this because there has never been any one general public to which historians could have responded. Rather, historians have faced at least three broad categories of audience, and those audiences themselves have not been static. The first was the potentially "mass" audience of "general" readers, film and television watchers, and radio listeners. From the 1910s to the 1970s, historians displayed considerable interest in connecting with and making their professional work relevant to such audiences, who they defined as part of mass culture. Second, historians dealt with the more structured and almost "captive" audience of schools and colleges. Gradually, though unevenly, they lost control, for complicated reasons, of curricula in the high schools. Few academics challenged elementary school teaching, except by implication, while most remained interested in university teaching throughout the period under investigation. It was at the level of high schools that most opportunities to influence a wider public came, since this was the last time many Americans from the 1910s to the 1950s would study American and world history. Third, historians faced the institutional structures of the state and (occasionally) private corporations in marketing history as a discipline relevant to state legitimation and public policy. The origins of public history can be found here, but the story has never been told in depth. It encompasses the origins of applied history, strong links with both state and federal governments, the professionalization of state and local historical practice, and the maturation of a history centered on the nation-state by the 1940s and 1950s. In short, historians have—despite the mythology—long been engaged with public audiences, but the particular audiences engaged have changed over time. In this book I lay out the different relationships and temporal rhythms for the multiple audiences discussed.

One can generalize and say that these interconnected practices linking diverse publics and historians had a particular trajectory. Before the 1950s, those scholars interested in public outreach and relevance were informed by new and dynamic approaches to history. Progressive historiographical trends made connecting with wider audiences easier than in subsequent periods because of the focus on the democratization of learning; on the utility of history for civic responsibility, rational argument, and empirical analysis; on philosophical

pragmatism; and on a national narrative of progress based on clashing political, economic, and social interests. However, concern over fragmentation
clearly began in these decades of Progressivism, too. Historians before the
1950s experienced the same pressures of specialization as later, but they used
the Progressive project to provide a largely coherent paradigm within which
to engage a variety of audiences and shape historiography on different levels.

The record suggests that the contemporary debate wrongly labels professionalization and specialization as the root causes of a perceived public irrelevance of history. The Progressives were both professional historians *and* advocates of outreach and public relevance. Moreover, their tradition of mixing
scholarship and wider involvement in reformist groups and institutions provides a useful model. It is one of historians working not as elitist public intellectuals, though there is a place for that, too, but rather as scholars reflecting
and shaping historical consciousness in university and public service. This tradition locates historians within the social formations and institutions of their
time. The record of past involvements of this type indicates that historians
need to be reflexive in their historical practice and should pay close attention
to changes in intellectual and institutional settings. Historians today cannot
follow the prescriptions of the past, but they ought to be more aware of them
and of the achievements accomplished under their rubric, lest they try to re-
invent the wheel. That degree of self-examination and circumspection would
give current debates the depth and context that they frequently lack and might
caution historians against some of the pitfalls that older generations of historians experienced in trying to make their histories useful—at a time when professional historians are desperately trying to reengage with public audiences.
To that attempt, its causes, and the lacunas in the discussion over the fragmentation of history we now turn.

Part 1

THE BROKEN MIRROR

1

What's Wrong with History?

The Contemporary Context

Allegiance to the United States is based, so the nation's founding myth goes, on ideas and beliefs. What links Americans together is not the ethnic, religious, or cultural origins of its citizenry but a shared civic culture. Those ideas require a particular reading of history—a collective memory. In the 1990s, the fabric of the collective identity appeared to many observers to be badly frayed, and historians seemed to be responsible. On 2 May 1998 the *New York Times* carried a story about a new national organization called the Historical Society. The founders included Eugene Genovese, a prominent Marxist of the 1960s, and a number of supporters representing both the Left and the Right of the political spectrum. These reformers aimed to "revitalize the study and teaching of history by reorienting the profession toward an accessible, integrated history." Not only did the move reflect academic disquiet over the perceived "fragmentation" of the discipline; the "culture wars" of the 1990s were joined to this theme to explain history's failure of duty. Genovese and his allies gave the impression that "fragmentation and over-specialization" were associated with "the politics of race and sex, a reliance on theory instead of evidence," and "rampant navel-gazing," an inward-turning impulse at odds with the spirit of free inquiry. The *New York Times* quoted the strident definition that the now-conservative Genovese gave to the identity politics of history: "the attempt to impose a particular ideological line and to compartmentalize" history so that it becomes a search for self-expression "rather than dealing with objective reality." Claiming the need for tolerance of differing opinions, Genovese lamented bitterly the apparent intolerance of his opponents. "These people are all for diversity, but if you don't take their line, forget it." The Historical Society and some supporters writing in 1999 in a flagship publication, *Reconstructing History*, attacked forms of multiculturalism that they claimed had verged on ethnic particularism, where truths were incommensurate and where claims were made for exclusive knowledge.[1]

Though the idea of a new national historical society supported by well-known academics was newsworthy, the criticisms leveled by that society were far from novel. The previous ten years had seen an increasingly shrill debate over political correctness, cultural fragmentation, and the sins of multiculturalism. This contemporary discourse was superficially like an onion: several distinct layers could be peeled off before the heart of the matter was revealed (and the peeling process was discomforting to the participants). At least three major layers were present: the dangers of multiculturalism and cultural fragmentation, the problem of academic specialization, and the professionalization of history and a concomitant academic distance from the public. Unlike the onion, however, these layers were not truly separate. Their interconnections and their origins need to be established. Glib though the contemporary arguments have often been, the deeper we probe, the more intricate and historically conditioned the problems appear.

Not only was the contemporary debate complex and confused, but it was also cumulative in effect. Criticism built upon criticism in the 1980s and 1990s to erode, apparently, the position of history in American culture and the role of professional historians as custodians of that culture. The attacks on multiculturalism were repeatedly linked to the state of historical knowledge among the general public. Commentators averred that knowledge of the history of the United States, its traditions, and its institutions was vital for national identity and social stability. A number, including Diane Ravitch, a contributor to *Reconstructing History*, had already in the 1980s declared deficient the knowledge that American youths had of their nation's past. They attacked the school history curriculum for promoting ignorance of great and powerful white men whose contributions were thought to be essential to the American creed. Finding the humanities wanting as a whole, E. D. Hirsch and Allan Bloom denounced cultural illiteracy and promoted ideas of a cultural canon.[2]

The main issues for public debate were political correctness and the survival of core political and moral values. To conservatives and even liberals, the study of minority groups and new ways of interpreting history fragmented the discipline and thereby undermined its role in the making of a citizenry's common culture. There was, put simply, too much *pluribus* and not enough *unam* left in American memory. Genovese's attack was one of several assaults on the allegedly divisive and particularistic impacts of multiculturalism in the 1990s. In 1993 historian Arthur Schlesinger Jr. criticized the failure to integrate minority history into a unified national story. In *The Disuniting of America*, Schlesinger defended the mainstream liberal tradition and attacked what he believed was a growing emphasis on ethnic separatism in school and college history curricula, which substituted for the shared history of "our national experience, in our great national documents, in our national heroes, in our folkways, traditions, and standards," a dismal and dangerous alternative. This was "the fragmentation of the national community into a quarrelsome spatter of enclaves, ghettoes, tribes."[3]

Schlesinger felt that these multicultural approaches could not be sufficiently critical and that it was necessary for multiculturalism's adherents to overstress the significance of their subjects and put a positive gloss upon minority cultures. This was close, in the view of some, to the ancestor worship of patriotic and genealogical societies. As Schlesinger put it, "Let us by all means teach black history, African history, women's history, Hispanic history, Asian history. But let us teach them as history, not as filiopietistic commemoration." Minority histories should be "integrated into the curriculum too." He also linked attacks on multiculturalism to the very survival of Western civilization. Schlesinger felt that "Western values" were essential to American democracy and required American unity for their transnational preservation. Both Europe and the non-European world had had their crimes, but Europe had been the source of the central liberating ideals of political democracy, the rule of law, and great movements such as the abolition of slavery. "Freedom of inquiry and of artistic creation" were central to this tradition and were threatened by multiculturalism, which exerted thought control through its policy of political correctness.[4]

When such critics pronounced history under threat, the attention they gave to the subject revealed its deep importance in American life. History became a controversial media topic because of these debates. A headline in *Time* magazine stated, "When a nation's diversity breaks into factions, demagogues rush in, false issues cloud debate, and everybody has a grievance." Art critic and *Time* contributor Robert Hughes sought to champion a liberal and tolerant center ground against the new intolerance of Left and Right over the issue of political correctness. At both ends of the political spectrum, he argued, cultural ideologues asserted their particularistic visions for America. While political correctness involved a number of disciplines, Hughes recognized the central role of history, claiming, "It's in the area of history that PC has scored its largest successes."[5]

Feeding the issue of political correctness and reflecting its importance in popular historical memory was the Columbian Quincentenary celebration, which shone a searchlight upon the meaning of European settlement in the Americas.[6] In postcolonial discourse, "settlement" had become "invasion." *Time* noted the rise of insistent radical views that deprecated the reputation of Columbus and highlighted the "Eurocentric theft of history."[7] The drastic demographic and ecological consequences of Columbus's "discovery" of the Americas were graphically portrayed in Kirkpatrick Sale's *The Conquest of Paradise: Christopher Columbus and the Columbian Legacy* (1990). The "first anti-Columbus book to achieve national attention," Sale's work heralded a rash of critical assessments of 1492 and its long-term implications, some scholarly, others highly polemic. These depictions of European settlement's genocidal impacts politicized the Quincentenary and provoked a conservative backlash. Robert Hughes derisorily dismissed Sale's work as "a current PC book,"[8] while conservative writer Russell Kirk denounced "whining radicals." The National Endowment for the Humanities' (NEH) conservative Republican chair Lynne Cheney weighed in, and funding was withdrawn for a television documentary on the Spanish conquistadors.[9]

These were essentially nonexpert debates over multiculturalism conducted in the media. Academics had already been forging their own version of the jeremiad about history, but their focus was on specialization rather than multiculturalism. Kenneth Jackson and other academics associated with the Bradley Commission on History in Schools, appointed in 1987 to survey the state of history teaching, argued that historians had lost their students because their interpretations had become too specialized. In *Historical Literacy* (1989), Jackson and his collaborators sought to turn the controversy over cultural literacy and knowledge of the canon to the advantage of history, which was perceived to have lost out to the social sciences and softer options in high schools and colleges. Among the contributions to *Historical Literacy,* several pointed to the internal, rather than the external, causes of the apparent rout of history by the 1970s. University of Chicago historian William H. McNeill noted, "Teachers found it exciting to teach the new kinds of history" on blacks, women, and the like. These courses "allowed them time to develop the new themes properly. It was less satisfying and much harder to combine old with new to make an inclusive, judiciously balanced (and far less novel) introductory course for high school and college students."[10]

The view that history had become fractured—a kind of broken mirror for viewing the past—gained support across most of the political spectrum of opinion within academic history. Senior scholars with liberal credentials such as C. Vann Woodward had already commented in the 1980s on the growing "fragmentation" of American scholarship. Once "a habitation of many mansions," history as a discipline had become "scattered suburbs, trailer camps, and a deteriorating central city."[11] Social history, thought by some to be at the root of the problem, had proliferated in the 1970s and produced strident attacks, including one by Eugene Genovese and Elizabeth Fox-Genovese. Eminent historians called for a return to either narrative history or the politics of history or both.[12]

The first major academic stocktaking of this debate came in 1986–87. New York University historian Thomas Bender called for a reintegration of American history around the concept of a public culture, drawing in part upon the older example of Charles Beard for inspiration.[13] Bender sought to incorporate new specialized histories through a critical debate, and his ideas attracted considerable attention. In both the *American Historical Review* and the *Journal of American History*, controversy raged over whether American history had become too specialized, esoteric, and narrow.

Yet the response from academics showed how fractured the profession had become and thus fueled perceptions of a weak and retreating discipline. Most historians respectfully debated the concept of a public culture and lamented specialization—but provided no new convincing synthesis. Some rejoiced instead over the diversity of American historical interpretation.[14] In a long review article in the *Journal of American History*, Wayne Urban dismissed the claims of Ravitch, Hirsch, and Bloom concerning cultural chaos and declension.[15] Evidence that many American historians recognized their inability to transcend the confines of specialization came in Peter Novick's *That Noble Dream* (1988), where, with a slight tone of resignation, he proclaimed that "there was no king in Israel."[16] *That Noble Dream* received great attention, but by and large commentators did not propose synthesis as the answer to the state of the profession as characterized by Novick. They concentrated instead on debating the implications for historical knowledge seen to be implicit in postmodernist approaches to history.[17]

Postmodernism's high tide of impact in the 1980s made it harder to get a serious hearing for opponents of fragmentation. The boundaries between history and literary studies seemed almost to collapse, and historians served up to each other an ever-more-eclectic range of subspecializations and interpretations. As Richard W. Fox explained in replying to Bender, "more and more writers in our postmodern, poststructural era wonder if it makes sense even to try to decipher an independent external reality" such as "all-encompassing narrative syntheses."[18]

Postmodernism gelled with a residual belief among American historians that history belonged to the people. The language of Carl Becker—"Every-man His Own Historian"—suitably modified to include race, gender, and sex, had become a democratic calling card. Postmodernist influences brought historians closer to their audiences by facilitating the telling of diverse memories. The traditional urge of historians to study the particular and their support for empiricist theories backed up these claims, too. As Darrett Rutman explained, "What is wrong with the fact that we are a disparate lot?"[19] Live and let live seemed to be the message. Ironically, every proposal for a new synthesis added further voices to the Tower of Babel that American historiography had apparently become.

Yet another part of this debate in academic circles was about neither multiculturalism nor the fragmentation of scholarship but rather the problems of remoteness from the public that specialized study seemed to produce. From the left, Russell Jacoby in *The Last Intellectuals: American Culture in the Age of Academe* (1987) lamented the rise of universities as the center of intellectual activity and the subsequent decline of the public intellectual.[20] Instead of academics dominating their own self-contained discourses and writing for esoteric audiences, Jacoby called for a reengagement with big questions and disputed the argument that "a reading public may be no more." This line of thinking has been congenial to some supporters of the Historical Society. A key contribution to *Reconstructing History* revived this theme in 1999, attacking academic work in which minute disputes, arcane topics and fields, and formidable jargon froze out "the uninitiated." Elizabeth Lasch-Quinn's "Democracy in the Ivory Tower?" drew upon Jacoby's "eloquent" work to stress the "overprofessionalization" of history.[21]

The sins of the professionals also provided the theme for a celebrated lament in 1987 from University of Wisconsin historian Theodore Hamerow. In the *American Historical Review,* he denounced history's "bureaucratization." For Hamerow, the rise of professional scholarship was actually a story of deterioration and decline. Hamerow rued the bitter divide between academics and amateurs and argued that the program of the former produced the specialization that "led . . . to the growing estrangement between the broad educated public and the world of scholarship."[22] Further attacks on the overprofessionalization of American history brought the theme closer to the center of historical debate and involved leading officials in the professional associations. By 1990 several prominent figures began to investigate the gap that had appeared between professionals and public audiences for history. Academics, said Louis R. Harlan in a presidential address to the American Historical Association, are "increasingly out of touch with the real world." In Harlan's view, "public historians" had "generally done more than academic historians to serve and promote . . . popular interest in history."[23]

In the 1990s, some writers sought to show how divorced academic history had become from public memory and yet how attention to popular memory could reinvigorate the discipline. The *Journal of American History* in 1994 featured this theme in a special issue, and a book, *The Presence of the Past* (1998), written by the editor of the *Journal of American History*, David Thelen, and by Roy Rosenzweig, undertook the first systematic survey of American public attitudes toward "the past." Building upon studies of popular historical knowledge already undertaken by Michael Frisch and other historians associated with *Radical History Review*, this work provided, indirectly, ammunition for the attack on the professionals as divorced from public audiences by questioning the idea that the latter were not interested in history.[24]

The Presence of the Past was perhaps affected by postmodernism, but the late 1990s, in which this book appeared, saw signs of a waning of that influence. A resurgence in and defense of expert knowledge and professional qualifications could be detected. Books such as *Telling the Truth about History* appeared in the United States, and *In Defence of History* in Britain.[25] Historians absorbed postmodern influences, as Patrick Joyce has pointed out, but they did not succumb to postmodernism.[26] Indeed, relativism came under attack once more, the autonomy of academic knowledge was reasserted, and syntheses began to come back into fashion.[27]

These themes were evident in the reception of *The Presence of the Past*. At one level, the response suggested that the historical profession had changed. The shift of the academic profession to incorporate wider perspectives, including nonacademic ones, was indicated in the reviews. The *American Historical Review*, the nation's premier historical journal, assigned a public historian to write a review, indicating a flexibility within the profession and accommodation to nonuniversity views and also the growing importance of public history beyond the academy in the nation's history making. From such sources, the book received favorable reviews.[28]

On the other hand, even public historians emphasized the importance of professionals in mediating between audiences and historical knowledge.[29] Every (wo)man might be his or her own historian, but all views were not equal. Academics, too, expressed reservations centered on the need to preserve academic autonomy and objectivity. Some were prepared to reassert the importance of professional identities and practices in the wake of the culture wars. In a long review in *History and Theory*, Michael Kammen argued that Rosenzweig and Thelen appeared to confuse people's interest in or enthusiasm for "the past" with knowledge about history and concepts of historical change. Professing great sympathy with the writers' ambition that "history-making be an autonomous and participatory process," Kammen anticipated possible concerns of professional historians. Rosenzweig and Thelen seemed, Kammen believed, "at least implicitly, to be relativists in the sense that one interpretation or vision of the past is just about as acceptable as another, at least for laypersons."[30]

If supporters for reconnecting history with wider publics met criticism from within the profession for their apparent failure to recognize expertise, they also faced public attacks from without. That criticism showed that academic historians had much in common with one another, despite their differences. Oddly, the historians who wanted to stress outreach were the ones most likely to be condemned politically. This was because they were the ones to test their views with audiences, and because the public they faced was diverse and "public" debate a robustly contested arena. Within that space, some wielded more influence than others. Access to popular audiences was conditioned by political power. In the United States, this meant that elite and conservative interpretations of the American past often had greater, though not exclusive, purchase in such debates. Powerful political lobbies and their representatives were, to say the least, not sympathetic with the ideas of multicultural diversity that had become orthodox in American historiography since the 1970s. That historians appeared to be broadening their views on relations with public audiences did not help very much when their professional judgments came under political attack.[31]

Academic history's apparent public powerlessness was revealed in the National History Standards controversy. In response to the reputed ignorance of American history among most high school students revealed by Ravitch and others, in 1991 the U.S. government set up through the NEH a project to create for high school history a set of National History Standards.[32] Despite the conservative origins of the funding in the administration of President Bush, the project relied on respected and influential professional historians and educators for its work. These were led by Gary Nash, of the National Center for History Education at the University of California, Los Angeles. The academic response reflected the historical community's liberal and left-liberal tendencies and its penchant for supporting historiographical diversity. Unexceptional to most professional historians as they were, the standards came as something of a shock to politicians, whose knowledge of American history appeared to be derived from old school textbooks or movies. The (relative) absence of time-honored themes and great white men from the checklist of required knowledge sent a shudder through conservative ranks. A symbolic vote on the standards in the Senate condemned them in 1995 by ninety-nine to one (the one negative vote was even more condemnatory of the standards). With no federal funding forthcoming to support the standards, they remained simply recommendations for state consideration. The result indicated that the nation's politicians dismissed the new social and cultural history and seemed to anticipate the claims of the Historical Society that academic history was politically irrelevant.

A second case concerned the cancellation of the proposed *Enola Gay* exhibition at the Smithsonian Institution's National Museum of American History in January 1995—very close to the time when the standards had been dismissed. The museum's attempt to present a multidimensional story of the dropping of the first atomic bomb, including the effects of the bomb on Japanese civilians, produced a massive outcry, in which the American Legion and the Air Force Association were vocal. Forced to back down, the museum lost some of its aura of academic independence from the Washington political machinery. The planned exhibit on the *Enola Gay* was abandoned, and the aircraft itself simply displayed without commentary. Again, as in the National History Standards debate, attacks on the political correctness of academic historiography flooded the media. Academics were allegedly "unable to view American history as anything other than a woeful catalogue of crimes."[33] Popular patriotism and nationalism prevailed. Only a pro-American position could have been presented in the museum without criticism.

This rebuff represented a defeat for a complex approach to the American past that would be in line with the received wisdom of professional historiography. Historians who objected to the changes to the script carried "little weight," yet even a revised script could not deter the exhibit's cancellation.[34] The entire episode placed historians, said Tom Engelhardt and Edward Linenthal, as "unexpected players on a public stage. They found their work debated or attacked, misused and abused, and themselves accused of aiding and abetting the post–Vietnam War fragmentation of an American consensus." On this public stage, professional historians were "relatively powerless and unorganized" and easily targeted.[35] As a result, the impact of professional historiography on the growing public history movement also received a check. As former Air Force historian Richard Kohn emphasized, the cancellation of the exhibit was possibly "the worst tragedy to befall the public presentation of history in the United States in a generation."[36]

These reversals could be interpreted in different ways. Senators and lobbyists for patriotic organizations stressed the out-of-touch multiculturalism of academic historiography. To historians alienated from the professional consensus, the fault lay with the profession. Victor Hanson highlighted the "increasing distance between the academic and the muscular classes that staff the all-volunteer, mercenary armies," together with the absence of large wars in the West for half a century, which meant that contemporary historians knew little "about what war is really like."[37] To some professional historians seeking more democratic political participation, however, politicians had misrepresented popular feelings, which would have tolerated diversity of interpretation and critical insights over the *Enola Gay*.[38]

It was possible to argue that this case was not representative. Special circumstances had rendered more difficult the professional historians' task. The conservative majority attained in the 1994 congressional election, the Contract with America that followed, and a range of discontents that veterans' organizations had with the Smithsonian prior to that time contributed to the controversy. Discontent over multiculturalism was only one factor, but the implications of the profession's inability to influence political actions and hence to promote the cause of history teaching, research, and critical debate were obvious. Whether academics supported specialization or not, whether they were of the Left, the Center, or the Right, and whether they supported more or less professional authority, the Smithsonian case was of a piece with others in the culture wars of the 1990s. It buttressed beliefs that American historians were marginal in political influence and at odds with large sections of mainstream American culture.[39]

But just how powerless were historians? Could a loss of power be measured over time? Did historians once have more influence, and when exactly was that influence exerted and why was it lost? These questions were rarely asked and certainly not answered adequately. Indeed, the responses were themselves confusing. Outside critics blustered that academics had too much influence, while insiders tended to think that they had little. The truth was probably somewhere in between, forged in the actual practice of historiography and its accumulated historical traditions. The impact could not be measured in the political response to a set of standards for American history or the vengeful and ill-informed comments of conservative politicians. Princeton historian Sean Wilentz, a contributor to *Reconstructing History,* implicitly contested the perception of powerlessness that many academics shared. The National History Standards highlighted the hitherto-unheralded "quiet conquest of the nation's schoolrooms" by "liberal academics" supporting multiculturalism and "a consensus of the historical profession on what and how children should be taught."[40]

Campaigners in the controversy in 2002 over Michael Bellesiles's *Arming*

America (2000) unconsciously provided further evidence of the ways in which the influence of historical scholarship operated. Conservatives revealed in these debates exaggerated anxieties about the power of a "liberal establishment" of academic historians. But more important, conservative arguments revealed that nonhistorians utilized expert historians and their methods to further their case. When Bellesiles won the Bancroft Prize for a work that deflated the historical traditions of the gun lobby, the National Rifleman's Association and other ultraconservatives expressed outrage. They brought out the usual range of columnists to contest Bellesiles's work, but the lobbyists were also quick to list and exploit *academic* exposés of Bellesiles's scholarship and relied on the profession's canons of objectivity to back their case. The Western Missouri Shooters Alliance directed Web visitors to the contents of the *William and Mary Quarterly* of January 2002 to reinforce its case. This issue contained, the shooters claimed, "several articles pertaining to the problems Professor Bellesiles [had] been having with his credibility." For conservative columnist Kimberley Strassel in the *Wall Street Journal*, it was "heartening to see members of the academic world work so hard to right its house." Those who upheld "the cause of truth" were "fitting role models."[41] The controversy did not prove that academic historians were powerful people in America. But it did indicate that relations between historians and nonacademic history makers might be more subtle and complicated than the laments of academics suggested.[42]

The most striking feature of the contemporary controversy was, however, not the failure to notice these subtleties in professional historians' engagement with different publics, but the discussion's lack of historical depth. Few academic or popular critiques revealed that "fragmentation" and "overspecialization" were not new. Neither the *Times* article on the Historical Society nor the book produced by the society as a standard bearer, *Reconstructing History*, made this point. Ironically, American historians have displayed remarkable amnesia over the intellectual history of their own discipline. They have failed to tease out what was old and what was distinctive in the contemporary debates. They failed to notice parallels between the complaints of the Historical Society and of the Society of American Historians, founded in 1939. Even in the matter of identity politics, the novelty could be overstated. Relativism and regionalism in the 1930s divided historical consciousness as multiculturalism and postmodernism do today.

Nor was history the only discipline at risk. Fragmentation has influenced other fields, as critics such as Hirsch and Bloom had maintained. Many of the attacks on cultural illiteracy were leveled at literature professors and cultural studies as much as at history.[43] More distant disciplines have suffered self-criticism, too. In 1986 geographer Sam Hillard deplored the tendency for specialization to result in large intellectual gaps in the center of that field. "The end result is that [the discipline] looks like a wheel. People sit on their own spokes and talk less and less to those on the other side. Eventually the whole may become a doughnut, with a huge intellectual hole in the middle."[44] In a similar fashion, *American Sociological Review* editor Sheldon Stryker noted, "Sociologists are in danger of losing their core identity, . . . as a consequence of the centrifugal processes set in motion by the increasingly specialized nature of the discipline and the profession."[45]

Historians thought they had lost their educated public, but sociologists also despaired at times of a wider social influence. In his presidential address to the American Sociological Association in 1988, Herbert Gans lamented the generally low opinion held of sociologists in the American community. Ironically, for Gans the pastures seemed greener in the discipline of history. "In their nonoccupational reading . . . many members of the educated public seem to specialize in literary and historical works." He noted that most publishing houses and important magazines like *Time, New Yorker,* or *Atlantic* continued to be run "by people from literary and historical backgrounds." Why the reading public remained "so fond of history and why it ignores—and perhaps dislikes—some or much sociology" was, he believed, "a research topic of fundamental importance."[46]

What is peculiar to history then? The answer remains obscure in the light of these comparative assessments. Sociologist Tony Becher analyzed historians in the Anglo-American world and found that, on both sides of the Atlantic, similar concerns about the discipline of history existed in the 1980s. But history did have distinctive problems of identity derived from its original historical mission and methods: "One characteristic which marks off history from many neighbouring disciplines in the social sciences is the limited scope historical argument affords for generalisation." This would seem to encourage specialization, but Becher also showed that historians preferred writers who could take in the broader sweep. Critical of too much specialization, his respondents actually aspired to generalization.[47] Historical inquiry continues to encourage such views through the ambition of historians to cover all of human society. It is no accident that sociology is the discipline most like history in its anxieties over fragmentation and loss of public relevance, because both speak to the issue of wholeness; yet only history maintains through its practice an aversion to theory—theory that could provide coherence. The fragmenting effects of postmodernism have been abetted by the distrust of large-scale theory, and yet at the same time, the proliferation of postmodernist theories—in the plural, not grand theory—has produced resentment as fragmentation has become obvious.

While these effects seem to be more serious for history than for other disciplines, whether they are more serious for history as practiced in the United States is less clear. Here the argument rests upon the alleged remoteness of American academics from the public, as well as on the huge amount of scholarship already produced. The volume of historical production and the range of special studies have provoked much comment. The late Robert Kelley compared the outpouring in American history—where the problems of specialization were seen to be more severe—to "watching a non-stop, monster fourth of July fireworks display, more and more fine works bursting in the historical firmament, tumbling up into the sky one after the other in a steady stream. There is never a moment of stillness."[48] The conventional wisdom is that U.S. history is inordinately large by volume and number of historians, with the *Journal of American History* reviewing some six hundred book titles, many from university presses, annually.

Yet if American history's specialization has perceived links to the volume of contemporary historical scholarship, anxieties about specialization have also been widespread in other countries where production has been less. English historian Simon Schama, though now based in the United States, wrote tellingly and amusingly in the *Guardian Weekly* on the theme of academic declension in the wider sphere of Anglo-American and European historiography. "What has gone wrong with historical education?" asked Schama. Once, historians "shared an instinctive ability to dwell in worlds separated from our own by time." Then, scholars brought "the closeness of that experience of the 'other' to their work, to give it voice and colour and texture." Now, according to Schama in 1991, the ability to write interestingly for the general public has been severely, perhaps terminally, compromised. Dreary textbooks the size of "telephone directories" have snuffed out historical imagination among the young. Schama presented an alarming picture of fact-grubbing scholars engaged in mindless disputes of attrition over interpretation. Instead of history as the "imagination of our hearts," we got articles on the Dutch margarine industry, circa 1750, or the meaningless me-tooism of multicultural history. The result was that "history in our schools may be genuinely threatened with a kind of extinction."[49]

Schama's complaint duplicated those by English historians such as David Cannadine, who focused in 1986 on the "real relative decline, increasing fragmentation, and loss of public function" in British history. "Much professional history," he declared, had become "more concerned with the increasingly introverted debates of separate subspecialisms, than in building bridges between them."[50] In France, Georges Duby echoed U.S. and British laments of lost influence, arguing that scholars had been "wrong to abandon the literary marketplace to amateurs."[51] Smaller countries have also felt the repercussions of intense specialization. Australian historian Stephen Alomes noted that more academic work had been done on Australian subjects in the last thirty years "than the preceding 170 plus." Yet this work exhibited a parochialism of approach: "The professionalisation of academic work" since World War II, he remarked, "led to a concentration on specialist scholarly study" and a "retreat" from "more general questions." The Australian case reveals that there is no necessary connection between the sheer volume of scholarship and the perception that history has become a fragmented discipline. Australian history is only a tiny fraction of the annual American output.[52]

The modern American jeremiad is not distinctive if we extend the comparisons back across time either. Anxieties about specialization have come in *waves,* and historians have at each stage sought both to transcend specialization and to use that debate to produce history that better reflects a diversity of interests in society. In effect, attacking or supporting specialization has been a tool for the promotion of such interests within the historical profession, just as it is today.

The more difficult and analytically separate issue of professionalization is not new either. It was repeatedly raised along with the invocation of a fragmented discipline. Anxieties over the latter phenomenon were in part a byproduct of the larger debate concerning the discourse of history, its concrete practices, and its political significance. American historiography emerged in a climate in which history was expected to be useful. The search for the uses of history in a democratic society has ranged far and wide over the course of the last 120 years of professional history making. In many ways the theme of the usefulness of history and its historians is the most distinctive throughout. And the advocates of history's relevance in turn helped, by attempts to be responsive to public audiences, issues, and pressure groups, to diversify the treatment of history—and ironically to fragment it.

2

The Great Jeremiad

The History of Historical Specialization

So common have criticisms of overspecialization been that their continuing appearance registers a failure of American historians to examine the history of historical practice. Far from being a recent blight upon historiography, specialization in "the minutiae of scholarship" went back almost to the beginning of the profession of history in America.[1] Criticism of academic narrowness followed soon after. It waxed and waned over the course of the first one hundred years of academic history in the United States, ever since the founders of the profession introduced the concept of "Scientific History" by the 1880s. Derived ultimately from German scholarship but modified by a strong dose of Anglo-American empiricism, Scientific historians' practice was based on objective facts, close analysis of documents, the treatment of history as a science in search of evolutionary laws, and the production of monographs and scholarly journals to achieve these aims.

Shotgun attacks on specialization over the next hundred years masked several problems and issues: narrow topics, specialized language, dull style, and loss of audience and narrative coherence. The perspective on what was "too specialized" differed according to one's point of view. For example, some very "narrow" topics had no contribution to make to the discipline's intellectual coherence even though articles and books on these topics (e.g., Civil War military subjects) could have very large audiences. Because of its specialized terms and language, history influenced by the social

25

sciences could be condemned as off-putting to a wider readership, though such writing often dealt with subjects having grassroots appeal. The most serious complaints throughout, however, concerned audience and coherence and were not separable from the question of the perceived power, influence, and social position of professionalized history. "Specialization" and "narrowness" quickly became pejoratives used, in effect, to advance other causes, such as the popularization of history, attacks on the nature of training for university teaching, and attempts to incorporate new themes in the discourse of history to make it more responsive to economic and social change or cultural diversity. In all these matters, historians displayed sensitivity to the underlying question of audience in ways that belied the image of cold adherence to scientific method and inward-turning professional development. Scientific historians, Progressives, counter-Progressives, and the New Left all recognized and to some degree deplored historical specialization; ironically, most did so while simultaneously advancing the process they condemned.

The early Scientific historians championed objective facts and professed to be in search of the universal. Writing in the early 1890s, Yale colonial historian Charles McLean Andrews already felt the carping of those who criticized his fledgling "science": "We hear complaints of the present tendency toward an undue contraction of the field of specialized work."[2] In 1895, William Milligan Sloane, of Columbia University, registered in the first article published in the *American Historical Review* (*AHR*) the criticism that "interest" in history had been "immolated before the Moloch of details."[3] Two decades later, the picture had not improved much. Lucy Salmon, of Vassar College, was asked as a member of the American Historical Association (AHA) executive to comment upon the content of the 1916 and 1917 annual conventions. "Personally," she wrote back to Columbia historian Evarts B. Greene, "I have deprecated the tendency of late years to split up the Association into sections and especially sections representing particular fields of history." She recommended instead that more sessions take up "some large subject of historical interest." This approach would "be more profitable than many of us have found the minute sub-division into special sections." Salmon lamented the presence of narrow specialists on the program committee and urged the AHA to appoint historiographer Frederick Teggart and Latin Americanist Herbert Bolton to reshape the programs. Such men, she argued, "represent not only the minutiae of scholarship but an interpretative insight and a skill in literary presentation of the results of historical research."[4]

Although the early generations of academic historians worried about the impact of their craft on the unity of historical knowledge, they believed that they had the answer in their historical practice. They urged adherence to the maxims of "universal history." Andrews sought to reassure anxious colleagues that "[t]here never will be any danger from such contraction" into "narrowness, detail and specialization if the writer remembers that he is producing a page of universal history." Rather, the problem came from the antiquarianism of untrained scholars whose practice was "directly hostile to historical learning." He assured readers that it was "not necessary that we stop writing special monographs, it is only necessary that we treat the particular with a full understanding of its relation to the universal." The comparative method would be the agency of this commitment, breaking up the "narrow lines upon which historical work has been and is still done." Comparative study would recognize the "oneness in all study in the search for truth." Interdisciplinary breadth was also essential. Andrews advocated the use of methods in the related fields of textual criticism, archaeology, and other "sciences" to broaden historical inquiry.[5] In a similar fashion, Sloane saw history as moving from the particular toward the general through the study of "epochs" and accepted "the doctrine of the unity of history" through "the inductive and comparative method."[6]

Whatever its risks, Scientific historians believed that specialization was as inevitable in historical study as it was in physics or chemistry. In the eyes of such an influential scholar as John Franklin Jameson, the first editor of the *AHR* and its leading light in its first three decades, only by specializing could the new "Scientific historians" hope to seek out, publish, and interpret the vast collections of hitherto-neglected primary sources. Only through specialization could scholarly ignorance of whole fields of history be eliminated. Jameson welcomed the "richer and more diversified historical studies" that he found characteristic of academic practice.[7]

The question was not whether to specialize but how to effect the division of labor required. Early professional historians saw history as like a jigsaw puzzle in which the pieces would be steadily recovered to produce a total picture of the past. In Jameson's metaphor, history could be considered a stately mansion for which historians were preparing the bricks.[8] Since the concept was of a house to be made of bricks and mortar, all contributions should fit together, not compete for space or design. With that caveat, he viewed specialization in a hierarchical fashion, crowned by general, or universal, history. Outlining the ideal situation, Jameson envisaged the consolidation of local history under academic leadership, the emergence of thematic groupings of historians (e.g., economic historians) that cut across national boundaries, and general histories of both national and international scope to sum up the field.[9] Jameson hoped to "set a standard"[10] for specialist work by encouraging principles of objective history through establishment of scholarly journals in each field. Thus, he praised the *Catholic Historical Review* (1915) because it was "conducted with

much energy and intelligence . . . and has done much to stimulate the many
local Catholic historical societies, and to create in them the sense of solidarity
and the belief that they have an important mission to be fulfilled by common
action."[11]

More important than the variety of tasks within historiography was control of the division of scholarly labor. Until the mid-1920s, the AHA sought to
supervise the activities of specialized societies, on the grounds that subfields
were, as Joseph Schafer of the State Historical Society of Wisconsin put it,
"merely history, and not a specialized thing."[12] The AHA had disbanded its
Church History section in 1903 because the work of the association was "so
broad and inclusive" that there was "no need of separating church history and
distinguishing it from general history."[13] Jameson feared "Negro" history's
program of research and also the emergence of the *Mississippi Valley Historical
Review* as a possible competitor for the *AHR* in the general field of reviewing.
But Jameson did not decry the emergence of specialization per se, provided
these diverse enterprises could be kept under the umbrella of the AHA.[14]

Jameson's attempt to control specialized studies was illustrated in the development of African American history. In 1916 he encouraged the work of
Carter Woodson and the recently established Association for the Study of Negro Life and History (ASNLH) and its *Journal of Negro History*.[15] "[D]istinctly
appreciative of the need of more work upon the history of the Negro in America," the *AHR* editor was instrumental in gaining Carnegie money for the
ASNLH in 1921 and aided its successful quest for Rockefeller funds in 1922.
Jameson favored a "thorough" study of Negro history but characteristically
told Woodson that he wanted to know what the new field could contribute to
a general understanding of the United States.[16] He also labored hard with
Woodson to ensure that the areas of work undertaken by each would be different yet complementary. Since Jameson's Carnegie-funded Bureau of Historical Research was engaged in collecting and publishing on the legal history of
slavery itself, he encouraged Woodson to focus on post-1865 history.

Some of the new specializations that Jameson encountered were informal
academic subdivisions within the AHA. Unlike other disciplines, region and
nation loomed large in the way the subject was carved up. Sections of the AHA
conventions were devoted to European, American, Far Eastern, and Latin
American history, though others concerned religious, military, or economic
history and still others practical issues, such as archives. Formal divisions
grounded in new associations and new journals came more slowly but just as
surely. Most prominent were the Mississippi Valley Historical Association
(MVHA; 1907) and the Southern Historical Association (1934). Jameson sin-
gled out for comment Latin American studies and the *Hispanic American His-*

torical Review (1918). He understood the need for scholars in such areas to develop networks for like-minded thinkers and to provide the "'aid and comfort' which resides in the sense of not working alone."[17]

Despite the appearance of new internal groupings, most specialized societies established before 1930 emerged from outside the profession, reflecting either the rise of allied disciplines or the pressure of nonacademic interests. Major sources were ethnic groups, who were becoming more conscious of the passing away of their traditions; one such group established the Norwegian-American Historical Association (1926). Others wished to defend themselves against negative stereotypes, as in the case of the American Jewish Historical Society (1892)[18] and the ASNLH (1915). Some organizations represented nostalgia, such as the Railway and Locomotive Historical Society (1921);[19] others were the result of the vogue for genealogy or family history, such as Chicago's McCormick Historical Society and Library, directed by agricultural historian Herbert Kellar (1915).[20] Most were concerned with popularizing history in one form or another because their survival depended on public support.[21] The ASNLH was especially concerned with the public reception of its *Journal of Negro History*, as evidenced by an early article: "How the Public Received the *Journal of Negro History*." The association's aim was to "popularize the movement of unearthing the Negro and his contributions to civilization." Yet this sensitivity to the public, spurred by the need for donors, was combined with a belief in Scientific History's article of faith "that facts properly set forth will speak for themselves."[22]

By the 1920s, major forces were at work within the profession to accommodate these new interests, whether popular or academic in origin. When academic historians accepted specialization, they were not retreating into a narrower professional life but embracing realistically the diversity of American society and attempting to respond to the expressed popular need for historical research. Women's history provides a key example. This field drew sustenance from the memory of the great crusades of first-wave feminism and the struggle for justice embodied in the suffrage movement. It also had professional dynamics. The Berkshire women's history conference (founded in 1930 under the name "Lakeville Conference") stimulated a sense of camaraderie among marginalized academic woman historians. These college women persistently lobbied the AHA in the 1930s for space for women historians on the annual program and for executive and committee positions within the association. These entreaties received support from such up-and-coming Progressives as Merle Curti and Arthur Schlesinger.[23]

The push for topical specialization was aided by the rise of Progressive history to intellectual dominance by the 1920s. Progressive historians and their

"New History" focusing on social and economic life provided a major impulse toward this greater acceptance of diversity, including women's history. Yet, paradoxically, the Progressives also strove for unity. They preached the wholeness of knowledge and the interconnections of facts. History would be the key discipline of synthesis, as outlined in James Harvey Robinson's *The New History* (1912) but later developed by Charles Beard through his voluminous writings and moral presence. The Progressives' insistence on incorporating social and economic life as topics for historical research encouraged this synthetic approach. Historian of slavery U. B. Phillips noted that in the writing of social and economic history a broad view was essential. The "very study of the history of American Industrial Society will itself not permit a narrow specialization."[24]

A further aim was to defend history against academic specializations that rivaled history as a whole, such as economics, political science, and sociology. Beard sought to integrate knowledge in the social sciences, with history "[c]rowning them all." There were, to be sure, "specialized histories of economics, politics, and military affairs," but "like the separate disciplines of contemporary life," they existed "for the sake of convenience" and did not represent "absolute divisions." History provided the required synthesis of social knowledge by taking for its data "all that has been done and said on this earth since time began." Beard's formulation was at one with the original aim of universal history with its philosophical, as well as cosmopolitan, overtones.[25]

Though Progressives tilted against the Scientific historians for producing narrow work, they consistently exaggerated their own separation from the practice of their forebears.[26] The Progressives themselves furthered the process of specialization. Embraced as a way of making history more relevant, New History responded to the demands of interest groups by broadening the range of subjects studied. New Historians could do this and support both Scientific History's universality and its specialization without fear of hypocrisy or inconsistency because they believed that the paradigm of Progressive history would contribute to a common project. Progressives had accepted, Herbert Kellar later recalled, a "revolutionary expansion in historical interest" that made "the full scope of life" their province.[27]

Notwithstanding criticism that they would fragment history, the special fields that the Progressives developed grew in number in the 1920s. Social history and the beginnings of urban history can be traced to the Progressive impulse. Labor history, pioneered first in the field of institutional economics, broadened during these years into the history of labor and the working class with Norman Ware's *The Industrial Worker* (1924) and pioneering community studies of factory towns by Vera Shlakman and others. But labor history as a subfield defined by a separate society and journal was much slower in developing.[28] The field had been so closely tied to institutional economics and public policy that its leaders felt little need for the cohesion that an association of like-minded historians could provide.[29]

A more prominent example of specialization came from the U.S. rural past. The rapid rise of agricultural history, with the formation of the Agricultural History Society under AHA auspices in 1919 and a specialized journal in 1927, furthered the aims of Frederick Jackson Turner to study the social and cultural impact of the frontier and promoted western history.[30] These initiatives had strong support beyond the academic community. In many ways the driving force behind the founding of this subdiscipline was, as with labor history, the desire to inform public policy. The federal government's Department of Agriculture and its leading officials strongly supported the society in its early years.[31] In turn, agricultural historians spurred the development of the broader field of economic history by proposing the formation of an "industrial history" society in 1940. Due partly to opposition from business historians who feared poaching upon their own territory, this move did not succeed, but the American Economic History Association was formed in 1941 and incorporated agriculture, business, economic, and even some labor history specialists in its ranks.[32]

The dynamics within the academy favored further specialization at the same time that these outside pressures mounted. The 1920s and the 1930s, the peak of Progressive influence, witnessed a proliferation of scholarly journals. This academic expansion was underpinned by the rapid growth of research infrastructure. More universities established doctoral programs, and more foundations emerged to fund research. As one index of growth, the period between the world wars saw by far the greatest increase in doctoral production in all of the years since the beginning of academic history in the 1880s. Sixty-six percent of all the history doctorates produced up to 1935 were conferred between 1920 and 1935, with the most marked rate of increase from 1925 to 1930.[33]

By the 1930s American academic historians were already classified in terms of specializations, principally of two types: chronological (such as Revolutionary, antebellum, Civil War, and Progressive Era subjects) and regional (western historians elaborating on the frontier thesis, southern historians on slavery and sectional conflict, and historians working on colonial topics, largely of Puritan New England). What was true of American history was also true of the rest, though regions or continents often defined the fields. European economic historian and University of Chicago professor John U. Nef observed in 1944 that history was "split up somewhat arbitrarily according to ge-

ography and chronology . . . with each professor brooding over his particular
preserve, frequently well armed with a view to poachers." This process produced experts "justly proud of their small reputations," but the effect was a
"splintering of history" that troubled Nef because of the consequences for humanistic inquiry and liberal education.[34]

In the case of American history, these divisions were neither arbitrary nor
purely professional. They reflected the sectionalism and regionalism that
Turner had identified in the 1920s as a major theme in American life. Many
academic participants in regional groupings sought to mediate between a vernacular sense of place and their own professional training and critical sense of
history. Especially important among these groupings was southern history,
which benefited from the resurgence of interest in American literary and historical traditions during the New Deal period. Southern history's professionalization received a decided boost from the founding of the *Journal of Southern
History* in 1935 shortly after the Southern Historical Association had been established. A parallel case was the work of Harvard's Samuel Eliot Morison and
Kenneth Murdock in the founding of the *New England Quarterly,* which com-
bated negative stereotypes of Puritan society and religion. All these historians
sought to rehabilitate their fields of research: New Englanders against the debunking tendencies of amateurs who had caricatured Puritanism, southern
revisionists by defending the South's position on the Civil War.[35]

Thematic specializations also matured in the 1930s. These tended to reflect the most innovative and radical sections of the profession influenced by
the Progressive tradition. The importance of these new topical divisions surfaced nationally in the 1939 and 1940 AHA conventions, though work in this
vein had long been under way in the 1920s.[36] Here, broad themes, often cross-
national, indicated that the shift to more specialized discourses was accompanied by an enriching of historical perspective. Organized by leading Progressive historian Merle Curti under the title "Paths to the Present," the 1940
convention displayed an impressive and strikingly modern range of concerns.
This convention was the first to hear a special session on women's history,
with Jeanette P. Nichols presenting "The Nurture of Feminism in the United
States," and W. E. B. Du Bois chaired a session on black history. In a session entitled "Class in American Labor History," Henry David questioned Selig Perl-
man's exclusively trade union focus and asked whether this did not exclude
"other significant aspects of the labor movement."[37] Local and cultural history also received new and invigorating treatment. At the 1939 convention,
Gerald R. Capers complained that "American history [had] been written from
the top down, and only recently [had] the necessity of studying it from the bottom up been recognized."[38]

This new bout of specialization brought something different to the debate which, though muted at the time, has become central to more recent disputes. For the first time historians took seriously the possibility that academics' specializations might be incompatible, not bricks that could be connected in a common edifice as Jameson had hoped. The discourse over specialization became intertwined with the debate over relativism reflected in the work of Charles Beard and others who stressed the historian's "frame of reference."[39] In *The Cultural Approach to History* (1940), Caroline Ware commented on this general philosophical problem and linked it to the aftermath of the Great War, to "the crisis of western civilization," and to the impact of new social sciences that challenged rational thought and raised anew "broad questions of historical interpretation." Although she pronounced historians increasingly aware of national bias, they were "less aware of the bias which reflected the class position, the fact of literacy, and the place in the total culture occupied by the historical profession."[40] This new disposition toward reflexivity shown in Ware's critique opened the door to arguments by minority groups and the self-appointed representatives of the economically oppressed. In these arguments, the existing Scientific practice stood condemned because it could not fully comprehend the cultural or class diversity of modern viewpoints. Thus, economic historian and Marxist Louis M. Hacker thought in terms of a "class identity" shaping historical interpretation and accused Charles McLean Andrews of bias against workers. He also denounced Carl Becker as among the "middle-class intellectuals."[41]

This growing diversity of historical scholarship in the 1930s brought criticism, but several quite distinct objections became mixed. For one group hostile to specialization, the real targets were the doctoral programs and the monographic focus of research. Some of these critics came from outside the profession of history entirely and reflected heated public debate over the outcomes of higher education. College educators inveighed against parallel trends in many disciplines. These attacks on "pure" researchers were partly budget driven by deans wishing to turn Ph.D.-laden faculties into teaching machines.[42] Colorless administrators worried about the effect of research training on teaching in colleges, normal schools, and high schools. The "unfortunate result" of the Ph.D., as one critic put it, was "over-specialization which may be of tremendous value for research in a given field but may also prove disastrous for college and high school teaching." John C. Granbery, a University of Texas engineering professor, attacked the obsession with research-based degrees in the *Texas Outlook* in 1937. His article attracted wider attention when reprinted in the *Journal of the National Education Association*. According to Granbery, "no special ability" was required to take the Ph.D. All that was needed was "money enough to see it through" and "the moral quality of sustained application in a specific field, with persistence and willingness to stay with it to the end." The subjects of research were "usually trivial, and the style uninteresting." The candidate's arduous labor "fitted him neither to teach nor to do creative literary work." Granbery reflected the thinking of Progressive education of the 1930s, which favored instrumentality over pure research. He cited Charles H. Judd, a University of Chicago psychologist who deplored the "modern concentration of attention" on narrow subjects, which often resulted in "atrophied personalities."[43]

The job crisis of the Great Depression compounded the problem of academic narrowness, making historians less marketable outside the research universities. Fueling the concern was doctoral overproduction. A "marked increase" in the number of graduate schools, especially outside the East, and "an expansion of their size everywhere" encouraged more doctorates. So, too, did the economic circumstances of the 1930s. If the depression "prevented some persons from pursuing graduate work," it "tempted many others" to stay out of the job market and upgrade their qualifications as they waited for an improved economic climate. This shelter from the storm of the depression was temporary, however. Excess doctoral production led to a job crisis in many fields, but history suffered more than most because job opportunities, apart from teaching, were "comparatively few."[44]

These professional pressures were frankly discussed at the AHA annual conventions, and even the higher councils of the two major professional organizations now conceded the dangers of narrow scholarship inherent in traditional historical practice. In 1943 Guy Stanton Ford, executive secretary of the AHA, admitted that "the tendency to over-specialization" could be linked to "what we call scientific methods of research."[45] Theodore Blegen agreed in his MVHA presidential address that "too many scholars, engulfed by their specialization, seem to write mainly if not only for their long-suffering colleagues."[46] Attempts to combat these failings came from both conservatives and Progressives. Establishment figures such as *AHR* editor Robert L. Schuyler reasserted Jameson's idea of the importance of generalist journals to provide syntheses and called for more articles appropriate to "the journal of a general, non-specialized historical organization."[47] In response to scholarly concern, AHA conventions in the late 1930s devoted sessions to the need for syntheses to aid the popularization process.[48]

A second approach to ameliorating the effects of overspecialization was the planning of cooperative publications which could pool specialized talents and help incorporate new work within the mainstream. The Progressives Arthur M. Schlesinger and Dixon Ryan Fox edited the History of American

Life series in the 1930s with this aim in mind. In a review, John Allen Krout, Columbia University social historian and Progressive, stated that he observed in this series "a demand for a synthesis" that would relate the new subfield of social history to "the conclusions of historical specialists who had already found centers for their interests."[49]

A third approach identified narrow and trivial subjects rather than subject specialization as the bugbear. The ideal was good writing and a feel for historical significance in connecting the particular to the general. Such important figures as Bernard DeVoto, cultural historian Howard Mumford Jones, and Columbia professor Allan Nevins and historians associated with the *Saturday Review of Literature* favored this approach. They viewed specialization as a much broader problem than one concerning only history and identified a looming crisis across the humanities. Echoing earlier complaints by Nevins, Jones moaned that "we are overwhelmed and exhausted by our knowledge." He claimed of literary studies that "the amount of scholarship" published had become "so vast that the problem of bibliographies, finding lists, and the cheap reproduction of materials" was the "most pressing practical problem before the scholarly world."[50] Such critiques heralded attempts to revive history as a form of popular communication, discussed in the next chapter.

This reaction could not effectively combat historical specialization, however. Nevins and Jones had to accept its growth because it corresponded to the desires of readers as much as to the necessities of academic life. In *The Gateway to History*, Nevins praised the type of reader that Theodore Roosevelt was: "In certain minds intellectual curiosity plays like an unceasing fountain." But Nevins admitted that "other men" did not display TR's "incessant intellectual activity." For this reason, it was "necessary to take a distinct channel of professional activity and relate it to the nearest branch of history. The business man has every reason to be interested in economic history and the careers of industrial leaders; the lawyer, in Constitutional history."[51]

While popularizers such as Nevins accepted a degree of specialization as essential, some partisans of research indirectly defended specialization by reasserting professional standards and disciplinary objectives against the attacks of college administrators.[52] At the 1941 AHA convention in Chicago, William B. Hesseltine, of the University of Wisconsin, spoke "against decreasing the specialized research training in the Ph.D. program." Hesseltine and Louis Kaplan's survey of history doctoral programs published soon after defended the profession against its critics and claimed a modest "improvement" in research and writing. These scholars took the critics of the overproduction of scholarship seriously but argued that standards had risen at the same time that monographic production had increased.[53]

World War II reinforced the position of the researchers, providing them with new defenses. These ideas departed from the old caricature of specialists who defended their territory grimly. Rather, historians now emphasized areas of expertise that served government policy or public interests. Guy Stanton Ford, of the University of Minnesota, noted "a wild scramble by the armed forces and a dozen civilian agencies for trained personnel with a knowledge of every corner of the world we have ignored." This "hasty effort" evidenced "the immediacy of the need for such specialization."[54] Strategic, military, and security demands benefited non-American history fields especially and fed into the area studies programs established after World War II.[55]

In the light of the new circumstances of war, historians increasingly recognized that they needed to manage specialization rather than simply to denounce it. Cultural and medical historian Richard Shryock was well placed to comment. Because of the "spread of professional interests," he argued in 1942, no longer could specialization be avoided. "Increasing complexity of subject matter on the one hand, and mounting bulk on the other, seem to threaten the whole future of historiography." Much history, Shryock argued, was already being done outside the boundaries of the historical profession in areas such as the law, medicine, and science. Shryock began to seek new ways to handle this complexity and help generalist historians cope with the information explosion.[56]

One way to transcend the confusion was essentially organizational, while another was theoretical and conceptual. Organizing teams of textbook writers would help to synthesize knowledge. Academics began to move away from the single-author textbook in recognition of the need for cooperation of specialists. The rise of the multiauthored text that reflected specialization dated from World War II. A prominent example was *An American History* (Harper, 1950), which linked Merle Curti with Thomas Cochran and Shryock. As Curti explained to another potential contributor who ultimately declined, Thomas Bailey, "It seemed to us that fairly likeminded scholars could, as a result of their special knowledge, produce a text which would be richer and more satisfactory than any single historian can now do in view of the status of scholarship in the several fields of American history."[57]

A second path was interdisciplinary and conceptual. Rather than treat history as a set of interlocking facts, historians began to examine their methods and materials more reflexively to seek commonalities. Shryock, among others, contributed to the search for a new cultural-historical synthesis that would draw upon the emerging discipline of cultural anthropology. Especially important initiatives began in connection with the 1939 AHA convention and were documented in Caroline Ware's *The Cultural Approach to History*. The search for the connecting elements in culture as a basis for historical synthesis, as contained in Ware's edited volume, was aimed at all history as practiced in the United States. Ware specifically recommended the cultural interpretation as a way of overcoming the "diverse approaches" of the New History that had "multiplied materials and ideas" and lacked "a basis for selection, organization, and interpretation."[58]

This cultural approach fed the nascent development of American studies. A signally important attempt to overcome disciplinary boundaries and grasp American culture whole, American studies functioned, in theory at least, as a countervailing force to the pressures of specialization within the field of American history. This concern with fragmentation and synthesis was central to the origins of the American civilization courses of Ralph Gabriel at Yale in the 1930s and of literature expert F. O. Mathiessen at Harvard, of Shryock at Pennsylvania, and of many others in the 1940s. At the AHA meeting of 1948, Shryock characterized American studies as "meeting an obvious need for courses integrating the study of the many facets of American life and cutting across the former limiting bounds of subject and departmental interests."[59] It was, Richard M. Huber of Princeton explained in 1954, "a movement in higher education which attempts to skirt the perils of specialization without losing the value of concentrated depth."[60]

American studies could not stop specialization, however. In practice, the field reflected rather than overcame growing fragmentation since most scholars in the field continued to identify with their literary or historical affiliation. As a method, American studies in some ways added a new specialization. It became, ironically, a new discipline focusing on the interpretation of cultural texts through the myth and symbol school.[61] Though more attuned to the claims of wider relevance and audience than many fields of history conceived more traditionally, American studies increasingly yielded in the 1950s to self-contained academic demands for a distinctive program of research and to professional pressures that "encouraged the formation of professional organizations, journals, and conferences."[62]

This fragmentation of history into area studies and geographic concentrations was not new, but it was clearly consolidated post–World War II.[63] In the first two generations of professional scholarship, students had sometimes been trained in American history and then forced by necessity to teach European topics, or vice versa. Carl Becker wrote his thesis on the American Revolution, but his writing included important work on European history.[64] This movement from European to American history and back again made for a lively cross-fertilization of ideas. Robinson, with whom Becker had studied in 1898–99,[65] provided another example, as did Beard, who had been trained in

English history and then wrote mainly on American topics. The absence of adequate research facilities and travel money contributed to the tendency for early Europeanists to do their later work in American fields. After World War II, the critical mass of Europeanists and Americanists as separate blocks grew, however, at the expense of cross-fertilization. As early as 1945, Carlton Hayes worried about a decline in the linkages of the two areas; he sought therefore to reassert the connection by interpreting European history as inextricably tied to the process of frontier expansion in American history.[66]

The figures for the postwar years confirmed Hayes's fears. Backed by the growing volume of historical scholarship, specialization threatened to dismantle important lines of communication between geographically distinct fields. The number of doctorates granted in 1948–57 roughly equaled those of the previous twenty years, and the percentage of doctorates in European fields rose from 33 percent before 1935 to 38.4 percent from 1955 to 1959.[67] Europeanists benefited from the critical mass achieved in history departments and also from the development of area studies in, for example, Russian and Soviet history. The change enhanced capacities to contribute freshly to European and world history but did not encourage continued collaboration with U.S. history specialists.[68]

By the 1950s, material changes in the conditions of historical production underlay the renewed growth of specialization. Technological innovations such as microfilm, which had been developed in the late 1930s, democratized access to primary sources by the 1960s and so put a premium on original research and monographic approaches. Though foundations supported the sciences and social sciences much more readily, the number of organizations making grants for historical research grew markedly post-1945. At the same time, university presses subsidized publications considered too narrow for the commercial publishing houses of earlier eras. This heavier focus on specialized research, together with a modest expansion of university positions, might have enabled historians to forget about the problem of specialization in the 1950s. But, paradoxically, they did not.[69]

The old aim of transcending specialization survived. A survey of graduate education begun in 1958 concluded that the dream to "understand universal history" had become "enormously more difficult" due to "the accumulation of knowledge," but historians kept trying.[70] The AHA's new executive secretary in the 1950s, Boyd Shafer, used his position as a bully pulpit on broad professional issues, proclaiming that the "greatest present need" was not for "skilled specialists" but "liberally educated historians."[71] The AHA Council also worried about the effects upon teaching. Through the Service Center for Teachers of History founded in 1956 and directed by George Carson Jr., the

AHA sought to "bridge the growing gap, which results from increasing specialization, between teachers of history in the schools and specialists in historical research in the universities."[72] Other scholars criticized their colleagues for failing adequately to resist the siren calls. In 1958 Arthur Schlesinger Jr. deplored the "steady withdrawal of the technical historian from general intellectual discourse."[73]

When the New Left emerged in the mid-1960s, its call for non-elitist history would further expand the topics historians attempted to cover, but it initiated few new trends. Much continuity could be detected with the depression era history written from the bottom up. The underlying call of the New Left for "relevance" and inclusiveness continued the project of the (now old) New History.[74] With the proliferation of the "new social history" in the 1970s compounding the problem of fragmentation, the scene was set for a renewed jeremiad in the 1990s.[75]

None of the post–World War II critics raised truly novel arguments, however. As Schlesinger Jr. stated in 1958, there was "nothing new about this separation between the technical historian and the cultivated public." Schlesinger readily identified the key theme that explained the attacks on specialization. It was not the volume of historical production, since this became an issue long after the specter of narrowness began to haunt historians' discourse. Rather, historians worried about their lack of influence over public policy, civic debate, and popular culture. Schlesinger complained that "the professional historian does not matter much in the general intellectual life of the United States," compared to Britain, where Isaiah Berlin, A. J. P. Taylor, D. W. Brogan, Hugh Trevor-Roper, and others "count for something outside the profession" as Turner, Becker, and Beard once did.[76]

Such concerns were rooted partly in the desire to write a more comprehensive and democratic history but also reflected the discourse derived from the earliest proponents of Scientific scholarship. From the time of its origins, history had the potential to explain the other social sciences and to situate human development more intelligibly by its commitment to including all of the human past in its stories. The comments of Charles McLean Andrews on this subject made in 1893 were typical of these universalist aspirations.[77] These aspirations made the discipline particularly vulnerable to the problem of specialization. Common was the viewpoint of George D. Lillibridge of Chico State College in 1958 decrying "the immense extent of specialization, which is naturally to be found in the oldest and broadest of the fields of human knowledge." He taxed the profession because it no longer seemed to supply some clear "meaning and purpose for the study of history."[78]

These imperatives rooted in the discipline's discourse help explain why historians so persistently looked over their shoulders as they specialized more, hoping for synthesis and popular appeal. But did historians ever command that general public appeal? If so, when and why did they lose it? Were the efforts of the 1980s and 1990s to reconnect with public audiences reruns of earlier attempts to broaden the appeal of history? What was the relation of historians to so-called amateurs and that illusive figure, the "general reader"? To these themes the next set of chapters turn.

Part 2

Historians and the Masses, 1890–1960

3

Searching for the General Reader

Professional Historians, Amateurs, and Nonacademic Audiences, 1890–1939

Professor Allan Nevins never forgot the sheer pleasure that the reading of history books produced. During his midwestern childhood, he learned their smell and feel and the joy they could convey. His "affection for history" began, he puts it, as "a child in an Illinois farmhouse, reading Macaulay and Parkman (for the family library was sizable and austerely serious) on the rainy days that meant a relief from labor."[1] In the 1930s, Nevins lamented the decline of history reading that he thought he had observed in the years since his youth. "Once historical study in America was tremendously alive," but, by 1939, control lay in the deadening hands of dry-as-dust academic pedants who had both spurned and in some measure stifled the demand from popular audiences for good history.[2]

So colorful and controversial a figure was Nevins that one can easily forget a simple fact. His attack was not unique, nor was it a complaint directed only by nonacademic critics at professional scholarship. Running through professional historical thought since the 1890s was a persistent theme of engaging with the "general reader" and a desire to combine historical scholarship with a better writing style and broader syntheses of history. Far from unique, Nevins's views were a product of conditions in the writing of history that promoted considerable interaction between a resurgent amateur group and sections of the professionalized craft. A former journalist and amateur practitioner himself, Nevins acted as a go-between with professionals, negotiating the revision of historical practice.

Writing for a wider public was neither stopped nor despised by the Scientific historians, as the common caricature of the discourse of history—fueled by Nevins's own extreme statements—assumes. Rather, history renewed its links with wider public audiences in the early decades of the twentieth century as a response to the surge in public interest in history reading, but by the 1950s, the power of this renewal was waning. How academic history's relations with the reading public and its nonprofessional historians actually improved—then deteriorated—from the turn of the century to the 1960s is the story of this and the next chapter.

Nevins's controversial attack on professional historiography undertaken in the *Saturday Review of Literature* in 1939 distorted and sensationalized this story. The attack stemmed in part from Nevins's anger that, late in 1938, the American Historical Association (AHA) had rejected his plans for a popular magazine of history. Nevertheless his effort to revive an older and more vibrant culture of history reading struck a responsive chord among many AHA members and sections of its executive that supported his attempt and helped to found the Society of American Historians in 1939. Academic historians were at the forefront of those trying to stem a perceived decline in the cultural authority of history writing. William Langer, of Harvard, was one of many who deplored a "gradual fading of historical-mindedness." Whereas once history had its Buckles, Macaulays, Thiers, and Michelets, when "history was popular," now, he lamented, "we write untold quantities of history, but no one reads us."[3]

Langer's grim comparisons paralleled those of an official report of the AHA entitled *The Writing of History* and published in 1926. John Spencer Bassett's contribution, "The Present State of Historical Writing," presented "unvarying testimony that history is less read to-day than formerly." History was "not wanted," and historians were no longer "treated with marked respect by the general public." The situation was a far cry from the days of George Bancroft, when magazines were full of history and leading writers were "received with great favor by the intelligent public."[4] According to Wilbur C. Abbott, of Harvard, in the same volume, Parkman, Prescott, Motley, and others "actually made money out of history, and good history," but few, if any, historians came close to achieving this in the 1920s.[5] This view was hardly confined to crusty conservatives. The prominent Progressive Arthur Schlesinger Sr. complained in 1929 of "a widening chasm" between "the professional historian and the reading public."[6] These views of academic historians were shared to a degree by their nonacademic colleagues. To *Publishers Weekly*, the historian was "no longer a social lion" and lacked "the rewards in fame and fortunes" of illustrious predecessors.[7] Correspondents to the *Saturday Review of Literature* broadened the lament to include all literature of substance. Books were on the way out, unable to compete with movies and radio.[8] But while the decline of reading was agreed upon, the cause was not. Nonacademics tended to blame the professors' excessive scholarly apparatus for the problems.[9]

★ ★ ★

Despite all of the lamentations over the loss of past glories, the state of history reading and writing was never quite as bad as declensionist theories suggested. The critics of academic history's impact imagined a larger and more literate general reading audience for works of history in the nineteenth century than ever existed. Most people had access to few books and did not read much history except in the form of newspaper and magazine articles that treated mostly local subjects. Even Nevins's own memory of turn-of-the-century Illinois was not an infallible guide. The audience for the much-vaunted histories of Bancroft and Parkman was restricted to an elite. The paucity of books was especially true of rural areas such as Nevins remembered so fondly. As Ray Allen Billington remarked, Nevins as a farm boy reader was unusually serious in his tastes. "Because his father, a stern Presbyterian, frowned on earthly pleasures, young Allan cut his intellectual teeth on the five hundred volumes of history, economics, and theology that comprised the family library, rather than on the dime novels and Horatio-Algerish fantasies usually read by the youth of that day."[10] A study of reading habits on farms in the 1920s suggested the limits of Nevins's boyhood experience, too, and concluded that only 38 percent of adults in rural families had read any books during the year. The chief reading matter consisted of newspapers and magazines.[11] Nor did things did get better during the depression decade, as a woman from rural Ohio explained in 1935: "Books are luxuries . . . to farm people, who have been facing drought, floods, and finance companies."[12]

Yet history reading, at least as measured in the enduring forms of production, sale, and circulation of books, was far from declining. By the 1920s, a growing and more broadly based audience for nonfiction could be detected. One indication—and cause—was the emergence of book clubs; by the late 1920s there were nine of these in the United States, of which the most important, serving over 100,000 readers each by the 1930s, were the Book-of-the-Month Club (1926) and the Literary Guild (1927). These clubs were sending out about 50 percent nonfiction, much of it history and biography.[13] While farmers did not read many books, by the early 1930s the rising numbers of col-

lege and high school graduates in the towns and cities did. *Publishers Weekly* analyzed the reading habits of these educated types and found an increased interest in nonfiction.[14] This new market was similar to that catered to by the
Book-of-the-Month Club. It represented the middle class, professional groups,
and those aspiring to professional status. Its aesthetic preference was what
Joan Shelly Rubin and Janice Radway have called middlebrow culture.[15]

Middlebrow tastemakers evidently had contempt for those who catered to
"only a small coterie of well-informed specialists." This is a conclusion of those
who have studied both the columns of the *Saturday Review of Literature* and
Book-of-the-Month Club pronouncements and book choices. Like some historians impatient with the rigors of Scientific History, the editors of the Book-of-
the-Month Club praised popularizers "who wanted to share their special expertise" with a "general audience" in a "comprehensible and manageable form."[16]
Henry Seidel Canby, who chaired the board of judges that selected the club's
books, was also a founder and editor of the *Saturday Review*. He stood for the
"cultured gentleman."[17] A representative of the "genteel tradition," he marketed to middlebrow tastes through the club and the *Review* and defined culture
to the professional-managerial class. Mediating between high- and lowbrow, he
and his group provided expert "certification" of culture.[18]

The audience was not the "general reader" that historians sometimes wistfully recalled. In fact, the market was diverse in interests and reflected regional, class, and gender divisions in American society. As editor and publisher
Henry W. Lanier remarked in 1929, "there are numberless special publics." It
took "but little experience of editing or publishing to convince one of the fu-
tility of arguing about 'the' public for books or magazines in this land of the
swarming free."[19] This democratization of reading created enormous opportunities, however. The elite who wrote, evaluated, and marketed books now
strove to take advantage of these opportunities and capture wider commercial
audiences by modernizing the older genteel culture.

What brought audiences together and allowed the marketing of middlebrow taste was the gradual development of a national culture. Detectable after the Civil War, it flourished in the early twentieth century and was extended
in the 1920s by radio and film. Both amateur and professional historiography
benefited from these profound changes. The national culture meant, not a uniformity of opinions or reading interests, but a common grid of debate shaped
by technological development and changes in business organization. In the
late nineteenth century, new communications in the form of the telegraph
and railroad brought different regions of the United States closer together.
Ideas, books, and writers from all over the country reached a national audience through magazines and newspapers. Southern writers could more easily

reach midwestern readers, for example.[20] High national literacy rates (over 90 percent of all adults by 1900 and 94 percent of native-born whites by 1890) and the expansion in the early twentieth century of public libraries swelled the national reading audience. Along with these changes, the growth of a nationally important review culture in the quality press can be dated from the founding of the *New York Times Book Review* in 1896.[21]

In response to these social and technological changes, publishing became organized nationally. In the decades in which academic history emerged, publishers strove to create a fairly uniform market across the United States. The firm of Henry Holt, founded in 1869, is a key, if early, example. In 1904 Holt began publishing the American Nation series, the first modern, academic, multiauthored history of the United States. The possibilities of a national market for books meant that publishers could be more adventurous, especially by the 1920s, when new firms such as Alfred Knopf and Random House produced both prestige books and cheaper editions.[22]

To an unprecedented degree, publishing houses came to be centered in New York City, a location that also boasted one of the nation's major private universities and was close to many of the other Ivy League campuses of the Northeast. Columbia University's administration of the Pulitzer Prize after 1917 furthered this sense of university/publishing collaboration and its centralization in New York. The conditions were created by 1920 for a closer cooperation between writers, intellectuals, academics, and the publishing houses, which were expanding in number and influence. Frederick Jackson Turner correctly noted in the early 1920s the "preeminence of New York City as the center for writers and journals which influence American thought."[23]

More immediate circumstances benefited history in particular rather than publishing in general. The total production of history books by 1925 was about three times as large as before World War I.[24] The war served as a major stimulus to curiosity about the past. History and biography became especially popular within the rising interest in nonfiction, due to "the concern with fact, information, opinion, argument, and history which began with the approach to the crisis of the war as far back as 1910." The economic "unrest and social change" of the 1920s and the catastrophe of the depression after 1929 provided further reinforcement.[25] From 1930 to 1933 history publishing rose by 8 percent and was the only field to expand. Overall, new books and editions in 1933 were down 10 percent from 1932 and 20 percent from 1930.[26] *Harper's Magazine* editor Frederick Allen explained the rising interest in American history in the 1930s as an attempt "to discover how such a disaster [as the depression] could have happened."[27] As interest in the American past became democratized in the thirties, American popular cultural traditions and heritage received further attention. Through its arts and writers' programs, the New Deal encouraged publications highlighting the traditions of America. In response to the uncertainties of the decade, regional cultures attracted renewed interest, and writings about them gained still wider national circulation.[28]

★ ★ ★

The thirst for history and tradition offered new opportunities for professional and amateur historiography alike. This vacuum in the provision of historical knowledge began to be filled, but in ways that posed a challenge to Scientific History. Historical fiction boomed. Though the resurgence of the genre was a transnational phenomenon,[29] the 1920s witnessed the development of a robust culture of novels on American history. A "keen interest" in historical fiction was already apparent by 1924 and strengthened over the next ten years.[30] Kenneth Roberts's Arundel series, Hervey Allen's *Anthony Adverse,* and Margaret Mitchell's *Gone with the Wind* were among the better known and more successful of the profusion of popular historical novels produced.[31] The audience for these works was rooted mostly in the middlebrow culture, but workers also began to participate as book clubs, public libraries, and expanding secondary education provided a wider audience for historical fiction and nonfiction directed at the social problems of the era. In the depths of the depression in 1934, Louis Adamic concluded that "the overwhelming majority of the American working class" did not read "books and serious, purposeful magazines." Nevertheless, demand for populist and left-wing fiction grew, and Popular Front writers joined the best- or better-seller lists through the work of Howard Fast by the early 1940s.[32]

The vogue for historical novels prompted self-searching and critical analysis among the intellectual elite. For some, the growth in the genre signaled bourgeois decadence; for others, an inexplicable tactical blunder—a simple abdication of ordinary storytelling by literature people obsessed with complicated strategies of narration.[33] For still others, the failure lay with academic history. Noting the "extraordinary number and wide popularity of historical novels" in the 1930s, Arthur Tourtellot attempted to explain their appeal, which seemed to eclipse that of conventional history. Historical novelists created the world the way the participants saw it, opined this *Saturday Review of Literature* contributor. In comparison, historians focused on "the distant, underlying causes of any historic movement." Tourtellot concluded that "the first duty of the novelist" was to shake off the historian's "verdict of posterity."[34] Historical novels had been popular in the United States before, notably around the turn of the century, but the difference in the 1930s was that Americans had "exchanged the romantic for the realistic." As Hewitt Howland, a Bobbs-Merrill editor and formerly editor of *Century* magazine, argued in 1934, "We still want historical novels, but they must have the flavor of reality."[35] Many of these books were snapped up by Hollywood producers, and some became the basis for the plethora of 1930s historical costume dramas on the screen.[36]

Such expanded market opportunities for history spawned a new breed of nonacademic historians. The rise of history as a university-based profession did not destroy its amateur competitors. Even though a "small army of professionally trained historians enjoyed high prestige" and had wrested "full control" of the AHA from their amateur colleagues by 1900, the power of the professionals grew unevenly and gradually.[37] More important, outside the ranks of the professionals, amateur historians thrived. The decades from 1910 to 1940 saw a rise in amateurism, not a decline, but it was a new kind of nonacademic history operating on a *national*, rather than a local, level. It was, in truth, not "amateurism" in any meaningful sense anymore since a new kind of professional writer replaced the old elite. The new authors made their living from their writing, unlike local historians or some of the prominent amateur historians of the nineteenth century, and saw themselves as members of the "professional writer" group.[38]

Who were these new professional writers of history? Mostly they came to history through newspaper work and often remained active journalists. Bruce Catton, later editor of *American Heritage,* preferred to call himself "a reporter, not a historian,"[39] while Bernard DeVoto was "apprenticed in the hard school of professional journalism."[40] Among the other journalists were Henry Pringle, author of an acclaimed study of Theodore Roosevelt,[41] and Mark Sullivan, the author of the multivolume *Our Times,* whom Allan Nevins praised because his magnum opus had "probably done more to interest people in American history than anything else written in our generation."[42] Marquis James, winner of the 1937 Pulitzer Prize for biography with a study of Andrew Jackson, had been a newspaper reporter in several midwestern cities and New York and served on the editorial staff of the *New Yorker.*[43] *Harper's* editor Frederick Allen was the author of *Only Yesterday,* a popular account of American society in the era of World War I.[44] Pulitzer Prize winner Carl Sandburg penned acclaimed works on Lincoln, including *Abraham Lincoln: The War Years.*[45] For many years he worked on the staff of that "proving ground of literary talent," the *Chicago Daily News.*[46] Walter Millis, author of Houghton Mifflin's *Road to War: America, 1914–1917,* worked for the *New York Herald Tribune.*[47]

Several authors juggled writing with the editorship of newspapers. Before he penned the widely acclaimed *The Tragic Era* on Reconstruction and entered government service as a Roosevelt-appointed ambassador, Claude Bowers's long career in journalism included a stint as editor of the *Fort Wayne Journal-Gazette*.[48] Herbert Agar, journalist and later editor of the *Louisville Courier Journal*, was the author of *The Price of Union* and the winner of a Pulitzer Prize; Douglas Freeman, the biographer of Robert E. Lee, served as editor of the *Richmond News-Leader*.[49] Most prominent in the 1930s, however, was George Fort Milton, editor of the *Chattanooga News* and author of *The Age of Hate* and *The Eve of Conflict*.

These authors blended thoroughly professional writing standards with enthusiasm for the concept of history "for its own sake." Milton, who wrote "as an amateur historian," best defined the attitude. Using the word "amateur" "in its pristine sense of love and affection," he liked to "emphasize the point of the pleasure afforded by the avocation of the search for the facts—and the truth behind them."[50] Of course, not all newspapermen made good writers, and nobody seemed to be able to pinpoint the precise qualities that made the transition possible.[51] But the fraternity of journalists had their own informal sense of peer review and judged academics by criteria derived from their own highly professional self-image. Thus, Henry Pringle praised Columbia historian Henry Steele Commager because he was a writer good enough to "hold a job as a reporter upon any newspaper in this country."[52]

Some of the new breed of historians were radicals, but, not surprisingly, these were less likely to come from the staffs of major newspapers, most of which were noted for conservative political opinions. In the 1930s, a host of Popular Front writers such as Jack Hardy and James S. Allen were associated with the Communist Party. Others were more independent radicals such as Millis and Louis Adamic, author of *Dynamite: The Story of Class Violence in America* and *The Native's Return*. In the 1930s, leftist progressive Matthew Josephson, who reviewed for the *New Republic*, earned money through assignments for such "slick" publications as the *Saturday Evening Post* and *New Yorker* to subsidize his serious writing.[53]

As in the regular historical profession, few of these nationally prominent writers were women. Gender patterns illustrated how much the academics and their journalistic compatriots had in common on this score. Henrietta Buckmaster was one of the few women writers of the time who, Darlene Hine points out, had "a long journalism career."[54] This lack of prominence reflected the male-dominated world of newspaper culture. Women writers tended to congregate in the local historical societies or wrote biography and historical novels.[55] In the latter fields and in specialist areas of history, however, women did provide ample evidence of amateur historical achievement. Women were not prominent in the mainstream history field, with its emphasis on politics and economics, but were active in such topics as reform movements and popular culture.[56] Amateur women often wrote about marginalized groups, as Margaret Bell did in *Women of the Wilderness* for E. P. Dutton in 1938, and as Buckmaster did on African Americans in *Let My People Go: The Story of the Underground Railroad and the Growth of the Abolition Movement* for Harper in 1941.[57] Women who did have experience in journalism tended to work for magazines rather than newspapers and served in peripheral positions as book review specialists or wrote freelance. The Canadian-born Constance Skinner was a partial exception; she held jobs on several major newspapers before moving on to prominence as the editor of the Rivers of America series on local history in the 1930s.[58] But like her peers, she gained her spurs by writing drama and poetry reviews rather than working on political and economic reporting. The outstanding woman among the nonacademic "outsiders" named by Allan Nevins in 1939 was, however, not Skinner or Buckmaster but Constance Rourke.[59] She had never been a journalist, though she did write reviews and articles for leading periodicals. Author of *American Humor, Trumpets of Jubilee,* and other pioneering studies of cultural history, Rourke died prematurely in 1941 and her influence on American historiography was cut short.[60]

It is significant that American women historians of the academic kind also focused on social and cultural issues, as Lucy Salmon had done. Salmon's posthumously published *Historical Material* (1933) was a theoretically sophisticated collection of the New History genre. Others, such as Alice Tyler, of the University of Minnesota, in her lively and eclectic descriptive survey of antebellum social history, *Freedom's Ferment* (1944), produced work hardly distinguishable in approach from that of the so-called amateurs. Women also tackled American minorities, with several working on the history of American Indian peoples.[61] Angie Debo, a noted authority on the latter and author of nine books, was trained as an academic but, like many women, could not get an academic job even though her *Rise and Fall of the Choctaw Republic* (1934) won the AHA's Dunning Prize.[62]

Men and women alike, these new writers were prolific. Whereas academics lamented in the 1920s that their protégés usually wrote nothing beyond the doctorate, nonacademics who lived off the proceeds of books and magazine articles were much more productive, and knew it, as James Trustlow Adams noted in a comparison of the "output" of both groups.[63] From the 1920s to 1940s, George F. Milton produced five books and numerous magazine articles, mostly done while holding down a full-time newspaper job at a time of enormous financial strain in the company's history.[64] The ability of authors such as Milton to churn out books was facilitated by the spread of the typewriter, which, as Turner pointed out in 1924, had "modified literary style."[65] Newspapermen were more likely to use typewriters in their day-to-day work because of the premium on speed, and they translated this urgency to their books. In some cases the speed of production was aided, as in Milton's case, by secretaries. Milton dictated work to his secretary and used the resources of his newspaper for research.[66] In contrast, academic historians were burdened with teaching.[67]

These new journalistic writers had other great advantages. The most effective reviewing in terms of book sales came from the daily press rather than learned journals. Many dailies routinely reviewed works of history, with the *New York Times* (from 1896) and *New York Herald Tribune* book review sections (1925 onward) being the most prominent outlets, along with periodicals such as the *New Republic* and *Saturday Review of Literature*. Newspaperman/historians had the contacts to get their books more widely discussed in the popular media. George Milton assiduously cultivated networks among his newspaper acquaintances to get both free publicity for and favorable reviewing of his books. He also used these contacts to lobby for the Pulitzer Prize.[68]

The rise of the new amateur historical writing represented both a challenge to and an opportunity for professional historians. It encouraged, especially, an often forgotten part of the professional project. Despite the widespread conviction, then and now, that academics and amateurs were at odds, academic historians had never expected to supplant nonacademic writing.[69] They simply assumed that the large volume of monographic work they hoped to produce would provide the building blocks for a new synthesis. Scientific History would, in John Franklin Jameson's view, indirectly transform the standards of all generalists, including nonacademic writers who used scholarly resources.[70] Academic historians did not oppose amateur writing and saw stylistically pleasing literary presentation as the end product of historical work. The issue of "style" and the possible decline of literary standards, topics that agitated amateurs, also concerned university-based historians. Thus, Albert Bushnell Hart affirmed the term "imagination" as central to historical writing and invoked the memory of Parkman, Motley, and Macaulay, with their "arousing style" and "dramatic instinct."[71] History was not simply the scientific scrutiny of facts, though this was an important prerequisite. William Milligan Sloane, author of the very first *AHR* article, anticipated an enlarged "reading public" for a history that "shall be alike scientific and artistic"[72] and in his AHA presidential address in 1911 referred to the public demand for "the truth told entertainingly."[73]

Though professionals envisaged a common enterprise with nonacademic historians led by themselves, they never included fiction in this coalition. Instead, they drew a clear line dividing what the novelist did from historians' practice.[74] The genre of the historical novel lay outside the discourse of Scientific History and its concern for facts and objectivity. Fiction was rarely raised as an issue in AHA circles before the 1940s, and then only tangentially. After an Oklahoma attorney complained about the alleged Tory bias of historical novels written by Kenneth Roberts, AHA executive secretary Guy Stanton Ford agreed "that there should be some provision for a critical review of all historical novels in terms of their historical accuracy." But Ford believed that evaluation of popular works of fiction should not take valuable space in a scholarly journal. The *American Historical Review* was "already overcrowded with reviews of serious studies on American history." More than that, the *Review*'s evaluations "would not reach the general reading public."[75]

As popular writing of history prospered, some academics felt that nonfiction constituted a graver threat than novels posed. Academics feared not so much that they were losing control over the discourse as that academic historians would split over the role of popularization and neglect serious academic work. The relativist controversy of the 1930s was tied to this theme. Opponents of relativism feared more than the possibility that epistemological anarchy would undermine the theoretical foundations of Scientific History. Those great debates were as much the product of changes in the practice of history and the reception of historical work among wider audiences. Replying in 1935 to Charles Beard's *American Historical Review* article "Written History as an Act of Faith," Theodore Clarke Smith noted that the chief threat to Scientific History was "the great development of what may be called nonprofessional history in the twentieth century." Mostly journalistic, this type of history did not "consider it necessary to be impartial or even fair; it prefers to be interesting and as a result popular." Smith felt that the relativist tide reflected a vogue for popularity spearheaded by nonacademic historians. Within the AHA, Smith identified this tendency with many of "the younger members of our profession," who were "already becoming affected" by the movement to make history more popular through nonfiction works.[76]

Smith wrote at a time when the definition of "amateurism" within the practice of historical writing remained unclear. In theory, professional historiography demanded the drawing of a boundary between academic history and amateur practice. Yet such precision was rarely reflected in the terminology used. Academics sometimes defined popular history that displayed bias, poor judgment, and incorrect factual information as "amateur" history. Arthur Schlesinger did this in a very disparaging review of W. E. Woodward's *A New American History* in 1936. But Schlesinger's comments stood out as blunt and rare. Some academics went so far as to treat amateurism positively, while others referred more neutrally to "non-professional history." Still others worried about "journalist-historians."[77] The category of "amateur" could conceivably include several different types, ranging from the old patrician scholar of the turn of the century to snappy journalistic writers. Most obviously, the concept included writers of general works of history who were not employed as academics and did not have advanced degrees. A larger group were writers of local history, but they in turn ran the gamut from genealogists and antiquarians to quasi-professional people who cooperated extensively with academics. The academics proposed to reach these local groups through their historical society campaigns (discussed in chapter 12). The work of amateur writing in the national publishing marketplace raised different questions about the hegemony of the professional discourse.

Far from totally rejecting the popularizers, academic historians conceded that nonacademics produced the most readable and often the best general histories. One who held this view was William B. Munro, a political scientist at Harvard who had trained as a historian and had written administrative and political histories. Another, Dixon Ryan Fox, stated that nonacademic historians were definitely superior to their academic counterparts.[78] His statement may have been made to please the hearer, James Trustlow Adams, who reported the conversation to Allan Nevins, but Fox's whole career suggested that he took nonacademic writing seriously. He was one of the stronger supporters of the popularization movement.[79] Another was Harvard historian Crane Brinton, who heaped colorful praise on the amateur as the "lover" of the past "whose passion is undulled by professional routine."[80]

The focus of the new nonacademic writers of the 1920s and 1930s made it easier for university-based historians to cooperate with them. For one thing, these writers concentrated on themes of national, rather than local, significance.[81] For another, academics and amateurs shared a common commitment to facts. Unlike later exponents of historical "faction,"[82] the historian-newspapermen professed objectivity. Though known to be "stridently anti-academic" at times,[83] James Trustlow Adams defended the Scientific History project. In his 1923 article "History and the Lower Criticism," he argued: "The public is necessarily somewhat behind the march of historical and scientific studies." Adams endorsed the academics' program of monographic production. "The historical field" was "now so vast that only a large group of workers" could cope with the volume of material. Adams praised the academic-inspired American Nation series as a culmination of thirty years of monographic work. Using this series as a model, he outlined how cooperation between amateur popularizers and academics worked. While history was not a science, the use of scientific method "led the American historian to judge his material with an impartiality" alien to the partisan spirit found, hitherto, in the works of Bancroft and the like. In this first stage of history production, specialists wrote the "books unattractive to the general reader and indeed usually unknown to him." Popular history then built upon these foundations to produce what Adams called "the true story of mankind in the past." In this support of truth, however, the amateur had a role as important as that of the university-based researcher. As an individual with a commitment to the truth and "whose ideals are those of the scholarly historian," the writer of popular history could serve a "mediating function" between the "scholar in his closet" and "the great mass of citizens."[84]

This acceptance of professional standards in a common scholarly enterprise was widespread among nonacademics. To *Publishers Weekly*, Scientific History could provide the foundation of synthesis: "To the advantage of history publishing is the great accumulation of monograph and thesis material awaiting the writer who can reinterpret these facts to a public whose appetite for history has been whetted by many successful biographies and biographical novels."[85] For this reason, amateurs regarded facts highly. As *New York Herald Tribune* reviewer and amateur historian Geoffrey Parsons put it in regard to Frederick Allen's *Only Yesterday*, "Objectivity is an outstanding trait of the volume." Allen's judgments were "amazingly careful and balanced." The reader was "splashed by the cold facts of America in 1919."[86] This shared discourse stemmed from a concern with "realism." As John Franklin Jameson noted, that disposition revealed "a discontent with rhetorical and imaginative presentations of human life" inherited by historical novelists and historians alike after the Darwinian revolution.[87] It is not surprising that both academics and nonacademics shared much of the modernist project.

Sometimes, these commonalities were obscured by antiacademic rhetoric among writers outside the universities. The latter could summon up envy over the aloofness of university-based historians from the hard grind of the market. Adams, Bowers, and Milton could be scathing about academic foibles.[88] Milton had little respect for the Ph.D. and professed in private that "I care little of a dam [*sic*] about the college professor groups." Bowers was said to refer disparagingly to "the perfessors" who wanted to "kill" history and "dissect it as a corpse."[89] The public comments of former newspaperman Nevins and of Nevins's wider network of friends about academic "pedantry" echoed the concerns of Milton and Adams.[90]

Yet, in practice, nonacademics depended on professional historians for a considerable amount of their research.[91] While Milton griped at the reliance of academics on the Ph.D., he simultaneously set up a network of academic contacts that he used for information. Especially deferential toward Wisconsin historian John D. Hicks, Milton stayed with him whenever he visited Madison. Milton rejoiced when the AHA annual meeting was held in his hometown of Chattanooga in 1935 and had worked with Hicks to achieve this aim.[92] The

Tennessean frequently praised Hicks's work,[93] especially his textbook *The Federal Union*. He admired Hicks's "capacity for extraordinary compression without at the same time either getting the style too bare-bones for pleasurable reading; or the facts too black and white for the necessary implications of gradations of gray." Such praise could at times be cynical, of course, since Milton actually coveted rather than despised the academic life and later hoped for a chair in a "top-flight University."[94]

Little-known figures consulted the experts as much as the well known did. Earl Bell, who worked for the *Augusta Herald* while writing a historical novel, sought advice in 1941 about the Ridge family and Cherokee Indian history from Ralph Gabriel.[95] Robert Wolf of New York City claimed to be writing a "pot-boiler" on American "morals" but conceded that he needed "expert advice" from academics "on sources."[96] Arthur Schlesinger did not approve of what appeared to be a sensationalist account of "vice" but offered Wolf help in the hope of improving a book that "would be read" because, as long as there was a "public demand" for such works, Schlesinger believed the supply would be maintained.[97] When academics wrote popular or readable histories, their work won the nonacademics' applause. A *Saturday Review of Literature* editorial called Morison and Commager's *Growth of the American Republic* "the most literary of short histories," with "crisp, vigorous, and lively" prose.[98]

Whether based on cynical motives or not, this pattern of interaction set the stage for academic influence. Constance Skinner carried on an "extensive correspondence" with Turner and testified to the influence of his frontier thesis. She championed an environmental explanation of American history in her books, "with their stress on rivers, mountains and forests."[99] Nonacademic interpretations of the history of slavery, the Civil War, and Reconstruction were similarly influenced by the growing volume and prestige of academic scholarship. The dominant interpretation of Reconstruction in the interwar period came, observes Kenneth Stampp, from "two books, neither written by professional historians": Bowers's *The Tragic Era* and Milton's biography of Andrew Johnson. This conservative, prosouthern view "crept into college textbooks and into books that surveyed the Civil War and Reconstruction period," but the group that "really began this interpretation" was William A. Dunning and his students, from whom Bowers and Milton had absorbed their views, "full of the racism of the period."[100]

★ ★ ★

Not only did academics cooperate with their amateur colleagues and influence their work, but from 1915 to the end of the 1930s, academics themselves undertook a series of pioneering projects in the popular realm. In 1915 Yale academics began the fifty-volume Chronicles of America. This followed the arrival in the United States of Robert Glasgow, a Canadian publisher who had already produced a similar series on Canada.[101] He persuaded George Parmly Day, president of Yale University Press and a strong supporter of the university's mission to spread scholarly influence beyond academia, to back the series.[102] Larned Professor of History Allen Johnson became general editor, which was an auspicious choice since the Yale professor proclaimed that "there is little point in writing history which will not be read."[103] The Chronicles had such leading academic contributors as Carl Becker, William E. Dodd, Carl Fish, and Charles McLean Andrews.[104] All volumes were to spare the "traditional sensibility of the general reader" by "the almost complete absence of footnotes." These were all lively narratives, wrote Columbia University's Evarts Greene approvingly, and the reader would be "not only entertained by the story in each volume" but also "given a real vision of the development of this country." A special effort had been made to reach "those of our citizens who are not in the habit of reading history." Volumes had illustrations in the form of "elegant" portraits, and Andrews's *Colonial Folkways: A Chronicle of American Life in the Reign of the Georges* had "admirably selected illustrations of architecture, household furnishings, and costume."[105] Academics by and large welcomed the series as nurturing the general reader, whom American historians wanted to be the end recipient of Scientific History's scholarship.[106]

George Parmly Day believed that the series enabled Yale to carry on its mission of "extension work" to the American people. Readers reported the Chronicles to be "as interesting as biography or, indeed, as fiction."[107] In the opinion of the *New York Tribune*, here at last was history "as it should be presented." The same paper praised the series as "a species of literary craftsmanship." Not only were the volumes superior in readability, but they were "painstakingly accurate," too.[108] *North American Review* declared the series "unexampled in our historical literature" for the historian and for the general public, whose prior reading, Day reported, had been "largely fiction."[109] In keeping with the plan for readability and general interest, the authors included such nonacademic authorities as Constance Skinner, who crafted the *Pioneers of the Old Southwest*.[110]

Too expensively produced to reach a mass audience, the series was nevertheless well marketed.[111] *Publishers Weekly* reported that "tens of thousands" of the narrative Chronicles were sold in the 1920s as a "popular yet authoritative history of America," mostly by "intensive subscription sale."[112] Yet the fifty volumes were uneven in quality, and academics regarded their main purpose as disseminating interpretations available elsewhere. For this reason they had little academic use. Most important, the Chronicles series was relatively conventional in comparison with the highly innovative attempts under way in the 1920s to make motion pictures from the series and to supplement the Chronicles with a truly pictorial history of the United States that would appeal to students in the classroom. This, the Pageant of America,[113] was unthinkable without the example of the Chronicles project but went far beyond it in influence.

The fifteen-volume Pageant series was the most important publishing initiative of the era that sought to bridge the gap between academic scholarship and public audiences. The impetus came from the same source as the Chronicles, Yale University Press, which turned to the young and rising Yale scholar Ralph Gabriel to develop the concept in 1924. As a doctoral student, Gabriel studied local history and cultural evolution and developed a lifelong commitment to historical synthesis, as seen in his undergraduate teaching, his textbook writing, his surveys of American civilization, and his pioneering in the 1930s of American studies.[114] The series reflected these themes. Consciously drawing from the success of the live history pageants that flourished in American towns before World War I, Gabriel and his associates strove to duplicate in print their celebration of American life and consulted with the American Pageant Association over the substance of the project.[115]

Although a narrative of American history, the series was conceived so that the illustrations would carry the burden of the story. Inspired also by the Chronicles of America Photoplays then in production at Yale, the series drew upon the opinions of school educators, who suggested the importance of visual elements in education. More than eleven thousand pictures, drawings— some specially done for the series—and maps were employed to make American history come to life. As justification for this heavy reliance on the visual, Gabriel noted that "pictures speak a universal language."[116] The Pageant was not unprecedented in its use of illustrations; in fact, illustrated histories had been commonplace in amateur historical writing in the nineteenth century, but the scale of the work undertaken for the Pageant was unique for professionals. The latter did not, as has sometimes been argued, abandon the tradition of popular pictorial histories; rather, they sought in the prominent case of the Pageant project to take over the genre and harmonize the visual tradition with professional techniques of historical research.[117] The series did not repudiate Scientific History despite its appeal to a mass audience. Rather, Gabriel and his collaborators sought to implement the long-term agenda of combining science and art. The fruits of scholarly history would be presented in an appealing fashion to both students and the general public. For Gabriel, "scientific history and popular history" were "not antithetical." The aim was the "popu-

larizing of history" to create a more enlightened citizenry who would invigo-
rate American democracy.[118]

Despite the emphasis on popularization, it was academic history and its
standards that would be conveyed. Among the editors were many associated
both with the motion picture Chronicles series and with Progressive history.
As a connecting link with the Chronicles book project, Allen Johnson served as
a member of the Pageant's board along with Yale's Charles McLean Andrews.
Also contributing were Dixon Ryan Fox and John Allen Krout of Columbia
and William B. Munro of Harvard. Herbert Bolton of California and Chicago's William E. Dodd provided regional diversity on the West and South,
and Arthur Schlesinger, the up-and-coming Harvard scholar, added expertise
on the new subdiscipline of social history.

To fulfill its ambitious aims, Yale assembled a publicity and marketing ma-
chine for an extensive campaign focused on the Pageant's role in active and
progressive learning.[119] In line with Day's policies, the press billed the series as
a de facto Yale University "extension course" on "current American life problems" and developed a radio campaign to sell the books. Consultation with
community groups, such as the United Daughters of the Confederacy, took
place to ensure the marketability of the series and wide readership throughout
the nation.[120] The press argued that extensive coverage of schools would pay
off by appealing to the "love of adventure [and] patriotism" among students
and a broader public. Gabriel and his colleagues provided an outline of study
for use in schools and colleges based on the series and pushed this in teacher forums such as the *Historical Outlook* magazine.

The visual focus of the series led to "an intensive and extensive search for
nonliterary remains" in the form of what is now called "material culture."[121]
So too did the heavy emphasis on social and cultural history. Pioneering work
on sports history in volume 15, *Annals of American Sport* by John Allen Krout,
was just one example of the adventurousness of the themes. Another feature
of the series was how broadly intercultural it was, with material on cultures
other than the English, including the early history of Spanish borderlands.[122]

Gabriel and his fellow authors drew upon Progressive Era scholarship and
attempted to convey its key conclusions and concepts to a wider audience.
They blended Turnerian concepts of frontier evolution with Beardian economic determinism, but the story they told was cast as an epic of achievement
in which American democratic civilization swept onward to the present. The
Pageant of America series swung sharply toward a bland but upbeat interpretation in the interest of popularization, a trend that muted the critical edge in
Progressive historiography in the 1920s. This provided short-term gains in influence and sales and was partly pushed by the Yale University Press staff, who

succeeded not only in structuring the series' concept but also, by badgering Gabriel with feedback from pressure groups, in influencing detailed interpretation as well. The result was a celebratory tone that helped make the books successful.[123]

The Pageant series won enthusiastic endorsement from nonacademics and was widely reviewed in the press. A *Boston Post* editorial of June 1927 hailed it as "history made visual."[124] The *Saturday Review of Literature* endorsed it as "surely the most fascinating text in American history ever compiled."[125] Academics were pleased at its popularizing value. Even scholars of dour reputation such as the historian of the first British empire, Lawrence Henry Gipson, praised it.[126] Others with a deeper interest in the problems of specialization such as Richard H. Shryock, of Duke University, acknowledged "the easy accessibility" of the collection, claiming that it was more visually valuable and educational than films.[127] Children, at least of the middle classes, enjoyed it as part of their recreational reading.[128] It was well received in schools, even before an accompanying lantern-slide illustration series was prepared in the 1930s.[129] The American Pageant Association's secretary, Lotta Clark, a teacher educator in Boston, praised the series as a vital part of "visual education."[130]

In the late 1920s, just as the Pageant series was being completed, the first volumes of a new attempt to popularize academic scholarship were well under way. This major successor to the Pageant and Chronicles was brought to fruition during the following decade. The History of American Life series provided a social and cultural history of the United States in an accessible form. This twelve- (ultimately thirteen-) volume series was planned and published by Macmillan (1927–48) under the editorship of Arthur M. Schlesinger and Dixon Ryan Fox. Noticeably more academic in tone than the Pageant, with nine of the twelve contributors academic historians, it maintained the Pageant's commitment to ample illustration and lively writing.[131]

The series appeared to mixed responses, however. Charles Beard was among those who criticized its eclectic focus. Yet it did stimulate the demand for more social history in college courses and in university research while at the same time winning applause from wider audiences.[132] At a special session devoted to it at the 1936 AHA annual meeting at Providence, Rhode Island, John Allen Krout analyzed the appeal of the series as rooted in its inclusiveness and attention to everyday life. The contributors also won accolades for readability and style. Bernard DeVoto, then editor of the *Saturday Review of Literature* and a trenchant critic of bad academic writing, called the series "so far superior to all other general histories that, with them, American history is acceptably written for the first time."[133]

A final—and better known—achievement in the great drive to popularize American history came in the joint works of Charles Beard and Mary Beard. In *Rise of American Civilization* (1927) and *America in Midpassage* (1939), they presented comprehensive narrative histories written in a forceful style. Immensely successful, these volumes served a generation as textbooks in colleges and high schools, winning critical praise from reviewers.[134] What is especially noticeable is how these works won acceptance for their literary achievement and public impact as well as for scholarly purposes. Academics such as Max Lerner, of Williams College, who fell under the Beards' sway, proclaimed of *Midpassage* that the Beards "have become literary artists without ceasing to be good historians."[135] For freelance writer and onetime editor of *The Freeman* Albert Jay Nock, the Beards had left "all the works and ways of the damned professor long behind."[136] But they had done more than that. They had successfully incorporated the New History, particularly the history of economic and social life, within a national narrative structure.

Reaching out to the general reader as Beard, Schlesinger, Fox, and the authors of the Pageant series did was one of the foremost achievements of Progressive Era historiography. Yet the effort did not satisfy the critics. The "damned professors" were still in control. Those discontented with this state of affairs would soon make new attempts to bridge the perceived gap with the general public. They brought together at the end of the 1930s leading amateurs and professionals in a crusade against pedantry. This work was almost inconceivable without the font of energy that was Allan Nevins.

4

The Crusade against Pedantry and Its Aftermath

Allan Nevins and Friends, 1930s–1950s

Allan Nevins praised the *Rise of American Civilization* by Charles Beard and Mary Beard as "the ablest compendium" of all United States histories.[1] Yet he could conveniently forget Charles Beard's academic background and professional leadership when he later came to dismiss this work as the aberration of a popularizer like himself. Despite the evidence of effort by academics, Nevins remained dissatisfied with their responses to the challenges posed by the growing public interest in history. Schlesinger and Fox's History of American Life series was for him uneven in quality and lacked the grand narrative that only a single author could impose. Significantly, it was the volume written by the amateur, James Trustlow Adams, that Nevins declared the best. Nevins's qualified praise—as one of the authors he could hardly condemn the series outright—signaled his dissatisfaction with the achievements of academic history.[2]

From the mid-1930s through the mid-1950s, Nevins was the most prominent critic of academic pedantry. At times his initiatives polarized relations between academics and their amateur colleagues, but he also served as an important bridge between the two worlds. He shared the methods and theories of academic historians to a large degree and differed with them chiefly on how far to accommodate amateurs within the academic agenda. Whereas academics had viewed amateurs as the (potential) popular disseminators of scholarship since the beginning of Scientific

History, Nevins saw nonacademics in a more creative role. Like some others who got their start in newspapers, he regarded amateurs as the more innovative branch of Clio's family. Nevins embodied the central characteristics of the new popular historical writers yet worked toward a resolution of the conflicts between popular and academic conceptions and provided leadership to those professors who wanted reform.

As a young man arriving in New York from Illinois in 1913, Nevins served on the staff of the *Evening Post* and later the *New York World* while producing several important works of history. By the mid-1920s, as his books won acclaim, he began to covet an academic job and took a temporary position at Cornell in 1927 before moving to an adjunct status at Columbia in 1928 and finally snaring the DeWitt Clinton Chair of History in 1931. Initially, he continued editorial writing for the *World*, but in 1931, he became a full-time academic, with normal teaching and research responsibilities. However, his literary production in no way diminished. A legendary figure for his immense energy and rapacious appetite for reading, Nevins staggered home at night laden with books and ducked from hasty evening meals with the family or guests back to his study.

Nevins felt like an "outsider" defending nonacademics, but he could articulate this theme more intensely because he was also an insider. As a Columbia professor, he had many of the privileges of academics but felt that, without a Ph.D., he lacked the necessary specialist qualifications to be truly accepted by the guild.[3] For a reputed outsider, Nevins cultivated considerable support within the historical establishment for his views on the discipline's popularization. He won increasing respect because, as Conyers Read, executive secretary of the American Historical Association, put it: "Nevins, after all, is a sound scholar with [sound] scholarly standards."[4] His credibility grew because of the academics' persistent anxieties over both specialization and the apparent gap between themselves and a wider public. Nevins's very appointment at Columbia reflected this concern and the desire of academic historians to do something about it. The most outstanding example of this position within the profession was Read. One of many who believed that serious history writing was being eclipsed by the popularizers and that historical consciousness was declining in public discourse, principally because of the rise of film and radio media,[5] Read aimed to spread a stronger sense of the past among those "in need of historical-mindedness."[6] When Nevins announced a scheme to produce a popular magazine of history with the commercial publisher Condé Nast, he struck a positive chord among some of these anxious academic colleagues. Read tried (unsuccessfully) to get the AHA Council to adopt this proposal at its meeting in Chicago late in 1938.

The AHA reputedly backed away because the proposed magazine would not be sufficiently scholarly,[7] but this was only part of the story. The magazine drew fire from within the AHA because it did not go far enough in popularizing history. The cost of the magazine was one sticking point. As Read pointed out, the AHA Council felt that a magazine subscription selling for ten dollars had, "rather obviously," a basis of appeal that was "exclusive, not popular."[8] Read thought that such a magazine would draw in people who were interested in history only "as a buttress of the status quo."[9] Another bone of contention concerned the financial implications for a cash-strapped scholarly association in the midst of the depression. Nevins's idea of establishing a fund of $300,000 to back the scheme and working in partnership with a commercial publisher threatened to undermine the AHA's own parlous finances by drawing off part of its potential membership dues.[10]

The concept of a popular magazine had its gestation five years earlier and the impetus came from within the AHA. The idea was debated at "considerable length" in 1934, shortly after Read became executive secretary.[11] During 1938, Read negotiated with the Philadelphia-based magazine *Events* (which in 1941 merged with *Current History* and which academic historians helped finance) for that magazine to be taken over by the AHA as a popular outlet.[12] A sizable number of historians within the AHA's senior ranks sympathized with the scheme, including former AHA secretary Dexter Perkins.[13] Even many of those who opposed the plan unveiled in Chicago in 1938 professed support for its general objectives.[14]

When the AHA Council rebuffed Read, Nevins rushed to print with an intemperate outburst, entitled "What's the Matter with History?" in the *Saturday Review of Literature* in February 1939. This attack on his "dry-as-dust" opponents expressed all of the frustrations, however inaccurate and unfair they might have been, that nonacademic historians felt. "Another thin and disappointing year in American historical writing," the opening announced. So caustic, so articulate and molten in its criticism, and so splendidly delivered was his riposte that one is tempted to quote it at length. Dividing the discipline into the popularizers, the pedants, and those mediating between them, Nevins counted the pedant, essentially interchangeable with the Scientific historian, to be the worst. The pedant traded only in facts and was the chief enemy of history's popularity and intellectual integrity. The "touch of this school benumb[ed] and paralyze[d] all interest in history" because its partisans had neither ideas nor literary talent. Despite these grave defects, the pedant had institutional power. "Difficult to dislodge," the narrow-minded type of scholar had "found means in our university system and our learned societies to fasten himself with an Old Man of the Sea grip upon history." The pedant had never published "a real book," and apart from the disparaged Ph.D. and perhaps one or two small monographs produced slowly over many years to vanish without a trace, "his literary production" was "confined to an occasional spiteful review of some real historian."[15] Real historians were those of expansive views, like Charles Beard and himself, as well as a host of so-called amateurs coming up through the ranks to shame the Scientific scholars.

So much did Nevins's invective polarize opinion that it has continued to hide an important truth: he sought a cooperative agenda with academics and adhered to the original goals of Scientific History as reinterpreted by the Progressives in the 1920s. The foibles of the popular writers were spared his harshest barbs, but he did make clear that not all was well in that camp either. Popularizers had interest only in form, not content. More important, they lacked critical insight, the basic requirement of good historians. He therefore dismissed these writers as the "Pangloss" school, claiming, "History proper recruits nothing from that bleak quarter." The ideal history came from the in-between group, which included himself. Such work would be factual and interpretively sound scholarship "in attractive garb," not "excessive popularization."[16]

Nevins's agenda was twofold: a new association to link academic allies and popularizers in the interests of good writing, and a monthly magazine to fuel the public's thirst for sound historical knowledge. Nevins hoped the new "Society" he had in mind would "cooperate with and strengthen the American Historical Association," encouraging allies within the association to "hold the pedants within bounds." But any new historical society needed its own journal "to educate Americans in the dignity and fascination of their own past." The American Historical Review was for this purpose beyond redemption, so enveloped in "esoteric aims" was that venerable periodical. Like the Review, the proposed magazine would be general in its topical scope. Nevins had become agitated mainly over the American past, but his critique also imprecisely touched upon the broader field. The new magazine would include "the historical backgrounds of many a world problem of today."[17]

Though the idea had already been rejected by the AHA, the magazine's chances were further undermined by Nevins's own public attack. Read warned that "I am not going into the new venture much further if it means that I must endorse our condemnation of all the hard spade work of history and all the hard spade workers." Popular history had to be "based upon the solid findings of scholarly research."[18] Nevins's intemperate assault also undermined academic support for the proposed Society of American Historians.

The effect of the outburst caused some, like AHA councilor Solon Buck, to refuse to join the SAH because the new society would be identified with the *Saturday Review* assault.[19]

In the light of this criticism, Nevins revealed his fundamental ambivalence toward academic history. That Nevins did not intend to break with the academics is shown by the way he quickly backpedaled in response to their outrage. Early in 1940, Nevins depicted history as "a mansion with many rooms" that contained "a place for the erudite specialist, for the coldly scientific historian, for the interpretive writer, for the historian of imagination (when held in check by fact), and for many other figures."[20] He reaffirmed this position in his public reconciliation with the academic community that came in his presidential address before the AHA in 1959, "Not Capulets, Not Montagues."[21]

Founded in 1939, the Society of American Historians (SAH) selected members by invitation only. The prominent amateur Douglas Freeman became president,[22] but academic historians were among the members and executive. Carl Becker was vice-president, Krout became secretary, and Read and Harvard's William L. Langer were councilors along with amateurs Henry Pringle, Marquis James, and Carl Van Doren. Despite the assistance of such eminent historians of both academic and nonacademic varieties, the SAH did not prosper in the 1940s. Wartime distractions for its members (Nevins spent a good deal of the war serving as a propagandist for the Allied cause abroad) sapped its strength and ability to tap funds. Read described it in 1943 as being "near death's door."[23] Several times the society revived proposals to found a popular magazine but without success. Various names such as *Milestones, Living History*, and, in 1949, *History* were floated without success. In 1949, a trial issue was mocked up to show potential investors. Not until 1954, when Nevins combined forces with the existing American Association for State and Local History's (AASLH) journal, *American Heritage*, was the dream achieved. The AASLH had founded *American Heritage*, a low-cost, unpretentious magazine, in 1947 and had expanded and in effect relaunched it in a more ambitious and attractive garb in 1949. The magazine presented an outpouring of efforts by historians of local history to make history more popular.[24] The AASLH executive struggled to perform editorial work on the magazine, given the association's limited resources, and saw a partnership with the SAH as a way to achieve its own aims to popularize history along with those of the Nevins camp. The latter still sought to combine academic and general audiences and eyed the AASLH's rising membership.

The shift in the direction of the magazine was decisive and confirmed some of the fears expressed by the AHA in 1938. With the SAH and commercial publisher James Parton involved, and journalist Bruce Catton as editor, it strayed from Nevins's original conception as much as it did from that of local historians. Nevins had earlier aimed to create a magazine which would be, Roy Rosenzweig observes, "a bridge between the academic specialist and the general reader and serve as a form of cultural uplift and adult education." With great weight given to the glossy format, hard covers, and profuse illustrations, the new *American Heritage* differed from Nevins's plans for *History* that had been revealed as recently as 1949. The latter had stressed public service, cultural improvement, international, as well as American, history, and a solid contemporary news focus rather than the deceptively apolitical stance of its successor. In contrast, the new periodical sought to highlight "heritage" and "sense of roots and place," tying nostalgia to the story of American exceptionalism and the nation's "daring dream about liberty and justice."[25]

In spite of this shift, or perhaps because the magazine strayed from Nevins's older and rather idealistic conception of history's audiences, the magazine was a runaway hit. Tripling its initial subscription list after five years and achieving many times the number of sales won by the original AASLH publication, *American Heritage* rivaled *Harper's Magazine* and *Atlantic* in circulation by 1959.[26] The way the new magazine succeeded pleased Nevins, despite its divergence from his earlier plans. In any case, Nevins always put U.S. history first and believed in the entertainment value of that history. Entirely compatible with Nevins's rhetoric of the 1930s were the promoters' plans to tell the "flamboyant" and "endlessly fascinating" story of how Americans were brought "together."[27]

Yet the holy grail of combining academic history's best with outstanding writing for popular audiences was not attained. Nevins had achieved only the superficial part of his agenda. Perhaps he deliberately compromised his aims as he grew older and more contented with himself and with American society. The compromise also reflected the conservative trend in American politics and culture that pervaded the 1950s. Like the *Saturday Review of Literature*, which in the late 1930s Nevins took as a model for literary culture, *American Heritage* reached an audience restricted in educational and socioeconomic terms. Unlike the former, which had a critical edge, the new glossy magazine was uncritical and circumscribed in its social impact. It found its broadest appeal "among America's upper middle class."[28] The history conveyed was static, reliving an older era with little sense of the major forces bringing change over time, and failed to incorporate understanding of the tumult that would mark American society in the 1960s. Class, racial, and ethnic conflicts disappeared in the magazine's eclectic gloss. It favored the medium over the message and so conveyed conservative messages.

The SAH itself did not have the impact that Nevins had hoped it would, but the 1950s proved a more successful period. Not until then, when it established a lecture bureau to facilitate public-speaking engagements by members, were its finances secure. Beginning in 1957 it awarded the Parkman Prize to encourage better writing in American history, and starting in 1960 it awarded a prize for the best-written Ph.D. as well.[29] Through Nevins and his friends, the SAH helped put on a number of radio and television productions of history, but it remained a small, if distinguished and elitist, body. Indeed, toward the end of the 1950s, as Nevins and the original founders began to retire, it seemed for a while that the SAH might collapse. In response, it chose to narrow its somewhat eclectic base of support, embarking on a campaign to cull its membership list.[30] Eventually, it affiliated with the AHA. Academic history had preserved its organizational hegemony despite the froth and bubble of the Nevins challenge. Meanwhile, academic history production grew exponentially and showed little influence from the SAH in the direction of better writing and a larger public appeal. The same complaints about unreadable and unread academic history appeared again in the 1960s, often—as earlier—from prominent academics.[31]

The difficulties of sustaining the 1930s and 1940s dream of academic and popular cooperation were manifest also in the History Book Club (HBC). Founded in 1947 by former newspaperman and self-confessed history buff Ray Dovell, this was another alliance of amateurs and professionals, but unlike the SAH, the emphasis was commercial from the start. The HBC enlisted as editor *Harper's Magazine* journalist and Pulitzer Prize–winning historian Bernard DeVoto, who, like Nevins, believed passionately in the role of history for the enlightenment of a wider public. At the beginning, DeVoto aimed to enlighten "without trying to 'educate' Americans." Adopting the strategy of cultural improvement was, he asserted, the professional historians' mistake. The audience had to be accepted on its own terms.[32]

Like other book clubs, the HBC marketed discounted books selected by a board of editors and offered dividends to members in the form of books for a certain number of yearly purchases. A newsletter, *America in History*, contained the panel of expert editorial advisers' reviews of their selections. The politics of selection reflected the club's perceptions of its audience. It was assumed that the demand would be high for American history, especially colonial, Civil War, and western. The club also felt it necessary to appeal to persistent regional disparities and cater to New England and the South as well as the West—in short, a geographically balanced list was essential.[33] The club's choices were eclectic; there was no attempt, as the academics wanted, at general synthesis. Rather, specialization was regarded as compatible with a "general" readership.[34]

Despite this eclecticism, the club's selections were ideologically narrow, reflecting the cultural climate of the Cold War era. DeVoto himself was a critical liberal and a crusader on conservation, but, as with ordinary academic history, political interference could hardly be avoided entirely. Dovell warned DeVoto about the need to be conciliatory toward the American Legion in book choices and reviews.[35] Both the club and prominent pressure groups shared, however, an emphasis upon what made the United States unique. According to a member of the Board of Editors, amateur historian Stewart Holbrook, the club proposed to tell "incomparably the greatest story on earth, the story of the United States of America."[36] This was similar to the position of Nevins and of *American Heritage*. Like *American Heritage*, too, the club favored the "romance" and nostalgia of human interest over dour academic priorities.[37]

But the ambivalence that Nevins displayed toward academics was also revealed in the HBC. Academics' books were included on the lists by DeVoto, some academics were used as advisory readers, and the editors also realized that professors could be a valuable market.[38] The club management believed that critical reviews of books by experts would convey a quasi-academic appeal and give marketing advantages over other, more indiscriminate clubs, lifting "promotion far above other book clubs both in intellectual content and in public appeal."[39] This approach was adopted not only to cater to the market but also to promote sound history. The editors functioned in part as those for academic series did, seeking critical, rather than purely entertaining, histories. The young Harvard historian Arthur Schlesinger Jr., already a Pulitzer Prize winner, was the most prominent adviser. He believed that the HBC could provide outlets for the best academic history and make history matter.[40] Dovell's populism and blunt commercial pitch notwithstanding, the club straddled, like Nevins's work, the middlebrow line between marketable popular writing and more serious history.

For all this high-mindedness, the beginnings were not auspicious. With just 3,600 members, the new club started on a parlous footing and almost immediately experienced organizational problems.[41] DeVoto charged that no one within the management knew much about publishing; nor did a dependable mailing system, adequate deadlines, or firm policies on selection exist. Within a year the venture was in financial trouble. When Dovell tried to cut costs, heated arguments with DeVoto ensued. The most important of these concerned how intellectually serious the club's selections should be and how ideologically critical of the American system.[42] The apparent liberal and antisouthern bias in DeVoto's editorial policies worried Dovell, who was ever conscious of the need to create a broad market, but the issue of quality publication was more divisive still. Despite his claims that the club would not serve to

educate, DeVoto consistently sought to raise intellectual standards, and he resigned in 1948 over Dovell's failure to support more serious and expensive titles.[43]

When DeVoto departed he predicted the venture would flop.[44] He was
mistaken, since the club continued in the 1950s under the editorship of the
eminent Jefferson biographer Dumas Malone, of the University of Virginia.
Though based in the academy, in 1937 Malone had already expressed a preference for bridging "the chasm between professors and readers."[45] To achieve
commercial success, however, the scope of titles had to be changed since, in
Malone's view, there were not enough good books on American history with
wide appeal. The HBC therefore turned to ancient and European history to
make ends meet[46] and remained frustrated in its inability to reach much of its
potential American history audience, a failure comparable in some ways to
that of professional historians.[47] As Dovell conceded in 1957, the HBC remained one of the "specialized clubs" without a mass audience.[48]

Ideologically, the selection policy's nationalist and exceptionalist focus
served the club's marketing strategy in the 1950s, but the civil rights and Vietnam conflicts of the 1960s unsettled its positive assumptions about the American past. In response, by the 1970s the club had to incorporate academic views
of social conflict through such subjects as slavery, as consensus views of the
American past came under attack. Professedly nonacademic aims notwithstanding, the club veered, due to outside social and political pressures and
reader demand, in the same directions as academic history.[49]

* * *

The aim of DeVoto, Malone, and Nevins to straddle the popular and the academic was partly realized. But the dreams of the 1930s to transform historiography and restore a more historically informed culture were not. Nevins's assault on the academics could not last because it had no secure interpretive
innovation or philosophical system that could be heuristically applied by a
generation of historians in the way that Charles and Mary Beard's work could.
It was concerned more with style than substance and in this sense was
ephemeral. DeVoto differed in his more consistently critical appraisal but
could not as a consequence influence the popular market as much as Nevins
did. The audience receptive to the ideas of either was more limited than they
had hoped.

Despite notable achievements, the climate for amateur-professional cooperation and for marketing serious written history to a popular audience in the
decade after 1945 did not match that before 1940. These changes partly ex-

pressed deeper shifts in historical consciousness. Whereas the Great War, the depression, and the New Deal had encouraged historical and critical explanation, their replacement as sources of anxiety by the discontinuities of the Cold War and consumerist prosperity produced an uncritical vogue for American tradition. Behind the apparent appeal to the past, what Michael Kammen calls an ahistorical "quest for timelessness" prevailed as a means of cultural reassurance. Rather than history as explanation for the present, people in the age of the bomb and American world power sought the less critical terrain of "heritage."[50] As Schlesinger Jr. observed in 1958, "the current . . . [historical] revival seems to have nearly everything except history." It dealt in "self-approbation" and "nostalgia" expressed through museums and television programs rather than books.[51] Meanwhile, the intelligent lay reader's attention had been partly captured by the "pre-occupation with popular sociology" that accompanied anxieties about the new mass culture.[52]

The impact of television on reading could not be discounted either, even though its effects on cinema attendances were greater.[53] Writers had weathered the challenge of radio and film, but in television they faced a new and formidable threat. Television "pre-empted the mass market" and, Daniel Bell observed, thereby changed "the pattern of magazine audiences."[54] Generalist publications lost out, but specialized markets—and American Heritage filled one of them—benefited from shifts in the way advertising allocated resources to sell products. Meanwhile, prospects for serious crossover books of the type that the HBC and Nevins had hoped to foster were not so good.

A less heralded change was the passing of the great cohort of interwar amateur historians. By the 1950s, key figures were retiring, dying, or moving on. Marquis James and Henry Pringle died in 1955 and 1958 respectively. Nevins himself had entered the last (though hardly inactive) stage of his career, retiring from Columbia in 1958 to the salubrious pastures of the Huntington Library, while DeVoto's premature death in 1955 removed an eloquent advocate for nonacademic historians, yet one who could appreciate the need to bridge the gap with professional colleagues. Claude Bowers had long since been an ambassador (to Spain and then Chile); Milton had financial woes and his force was spent. The interwar dominance of the newspapermen ebbed as journalists' training and practice became more specialized and focused on the present.[55]

A further cause of the amateurs' relative decline came from changes in publishing. By the early 1950s, history book publication had declined from the heady heights achieved before World War II. Book production in all fields fell during the war due to paper shortages, and when it recovered, higher prices prevailed. Then, history publishing did not rebound as robustly as the book trade as a whole. One index for which data are available is for titles produced. For history the proportion fell from 7.56 percent to 4.83 percent of a slightly expanded total production from 1939 to 1949.[56] This trend continued into the next decade. By 1951 history commanded just 4.65 percent of the book market and was still at 4.8 percent in 1957.[57]

It was not just the somewhat lower overall profile of history that mattered. Many commercial publishers began in the 1940s to steer away from serious written history and left fewer venues in which both academics and amateur historians could mix.[58] Academics were less affected by this change, and this fact solidified their position vis-à-vis the amateurs. Academics could now publish more often in the low-royalty, lower-volume university presses, which aimed to "reach special markets" rather than the "large amorphous markets" of commercial publishers.[59] However, the expanding university press sector did not yet match the volume of activity of the commercial presses and made up only 10 percent of the market by 1953.[60]

The new structure had consequences for the types of history written. In a 1947 address on publishing, historian Dixon Wecter held imitative and timid commercial presses partly to blame for what he saw as some academics' desertion of the general public. With "current printing costs so high and book prices lagging," the "fickle patronage" of "prestige titles" by commercial presses had collapsed. With these changes, the academics' nexus with the wider market seemed under threat. The publishers themselves were, Wecter concluded, encouraging the "vocabulary of pedantry" among scholars.[61]

This dire appraisal of trends proved only partly correct. In the light of 1950s prosperity, potential audiences reappeared. Nonetheless, it was mostly the innovation of the paperback that compensated in the decade after 1955 for the declining nexus with commercial publishing for the majority of historians that Wecter had identified. This further "revolution" in publishing, discussed in the epilogue, would help the sales of academic history books from the mid-1950s, but their increasing output mostly appealed to specialized university and college, rather than more general, audiences.[62] Popular historical writing did not vanish, but it was less often in the best- or better-seller lists. Some major nonacademic figures such as George Dangerfield and academic crossovers such as Schlesinger Jr. and Malone continued to write successfully for a wider public, while new luminaries such as Barbara Tuchman, William Manchester, and William L. Shirer emerged to carry on beyond the chronological limits of this study.[63] In practical ways the gap had widened between the majority of academic historians and their amateur colleagues, but the two had much in common. The SAH had not seriously challenged the sphere of academic writing, which became increasingly the dominant one, intellectually and institutionally speaking. Academics and nonprofessionals seemed in some measures to have grown together ideologically in promoting consensus views of the American past.

* * *

Neither this denouement nor the idea of popularization was entirely peculiar to the United States. The striving to create popular audiences for written history was more widely shared in the Anglo-American world. In part, the impulse was a product of transnational intellectual and professional debates within Scientific History. At the same time that Nevins flourished, George Macaulay Trevelyan functioned as a similar figure caught between professional and amateur in Britain, encouraging literary excellence, narrative, and the exercise of imagination in history. Like Nevins, Trevelyan was a prodigious writer and best-selling author. He reentered academic life at Cambridge in 1927 just before Nevins went to Columbia. Trevelyan was president of the Historical Association from 1946 to 1949, when the critical development of the popular magazine *History Today* took place under the association's wings. Uncannily like Nevins's pet *American Heritage* project in concept and timing, it had first been planned in 1939 but did not appear until 1951.[64]

Trevelyan, to be sure, had more prestige within the English historical community than Nevins did in the United States for much of his career. Trevelyan served as Regius Professor of Modern History at Cambridge from 1927 to his official retirement in 1940 and as Master of Trinity College (a Crown appointment) from 1940. Nevins took longer to gain comparable honors, including recognition as president of the AHA in 1959. Trevelyan's place was more established because the transition to professionalism was more attenuated in the British case.[65] Class also contributed. Gentlemen amateurs or semiprofessionals like Trevelyan were tolerated in part because gentlemen were tolerated, or even encouraged, academically speaking. Such differences mattered mainly in the short to medium term, however. The Historical Association in England blended amateur and professional interests during Trevelyan's prime, but its journal, *History,* switched after 1956 to pure academic research scholarship, and its columns devoted to local history and teaching disappeared. From that time, *History* became indistinguishable from any other academic journal. Just as the search for public audiences had been stimulated in both countries by the shock of world wars and the Great Depression, in both (though more extensively in the American case) professionalism received a boost from the post–World War II expansion of the university system. In Britain, the new red brick universities and the belated growth of the social sciences provided enlarged opportunities for professional scholarship of a more rigorous and rarefied kind than Trevelyan favored. Like Nevins, he had always been subject to criticism for fluffy work, but after the solidification of academic history as a profession, his reputation went into eclipse, only to be partially revived by the 1990s as historians reengaged with narrative strategies. Nevins and Trevelyan had failed to transform historical scholarship in the Anglo-American world, but both left substantial legacies.[66]

Neither the popularizers such as Nevins or Trevelyan nor the defenders of purely academic historians had their way entirely from 1900 to 1960. Both academic and nonacademic history had survived and even reached an accommodation, but the audiences they addressed, at least in the United States, were now more separate than before the 1950s. The boom of popular "written" history had passed. Both amateur and professional history faced new challenges from the electronic media, as shown clearly in the 1950s with the rise of television as a mass medium. But history had met such challenges before. The story of history's relationship with public audiences is one of changing means of communication. Since the 1920s, academics had grappled with the problem of new media. The challenge of nonprofessional history makers who rivaled academics in print was by no means the only one, and in the long run not the greatest. Motion pictures and radio both threatened the discourse of professional history, and, once again, historians sought to meet the challenge by connecting with a broader audience.

5

Movies Made History and History Made Movies

When historians discuss film and history, a long list of unflattering self-indictments often accompanies the debate. The critique goes something like this: Scholars have ignored the significance for their craft of the powerful visual medium of motion pictures. Despite film's enormous significance as a cultural artifact, historians have adopted inappropriate standards for assessing its influence and have missed its potential for shaping historical consciousness. They thereby abdicated a role in the critical assessment of popular culture and may even have contributed to a loss of audience for history. When historians have given scholarly attention to film, they have focused on whether films are accurate in historical detail rather than entertaining or interpretively "true" to their subjects.[1] The analytical perspectives of cultural studies and postmodernism strengthened this critique of academic history. As Robert Rosenstone put it, "the notion of history as constituted and problematic" has not been sufficiently understood. We tend to see written history as epistemologically different from film, whereas it is just another representation of reality.[2] Rosenstone recalls historians' neglect of film in the 1960s: "thirty years ago, when I completed my doctorate, the idea that historical film might be worthy of attention as a medium for seriously representing the past was unthinkable."[3] Other authorities have found a dearth of critical commentary and little use of film as evidence of popular cultural trends.[4] Peter Novick's *That Noble Dream* made just a single reference to film in its more than six hundred pages on American historiography in the twentieth century. In this emblematic example, Louis Gottschalk, a University of Chicago historian and later president of the American Historical Association, wrote to the president of MGM in 1935 to attack historical inaccuracies in the costume drama *The Scarlet Pimpernel*. Gottschalk thought that boards of historical advisers ought to be created for Hollywood films in order to correct such mistakes. This call for historians to vet films Novick described as a "quixotic" attempt to bring history to the masses.[5]

The example is misleading when taken out of context. Contrary to much recent discussion, historians discussed, tried to influence, and even tried to make movies from a much earlier time than is commonly recognized. But they did not treat movies in isolation. They regarded film as part of a larger problem of "mass" media. The democratization of knowledge, the spread of high schools, the rise of "yellow" journalism, and, most important, the rise of the radio were common features of the decades in which professional history emerged. Any account of historians and public audiences must deal with all of these and, especially, with *both* radio and film as expressions of the problem of the democratization of information and as examples of the challenges this process posed to historians. Though by the 1930s historians came to see radio as potentially more significant for disseminating historical knowledge than films, the movie challenge came first, and historians responded accordingly. Already by the end of World War I, the role of movies in history making was a public issue because of the controversial D. W. Griffith film *Birth of a Nation* (1915). Griffith himself claimed the right "to present the facts of history as we see them."[6] That President Woodrow Wilson, a Johns Hopkins history Ph.D., initially endorsed the racist classic as authentic continues to embarrass historians, but this endorsement was just one of many ways in which academically trained historians evaluated the role of feature film before the 1960s.[7]

Academic historians shared with the wider American culture serious moral and social apprehensions over movies.[8] The public indictment in the twenties verged on moral panic: movies conveyed morally questionable values because of their seemingly endless portrayals of sexual transgression, gambling, drinking, and smoking; movies were mind-numbing and likely to brainwash young viewers, making them uncritical and passive. Of special concern was the fear that viewing movies would discourage reading. Many of these preconceptions continued through the depression era, fueled by the Payne Fund Studies, which investigated film's moral and social impact. In what was essentially a historical study of the social content and possible impact of movies over time, sociologist Edgar Dale contributed one of the most important pieces of research to this early literature. His *Content of Motion Pictures*

(1935) showed shifts in morality. Movies depicted drinking and smoking as common and gave increasing space to sex and crime themes in the 1920s.[9] Other commentators were more alarmist. Henry James Forman's *Our Movie-Made Children* conveyed the findings of the Payne Fund Studies to a wider audience and emphasized their more sensational aspects.[10]

As largely middle-class and middlebrow people, historians were hardly likely to be immune from these broader public concerns. Some historians responded to the perceived moral threat by joining organizations committed to the uplift of the cinema. In California, Edgar Robinson, of Stanford, joined the Motion Picture Research Council, a moral reform lobby group that instigated the Payne Fund Studies.[11] Edwin Seligman, an economist and occasional economic historian, was a vice-president of the national body. The council declared that the "welfare of youth is in the balance" and claimed that lobbying from religious bodies had not stopped pernicious and immoral movie influences. This was not an exceptional view within the social sciences or within the historical profession. The AHA's Commission on the Social Studies (1929–34) reported on the "degradation of morals and taste" and the emphasis on sex and crime in "sadistic" movies and other commercialized entertainments.[12]

More obviously aligned to their professional interests was historians' criticism of film for inaccurate depictions of the past. This indictment extended to fears that foreign perceptions of American life might be warped irrevocably by movie misrepresentations. Before his return in 1925 from a stint occupying the inaugural Harmsworth Chair of American History at Oxford University, a young Samuel Eliot Morison urged inclusion of American history in British school and university curricula to combat movie-inspired misrepresentations. "American films . . . presented a distorted view of life in the United States," he advised a British audience. Produced "for an American market," such films ought not to be taken seriously, because they provided merely a compensation "for humdrum life on Main Street."[13]

Yet the reaction to film was not as unremittingly negative as these indictments suggested. Positive support jostled with criticism from the 1920s onward. Historians' interest, both positive and negative, in the movies began as early as 1913, when the role of movies as an aid to teaching was aired at a history teachers conference in Indiana.[14] Interest in the educational possibilities surged in the 1920s, when feature films and Hollywood dominance became unmistakable trends. The ever-thoughtful Frederick Jackson Turner commented in 1924 that film had "deeply influenced the psychology of youth, for evil as well as for good; but in any case it has added new means for seeing the world and has profoundly modified the simplicity and localism of our life."[15]

The contribution that film could make to the wider public's knowledge about the past excited some historians. Dixon Ryan Fox called motion pictures "the popular drama of today; a hundred see the hero foil the villain on the screen to one who sees it on the stage." Fox also backed Turner's observations about film's revolutionary effects on American culture. In Walter Benjamin's phrase, Fox foresaw a new "age of mechanical reproduction." Unlike the theater or classroom presentations, film afforded "permanent form with almost infinite re-presentation."[16] The new medium could, as other enthusiasts put it, supplement classroom teaching and provide students and the wider public with a better understanding of the American past. Historical film could even be a way of compensating for professional historians' neglect of the general reader.[17]

At the time Fox wrote, American historians were beginning their first serious effort to engage with movies as a form of history, through the Chronicles of America Photoplays. This was an ambitious attempt by Yale University Press to translate the success of its fifty-volume Chronicles of America series onto the screen in thirty-three films depicting American history from the Puritans through the Civil War. Though the film series had vital support from the press's president, George Parmly Day, the Photoplays concept was the brainchild of Robert Glasgow. The Canadian-born publisher convinced Yale first to do the book version, modeled on the Chronicles of Canada series that Glasgow had developed. In the wake of widespread success and critical acclaim for the American version, he convinced the press to form the Chronicles of America Pictures Corporation to produce a film equivalent.[18] Yale agreed to this venture only after insisting that prominent historian Max Farrand and other Yale academics retain a supervisory role. Farrand was positive about the effects that movies and other new media could have on the elevation and standardization of American culture.[19] A number of other historians were drawn into the project as advisers. Among these was College of Charleston historian Nathaniel Stephenson, who was at the time (1920–21) a visiting professor at Yale. He became the guiding light of the Photoplays series, especially after Glasgow's death in 1922, and served as editor till 1927.[20] Edging out the influence of Glasgow's partner, Arthur Krows, whose background was in film, Stephenson turned the series more steadfastly toward historical veracity rather than entertainment. Charles McLean Andrews participated, along with Farrand, William Wood (one of the Chronicles book series authors), the State Historical Society of Wisconsin's Joseph Schafer, and Stanford's Edgar Robinson as expert advisers to ensure the historical accuracy of the scripts.[21] An educationalist reported that "distinguished professors of History had given their help," and for this reason, "for the first time the films were both accurate and artistic."[22]

The series received enthusiastic endorsements from academics. Those at the annual AHA convention held in Columbus, Ohio, in 1923, were treated to an important symbolic gesture of professional involvement with a special screening of one of the films, *Vincennes*.[23] Dixon Ryan Fox called the Photoplays a series of permanent value. "Year after year these thirty-three Yale pictures will go on presenting at numberless times and places the historic experience of the American people."[24] Fox was one of a number who argued for the link between seeing the films and an increased interest in reading about American history. The *Ohio History Teachers Journal* promoted and Yale marketed the books of the Chronicles series together with the films and a Yale course of study designed by Ralph Gabriel and Arthur B. Darling. Fox recommended history titles for booksellers to display after the Photoplays had been shown across America,[25] and some professors used the films in their classrooms, as Robinson did at Stanford.[26]

Outside observers also praised the series.[27] While for the *New York Times* the original fifty-volume set of books was good, the films "multiplied" their value "many times by endowing these figures with power to move about in scenes which were familiar to their originals."[28] The Englishman W. T. Waugh, who in 1926 lectured in western Canada, used *Wolfe and Montcalm*, a film based on the Chronicles book by G. M. Wrong, for illustrative purposes. Noting that the film "made a great impression on spectators of all ages," Waugh interviewed many theater managers who disputed the claim, repeated by later film historians, that the series lacked audience appeal. He added that "the teachers who saw the film were almost without exception loud in their approval."[29] However, the general public within the United States proved less enthusiastic. The grassroots analysis of moviegoing conducted by sociologists Robert Lynd and Helen Lynd in "Middletown" (Muncie, Indiana) pointed to the weakness of these films as entertainment. One exhibitor discontinued the series after the second picture was shown. "[P]eople do not go to the movies to be instructed," concluded the Lynds.[30] Rather, they wished to be entertained, and the Photoplays failed as general entertainment.

Though the Chronicles were marketed to the general public in order to cover costs, fundamentally the series was aimed at schools.[31] The Yale University Press Publicity Department documented extensive testimony from school boards and individual teachers showing interest in and approval of the series.[32] Yale could not have orchestrated all of these favorable comments. The Nebraska State Teachers Association was one of many organizations which, quite independently of the Yale University Press Film Service, recommended use of the Chronicles and gave teachers advice on how to obtain the films.[33]

To assess the impact, Yale employed educational experts working with his-

torians. In 1929 Daniel C. Knowlton and J. Warren Tilton published the results
of their experiments in which seventh-grade teachers had used the Photoplays; they found that the films "produced more pupil participation in classroom discussion" and "contributed materially to the gaining and retention of
worthwhile knowledge."[34] The researchers also praised the tendency for the
series to generate independent reading of history. They thereby undermined
the common assumption that watching films necessarily corroded reading
habits. The study of the educational impact of the Photoplays paralleled
efforts on the other side of the Atlantic to measure film's potential role in
schools, and yet the result was slightly different. British experiments stressed
stimulating interest in the past, while the American investigators favored the
immediate acquisition of factual knowledge.[35]

The difference highlighted the major criticism of the role of historians in
evaluating film: that the series failed financially and artistically because of in-
compatibilities between filmmakers and pedantic, fact-grubbing historians.[36]
Ultimately, the Photoplays were indeed failures, and only fifteen of the anticipated thirty-three films were exhibited. Historians complained about the
scripts, and Stephenson vetoed some to satisfy the demands of the historical
advisers. The most celebrated case concerned *The Declaration of Independence.*
There the original scriptwriter seized upon the dramatic device of delegate
Caesar Rodney's dash by horse to reach Philadelphia in time for the crucial independence vote in 1776. For Stephenson, this made the script revolve around
the clichéd melodramatic device that a "favorable vote could not be had unless
Rodney arrived." Therefore, "all subsequent American history turned on the
speed of Rodney's horse." Rather than highlight such individual contingencies
and emotions, Stephenson insisted that "the true objective was the public
event." He unceremoniously dumped the melodramatic script for a more dig-
nified, balanced account.[37]

Was the series trapped in a sterile search for factual accuracy? Perhaps, but
the positive side to its search for realistic portrayals of the past has to be mentioned. In commenting on a script on gold mining in California, Stanford's
Robinson objected to melodramatic racial stereotyping.[38] He argued against
ethnic typecasting and complained that "I suppose there must be villains in
any scenario, but is it essential that the villains be Southerners, Englishmen
and Mexicans?"[39]

In most cases, the issue was never so simple as one of factual accuracy versus audience appeal. The series was pulled in different directions by conflicting
audience responses and blatant pressure-group activity. Pacifists objected to
the pro-war content in those films that dealt with the American Revolution,
and prohibitionists banned the use of some of the films in Detroit public

schools in the late 1920s because they showed drinking. Laura Osborn, a pro-hibition supporter on the Detroit School Board, did not find the films boring for their adherence to known historical facts. Rather, they were not bland enough. She condemned the films morally as "too realistic" for children.[40] In this case, the producers had failed to bow to popular stereotypes, which typi-cally projected George Washington as a saint, not a drinker.

Though Stephenson expected the films to conform to known historical fact, in practice compromises had to be reached, especially where gaps in knowledge existed. The standard applied was "plausibility." When no "pic-turesque historical fact"[41] conflicted with the script, Stephenson allowed much leeway. The scene merely had to be believable. Rather than slavishly follow facts, each Photoplay attempted to evoke the atmosphere of an era.[42]

Not only did the series depart from the canons of purely factual content. A more serious problem was the flirtation with the heady patriotism and popu-lar prejudice of the 1920s, which gave the films an ideological bias. American-ization pressures provided a strong rationale: the series would instill Ameri-canism among the new immigrant groups, suggested Dixon Ryan Fox. "Is it likely, speaking in hard realities, that the mass of new Americans" would ab-sorb patriotism as effectively "in any other form?" The pictures gave these im-migrants "roots with which to draw moral and intellectual nourishment from America's past."[43] With immigrants Americanized through motion pictures depicting positive national values, the negative influences of Hollywood could be neutralized.

Among the Photoplays' target audiences were the patriotic and hereditary societies whose influence peaked around World War I. In a telling example of attentiveness to particular publics and their prejudices, the series' editors at-tempted to appeal to prosouthern groups. These were vitally important in the selection of school textbooks and in shaping local attitudes on the themes of historical memory in the American South. The films therefore projected con-ventional views on race relations and the North/South divide. *Dixie*, the film on the South before the Civil War, won praise from the United Daughters of the Confederacy (UDC). A Mobile, Alabama, member of the UDC, Irene Se-wall, said *Dixie* "was a great success—everybody that attended thought it was splendid."[44] The UDC embraced *Dixie* not because it told a more interesting story than the other films but because it appealed to southern prejudices.[45] Ruth Lawton, president-general of the UDC, viewed the Yale venture as a po-litical statement, useful in the process of national reconciliation going on as a result of the resurgent power of the white South. Attacking midwestern "domination" in historical interpretation, Lawton saw *Dixie* as helping to "obliterate the bitterness of sectionalism." When she claimed that the treatment of slavery in American history was "out of proportion"[46] to the injustice done, her special plea was no different than what had been argued in *Birth of a Nation* or in several prosouthern feature films of the 1920s. Nor was it different from the literary outpouring of Lost Cause novelists and historians.[47]

Rather than being unpopular because they followed academic standards, these films pandered to regional and national historical consciousness and to popular conceptions of American history without providing any serious intellectual challenges to dominant themes. In 1929 the UDC president-general did not single out *Dixie* but publicized the entire series, proclaiming that there was "no more effective aid in the teaching of America and in stimulating patriotic American citizenship."[48] If anything, rather than demonstrating ivory tower remoteness, the Photoplays editors strove too hard to tap popular patriotic sentiment.

Yet neither content nor presentation brought about the failure of the series. The films were, in truth, too much a part of their time, not too little. Their melodramatic features were concessions to script writers and to the popular conception of moviegoers' tastes. While this was common for the motion picture genre of the 1920s, the Yale films were meant to last. Acting fashions soon changed, leaving the films as period pieces. Moreover, they were trapped in the silent-film technology, which soon made them partly obsolete and prompted student and public complaints.[49] If the series was technologically dated in the 1930s, in the 1920s it was ahead of its time in the sense that school and even college resources did not support the widespread showing of feature films. Projection equipment was simply not available in many cases. Even a well-endowed institution like Stanford lacked some of the suitable equipment.[50] This weakness was part of the larger technical problem of distribution. The films did not have the budgets (or the industry contacts) for the publicity and block-booking techniques that the studios used to promote commercial films.[51]

Ultimately, the twists of the national economy sealed the series' failure. The depression's onset in 1929 came as the final blow, and plans to extend the venture to talkies were shelved, but not before Henry Johnson, professor of history at Teachers' College, Columbia University, worked on productions planned by Fox Films. Fox completed a series entitled "When Our National Songs Were New," working from "Yankee Doodle" through "The Battle Hymn of the Republic." "[T]he actual writing and singing," Johnson recalled, was "dramatized by professional actors." Shortly after, the studio planned a thirty-six-picture series on a "connected history" of the United States. But the depression intervened while four films were being made. Litigation over ownership followed and the completed pictures remained unreleased, locked in the

Fox film library.[52] The "vast amount of money" required had now put a "commercial mark"[53] on the use of film that stymied the contribution of historians except as occasional consultants, leaving the Yale project as the major monument to historians' early, lively interest in film. Yet Yale continued to promote the series during the depression era and marketed photographic slides to be used in classroom discussions.[54] One broadcaster in the 1930s called the Yale effort "the greatest contribution in the field of visual instruction" made to that time.[55]

Debate over historical movies took a new turn in the 1930s with the profusion of commercially produced historical costume dramas on both American and European themes. It was at this time that historians wondered most about the historical accuracy of feature films.[56] Louis Gottschalk's 1935 letter of complaint to MGM was by no means the only critique of such costume dramas. Allan Nevins lamented in 1939 that "even intelligent and reading Americans" had their views shaped largely "from the movie distortions of our nation's past,"[57] while a 1944 report on American students' knowledge of history conceded that movies sometimes presented oversimplified motives, "sentimental interludes," and a "romantically unreal impression."[58]

Such criticism was not unique to historians. It was widely shared in literary circles among creative writers, journalists, and radicals. Particularly active in the left-wing press were those who objected to prosouthern material. Some panned *Gone with the Wind* and its portrayal of the "waning Confederate mythology."[59] African American historians, notably W. E. B. Du Bois, objected especially to rampant racial stereotyping. They did this as part of the work of the National Association for the Advancement of Colored People (NAACP), which condemned anti-Negro stereotypes in films. In 1939 the NAACP attacked "powerful movie moguls" and denounced *Birth of a Nation* as "the parent of an apparently never-ending storehouse of pictures based on the old South with its crooning black mammies, obedient colored servants, and psalm-singing workers who tip their hats graciously to white southern plantation lords."[60] African Americans deplored these films for their unrealistic portrayals of southern society, just as academic historians did for historical pictures as a whole.[61]

Even though the first full review of a work on the American movie industry did not appear in a major historical journal until 1948,[62] serious academic assessments of the movies began in the 1930s. Charles and Mary Beard developed an incisive cultural and economic critique of the movie industry as mass production. Briefly anticipating the theme in their 1927 volume, *The Rise of American Civilization*,[63] the Beards devoted a whole chapter of *America in Midpassage* (1939) to mass commercialized entertainment, in which they examined the social and economic history of the movies at length. They noted that historical costume dramas were part of a pattern of film culture that included sex and make-believe—"the perfect illusion snatched from a world of fantasy occupied by gnomes, talking animals, and dancing quadrupeds." With their "exotic scenery and costume," historical films had a similar impact. By placing "action in remote circumstances," history offered "a retreat to the land of make-believe." The Beards came close to regarding Hollywood movies as a product of consumption-oriented capitalism's creation of the false consciousness of the masses. This had implications for the survival of republican values. The Beards found it ironic that "American democrats were entertained by kings and queens in a succession of historical pictures."[64] This social phenomenon could only be explained as an example of the escapism that the Beards believed had perverted the movies. Although the industry could conceivably be harnessed to a higher good and thereby advance American civilization, they found only scattered examples in the feature films of the 1930s to commend and weighed in heavily on the deleterious effects of most films on tastes and morals.

Mary Beard is reputed to have been the major author of materials on cultural and social history in this work, but this did not stop Charles Beard using his prestige to push such views within the AHA's Commission on the Social Studies when it deliberated over the state of history in the schools in the early 1930s. Beard's influence was especially clear in part 9 of the commission's report, written by educationalist George Counts, Beard's close collaborator. In *The Social Foundations of Education,* Counts lamented the deleterious influence of the cinema. Through it "boys and girls are admitted to the adult world, with an unnatural emphasis on sex, sadism, crime, and generally a life of luxury and ostentatious display."[65] A moral and cultural critique was also manifest in the volumes that Beard himself wrote. In *A Charter for the Social Science* (1932), he declared "one of the problems of education" to be how to combat, in the interest of higher civilization and morality, the undesirable effect of "abundant" leisure exploited "by cheap and often degrading commercial amusements."[66]

The view of the Beards (and of Counts) had contradictory impacts. On the one hand, it allowed for the first time a serious consideration of the social and economic history of film as an American institution and provided a critique of film's historical functions. In this respect the Beards went beyond the moral panic of the 1920s. This aspect of the Beards' work would, however, languish in the post–World War II period as much as Charles Beard's economic interpretation of history did. A similarly trenchant critique of cinema's influence did not reemerge until after the New Left appeared, when radical historians discussed the way Hollywood dehistoricized historical plots and thereby undermined rather than strengthened historical consciousness.[67] On the other hand, the Beards' work did draw upon the preexisting moralism and gave new depth to intellectuals' disquiet over popular culture. In this way the Beards helped to distance historians, along with other intellectuals, from film as an interpretation of the past. They reinforced the sense that historical films might provide illustrative material but not adequate representations of history. Motion pictures they mostly relegated to the category of lowbrow entertainment.

The two sides of the critique appeared in Margaret Thorp's *America at the Movies* (1939). Thorp, a niece of prominent historian Max Farrand, argued that the movies touched every "phase of American life" and thereby illustrated the importance of movies as a social institution. But the concluding chapter, "The Lure of Propaganda," drew on Beards' distrust of the power of movies and asserted that they perverted the truth about the past. In the *Mississippi Valley Historical Review* Elmer Ellis held Thorp's claim to be "especially significant" among the findings of the book and urged social historians to take notice.[68]

When scholars such as Ellis and Thorp recognized the capacity of the cinema to exert power over social and political life, this was not a one-sidedly negative view. The movies could be a positive force. Several of the AHA's Commission on the Social Studies reports considered, as Counts put it, that film could become a "fine cultural instrument," depending upon "the appearance of a more critical and intelligent public and the removal of the domination of the commercial spirit."[69] When Du Bois criticized *Birth of a Nation*, he was careful to note the work's artistic advances. It would have been "a great step in the development of a motion-picture art" if the film were not "the vehicle" for "one of the least defensible attacks upon the Negro race."[70] Similarly, the 1944 report on the teaching of American history in the high schools written for the major organizations of professional historians stated that motion pictures, when "carefully made," were "one of the most effective complements to formal history" and found films especially useful in "the reproduction of the details of everyday life, an achievement difficult for the writer of history."[71]

Although Allan Nevins criticized the potential of film to tell lies about the past, he did not oppose Hollywood's use of historical themes. Indeed, he had offered his own book *Fremont: Pathmarker of the West* to MGM Studios as a possible source for a film in 1939. But MGM wrote back saying that the studio had already committed to a heavy dose of historical productions and the market could bear no more.[72] It may well have chagrined Nevins that all of the stories preferred by MGM were based on historical novels. But Nevins did not believe that the distorting impact of movies could have a long-term negative effect because, unlike the Beards, he saw movies as an intellectually ephemeral medium. It was of some consolation to him to believe that only books could provide sustained coverage of a historical theme.[73]

Given the ambivalent views of historians toward feature film in the 1930s, the appearance of an alternative genre in the form of the historical documentary was welcome. This could be more easily turned to school or college use since educational films were cheaper, shorter, and more suitable for classrooms.[74] Moreover, the use of documentary techniques seemed closer to the idea of a neutral rendering of a topic, though some historians were already aware of the creative and imaginative role of the filmmaker, as well as the presence of social and economic interests determining which documentaries would be made. One stimulus to academic historians' interest was the appearance of Pare Lorentz's *The Plow That Broke the Plains* (1936) and *The River* (1937); both were essentially historical works documenting the background to New Deal reforms in conservation policy.[75] Of equal importance was the establishment of a Division of Motion Pictures and Sound Recording within the National Archives at its founding in 1934.[76] At the 1940 AHA annual meeting, the chief of that division, John G. Bradley, gave the very first paper dealing with film to the major professional historical organizations, in which he discussed differences between "naïve" and more obviously and artfully constructed documentary sources.[77] During the previous year, Charles and Mary Beard had already discussed the political aspects of documentary film's constructed character. They agreed with the idea that documentaries offered more hope to historians than the run-of-the-mill feature films of the 1930s, noting among their positive comments that "[t]o the large store of federal [government] films, teachers and leaders interested in the future of American democracy could turn for concrete information . . . and for inspiriting scenes of public service." Yet this approval of documentaries was compromised by the Beards' belief that big capital dominated the movies in alliance with the state. The highly organized and lucrative industry might, in the dangerous situation of the late 1930s, be easily turned to pro-state propaganda in commercial or semiofficial documentary films and newsreels.[78]

From the 1930s onward, academic historians had little or no direct input in the conception and production of historical films, either feature or documentary. When the wartime Why We Fight "documentaries" directed by Frank Capra were made, historians took no part as writers or commentators, and only rarely as critics. This absence of activity partly reflected the Beardian atmosphere of distrust of wartime propaganda, though, looking back, one well-known historian remembered these films as boring as much as propagandistic.[79]

Not all younger historians shared the Beards' sense of the hopelessness of Hollywood. Arthur Schlesinger Jr. submitted a piece in 1940 to *Harper's Magazine* disputing a Beardian indictment of 1930s films by editor Frederick Allen. *Harper's* refused to publish the article, in which Schlesinger, already a movie buff as well as a historical prodigy, accepted motion pictures affectionately as an integral part of modernity. Film was also, Schlesinger realized by the late 1940s, a resource for future social histories because it provided insight into "those deeper layers of collective mentality which extend more or less below the dimensions of consciousness."[80] Nor did the exclusion of academic influence from moviemaking worry all historians. Some simply accepted that they could not shape popular consciousness of the past in significant ways; only the mass media could.[81] Academic specialization meant, in any case, that historians could not easily indulge their now-casual interest in the silver screen. During the post–World War II years, the growth of film studies fell into the province of other disciplinary areas focused less on written documents. Cultural analysis of film became material for interdisciplinary American studies journals, not the *American Historical Review.*[82]

This did not mean that historians ignored the rise of visual education. The *Mississippi Valley Historical Review* had announced in its teacher section in 1945 that the time had come to join "Clio and the Camera."[83] Colonial historian Carl Bridenbaugh enthusiastically endorsed filmstrips and documentaries to aid "visualizing the life of earlier times,"[84] while Ralph Gabriel likewise encouraged audiovisual aids in the post–World War II period. Illustrations from the Pageant of America books were used for this purpose by the Yale University Press Film Service in the 1950s under Gabriel's editorial direction. Yet this new industry was dominated by educationalists and usually directed at high school needs and was not a subject of historical research.[85]

Though film temporarily slipped from academic historians' agenda, their efforts to reach wider audiences must be seen in terms of their overall response to media. The appearance of new technologies and the changing nature of the audiences that those technologies spawned created a series of challenges diverting historians' attention. Film's early promise for conveying academic history was eclipsed by the rise of mass radio audiences in the 1930s, then by a post-1948 television industry that once more encouraged popular visual representations of the past. Historians soon realized the potential of these new media, even though they could only be largely reactive to new technologies, given the capital involved in their creation. In the 1930s and 1940s, historians concentrated on facilitating the spread of radio, which they found to be a more promising field than film. Radio had a certain linearity that appealed to historians' sense of progression through time; its focus on sound could privilege words, making the medium seem a useful vehicle for intellectual argument rather than a stimulant to the senses; it was less evocative, more rational than emotional. For these reasons, radio seemed potentially superior for communication of serious history. Moreover, radio offered broader and simpler distribution networks and less costly programming possibilities. It was therefore better suited to serving historians' desire to influence the public.

6

Radio Days

*How the American Historical Association Sought
to Meet a Mass Culture*

Radio occupies an inferior place in the contemporary discourse over history's relationship to the media. Historians now regularly review movies, recognize film as a legitimate representation of history, and write substantial histories of the cinema, but until recently, radio has received less attention.[1] It was not so in the 1930s, when radio rivaled film for the allegiance of the millions and when historians explored the possibilities of the new medium. Far from deserting the general public, prominent historians made a major effort to connect the American Historical Association to a "mass" audience. For ten years from 1937, the AHA had its own national radio program, and individual historians also contributed advice, research, and commentary to commercial programs about history. They were convinced that radio was superior to film as a vehicle for both educational and mass enlightenment. By 1944 radio could be called by the leading professional associations "one of the most active and aggressive agencies for the dissemination of history." It was "a rich and colorful supplementation" for history teaching "within the limitations imposed by the nature of broadcasting."[2] Long before this, Frederick Jackson Turner had observed radio's potential revolutionary impact. "Truly the planet is shrinking," Turner argued in 1924. "Even more striking" than film was "the rise and spread of radio."[3]

The AHA's chance for influence came from startling advances in the new medium's organization. By the early 1930s, improvements in transmission technology and the emergence of national networks created a mass radio audience. More important still was political controversy over control of the airwaves.[4] Historians were not alone in seeking improvements in program quality. Politicians, experts, churches, reformers, and public-interest groups demanded in the New Deal era that the new medium's communication and educational potential be marshaled for the common good.[5] The Women's National Radio Committee and its affiliates such as the Woman's Christian Temperance Union attacked the debasement of popular culture in mass media and urged use of radio to provide cultural and educational programming. These community organizations sought to raise broadcasting to "the highest possible plane" and looked forward to the development of "an American standard of culture."[6] A lively radio lobby developed through groups with confusingly similar names but different agendas. The National Advisory Council on Radio in Education (1931), with Rockefeller and Carnegie funds, produced *Radio and Education*. More politically progressive was the National Committee on Education by Radio. It favored government ownership of part of the airwaves and government control to promote educational use.[7] Although the National Advisory Council similarly concentrated on the "larger social and governmental policies of radio education," it did not advocate public ownership. In addition, Ohio State University's Institute for Education by Radio (1930) held annual conferences and produced *Education on the Air*. The institute focused on "the techniques of educational broadcasting" and gave space at its meetings to advocates of the commercial networks and government control alike.[8] The networks themselves promoted educational programming through the National Advisory Council because they wished to avoid the direct government control—or public station competition—that distinguished radio in many European countries. This combination of politics and technical changes gave historians the opportunity to exert influence and shape public audiences.

By working within the framework of commercial radio through the National Advisory Council, the AHA became aligned de facto with its policies against the alternative of a government-owned radio network or some other form of public control. This choice was a pragmatic and realistic one with short-term benefits for academic history's public outreach. (After all, the New Deal produced only a series of temporary agencies in the area of culture, agencies whose funding was ultimately eliminated just before and during World War II.)[9] But the decision to utilize national commercial networks did limit the freedom of academics to communicate their concept of history and contributed to the ultimate demise of the AHA's radio program.

If the possibilities of mass communication outlined by Turner in 1924 were national and global, radio and history came together first at the grass-roots level through state and local historical societies. The State Historical Society of Iowa gave a series of radio talks in connection with Iowa History Week in 1928. In Minnesota, more than twenty talks were given in 1927–28, with the result that family papers and diaries were turned over to the Minnesota State Historical Society.[10] Such programs multiplied in the 1930s and early 1940s. In 1942 the Detroit Council on Local History produced an award-winning series on the history of Michigan, with historian Sydney Glazer of Wayne State University providing research.[11]

While several midwestern state historical societies undertook such programming during the Great Depression, academic historians had already pioneered another local avenue for the dissemination of historical scholarship. The 1920s witnessed a flurry of educational programs as universities founded their own radio stations and rushed to sponsor outreach activities that might extend their public profile or provide cheaper ways of providing courses. Station WSUI broadcast both University of Iowa history lectures and state history talks as well as programming visiting speakers such as Dixon Ryan Fox.[12] The University of Illinois started similar work in 1931 with James G. Randall's lecture series, "History of the South since the Civil War." By that time, the University of Wisconsin, which boasted of having the nation's first educational radio station, broadcast lectures all over the state as WHA radio's part of the university's extension program, the Wisconsin College of the Air. After 1933, John D. Hicks's lectures in American history and those of Pulitzer Prize winners Paul Buck and Merle Curti were among those recorded.[13] Through the College of the Air, Curti found a wider audience for his Social and Intellectual History of the United States course.[14] While the Midwest forged ahead with this work, in the South less was done, with Tennessee and North Carolina being the most prominent.[15]

The early stations were often skeptical about broadcasting actual college classes—of which history was the first chosen in the pioneering case of Illinois. But the unsolicited audience response was strong and positive. Listeners asked for more educational programs and criticized stations for not having started them sooner. An old Civil War veteran wrote to say how much he had appreciated Randall's talks.[16] Such lecture programs extended classroom teaching, but they did more than give course credits. These programs provided a wide access to the general public, reaching people who could not get to libraries to borrow books and who were too poor to buy them. Mrs. E. M. Shuart of Kenosha, Wisconsin, liked WHA's broadcast of the addresses given at the Southern Wisconsin Teachers Convention at Madison:

My job as farm homemaker is a full time one and even if I could afford to buy the books we ought to read I should not have time enough to study them; so I have to get what I can just by listening to the lectures whenever it is possible for me to do so. Even that way I have been learning much that I did not know before. When I was in high school I used to dream about attending the University although I knew it was impossible; but now, almost twentyfive years later I am at least able to listen to some of the professors teaching there.[17]

University stations also offered a variety of specialist programs appealing to different local constituencies. Those about the history of labor and immigration reflected the growing emphasis on social and economic history in academic circles, as well as the surge of industrial unionism after 1935 in midwestern states such as Michigan.[18] Other courses covered minority groups and cultural history, as well as the standard political fare. Wilberforce University's *Music and the Negro,* broadcast through WLW Cincinnati, traced the history of African American music "from its jungle rhythms, through the spirituals of slavery days to the swing music of today." This program won first prize in 1939 from the Institute for Education by Radio with a citation as "restrained and sincere" in its portrayal of African American life.[19]

The state and university programs had their limitations. In the 1930s, not-for-profit radio was heavily concentrated in the land grant colleges and state universities. Moreover, educational radio was contracting at the grassroots level. In many states, transmitters were weak, finances were poor, and coverage was restricted. In North Carolina, for example, WPTF Raleigh, the commercial radio station carrying history broadcasts, reached only a quarter of the state's population in 1933.[20] Federal regulatory requirements and depression era budgetary problems led some universities to cut their commitment to radio, and many stations closed.[21] In those that remained, programmers often preferred such subjects as poultry raising, soil management, and cooking, though history crept in not only directly but also indirectly through social science, government, and citizenship offerings.

These grassroots initiatives were overshadowed in the mid-1930s by the development of the major networks and their affiliated programs. Because educational radio had a vocal lobby, and to prevent the possibility of extensive government regulation, the networks began to extend their own educational content. In addition to such formal educational initiatives as the Columbia School of the Air, which included history, the networks began programs of general historical interest aimed at the whole family and slated for evening listening. The Columbia Broadcasting System (CBS) introduced the most prominent, the *Cavalcade of America,* in 1935. By 1940 it had an audience of 6 million

"devoted fans." Other programs dealt much more with current events, including the popular *Town Meeting of the Air* on NBC (National Broadcasting Company), with an audience that reached 2.5 million listeners by 1938.

The AHA Council saw this network expansion as precisely the opportunity
that they needed. In cooperation with the networks, the AHA promoted a program called *The Story behind the Headlines*. Driving the AHA intervention was
the work of Conyers Read, executive secretary of the AHA from 1933 to 1941,
and his future wife, Evelyn Plummer Braun.[22] Read was different from the average member of the AHA in ways that partially explained his sensitivity to
public audiences. With a Ph.D. from Harvard, he had taught at the University
of Chicago until, in 1920, he took over the family textile business in Philadelphia. This experience in business through the 1920s seemed to orient him toward the problem of marketing history, but his commitment to Progressive
history also helped. As the AHA's full-time executive officer for eight years, he
became an activist—supporting applied-history projects, intervening in debates over history and the schools, negotiating to establish a popular magazine
of history, and, most important, pursuing with vigor the idea that the new
technology of radio should be used to make history more popular. Read's restless style matched Allan Nevins's own impatience with academe. It included
a penchant for the Dictaphone to pen "brusque" directives to colleagues
through a secretary. Like Nevins, Read cared deeply about history, and in this
he had a strong ally in Braun. For the detail of the radio work and tireless publicity, Braun was indispensable. As the American Association for State and Local History put it, the AHA program's success was due "primarily to her constant zeal, her driving power, and her tact in dealing with people."[23]

Read, Braun, and their allies in the AHA were not interested in purely local
or state efforts. They wanted a national approach, because they saw this as the
way to attract a larger and more general audience. Local efforts were, as Vassar
College historian Elizabeth Yates Webb put it for the AHA's Radio Committee
in 1934, "good enough as history, but not good for popular consumption." The
local programs had not solved "the educational problem with which we are
concerned—that of attracting and of educating the general public."[24] Once
the programs began, the AHA committee members were delighted that the
series reached a nationwide audience.[25]

National network programming would allow the AHA to fulfill its agenda
on the Scientific History discourse. Since the 1890s, under the influence of J.
Franklin Jameson, the association had been driven by the equation of "general" history to national and international history and by the desire to transcend parochial and particularistic concerns of local history groups. Network
radio time could address the national and not the local audience, bypassing

the antiquarian. It was never intended that the audience's interests would be purely American, however. The field was history considered broadly to include European and other international events of significance to better-educated Americans.

The AHA's radio involvement began in the early years of the depression, just as the movie effort at Yale faded. Several of the same individuals were involved. In December 1930 the Executive Council of the AHA appointed a special committee to work with the National Advisory Council on Radio in Education. Columbia's John Allen Krout served as chair of the Committee on History as part of the National Advisory Council's annual assemblies.[26] The committee included Ralph Gabriel (Yale), William E. Dodd (University of Chicago), Raymond Buell (Foreign Policy Association), and R. D. W. Connor (University of North Carolina). They planned a number of historical series—the first on the American Revolution to accompany the bicentenary of George Washington's birth, to be celebrated in 1931. In pushing this plan, Krout had a strong commitment to spread public knowledge of American history. He had been one of the authors of the Pageant of America, the popular pictorial history series edited by Gabriel. Through Gabriel came Yale links that stemmed from the Chronicles of America film project. The committee enlisted Nathaniel Stephenson, the chief architect of the Photoplays, to develop a radio series on the American Revolution, with a strong ideological purpose "to set forth the American point of view" in the dispute with Britain and "make clear how that great drama advanced the cause of democracy." Krout and his allies foresaw the dangers of esoteric knowledge, warning that "[w]henever possible," the phrasing of "the specialist should be avoided." Therefore, the committee advised that the "wider appeal" of "dramatic sketches," not well-written lectures, should be used.[27]

Nothing came of this initial venture, though the George Washington Bicentennial Commission of 1931 made historical broadcasts using Albert Bushnell Hart, of Harvard.[28] For the AHA, dramatic sketches turned out to be too expensive, especially if the job were to be professionally done.[29] In 1934, the committee detailed what the AHA planned to do in a paper presented by Elizabeth Yates Webb at the National Radio and Education conference. Here the AHA's hopes and fears were set out in a model document still referred to years later. She told how history had lost ground to mass media. Underlying this loss was the division between popular history and the academic exercise. "The listening public has learned through experience to expect its history in highly colored, sensational episodes," as in public or media representations, or in "dull, remote lectures about events which once happened." The gap would somehow have to be bridged.[30]

The objective was to show history's value, but the historians' group conceived of their discipline as valuable in two potentially contradictory ways: the cultural aim of "enlarging [people's] individual capacities for pleasure and cultural pursuits" and the democratic aim of helping them to live "intelligently as a part of a very complex modern society." In theory, and in the committee's view, these two aims could be reconciled: the audience would be large because it would be based on that sizable body of listeners thought to be passive and simply in need of something better than the low standard of programming common in commercial radio. Once good material able to serve the first aim was presented, a mass audience of "habitual listeners" would flock to the historian's fare instead of remaining addicted to the existing dross. To achieve these twin aims, the AHA committee would have to tread a middle ground—not too academic but not sensational either. "We are determined to be interesting to the populace" and "not to talk down to our audience," Webb wrote. Yet with the same stroke of the pen she affirmed the need "to maintain our scholarly integrity." The contradiction could be resolved, according to the AHA committee, by conceiving history, not as facts, but as "historical-mindedness." History would enable the public "to see that society is not static," that the past was not simply "the present" in an earlier period.[31]

Read and Braun (they were married by 1940) were, along with such supporters as Webb and University of Pennsylvania historian Roy Nichols, greatly influenced by the debates of the 1930s over history as an instrumental activity. With such figures as Henry Steele Commager, Krout, and William L. Langer, Read and Braun shared the view in the debates over amateur and professional written history that "the end of learning is not the writing of a learned monograph." They felt the isolation of the academic who discovers that "ivory towers are lonely places" and blamed this powerlessness on historians for retreating into obscurity. Adapting the ideas of the Progressives, Braun argued that "the aim of broadcasting sound history was to clarify the present."[32] Hence, they chose to do a program that would, like some contemporary high school social studies courses, move from the present to analyze the historical background of current events. This activity would have "political" content in the sense of commenting on important issues of the day. Like Charles Beard, the AHA committee felt that history must be "controversial," as Webb put it, and turning attention to the past would not necessarily be a conservative move. Rather, history through radio would open up alternative possibilities and so question why things were done the way that they were. This could well be radical.[33]

Despite this talk about conservatism and controversy, the new public activism could be reconciled with objectivity. Historians must present facts impartially, though they would select for presentation those that would highlight relationships of contemporary significance. This approach again drew upon Beard. Objectivity equaled the ability of the writer to get outside himself or herself: the historian must, as Braun put it, "be objective" by thinking of history, "not in terms of his own interest," but those of the audience, "an audience made up, not of students respectfully attending to their teacher," but "of men and women living their lives amid the realities of a stern and very confusing modern world."[34] In this view, the audience of a mass democratic citizenry determined the truly "objective."

Greatly influencing this formulation were commonplace ideas of a "mass" society swayed by the rampant influence of new "mass media." Webb's report mixed the influence of both conservative and radical critiques of mass culture, showing how closely these were intertwined as culturally conditioned, elitist responses.[35] She entitled her report "A Broadcasting Venture in Mass Education," vowing to tackle radio on its own "mass terms." This was a time when the American Association for Adult Education was promoting "mass education" for the many Americans who never went to university. Some authors noted the negative connotation of the "mass" as an undifferentiated public swayed by "emotion rousing" methods,[36] since Nazism, Fascism, and the Soviet Union were never far away when the media's potential was discussed. Phillips Bradley, a Queens College political science professor and contributor to the AHA radio program, found impressive the "powerful influence of mass opinion in making policy" in the "dictatorships" of Europe.[37] Equally worrying was the impact of mass media on culture in the United States. Like other academics and intellectuals, historians were apprehensive, believing that in the mass media minimal taste and much ignorance prevailed.[38]

Serious research on mass media was more measured in response than these fears would indicate. Paul Lazarsfeld had already begun his Princeton Radio Project research, which stressed the variety of audience responses and the existence of separate markets within the mass that could be tapped.[39] He greatly disparaged the potential for disseminating high culture to the mass and saw a deterioration in the quality of the listeners for news and serious cultural programs even while showing that a broader coverage had been achieved.[40]

Historians veered uncertainly over the next few years between acceptance of the limits that Lazarsfeld identified and much broader ambitions. They dreamed of the widest possible market but constantly compromised this aim by vowing to keep standards acceptable to professionals. Aware of the possible negative aspects of mass media, historians responded to the threat that these new media seemed to pose for rational thought and intellectual life. Webb drew attention to the "ideas and attitudes, emotions, tastes and actions of people" that were "almost determined by the influence of popular journals, the cinema and the radio. . . . The information available is frequently so distorted by bias or sensationalism that most of it cannot be called educational." Allied to this problem was the role of advertising, which meant that snappy and appealing programs must be made. "[O]ur broadcasts will be heard by people whose consuming habits have been built up through the persistent and spectacular din of advertising." The committee realized that advertising itself distorted history, noting the use of historical icons in commercials to sell dog biscuits.[41] Despite its desire to reach the masses, the AHA committee refused to pander to mass culture in the way that advertising did. As Krout put it, "it is better to have a small audience of intelligent listeners to a program of real merit than to have an audience of several millions for a dramatic program which is mediocre."[42]

Although the mass media posed a threat to culture and historical consciousness, it could still be history's savior. The new medium might solve the problem of historians' influence and provide a mass market for history if programs were properly presented. While some European examples were negative, others were positive, and the AHA looked to the BBC's effective and responsible programming of culture. Indeed, the AHA added Felix Greene, the BBC's American representative, to its committee to give advice. The committee rejected any idea for a deliberately segmented market approach to the audience and also declared university programming too limited for its purposes. Webb believed that "the social significance of the radio" lay elsewhere, "in its potentialities as an instrument for mass enlightenment."[43] Radio gave unparalleled opportunities in this regard because "for every one who quotes the columns of the newspaper during his daily rounds, a dozen would quote the radio." If news could be spread that way, then history could be diffused better than through books or classroom lectures. It was no good simply opposing new media, because these tapped instinctual behavior. "We are born listening," Braun argued, whereas reading must be learned and remained a conscious activity. Historians must utilize this habitual and deeply rooted desire to listen and thereby appeal to the public on "its own mass terms."[44]

Yet the aim was not simply to stimulate interest in history but to complement reading and to expand the domain of traditional historical discourse. Historians saw new media not as alternative ways of structuring historical perceptions but as ways of reinforcing the professional project. Radio would not produce a change in consciousness—it would truly be the medium, not the message. A great deal of community debate in the 1930s concerned fears that reading would decline due to the influence of film and radio. Not everybody agreed, however. Historians were among the hopeful: the proposed AHA program's "real significance" would depend, "not on how widely we are heard, but on how widely we are successful in inducing listeners to go further in their reading."[45] In turn, reading would drive work analogous to that of the Association for Adult Education and thus reinforce history's role as the foundation for citizenship education. Conyers Read envisaged correspondence with the audience, organizations of listeners, and the cooperation of public libraries in the preparation and distribution of supplementary history reading lists: "One can conceive of a whole system of adult education developing around a nucleus of this sort."[46]

If one had to choose among the mass media for the AHA's purpose, the prospects for radio seemed better than for film. Radio programs were cheaper to produce, more flexible in format, more extensive in their distribution networks, and hence more accessible to families and schools. Intellectually the medium was more closely aligned with print, and so historians felt more comfortable with it than with the visual. Radio was not as revolutionary as film, which transformed ways of "perceiving reality." As Eric Hobsbawm has argued, the medium produced no new ways of "seeing or establishing relations between sense impressions and ideas," yet "its capacity for speaking simultaneously to untold millions, each of whom felt addressed as an individual, made it an inconceivably powerful tool of mass information."[47] The work of the AHA's Radio Committee testified to the accuracy of these points. For Braun, radio's great advantage was its sense of "intimacy." The audience felt that it was being spoken to directly. Listeners gave greater attention to the words precisely because they could not see the presenter reading from a book.[48] More than intimacy, however, radio had an "immediacy" it would later share with television. As Cesar Saerchinger, the AHA's radio presenter emphasized, "The imaginative appeal of being present, even though only through the aural sense, at an event that is taking place now, is so great that the impression on the listener is bound to be permanent." The committee treated this instantaneous quality as linked to history. "The only difference between news and history," Saerchinger remarked, was "a difference of tenses; when you broadcast news you broadcast history."[49]

★ ★ ★

The goal was clear enough. The means were not so clear in the early 1930s. There was a long gap between the conception and the appearance of the AHA's first program in 1937. Running initially on CBS as *History behind the Headlines* and later on NBC as *The Story behind the Headlines,* the program lasted until December 1947.[50] The initial idea of a dramatic series was rejected. Not only would drama be too expensive, but it might undermine the program's high-mindedness. The fear was that episodes might be chosen for "their dramatic possibilities rather than because they had historical validity in themselves or in relation to the present day." Instead, Read and his allies picked a format that would reflect on current events by mapping out the historical background and significance of those events. Each week a headline would be chosen for comment and academic historians asked to provide draft material at short notice, from which the presenter would write the script. This in turn would be checked by the historian consultant and then by a member of the AHA Radio Committee. "In this way historical accuracy would be insured, as well as freedom from obvious bias or special pleading."[51]

The scheme seemed a trifle unwieldy, but the committee could alleviate the obvious logistical hurdles by using researchers from Philadelphia to New Haven, close to the major studios and to Read. The presenter was crucially important and needed to "combine the skill and popular appeal of a professional broadcaster with the learning of a professional scholar."[52] Read envisaged the presenter, not as shaping the material, but as a conduit. Akin to the family doctor, he would diagnose society's contemporary ills, using the scientific knowledge provided by specialists.[53] Consultants would supply the expertise. These included Max Lerner, editor of *Nation* and Williams College academic; prominent Columbia historians Krout, Harry Carman, and Carlton J. H. Hayes; Roy Nichols; Commager, then of New York University; Charlotte Muret, of Barnard College; J. Salwyn Shapiro, of City College; and Stanley Pargellis, of Yale. Most of these, particularly Pargellis, Krout, and Commager, became associated with Nevins and the Society of American Historians in the promotion of the proposed popular magazine of American history. Raising its own money and essentially run by Read and Braun after 1936, the Radio Committee was functionally independent of the AHA. But the idea of a radio program was much more widely shared, as the committee activity and the support given by historians as consultants indicated.[54]

The first series began with support from the Keith Foundation and later from the Carnegie Corporation.[55] Through the support of broadcaster Edward R. Murrow, then educational director of CBS, thirteen talks were broadcast over CBS in 1937, with regular news "spot" reporter Bob Trout as the presenter.[56] As Braun confided, "He's not a scholar, which is probably a good thing, as we're not aiming the broadcasts at scholars."[57] However, Trout was almost immediately declared unsatisfactory. Of this first set of talks Braun admitted that "as literary gems they are, I think, uniformly not good,"[58] and the committee decided to dump Trout. They needed someone who gave his whole time to the project, whereas Trout did the job part-time and for nothing. CBS and Murrow disagreed and so did not renew the series.[59]

For the second series, the AHA was fortunate to get the support of NBC. James R. Angell, former president of Yale, was educational counselor for the network and anxious to expand educational programming. It was Angell who changed the program's title from "History" to "Story" to make it more listener friendly.[60] Saerchinger was chosen as presenter. With a background as foreign correspondent for the *New York Evening Post* and the *Philadelphia Ledger,* Saerchinger was a more experienced writer and broadcaster than Trout.[61] In fact, Saerchinger's "long European experience" documented in *Hello, America* (1938) was decisive. It gave him "additional understanding of areas and peoples to which we should be called upon to give much attention."[62] As *Radio Daily* pointed out, Saerchinger was also a good communicator who "talks with quiet authority, and both his voice and manner of speaking are pleasant to the ear."[63] The series began on 8 March 1938 and continued weekly (at first not during the summers) until 1947 with the same presenter, though guests such as James T. Shotwell, Read, and, in 1943, AHA president Nellie Neilson appeared.[64] Saerchinger's first talk, "England's Foreign Policy," detailed the background to and implications of the resignation of Anthony Eden from the British cabinet.[65]

Befitting Read's plan that radio should enhance reading, not supplant it, the talks did not take place in isolation. They were complemented by the *Bulletin of "The Story behind the Headlines."* This weekly periodical appeared during the first two years of the NBC series. Under the influence of Krout, the Columbia University Press generously subsidized the publication, which strengthened the proposed links with adult education. Each issue contained an article based on the talk and a bibliography. Editorials extolling the importance of history and articles on historiography and philosophy of history were added. There, Read and others explained what history was and how the practice of history related to present-day concerns. Read told his audience that history was not merely an assemblage of facts but that "the facts selected for emphasis" were crucially important.[66] In another contribution, Webb attacked censorship of textbooks and reminded readers that patriotism had engulfed textbook writers during and after World War I.[67]

Even the trial CBS series got a good response, even though no effort was made to solicit fan mail because the funds available were not sufficient to answer correspondence in any quantity or to distribute copies of talks. In spite of that, many listeners wrote to express interest, to ask for further reading on the subjects broadcast, and to support the extension of the series. Read and Braun replied to each letter individually, gave advice on bibliographies, and suggested locations of suitable libraries. "With sufficient money available," Read predicted, "a very significant educational work could be done in follow-up."[68]

* * *

The initial talk of *The Story behind the Headlines* conducted by Saerchinger in 1938 won first prize for an educational program on a commercial network at the Annual Institute for Education by Radio in Columbus, Ohio. The award cited "intimacy of appeal, striking statements," outstanding "visualization," and "well-balanced, unbiased interpretation."[69] NBC official Franklin Dunham found the series "so good" and "so complimentary to NBC" that he praised Saerchinger for the "fine work he has done in our interest."[70] Though the focus was on national and international events, the series inspired efforts in new media among local historical groups. State historical societies expanded their radio offerings and introduced more variety and lively programming. The American Association for State and Local History praised radio as "a channel for reaching the public which has limitless possibilities" and applauded the pioneering role of the AHA in demonstrating the potential.[71]

The listening audience was also impressed. Ratings were respectable, if not outstanding.[72] As a result of its success, for the first time in 1941 the program continued through the summer at the request of NBC,[73] achieving in 1943 a Crosley C.A.B. rating of 6.5. "This is exceptionally high for such a program and is the highest of any sustaining talks program on N. B. C.," noted Braun—despite the fact that the series constantly had to battle against poor time slots and was broadcast mostly in the late evening because of its noncommercial nature.[74]

The program's content was largely political, not social and cultural. Before World War II, domestic and international topics were equally well represented, but after 1940, foreign and military affairs dominated. The AHA made the series "a definite war activity for the A.H.A., for the broadcasts have inevitably been concerned with backgrounds of the war." War exigencies exerted great influence. The script for 8 November 1942, for example, had been finished when the Allied invasion of North Africa was announced. A late switch resulted in desperate but successful efforts to arrange a talk on the French African empire "with the aid of back scripts" and hurried late-night "telephone consultations" with historians. Wartime allowed the series to concentrate on its mission to present information for the "public good," rather than its other original aim of cultural enrichment of the individual. On 8 March 1942, on-air remarks by James T. Shotwell and Read stressed the "im-

portance of radio in the world today and how much history has to contribute
to a better understanding of the complicated and bewildering present."[75] After 1945, foreign affairs remained important, but the program also covered
such domestic issues as the steel strike of 1946 and employment readjust-
ment.[76]

Though the AHA Radio Committee boasted that management never interfered with scripts, internal NBC criticism of the presenter's supposed liberal
bias did occur.[77] In 1938, Saerchinger wrote an article disturbingly in favor of
European-style government ownership of radio. Educational director Angell
commented that "he is allowed his views" but "cannot expect wholly satisfactory relations with the American industry, if his convictions lead him to a position which would in effect destroy that industry." Angell believed that "with all
its shortcomings, the American system" was "far more expedient and, politically, far less dangerous than the continental one." However, the program survived, as Saerchinger's views were not expressed on air. He also came under attack from listeners over the program's obvious alliance with the New Deal
tradition. A documentary recording of FDR's speeches, called *Rendezvous with
Destiny,* with historical narration by Saerchinger, supported claims that the
presenter was of decidedly liberal views.[78] These continued postwar, with a
Florida resident responding to a 1946 program that "[t]the address of Mr.
Saerchinger was pure propaganda for Chester Bowles and the O.P.A [Office of
Price Administration]."[79] Saerchinger's postwar addresses undoubtedly supported President Truman against both business and unions in political and
economic conflict. His talks seemed an extension of Fair Deal liberalism.

Opposition from within the historical profession also surfaced. *The Story
behind the Headlines* had initially been linked with Read, and resentment toward his executive style had grown toward the end of his tenure, complicating
efforts to run the radio series. As Thomas Bailey, a critic of Read explained,
"He made a lot of enemies while serving the Association, largely through his
lack of tact."[80] After 1941 Read had ceased to be executive secretary and the
Radio Committee's influence declined. There had always been reservations
about such a present-centered program within the AHA, just as there was
against Beard's activist and present-centered written history. In 1938 Solon
Buck had advised Braun that the broadcasts were "well written and objective,"
but he found the presentist emphasis in the *Bulletin* overdone. An article by
William Langer would have been more appropriate in a journal of "opinion"
than in a publication sponsored by the AHA.[81] The issues often seemed to be
oversimplified by the program, even though historians regarded the series as a
good idea in principle.

But finances, not academic politics, threatened the program most. The first blow came as early as the end of the 1939–40 series, when Columbia University stopped producing the *Bulletin*. The press could not continue to subsidize the book version, as it "was a losing venture." NBC continued to offer mimeographed copies free on request, but their availability was no longer advertised over the air because the budget did not allow a wide distribution. A more important threat came from NBC financial contributions. The *Headlines* program depended heavily on the network. The subsidy by 1944 was said to be in excess of $50,000 a month measured by lost commercials. "[T]he demand for advertising time on the networks greatly exceeds the time available," Read told Guy Stanton Ford, "and the pressure to convert public service programs into sponsored paying programs is almost irresistible."[82]

Commercial sponsorship seemed the answer, but this brought out latent professional opposition to Read and the program. In 1944, an offer from the Leaf Chewing Gum Company, which supplied American troops, led to conflict within the AHA. AHA council members, such as W. L. Westerman, called this attempted sponsorship the "final degradation." Even those who listened to the program called it "moderately good—mediocre rather than excellent."[83] Nevertheless, the sponsorship was narrowly accepted, and *The Story behind the Headlines* continued for another three years before NBC finally dropped it.

Though historians continued to contribute as researchers and broadcasters to commercial programs in the 1950s, they never again had an official AHA series under their control. Dumas Malone wrote *The Jeffersonian Heritage* for the National Association of Educational Broadcasters and the Ford Foundation in 1951–52,[84] while Allan Nevins and the Society of American Historians worked extensively with Broadcast Music Inc. (BMI) on its *American Story* radio talks, which were distributed to hundreds of stations across the country; many historians wrote scripts for the latter, among them Max Savelle, of the University of Washington, and Thomas Cochran, of the University of Pennsylvania, who contributed "Roger Williams, Dissenter and Democrat" and "The Factory Comes to New England" respectively.[85] None of these programs, however, had the continuity of *The Story behind the Headlines*, nor the official input from the AHA.

Hardly a total failure, *The Story behind the Headlines* had survived for ten years and exerted a far greater influence than any other attempt by academic historians at influencing the mass media. Yet its demise and its limitations both as history and as a vehicle for public outreach must be recognized. The AHA program had helped legitimate commercial radio by siding with the National Advisory Council on Radio in Education against the progovernment ownership group, the National Committee on Education by Radio. It is unlikely, of course, that any permanent national public broadcasting system on the model of the BBC could have been implemented.[86] But the failure of public broadcasting to proceed beyond university stations and public-service content on commercial radio circumscribed from the outset the AHA's chances of success. The program rose and fell on wartime audience demand and the availability of commercial sponsorship and network support, which proved transitory.

★ ★ ★

Comparing *The Story behind the Headlines* with its commercial competitors exposes these limits. The most interesting comparison is with the *Cavalcade of America*. Running from 1935 to 1939 on CBS, from 1940 to 1953 on NBC radio, and then for several seasons on television, *Cavalcade of America* differed in being a dramatic series with prominent actors in leading roles.[87] The series differed also in exploring social history more than political, and it focused on the United States alone. Moreover, it had a strong commercial sponsor in Du Pont and a better time spot (7:30 P.M. in the East, later 8 P.M.) than *The Story behind the Headlines* (which in its later stages aired at 10:45 P.M.).[88] NBC publicity emphasized that the series combined "dramatic interest, historical authenticity and significance." With the use of Robert Sherwood, Arthur Miller, Marquis James, and other popular authors as scriptwriters and with music by Don Vorhees and his orchestra, "radio's finest actors" would from time to time be featured. Occasionally, a famous star of stage or screen would "share the spotlight."[89] All these advantages gave *Cavalcade* an easier road to success than *The Story behind the Headlines*.

The drama, music, and colorful detail of human interest in the *Cavalcade* series appealed to a broader audience. While the *Headlines* program had many fans, *Cavalcade* had far more of them, and it had more political and social influence. The American Legion Auxiliary judged *Cavalcade* "the radio program most acceptable and worthwhile to the general family audience." The Women's National Radio Committee approved of the program's content for children, while students at one junior college rated *Cavalcade* highly among their "favorite educational programs."[90] The scripts were reprinted as school textbooks by the Milton Bradley Company.

This was not simply a story of scholarly ineffectiveness against commercial success, however. The harnessing of scholarly support was important for the acclaim that *Cavalcade* enjoyed. Indeed, in 1935 the AHA expressed "great interest" in the series, and five historians served in turn as research consultants.[91] Dixon Ryan Fox was the initial historical adviser for the show, followed

by James Trustlow Adams, Arthur Schlesinger Sr., and, in 1940, Frank Monaghan, and then National Parks historian Francis Ronalds from 1944. Monaghan, an assistant professor at Yale, also wrote scripts and made some of the
on-air announcements, while Schlesinger and Fox edited and published talks
from the program.[92] Through scholarly support, *Cavalcade* had gained the
professional imprimatur of historical accuracy without which it could not
have had such wide circulation. The show's "historical consultant" had a veto
over the factual content, which appealed to educators, who used the program
in their classes. The journal *Social Education* called *Cavalcade* "[o]ne of the outstanding radio programs of interest to the social studies teacher" because of
the "authenticity" imparted to the series by Monaghan's knowledge. When
Monaghan found that an episode did not accord with historical "accuracy," as
with one on Teddy Roosevelt scripted in 1941, the story was dropped.[93]

Accuracy was not what divided the academic-led *Story behind the Headlines*
from the commercial *Cavalcade*. Rather, differences centered mostly on power
and politics. Whereas the *Headlines* program adopted a critical and often liberal tone, influenced by the New Deal and Beardian ideas, the *Cavalcade* survived the 1940s better because it was a more ideologically conservative program that aligned well with commercial interests. *Cavalcade* self-consciously
sided with those who deplored the Progressives' debunking of American history in the interwar years and sought to provide a "cherished memory" of individual greatness by fostering among Americans a "respect for their own history."[94]

To achieve its conservative aims, a strong parallel was drawn between past
and present, but in the opposite way to the *Headlines* program. *Cavalcade*
sought to use the past to legitimate the present, whereas the *Headlines* sought
to use the present as a window to stimulate critical interest in the past. "[B]ased
upon American history and devoted to the preservation and appreciation of
the historic foundations of the American tradition," the *Cavalcade* program's
ideological pitch concerned the value of pioneering ideals and the parallels between these and modern American scientific and economic progress through
the slogan "Better Things for Better Living through Chemistry." Many of the
episodes concerned inventors, such as Samuel F. B. Morse, others celebrated
explorers, and still others the innovators of democratic or religious "experiments," such as those of Roger Williams and William Penn.[95] On an obvious
political level, the series also provided a public-relations coup for a previously
demonized company. In the late 1930s, *Cavalcade* legitimized the role of Du
Pont, which had been roundly criticized by isolationists for its complicity in
arms manufacture in World War I and for its role in dragging the United States
into armed European conflict.[96]

Before 1940, the series was in one sense comparable in its appeal with the *Headlines* program. Its audience "would not have satisfied many major sponsors."[97] Du Pont's interest in legitimizing its business led it to underplay the importance of ratings in the early days. But the company discovered that the audience responded especially to the stories of individual heroes portrayed by famous actors. In 1940, under Monaghan's historical guidance, the series shifted to NBC after a short interregnum. There it adopted a more expensive style of production, utilizing big-name stars like Lionel Barrymore and Henry Fonda. Like *Headlines,* the program was also aided by wartime patriotism and highlighted military conflicts and stories that showed American perseverance and courage, such as "Valley Forge." Simultaneously, the series could channel in a conservative direction the revival of American popular traditions that the New Deal had stimulated. The series was now self-consciously pitched at "those things that Americans cling to in a world that seems to have lost its sense of security, and its balance."[98] With this shift the popularity of the program rose to an all-time high during the war.

The response to *Cavalcade* in fan mail suggested that the program was remarkably successful in sanctioning the role of business, free enterprise, and Du Pont in American life. One fan, "CHR" of Seattle, wrote: "You have provided me with an entirely different perspective of the aims and purposes of the Du Pont company and what you are really doing to provide 'Better Things for Better Living through Chemistry.'" For "C O'D" of Denver: "Under these unsettled conditions this program has added value by bringing home the fact that there was good government before all the present half-baked ideas." After this thinly veiled attack on the New Deal, the Denver writer praised the program for "acquainting us with the progress made through science and invention today." *Cavalcade* "should make us all proud of the America in which we live."[99]

But fans can be fickle, and markets change. Even for *Cavalcade,* the 1950s saw the program's fortunes slide. The ratings in 1941–42 easily exceeded those for *Headlines* but fell by 1952–53 to about half the peak audience. Television's appearance and changing audience tastes made the program appear dated. When the series moved to television, it soon adopted a more contemporary focus and lost its pretensions to cover American history.[100]

In 1939, Lazarsfeld had claimed that "among the population little desire seems to exist . . . for educational broadcasting." The audience was small, but "the cultural level" of these listeners was "high." This finding indicated that educational radio was not hitting its intended target: "the great mass of population whose members may be more in need of the educational material."[101] Lazarsfeld was right. Neither *Headlines* nor *Cavalcade* could sustain a mass audience for educational programs that subscribed to scholarly standards. *Head-*

lines veered markedly toward the scholarly and thus limited its appeal; *Caval-cade* favored entertainment and ultimately lost out to the changing whims of television audiences. But the contribution of academic historians to all of these programs showed that, far from being locked away in an ivory tower, many were prepared to engage in grand plans for mass enlightenment.

Part 3

The Problem of the Schools

7

Contesting the Retreat from the Schools

Progressives and Teachers before World War II

In the depths of war in 1942–43, the *New York Times* carried alarming reports about the failure of historians to do their duty by the nation. The youth of America, in colleges and in schools, knew little about their own country's history. Some high schools did not teach American history at all. In a surprising number of states the subject was not required for graduation, and basic facts about American presidents, battles, and important legislation remained unknown to the great majority of citizens. With such immense ignorance about the traditions that Americans presumably shared, how could the United States assume the world leadership that war seemed to thrust upon it? This campaign was no passing whim: the *Times* series on this theme won nationwide headlines and support in other papers and endorsements from politicians and lobby groups and earned reporter Benjamin Fine a Pulitzer Prize for journalism. Schools and colleges, presidents and principals, strove to assure American political leaders either that the campaign claims were not true or that something was being done to remedy this deplorable neglect.

The campaign had begun with the restless and ever-energetic Allan Nevins. This time his platform was the *New York Times Magazine* in May 1942. Nevins seized on the statistic that twenty-two states required no high school instruction in American history. This amounted to cultural suicide, he argued. A people would "always find the richest source of cultural interest in its own past."

For Nevins, the arguments were "particularly forceful" in the wartime situation, since "national identity and national ideals are both rooted in history." War had, "like a sudden flash of light from a terrific explosion," thrown "illumination" on the question of "the patriotism and unity of the country." Historians must come to the rescue.[1]

Urged on by Nevins, Dixon Ryan Fox, and others, and backed by Iphigene Ochs Sulzberger, wife of the publisher of the *Times*, that paper began its series of investigations into the condition of American history in the schools and colleges.[2] In June 1942 the *Times* turned to the higher education system. It announced that U.S. history was not required by 82 percent of colleges for graduation, and that 30 percent of the college freshman class enrolled in world or European history, compared to 8 percent for U.S. history. In 1943 the *Times* published a survey of seven thousand college freshmen undertaken by Nevins and his supporters in the Committee for American History, the self-appointed watchdog. It was this survey that purported to uncover students' widespread ignorance of basic facts of American history.[3]

This public and political campaign was no isolated event. Time after time throughout the twentieth century, history teaching in American schools came under attack for its content and consequences. In recent decades American historians have rejoined the chorus of criticism initiated by Nevins, indicting both the history profession for omissions of duty and soft school curricula for the neglect of American history. In the 1980s and 1990s, the controversy over "cultural illiteracy" bore a striking resemblance to the Nevins/*New York Times* campaign. Diane Ravitch led the way in 1985 and 1987 with a series of articles and, with Chester Finn, *What Do Our 17-Year-Olds Know? A Report on the First National Assessment of History and Literature*. The answer seemed to be—demeaningly little.[4] In part agreeing with these criticisms of curricula and the state of knowledge, academic historians and their allies reasserted the importance of their discipline within social studies and over other social sciences. The Bradley Commission on History in Schools, established in 1987, wistfully surveyed a time when history was dominant in the social sciences and blamed historians and other educators for failing in their duty. Prominent historians and educators, including Kenneth Jackson of Columbia University, served on the commission. In the larger profession, historians such as Louis Harlan and David Kennedy became prominent advocates for the teaching of history in the schools.[5]

A chorus of voices recalled the years before World War I, when history professors played a major role in the shaping of school syllabi. Critics differed on the details whereby academic history came to lose its influence and on exactly when this happened. Generally, the critics portrayed a steady erosion from the time of World War I and dated the final abdication to the 1930s or 1940s. Academics no longer knew or cared what went on in the nation's schools. They, in Gary Nash's language, "walked away" from such involvement by the 1940s. Hazel Hertzberg, an education professor at Columbia University, blamed the change on increasing professionalization. As a contributor to the Bradley Commission, Hertzberg portrayed assaults by educators that steadily eroded history's position since around 1910 but then taxed historians for allowing this sad state of affairs to come about: "Professors who once taught the synthesizing survey courses now spent their time working with graduate students on specialized research, not on teaching. The survey course, often taught by those same graduate students, lost prestige and intellectual power in the colleges and universities."[6] Peter Novick was an agnostic on this issue of the public roles of historians, but his analysis in *That Noble Dream* likewise focused on the advance of professionalization as making historians ever more remote from the schools. According to Hertzberg, Nash, Novick, and earlier critics such as W. Stull Holt, the last (and very ineffectual) intervention by professional historians in the school curriculum came in the early 1930s.[7]

All of these views testified to the vitality of contemporary debates over history's place in civic education. As accounts of the problem of history teaching and the role of academic history within it, however, the critiques neglected several past attempts to reform history teaching in the schools, misinterpreted others, and exaggerated the extent of the decline by the 1980s and 1990s. For example, Kenneth Jackson and Barbara Jackson wrote in 1989 that "a shocking 15 percent of the nation's youngsters do not study American history in high school,"[8] and four states did not mandate any American history in high school. But compared to the 1940s, this implied a massive increase in the exposure of American students to their national history. In fact, the number of states in which American history was not mandated had dropped to less than one-fifth of its level forty years before. The Jacksons and others were closer to the mark in noting the neglect of non-American history, but the point remains clear. They exaggerated the long-term decline in the discipline.

These attacks lacked understanding of the politics of how American historians came to their present relationship with the schools. They have generally assumed that history's professionalization and academic specialization lay behind the divorce from this segment of the public; they have tended to treat the struggle as one between schools and historians, the latter usually symbolized by the American Historical Association; they have underestimated the divisions within the profession with regard to history teaching in elementary and high schools; and they have neglected the complex variety of forces contribut-

ing to the evolution of history teaching, from teacher educators, school administrators, and schoolteachers, through academic associations in competing disciplines, to political and public pressure groups. They have often failed
to distinguish between the fate of American and other histories; did not take
account of the difficulties of catering to a mass high school audience; and did
not appreciate the extent to which political interventions by pressure groups,
politicians, and some academic and nonacademic historians, particularly during the *New York Times* campaign, undermined cooperation with teachers.
Ironically, the efforts of some university professors to reassert a political and
national history during the 1940s contributed to this distance from schoolteachers and teacher educators.

★ ★ ★

The study of the long "retreat from the schools" by academic historians is a
complicated one. So many commissions of inquiry litter the record that it is
too easy to miss the main outlines of change. Far from academics abandoning
the schools from the 1910s to the 1940s, the period was marked by seemingly
endless debates over and reviews of that relationship. Reports issued forth in-
vestigating and proposing curricula every few years. Conflict erupted over the
attempts of advocates, especially located in the National Educational Association (NEA) and, after 1921, the National Council for the Social Studies (NCSS),
to introduce integrated and present-centered social studies programs. These
changes would include elements of economics, politics, and sociology along
with civics. The content of the history to be taught would change and its quantity would shrink to make way for these new, more utilitarian subjects.

But the underlying contest was not simply between social studies and
increasingly remote and ineffectual academic defenders of the status quo.
Rather, the struggle was multilateral, with historians themselves divided between Progressive reformers allied to social studies and more traditional historians. It was not "historians" who lost influence. In fact, they maintained a
remarkable degree of influence in comparison with other academic subjects.
Progressive reformers gained the upper hand within the profession during the
1920s and exerted some (albeit contested) sway over the evolving social studies. The greatest impact came from the work of James Harvey Robinson and
Charles Austin Beard, though tireless advocacy in the 1920s from that intellectual gadfly Harry Elmer Barnes and in the 1930s from other figures such as
Merle Curti contributed. Barnes wrote *The New History and the Social Studies*
and viewed the learning and teaching of history as inseparable activities that
would be revolutionized by the New History.[9] But above all, it was Beard

whose views came to be widely disseminated in school texts and syllabi in the 1930s.[10] Though Beard left the orthodox teaching profession with his resignation from Columbia University in 1917, he did not abandon his attempt to influence the wider sphere of professional historiography. Having stepped outside the formal confines of academic life, he became more committed to reform of its institutions. He denounced the "scribes" who ran the AHA and, with Robinson, helped to organize a rival to traditional universities through the New School for Social Research in 1920.[11]

A wild card in this complicated contest was the role of political interference and "public" pressure. From the 1910s onward, politicians, newspaper editors, and interest groups lobbied to boost U.S. history, change the content of British and European history, and force American school history to conform with patriotic ideals. This drive began during the hypernationalist phase of World War I. In the 1920s it took a new twist as Irish Americans and Catholics strove to defeat what they saw as Anglo bias in university-authored history texts circulating in the schools. In the mid-1930s the focus sharpened into anti-Communist pressure to expose Marxist influence on textbooks, led by the Hearst press. When the *New York Times* campaign began in 1942, it capitalized on a long history of public pressure to influence the role of academics.[12]

Until the 1940s, academics were attacked by these ethnic, populist, or right-wing groups as either too radical or as unpatriotic and pro-British. In the 1920s, academics and their amateur allies upheld scientific objectivity and insisted that the profession was not biased. Even the *New York Times,* soon to be so critical of school histories, defended historians against such populist pressures.[13] The AHA passed strong resolutions condemning legislative interference in the content of scholars' writings, and by defending their authority, academic historians became adversaries of "the public" in the form of lobby groups that included the American Legion and Irish Catholic organizations.[14]

In the 1940s, however, substantial numbers of historians sided with interest-group claims about distorted and inadequate history teaching and textbooks. Nevins was one of the leaders in this shift. These specialists (mostly of American history) not only sought alignment with a wider public but also agreed with the pressure groups' chief demand that American history should be favored over non-American history. For a significant section of the American historical profession, this was a shift from the orthodox position before World War II, which had defended through the AHA the teaching of non-American history. As a result of the wartime agitation, academics gained for a time what they had not achieved in the 1920s and 1930s, a bulwark against social studies and a reassertion of political and national American history taught in a conservative way. Historians of the United States used the wartime crisis to cement the role of professional historians and the role of U.S. history over other histories and gained advantage over non-U.S. historians and over the social studies teachers in the schools. Their position was further strengthened in the anti-Communist phase of McCarthyism from 1947 to the mid-1950s. As in other aspects of their public outreach, historians increasingly aligned themselves with the nation-state.

Leading high school history teachers, trained by the 1940s in the methods of social studies, opposed these developments. By siding with the pressure groups, the academic historians who supported Nevins and the *Times* campaign thereby undermined their ties with grassroots history teachers and their allies in teacher education whose orientation was toward the Progressive history agenda of the 1930s. Anxious to escape another Red Scare, after 1945 the AHA studiously avoided the pleas of teachers to intervene with the NCSS in disputes over the content of textbooks. The change coincided with the beginnings of a critical, anti-Beardian approach to American historiography in the research work of historians in the 1950s.[15]

* * *

These crucial shifts in the alliances of academic historians are easily obscured by the bewildering number of inquiries into the schools coming from historians and social scientists. These reports reflected the fact that in the United States, education was decentralized. States and even the school districts within them could not be changed overnight by legislative fiat. No mechanism for imposition of a national curriculum existed such as in France. Any curriculum reform had to be achieved by constant discussion and by education and guidance by experts. Curriculum change was easiest to implement in the crises of war, particularly 1941–45 but also in 1917–19. However, the cultural battles were protracted. None of the plans were implemented in their entirety, and change came in a slower and a more evolutionary fashion than reformers would have liked.[16]

The AHA exercised considerable sway over the high and elementary school curriculum from 1890 to World War I. Essentially, this influence was deployed through a series of committees in which academic historians designed detailed curricula for the schools. As early as 1892, only eight years after its founding, the AHA had built an alliance with the NEA and its teacher educators, administrators, principals, and some classroom teachers. That alliance cemented the early role of history in the curriculum. The Committee of Ten chaired by Charles K. Adams and including Woodrow Wilson had been invited by the NEA to review the teaching of history in the high schools and had laid out a general plan in which "history and civil government became the back-bone of the social studies" from grades 7 to 12.[17] The AHA's Committee of Seven (1899) laid down a clear program of four years of study in grades 9–12, with ancient history typically followed by medieval and modern European history, English history, and finally American history and civics in the final year of high school. This sequence was complemented by the Committee of Eight's report (1909), which secured in similar fashion the place of history, especially American history, in the elementary school system. In 1911 a Committee of Five submitted a review of the high school syllabus for the AHA and presented only relatively minor changes strengthening the role of modern history as against ancient. So far, so good.[18]

In these early efforts, the balance favored non-American courses. This accorded with scholarship of the time and with the power of the different specializations within the AHA. Historians agree that the recommendations of the 1899 AHA report were probably as widely adopted in the schools as humanly possible, given the diversity of the system. This report won for the early professional leaders the reputation of deep involvement in the schools, a position that later generations abandoned as professionalization and research orientation intensified. Actually, it was relatively easy to get the earliest recommendations, with their strong support for European and ancient history, adopted in schools since the system was oriented toward university entrance study. Only 6.7 percent of fourteen- to seventeen-year-olds were students in the 1890s, and college degree credit enrollments were a mere 2.3 percent of Americans in the eighteen to twenty-four age-group in 1900.[19] Moreover, historians did not face an organized lobby for rival subjects such as economics, political science, and sociology, as their professional organizations had emerged somewhat later than the AHA. Without competing academic pressure groups, the AHA was able to maintain the influence of history and hegemonic relations with the teacher educators/administrators through the NEA and cooperated with the latter in its early reports. As evidence of its commitment to influencing the schools, in 1912 the AHA also began to subsidize the *History Teacher's Magazine,* which had been founded by University of Pennsylvania historian Albert McKinley in 1909. Leading academic historians regularly wrote for this periodical, thus demonstrating their interest in high school issues.

These apparently rosy conditions changed during and just after World War I. The social context of Progressive America, with its vast numbers of immigrants and eager reformers equipped with ideas of national and social efficiency, could not be denied. Another factor was the rise of the junior high school after 1909, which spurred a reorganization of the curriculum wherever it was introduced, since it split up the four-year block on which the AHA's 1899 scheme depended. As John Franklin Jameson noted, the junior high school "must now be reckoned with."[20] With a senior high curriculum to be reorganized into a three-year sequence, the opportunity arose for social studies supporters, academics in the nonhistory areas, and school administrators to reduce European, ancient, and medieval history into a single block of world or general history, thus allowing space for American government, sociology, and economics, as well as civics.

Evidence of reform already existed before 1917, when the United States entered the world war. In 1916 a committee of the NEA's Commission on the Reorganization of the Schools—the Committee on Social Studies appointed in 1913—made its report. The change in the nature of the school population lay behind the findings.[21] Rising retention rates in the upper levels of the high schools boosted the numbers of students who would never go on to university, and with this change came the demand that their curriculum be useful in their working lives. School administrators and teacher representatives dominated this committee, and the only academic representative of substance was the historian James Harvey Robinson. He quickly exerted influence, articulating the Progressive demands for reform as part of the agenda for the New History set out in his book of that title in 1912. Drawing on Robinson's seminal work, the 1916 report argued for a reorganization of school syllabi to give more space to recent, particularly American, history at the expense of ancient and medieval, as well as time for current events and other subjects in the social sciences.[22]

The war and its aftermath provided the perfect setting for the dissemination of this plan. War frenzy begat a swelling in national pride, which in turn begat pressures for separate instruction in civics and American government and for a more useful, present-centered history. Historians did not need to share the extreme enthusiasm for war or patriotism to join in this effort. They had organized the National Board for Historical Service (NBHS) to weld professionals to the war effort, and leading scholars took part. At the request of the U.S. Bureau of Education, the NBHS produced high school pamphlets telling teachers how to restructure syllabi to highlight the struggle "between autocracy and democracy."[23] The AHA and the NBHS formed a committee in 1918 to investigate the teaching of civics, first under the directorship of NBHS official Samuel Harding, of Indiana University, then under Joseph Schafer, director of the State Historical Society of Wisconsin. This group again demonstrated close cooperation between academic historians and educators such as Daniel Knowlton, who taught history and civics at the Lincoln School at Teachers College, Columbia University. The Schafer committee reflected the influence of the new social studies. Its chief adviser was historian and educator Henry Johnson of Teachers College.[24] Reporting in 1921, the committee appeared to give way to the social studies, advocating for years 9–12 only two years of straight history instead of the four recommended in 1899.[25] The committee went along with the idea of an amalgamated world history in the senior high years, together with U.S. history as the second history subject. This was similar to the social studies proposals of 1916. Yet this committee adopted a strategy that Progressives would use throughout the 1920s and 1930s. It endorsed history's central role and separate history courses while maintaining that the other social sciences had an important but subsidiary place in the social studies curriculum.[26] To appease those in the historical profession who would decry the loss of specializations in the schools, such as the elimination of the English and French history courses that were often still taught separately before 1918, the committee proposed an elaborate series of electives. Nevertheless, the committee's findings were shelved by the AHA because they seemed to side too much with the Progressive insurgents.[27]

As a body, the AHA had rejected the reformers, but the latter would not go away. Backing their stance was the pressure of the social scientists, who wanted recognition and believed history was unduly prominent. Economist Leon C. Marshall noted in his *Social Studies in Secondary Schools* in 1922 that "the grip of history is strong" but predicted the imminent breaking of "the monopoly." What history would remain would be "more definitely pointed toward understanding the society of today."[28] But the representatives of neither political science nor sociology were as insistent on the need to overthrow history's leadership as Marshall. In the case of political science, a strong alliance developed with history through the work of Chronicles of America contributor W. B. Munro, of Harvard. Charles A. Ellwood, president of the American Sociological Association, also favored cooperation with history. Ellwood was impressed with the work of the Progressive historians and noted, "The best work in the field of history . . . closely approaches what might be called illustrated sociology." Indeed, he saw the New History as providing the leadership for social studies reform since, for sociologists, "all the social studies" depended on "the work of the scientific historian." Ellwood looked forward to "less bickering" and more interdisciplinary cooperation under the plans of the Progressives.[29]

The formation of the NCSS in 1921 gave historians a concrete opportunity to take the hand of cooperation with the social sciences in the schools that many other disciplines offered. The AHA was officially represented in the new organization. Albert McKinley served as inaugural president, and Bessie Louise Pierce, then at the University of Iowa, and Henry Johnson were among those elected as office bearers.[30] Renamed the *Historical Outlook* in 1919, the *History Teacher's Magazine* underwent a facelift to reflect the changing orientation from history as a discipline to history as an approach to the past that encompassed the newly emergent social sciences.

Hardly had the Schafer report been shelved when in 1923 the AHA appointed a new committee to survey the changing offerings in history. Under the directorship of Edgar Dawson, of Hunter College, this committee found that, since 1916, the trend had indeed been to erode the position of ancient and English history in favor of American and recent history. That this committee's work was a survey, without curriculum recommendations, showed the extent to which the AHA remained split over the Progressive challenge. AHA Secretary John Spencer Bassett referred to "a divided opinion" in the AHA: "Some of us are quite conservative and wish to follow the old lines. Some others are modern."[31] But the prevarication did not mean that historians lacked interest in or influence over the changes. According to Dawson, about one-third of the schools had already adopted the new plan, a fact that pleased the Progressives within and outside the AHA.[32]

Ironically, the work of the Committee on Social Studies of 1916 and its gradually widening impact was no disaster for history. As a modern commentator has observed, though the history content was compressed and ancient history made way for civics, "history fared remarkably well." Under the Committee on Social Studies, "history in general was granted the lion's share" of the curriculum. Unlike the social sciences, it retained its identity "as a separate discipline." Part of the success could be attributed to Robinson's role on the 1916 committee,[33] but this coup did not please conservatives within the AHA anxious to preserve their own ways of history and specializations.

Undeterred, the Progressives pushed for further reforms within the AHA. Their objectives were the reshaping of the discipline, greater cooperation with social studies, and a redefinition of the mission of history as reform of society. The AHA's Committee on Teaching included Arthur Schlesinger, then at the University of Iowa and a Beard disciple, as well as Columbia Teachers College academic J. Montgomery Gambrill. Schlesinger told Bassett that "the time is past when a group of learned men can . . . promulgate a uniform history program for the teachers of the nation." It was important to cooperate with "organizations representing active history teachers" and to "encourage experimentation."[34] Though later professing no knowledge of what went on in the schools, Cornell's Carl Becker argued that history should be replaced by a three-year integrated social science course in which two years would be devoted to the European and American past.[35]

The Progressives' arguments gained force among academics because demands upon the universities themselves were changing. The war's impact and the educational influence derived from teacher educator disciples of John Dewey—more than from Dewey himself—increased pressures within colleges and universities for a more student-centered and present-centered curriculum.[36] Equally important, surging undergraduate enrollments in the early 1920s spurred administrative demands that humanities faculties provide large introductory "service" courses for freshmen in large state universities. Together with the war experience, this stimulated the growth of survey courses, most notably Western civilization and world history, though the latter remained little more than an extension of European history courses in content. In American history, more emphasis went to recent events and to social and economic content because administrators, students, and academics themselves urged it. With the universities moving in the direction of the Progressives' program, demands for changes in the school curriculum had a firmer backing that could not be long ignored.[37]

Under the force of Progressive arguments and these institutional changes, the AHA agreed in 1925 to follow up Dawson's 1923 inquiry with "a thorough investigation of the whole field."[38] With $10,000 from the Commonwealth Fund, August Krey, a University of Minnesota medievalist and chair of the AHA's Teaching Committee, undertook a yearlong survey. "No report excited more interest" than Krey's, observed Jameson, but it did not advise immediate reform.[39] The committee realized the need for a longer-term study that would resolve the internal conflicts within the profession preventing reform. They urged a thorough and protracted study of "history and the social studies in the schools" to cover the entire school system.[40]

★ ★ ★

In response to the Krey survey, the Commission on the Social Studies was convened in conjunction with the NCSS. Five years of work followed the acquisition of funds from the Carnegie Corporation in 1929. This cooperation represented the growing alliance between elements within the historical profession and influential teacher educators such as George S. Counts, of Columbia. For inspiration and intellectual leadership the commission drew upon Beard, but within the AHA's formal structures, the genial Krey took control as chair of the committee.[41] Though political science, economics, sociology, and geography each had a representative, along with other interests, no discipline was as heavily represented as history, with Guy Stanton Ford, Evarts B. Greene, Krey, William E. Lingelbach (University of Pennsylvania), Henry Johnson, and Beard as members. Beard joined Krey and Ford on the Advisory Committee that framed the formal objectives of the commission. He became its leading intellectual spokesman and driving force over the five years of the study to 1934.[42]

Foreshadowing the agenda and the drift of the commission, in 1929 Beard attacked the neglect of social and economic life in dull texts and championed "the living present."[43] In line with this strategy, the commission cooperated to an unprecedented extent with the social sciences. Beard wrote two volumes of the commission's report urging this approach—*A Charter for the Social Sciences* (1932) and *The Nature of the Social Sciences* (1934)—and was, with Counts, the de facto coauthor of the *Conclusions and Recommendations* volume (1934).[44]

Reviewers charged that these key volumes, especially the *Conclusions and Recommendations*, failed to lay down a specific curriculum.[45] Yet this was not the commission's aim. Rather, it was to provide a curriculum strategy that would accommodate the social sciences while maintaining the hegemony of history as a discipline. Beard sensed that this approach would serve both the interests of academics and demands from social studies teachers and teacher educators to make sense of a crowded school program.

Secondarily, Beard asserted the role of the university specialist in general and the professional historian in particular within social studies. Academics could not impose curriculum, he conceded, but teachers would listen to the arguments of academics if these were relevant to the concerns of the time. Beard believed that the commission's agenda could be translated into curricula, as the recommendations of previous reports had been, only by action among local and state groups. The important point was to seize the intellectual agenda, and in this aim he essentially succeeded, at least in the short term. He deflected the potential for competition *between* academics by recognizing and asserting the need for university leadership of debates over teaching in the schools.[46]

This was very much in line with the AHA's strategy since the mid-1920s, when the Progressives gained the ascendancy. Beard did not hijack this agenda. He implemented it. As Krey's preliminary 1926 report planning the study put it, innovation in the social sciences was moving at a pace virtually impossible for teachers themselves to assimilate. Only specialists could supply the knowledge that the rapidly changing society demanded. Expertise would, Krey and Beard hoped, be welcome because schools would thereby receive professional support against outside pressures such as business, patriotic, and other community groups.[47]

Instead of a definitive curriculum, the commission of 1929–34 produced thirteen individual studies on subjects as diverse as educational testing, the role of teacher training, the social context of education, and political pressures upon schools.[48] Capping the lot were the general recommendations of the 1934 volume authored by Beard and Counts toward "an activist and reformist program" rooted in "orderly progress" through social education.[49] Rational thought, critical analysis, skepticism toward theories, and use of evidence represented skills that other social sciences could provide, but history would provide foundational content as well. There should be "a broad and comprehensive conception of the evolution of civilization" that all students grasped.[50] This would be the first step toward a new curriculum. Beard envisaged debate over the recommendations in the education community through a variety of channels, beginning with the *Social Studies,* the newly named AHA-sponsored successor to the *Historical Outlook* in 1935.

Not surprisingly in view of its relationship with the AHA, the new journal took up the report and championed it as the first "task before us."[51] But more important was the creation two years later of a replacement for the *Social Studies* after a commercial dispute with the publisher. As editor of *Social Education,* the new journal backed by the AHA from 1937, Columbia Teachers College historian Erling Hunt became a major contributor to the debate and supporter of Beard's position. Other teacher educators with links to the history discipline also favored Beard. The University of Minnesota's Edgar Wesley claimed that the report showed "not only how the schools can serve society but how in the long run they can make society."[52] Endorsing the *Charter for the Social Sciences,* the University of Wisconsin's Burr W. Phillips stressed its insistence on history's central and autonomous place in the curriculum.[53]

Representative schoolteachers and administrators viewed the report more ambivalently. Some endorsed the general recommendations, as Michael H. Lucey, principal of the Julia Richman High School in New York City, did, but noted the lack of specific detail on courses.[54] Others were more positive. For Vierling Kersey, superintendent of public instruction and director of education, Sacramento, California, the report could develop "a school program more definitely geared into its right place in a social order in transition."[55] Tyler Kepner, head of social studies at Brookline High School in Massachusetts, hailed the "boldness and virility" of the report. Its many useful volumes, he claimed, would help to prevent depression-inspired curriculum cuts in social studies as a whole and to assert their importance within education as being "so great that they may well be considered as the 'core' subjects."[56] The snag, which Kepner did not initially mention, lay buried beneath the general recommendations. The bias in favor of history only became clear when the AHA began to develop specific curriculum initiatives based on the report.

The Progressives' attempts to reform the system did not stop in 1934. With the activist Conyers Read as executive secretary and the influence of the Progressives growing among the profession's rank and file, the AHA immediately undertook a report on courses for university preparation at the request of the influential College Entrance Examination Board (CEEB). Since before World War I the board had run examinations for university entrance, and the structure of these exams influenced the school curriculum.[57] By working through the board, Read aimed to advance history by refocusing the curriculum around college entrance requirements. The CEEB Commission had the potential to create, indirectly, high school social studies courses both more rigorous and more history oriented. This report should, therefore, be considered an integral part of the AHA's work in the Commission on the Social Studies and an attempt to capitalize on its findings to the discipline's advantage.[58] Read headed the new commission and in his 1936 report adopted a strongly Progressive viewpoint, denying as Beard did the conceptual differences between history and the other social sciences. He argued for historical mindedness rather than for the survival of the discipline. Whether he was "really advocating history or sociology" did not matter. "What matters is the idea," Read stated in embracing the New History.[59]

The CEEB report dispensed with separate courses on ancient and medieval history but maintained a four-year set of history courses as the center of the social studies program for grades 7–12, including a Western civilization or world history course combining ancient and medieval history and separate courses on modern Europe, American history, and "contemporary civilization."[60] In another reformist move likely to upset traditionalists, the report favored simplifying the College Board's examination process in line with the reduced emphasis in schools and colleges on ancient and European history. It recommended abolishing separate exams for the different units of history other than American, which was given a five-year extension.[61]

These recommendations were not hostile to history. The "historical approach," said the report, was "the natural and easy method of approach to the so-called social studies." Academic history was well represented on the CEEB Commission by such leading scholars as Yale's Wallace Notestein and Harvard's William Langer, as well as the private academies, public high school teachers, and educational administrators. The CEEB Commission's membership was weighted in favor of history's survival as a separate sequence of subjects and its key position within the social studies program. With Read articulating a Beardian viewpoint, the commission urged deferring of economics and other social sciences as distinct subjects to the college years.[62]

Despite its prohistory bias, anything associated with Beard's ideas was likely to raise the hackles of conservatives in the AHA. *American Historical Review* (*AHR*) editor Robert Livingston Schuyler and Eugene Barker, of the University of Texas, already regarded Beard's Commission on the Social Studies as too radical and rejected its "militant" collectivist plan and its "propaganda" for what Barker regarded as the establishment of Utopia.[63] The CEEB Commission was tarred with the same brush, and its report compounded the split over relativism raging within professional ranks and demonstrated that when the arguments over the schools moved from generalities to curriculum implementation, the profession was still divided. Some Harvard academics felt that Read's report leaned too far in the direction of the social sciences.[64] These political and ideological objections backed up the reservations that conservatives like Theodore Clarke Smith had over Beard's attacks on objectivity. In the same *AHR* article in which he denounced Beard's AHA presidential address, Smith charged that for Beard "the only valid history was that which traced the forward movement toward a collectivist democracy," precisely the objective laid out in the Commission on the Social Studies. Smith attacked as socially dangerous and functionally ahistorical the teacher educators whom Beard courted. Smith was alarmed at the frankly instrumentalist view of one teacher educator, who informed him abruptly: "Tell me the kind of citizen you wish to have and I will arrange the kind of school history needed to produce him." For Smith, such a view was "a very short step to history as written or taught in Italy, Russia, or Germany."[65]

As soon as the AHA attempted, through the CEEB report, to implement the program of the Commission on the Social Studies, it encountered opposition in the schools, too. The report's tilt in favor of history produced strained relations with some teachers and teacher educators, particularly those determined to implement in its entirety the idea of social studies as learning for life. This opposition was expressed by the lone dissenting voice on the CEEB Commission, Tyler Kepner, a high school representative. A definite demand for separate economics and sociology courses existed, Kepner felt, and any curriculum neglecting these subjects could not be handed down from on high by academics.[66] Despite such dissent, the report pleased some in the social studies movement who saw it as a genuine move toward their approach. Read succeeded at least temporarily in getting wider support. Among the allies were the same people who endorsed the Commission on the Social Studies, including Hunt and Wesley, who edited the *Mississippi Valley Historical Review*'s Teachers' Section from 1936.[67]

Like its predecessors, the CEEB report's effectiveness depended on its reception among interest groups and its diffusion through educational institutions. It had little influence either on state universities or on many private colleges that could not afford to be so discriminating about entrance requirements. The effects were felt mainly in the "conservative endowed institutions

of the East," the Ivy League in particular.[68] Yet as Kepner pointed out, the report was a "far-reaching and conservative influence" on school education.[69]
Whatever their commitment to critical teaching and exploration of different
topics, teachers had to teach to examinations.[70] By 1939 the College Board had
begun to introduce new examinations combining different fields of history, as
Read's commission had recommended. Led by American University historian
Caroline Ware as chair of examiners, and with such strong academic representation as Columbia's John Allen Krout, academic historians continued to exert
influence over the board's policies.[71] Building links with the elite of history students in this way began a tactic continued in the 1950s through the advanced-
placement scheme. In this approach the AHA and its allies sought to conserve
serious history students for the discipline and for the elite universities.[72]

⋆ ⋆ ⋆

While the academic historians were asserting new leadership, they faced fresh
radical challenges from the disciples of social studies. At the end of the 1930s
some teacher educators, teachers, and administrators began to demand that
history be delivered in specialized topics, called "unit" studies. Here, such
themes as transport, science, or agriculture could be treated across time without reference to political events and the wider narrative record.[73] These unit
courses were not necessarily incompatible with a pluralist version of history
within a frame of reference such as Beard proposed. The unit system was already employed in Britain, but in the United States it emerged within a university system in which the social sciences other than history were growing
stronger, and hence unit history was more potentially dangerous to the discipline's power.[74]

The argument for units stemmed from demands for relevance to the present and from the desire of educators and administrators to deal with the clut-
tered nature of the curriculum, particularly in world history, where so much
had to be crammed into a single year. For these people, the example of the social sciences suggested topical, rather than narrative, coverage as a solution to
curriculum overload. As argued by Donald Alter, of Eastern Illinois State
Teachers' College, in high school world history courses teachers should give
up trying to cover everything. "Our brethren of the social sciences fields of
economics and sociology have already made or are rapidly making this discovery of concentration." History seemed old-fashioned and lagged behind.[75]

Equally disturbing, others wanted, not the teaching of history in self-
contained functional units, but rather the abolition of history courses and the
creation of a "fusionist" social science.[76] The most extreme threats came from

the Progressive Education Association (PEA), which sponsored a variety of experiments in the schools from 1930 to 1938 in which traditional history was replaced by present-centered learning objectives realized through integrated social studies courses.[77]

Yet here as elsewhere, the detailed picture was more favorable to history than appeared on the surface. Some of these PEA experimental offerings were clearly based upon history and compatible with the objectives of the Commission on the Social Studies. At New Trier Township High School in Winnetka, Illinois, abler students studied "the history of civilization" in the freshman and sophomore years. American history occupied the junior year, with "much attention to current events," and the fourth year program dwelt on the world since 1918. Other versions departed more from history as traditionally conceived. At the John Burroughs School in Clayton, Missouri, in place of history there appeared an "introduction to the social, political, and economic pattern of American life," and in place of world history "the foundations of our world culture."[78] In some places, as in Mississippi, the new curriculum did away with history courses entirely, with units on "the peace problem," art and architecture, and the performance of duties of citizenship in wartime, making up vacuous "Areas of Human Activity" to be studied. But as Leon Wilber of University High School, University of Mississippi, pointed out, history was "probably the most abundant source of materials for such units."[79]

Nonetheless, this was not history as the integrated sequence of events that most historians knew and accepted. When educationists and teachers spoke as the PEA did of "social living," the ability to cooperate with others, the "habits of work that make for effectiveness in civil life," and the need for guides to "intelligent action" to improve the world, the goals seemed ahistorical and insipid, even if the content was derived from recycled history courses, as it was in some experimental cases.[80] Not even the word "traditions" appeared in some of these courses but rather the "social pattern" of American life.[81] These trends and demands coalesced in a 1940 PEA report in which the recommendations of the Commission on the Social Studies, let alone of earlier, more traditional reports, barely rated a mention.[82]

A further but more ambiguous challenge came from demands for a more internationally oriented content. Social studies had been conceived originally as emphasizing the United States rather than European topics. Many Progressive historians worked to further this objective in the 1920s. By the 1930s, however, social studies advocates sympathetic to history began to demand a shift in the geographic orientation of courses toward the comparative study of the Americas, the Pacific, and the Far East and toward recent international relations. This reflected Progressive educators' wish that history and social studies

deal with the worsening contemporary international situation. Thus, Franklin
Roosevelt's Good-Neighbor policy stimulated interest in Latin American topics, and the rising threat of Japan spurred interest in Pacific and East Asian history. Such internationalizing developments were potentially compatible with
the thinking of large sections of the academic community. Beard himself emphasized in the Commission on the Social Studies that history must include
the world context of U.S. history.[83] The AHA, with its strong representation of
histories other than American, might have been expected to support a new international focus, but the Progressives' tendency to push hemispheric history
over European and Western civilization was a possible point of conflict with
the AHA, where European history was still a strong field. Of greater concern,
the study of international history in the schools was becoming shallower. New
courses turned from longer surveys to the study of the recent past and current
events.

Even architects of the New History such as Beard baulked at the pace and
direction of change. He warned in 1938 against those "social studies which dis-
card or minimize history." These curricula were "superficial in the worst sense
of that word." He attacked the "wishy-washing [sic] slovenly, third-rate style"
textbooks that circulated in so many social studies courses. In the journal *Social Education,* Beard announced, "Any treatment of a current system of
thought which does not deal with its development or dynamics and with the
forces outside that impinge upon it is as unreal as the old drum and trumpet
history once taught in the schools." Courses on current "problems" lacked
"the substance of life," which was dynamic. Only out of history could knowledge come.[84] Not only did social studies treat "matters within a shallow time
depth," but in Beard's understanding, it dealt with the "alleged present which
does not exist" apart from the traditions, ideas, values and institutions derived
from historical knowledge.[85] This philosophical point may have been lost
upon his likely audience, but his most damning criticism, derived from
broader intellectual anxieties about mass culture, could not be mistaken.
Beard dismissed the most radical trends in social studies as no better than the
popular trashy entertainment he condemned as a dream world in *America in
Midpassage.* Too often these courses "belong[ed] with the movies and sports
rather than with education as preparation for dealing with the world and its
works, its tough heritage which is ever with us, and its grand and universal
conceptions."[86]

Beard was not abandoning the New History, but he was, like Read, seeking
a middle way to reform historical practice while keeping it at the center of the
social studies by making it useful. The problem with the other social studies
was that they were not truly useful in understanding the world because they

dealt with "abstractions" rather than "realities." They represented the old formalism that Beard had condemned throughout his academic career. "Some economists are fond of saying . . . that their system would work all right if it were not for politicians and wars," Beard charged. They might be correct in theory, Beard argued, but reality got in the way. Realistic social science could not avoid the historical facts of "politicians and wars." Reason itself could "do little" without facts.[87] But what if the charges of the social studies people were correct and history were not "useful"? Beard blamed the Old Guard for their failure to speak effectively to public issues. "If history is being shot out to the rubbish heap, no small part of the responsibility rests with the historians themselves." The New History that was taught within the social studies remained a "healthy revolt."[88]

Under the impact of World War II, Beard would become even more concerned about the neglect of history, but tied to this was alarm over the neglect of the political and constitutional history of the United States. In the midst of war, Beard would join those who, under the banner of the *New York Times*, attacked the neglect of the facts of American history in the schools.[89] He would thereby give comfort to those who sought to reassert the traditional political narrative and history as a discipline over the interdisciplinary but historically grounded social science he championed during the 1920s and 1930s. This apparent shift was a product, not simply of war, but of the war's impact upon the long record of public pressure and political criticisms of the content of American history. The battle that American historians had waged in defense of history since World War I always concerned more than the rival professional interests of teachers, educators, and social scientists. The role of wider political pressures and of patriotic lobby groups was particularly important, a subject to which we will turn in the next chapter.

8

The Patriots' Call

American History and the School Curriculum in War and Peace

History became a very public and highly contested matter between the two world wars. The social studies lobby was not the only interest group that historians faced. Virulent attacks on the work of the teachers and writers of history as pro-British and antipatriotic came from voluntary organizations, lobby groups, newspapers, and legislators. The Sons of the American Revolution, the Veterans of Foreign Wars, Grand Army of the Republic, and the Knights of Columbus were active in these post–World War I campaigns. Patriotic and antiradical hysteria that accompanied American entry into World War I was joined by the discontents of ethnic groups, particularly the Irish, who sought to identify their histories with that of the United States.[1] The agitation forced greater concentration on American history within the schools and even the colleges. Academics reacted by emphasizing their expertise and seeking authority to determine content. Though stung by the attack on their professional autonomy in the 1920s, during World War II some historians used the resurgence of nationalist feeling to reassert their professional authority and specifically to strengthen the position of American history. The Cold War merely reinforced these tendencies.

★ ★ ★

A good part of this attack on academic autonomy in the 1920s was fueled by smoldering Irish American resentment against the

British handling of the "Troubles" in Ireland after 1916. Thus, the *Western Catholic* published Rev. M. J. Foley's comparison of George Washington and Eamon De Valera as revolutionary heroes, and the *Irish World and American Liberator* of New York ran articles on the role of Irish patriots in the American Revolution.[2] Especially targeted were allegedly pro-British history books. In his *Treason to American Tradition* Hearst journalist Charles Miller denounced on behalf of the Sons of the American Revolution the Anglophile and anti-patriotic bias in school history texts written by Columbia professor David Muzzey.[3] In response to complaints from patriotic groups, state legislators in California, Oregon, and Wisconsin sought to control academic input to text-book content. The Oregon legislature decreed in 1923: "No textbook shall be used in the schools of this state which teaches un-American principles, or which speaks slightingly or contemptuously of the men who founded the re-public, or who preserved our federal union."[4] Throughout the country, politicians employed similar tactics. Harvard's Albert Bushnell Hart, a former AHA president, was called before the Massachusetts legislature in 1925 to defend his interpretations of Thomas Jefferson.[5] City school boards where Irish or German groups could provide blocks of votes to politicians became the most active sites of criticism. Texts by leading AHA members were officially investigated and censured in 1923 by the New York City Board of Education and separately by the city government of Mayor John F. Hylan.[6] The tail end of this early phase came in 1927, when a politically motivated attack on Anglophile bias in textbooks occurred under the leadership of Mayor William Hale Thompson in Chicago.[7]

The AHA's response was to defend vigorously the separate realm of scholarly objectivity. The annual meeting at Columbus, Ohio, in 1923 passed a strong resolution attacking as "propaganda" the work of "certain newspapers, patriotic societies, fraternal orders, and others" in favor of "official censorship." It noted that if this campaign continued, academics would stop writing textbooks, since "self-respecting scholars and teachers will not stoop to the methods advocated."[8] The threat of a disengagement from the public was made clear. In 1927 the AHA had to reaffirm this resolution in the face of Mayor Thompson's Chicago campaign. The 1927 controversy, however, saw the AHA try to use divisions within the patriotic societies by supporting a resolution of the Vermont Society of Sons of the American Revolution. In this intervention the Vermont group deplored "as dangerous to the spirit of free speech" such attempts to dictate "the facts and conclusions that scholars shall be allowed to place in text-books and other historical works."[9]

By the late 1920s, the Americanization anxieties and Red Scare hysteria that fueled these populist interventions had subsided, and it was not until the mid-1930s and early 1940s that another wave of intervention threatened the independence of educators. Now the attack shifted to focus on alleged radicalism in social studies textbooks. The *San Francisco Examiner* and other Hearst newspapers sought out Communists and left-leaning types. The work of social science educator Harold Rugg was the principal target of this phase of textbook inquisition. Though aimed mainly at social studies texts, the crusade included a 1935 attack by the *Washington Herald* on the book *Modern History* by eminent scholar Carl Becker, of Cornell, whom the newspaper called "a well known communistic writer."[10] In 1940 the National Association of Manufacturers (NAM) followed up the Hearst campaign by appointing its own committee to review antibusiness statements in American school histories. It commissioned abstracts of eight hundred textbooks from an obscure assistant professor of business at Columbia University, Ralph Robey, that purported to show undue and systemic un-American bias. These abstracts detailed "attitudes to our governmental system and to private enterprise" and were distributed among NAM members for use in initiating school board investigations of texts.[11] A spate of such inquiries and textbook bans ensued in New Jersey and Iowa.[12]

Until the early 1940s these attacks focused on schools rather than universities and on textbooks rather than the wider issue of the history curricula; and they promoted overtly patriotic interpretation rather than factual knowledge. They did not involve professional historians on the side of the inquisitors, nor did professional historians respond favorably to the attacks by trying to align their expertise with the expectations of superpatriots. World War II changed all that, and the content of the curriculum became critical in professional and public debates.

* * *

The wartime assault initiated by Allan Nevins and the *New York Times* highlighted different questions concerning the content of history courses. What was the correct balance between American and non-American history? How much American history was taught, and of what type? And how much attention should be given to social and economic, as opposed to political and constitutional, history? Nevins's attack reasserted the value of the "national identity and national ideals" that were "rooted in history"[13] and widened the front by including a vigorous assault on college history teaching.[14] This campaign was more complex than a simple reaffirmation of earlier patriotic hysteria. It capitalized on growing discontent among professional historians, as well as conservative political groups, over "soft" social studies curricula.

Nevins's supporters sought to reinject into the minds of young Americans a historical rigor, knowledge of the facts of American history, and awareness of time as a chronological sequence. The existing courses were too present centered for their critics and did not make students aware of their own traditions. Journalist Hugh Russell Fraser, chairman of the Committee for American History and a strong Nevins ally, sought more room for "the history of the nation" defined as "the development of our political democracy." Fraser criticized "the tendency to ignore major phases of United States political history and to substitute for them economic, social and industrial history." These vendettas against the social studies could exploit the wartime situation. A "soft" curriculum and the failure to teach the political traditions of the American nation seemed anomalous to Fraser (and Nevins) in the ideologically charged atmosphere of war: it was "precisely against the background of America's political history that we are seeking to liberate the forces of freedom everywhere in the world today."[15]

The political pressure groups active in the 1930s vigorously resumed their activity under cover of war. Stories about deficient teaching in and knowledge of American history ran on for months, spread to the *Pittsburgh Press, St. Louis Post-Dispatch, Cleveland Plain-Dealer, Baltimore Sun,* and other major newspapers across the country.[16] Republican politician Wendell Willkie was quoted by the *Times* as saying that "it is about time that United States history should be taken up in United States schools." Two-thirds of college and university presidents agreed that U.S. history should be a compulsory subject for college entry. A joint meeting of the National Education Association (NEA) and the NAM urged U.S. history to be taught through elementary, high, and college levels in every state. Mrs. William H. Pouch, president general of the National Society, Daughters of the American Revolution, supported compulsory study of U.S. history with the misleading statement: "It appears to have been the fashion to study every other form of government except our own, to study every history book except that dealing with our own country."[17] Behind these pressures lurked an American national pride fed by the wartime turmoil in Europe and by America's new world role. Nicholas Murray Butler, president of Columbia University, concluded that knowledge of "the history of the United States from the settlement of this continent down to the present day is probably now the most important subject of study in the whole field of modern history."[18]

* * *

Acutely aware of the charged patriotic atmosphere and anxious to avoid a repetition of their action during World War I, the AHA's officials, led by new Ex-

ecutive Secretary Guy Stanton Ford, were initially reluctant to join another political brawl over American history in the schools.[19] However, the attack on the
colleges meant that academic historians could hardly avoid becoming implicated. Moreover, within the Mississippi Valley Historical Association (MVHA),
historians such as Merle Curti believed that academics should reassert a
stronger role in the schools.[20] A joint committee was appointed with Ford and
Theodore Blegen, president of the MVHA, as chairs to represent the two premier professional bodies. The National Council for the Social Studies joined as
the third partner to investigate the allegations.[21] The project was directed by
Edgar Wesley (University of Minnesota) and included in its ranks such well-
known historians as Dwight L. Dumond (University of Michigan), Joseph
Strayer (Princeton), and John D. Hicks (University of California).[22] Two of the
eleven members were high school history teachers, and teacher educators
were also represented.

Wesley's committee defied political pressure to increase the amount of
American history taught in both schools and colleges but urged coordination
between school and university courses to avoid repetition.[23] It concluded that
American history was adequately represented in the schools but that the subject was poorly taught; that the quality of instruction needed to be improved;
and that the emphasis on factual knowledge of great Americans of the type
tested by the Nevins/*New York Times* approach would not create a sense of history or reduce historical ignorance. The committee recommended that all students study U.S. history on at least three levels: elementary and junior and senior high.[24] For colleges, the report urged a more cultural and social approach
that utilized the idea of American civilization, but it also recommended the
United States in its world setting as an alternative. The synthesis of the new
"cultural approach to history" highlighted at the 1939 AHA convention and in
the nascent field of American studies influenced these findings.[25]

Published as *American History in Schools and Colleges* in 1944, the Wesley report was the last major institutional intervention by American historians into
the schools until the mid-1950s and was the last attempt to shape the school
syllabus directly until the 1980s. It laid out a detailed plan for the content of the
curriculum and specified a test of the range, structure, and types of knowledge that students should acquire in the course of their education. This report
demonstrated that many historians still took a serious interest in high school
history ten years after the Commission on the Social Studies had reported.[26]

Though the committee focused only on American history, its refusal to
join the call for more such history reflected the diverse interests of academic
scholarship. As an organization dealing with all fields of history, the AHA was
not likely to favor a greater concentration on the United States. But the re-

port's emphasis on better teaching and the need for a minimum three-year sequence in U.S. history did confirm the subject's hegemonic position, and the report did nothing to redress the growing imbalance between U.S. and world history. Nor did it do much to integrate American topics with the latter.[27] Like all such reports, its influence depended on its implementation. Though textbook writers claimed to follow it closely in the years immediately after World War II, more realistically the report served as yet another public intervention, one more salvo in the never-ending history wars. It described changes already occurring in history curricula, as well as registered academic historians' continuing involvement with high schools.[28]

This national crusade for American history was reinforced by academics at the local level. One result of the *Times* controversy was to spur historians to hold summer schools or institutes for teachers of American history. Such initiatives were not entirely new. The University of Wisconsin held annual conferences for history teachers throughout the 1920s and 1930s, but the shrill wartime debate encouraged such schemes. At the University of Washington, the history department worked with teachers, students, and lay groups, taking "a more active part in the movement to encourage a wider popular interest in American history and to improve the instruction in that subject in the secondary schools."[29] At the University of California, Los Angeles, and at Stanford, history departments held well-publicized conferences of university, college, and high school teachers and framed demands for an extension of U.S. history teaching in California. Elsewhere, professors worked alongside schoolteachers within the established teachers' groups—such as the Middle Atlantic States History Teachers Association—to strengthen history's role and further the objectives of the Wesley report.[30]

Of all these initiatives, Stanford's was the most revealing of academics' desires to take leadership of the public debate. As a result of the *Times* push and fearing that the Hearst press would put pressure on the California legislature for change, Edgar Robinson engineered the creation of the Institute of American History to improve the content of American history taught in schools and to discuss matters of curriculum through conferences of high school, junior college, and university teachers. These began in August 1942 and were held annually into the 1950s. A student of Frederick Jackson Turner's at Wisconsin, Robinson convened the citizenship program at Stanford in the early 1920s and was bruised then by attacks on the patriotism of academics. In response, he became a strong advocate of both "Americanism" and the special knowledge that experts could convey to lay people about American democratic values.[31] The job of specialists was to deliver the broad narrative of American democracy that the public wanted and that would perform the civic functions demanded by pressure groups. As Robinson's career developed (he became chairman of the Stanford history department), he emphasized American exceptionalism, referring in the Stanford Institute of American History debates in 1942 to "our unusual history in building a nation where none existed." Universities and schools "ought to teach that story of Americanism."[32] The sympathetic response to Robinson's reasoning showed that historians were determined not to become implicated in a revived attack on leftist content in high school courses. They saw a way out of the dilemma by insistence on their role as advisers on content rather than as political lobbyists for curriculum changes. But these experts could not defy public opinion; they could only influence the detailed implementation of policy. "There will be a public insistence upon the study of American history," Robinson predicted. If the subject were to be a required field for high school and college graduation, experts should control the content, not the general public.[33]

More extensive than the institutes and summer schools was change in university curricula. Academics sought to accommodate the charge of neglect of American history at the collegiate level. They aimed to make their teaching more relevant to concerns about the changing world role of the United States. Far from abandoning curriculum intervention, World War II saw universities advising the federal government on how to adapt college education to the new position of the United States. Two seemingly contradictory trends competed here. Should American history's dominance be enhanced, or should American history be presented in terms of a broader international context? At first, internationalizing seemed persuasive, but as the war and the debate over American history raged on, the development of an exclusively American focus gained ground.

Academics played a vital role in this debate in 1942–43. At the AHA's request, a committee headed by Bessie Louise Pierce and staffed by members of the University of Chicago history department provided the Federal Security Administration in Washington with model courses on American, European, and world history. These models were distributed to about three thousand educational institutions for local use.[34] The Pierce committee's syllabus was both a stimulus to and a symptom of change evident in a variety of college programs. Eugene Hugh Byrne (Barnard College) developed a new course that was strikingly similar to Pierce's proposal in chronological limits and terminology and was announced as "De-isolationized U.S. History: World History from the American Standpoint—1500–1942." Let American colleges, Byrne proclaimed, "stop teaching American history in a vacuum."[35]

The spread of American studies was the other, potentially conflicting response to the wartime debate. Historians such as Ralph Gabriel at Yale and

Richard Shryock at Pennsylvania took leading roles in laying the groundwork for the postwar expansion of this field and made history, along with literature, the foundation of that study for a generation. In 1944 Brooklyn College began an "American Civilization" course required of all freshmen, while both the University of Kansas and Indiana University planned new programs, and Maryland introduced a compulsory freshman course in U.S. history that was part of a new American studies major.[36] Historiographers and scholars of education have neglected this wartime change. Though some American studies courses such as those at Harvard (focused on literature) and Yale (influenced more by history) predated the war, and though the Cold War consolidated American studies, its true origins nationwide lay in the wartime enthusiasm to make American history more relevant to a wider public.[37]

As academics debated the introduction of American studies in college courses, they remained equally interested in promoting history in schools. But they did so differently from in the 1930s. Historians renounced, almost by necessity, any attempt to impose curricula directly. The emphasis on improving American history shifted to the servicing of teachers' needs for course materials. The establishment of the Service Center for Teachers of History, first proposed in 1953 and established in 1956 under AHA control, signaled the new strategy.[38] The AHA acknowledged the schools' need for "[d]irect assistance . . . in strengthening courses and in increasing the effectiveness of teachers and teaching materials." The problems created by "increasing specialization of historical research" meant that "new topics and areas must be treated and all interpretations must be revised." It was difficult for "busy teachers" to keep up with this knowledge explosion. The AHA's leaders believed that its "best contribution to improvement of the teaching of history" lay in providing this research, not through monographs but by summarizing trends in historiography. Herein lay the origin of the AHA's Pamphlets on Teaching series. The traffic would be two-way, however. The center not only provided information to schools but allowed "specialists in history" to become "acquainted with the nature and limitations of the teaching and learning process at various grade levels."[39]

Historians had been doing much along these lines locally and regionally since the mid-1940s. The Service Center merely sanctioned and consolidated this nationwide endeavor. The Stanford Institute of American History had evolved into such a forum, as did the equivalent at the University of California at Los Angeles.[40] In the 1950s historians elsewhere in the country established similar service roles. Starting in 1959, four colleges and universities and five adjacent high schools in western Massachusetts together planned a new eleventh-grade curriculum in American history, and teachers were brought to a summer institute at Amherst College for in-service training.[41] Meanwhile, the University of Washington's Thomas Pressly extended the summer institutes established there in the 1940s into the 1960s.[42] At Duke, beginning in 1953, educationalist William H. Cartwright and historian Richard Watson similarly cooperated in a series of annual seminars for teachers, administrators, and college academics that ran until 1975.[43]

A second postwar initiative was the development of advanced-placement courses such as that promoted by Thomas A. Bailey at Stanford, who sought the "revitalizing" of American history teaching.[44] The scheme started nationwide in 1956 and, by 1959–60, history enrollments had risen seven times in comparison with a fourfold rise in overall numbers of Advance Placement enrollments. American and European history were two of the eleven subjects in which advanced placement could be undertaken and contributed 21.4 percent of candidates in all fields of study in 1959, up from 10 percent in 1956.[45] Enrollments in U.S. history made up more than three-quarters of all the history students participating. And it was not just American history but the "political aspects of American history" that dominated advanced placement in its early years. The scheme strengthened academic links with elite preparatory schools, encouraged a more coherent and substantial history curriculum in high schools, and disseminated the counterreform in historiography against Beardian economic interpretation going on in academic research.[46] Academic historians had a strong role in this program from the beginning, with the director for the first two years being Charles R. Keller, a professor at Williams College.[47]

★ ★ ★

Assessing the impact of these war and postwar initiatives by academics is complex. On the one hand, change in the interpretation and content of history reached down into the high school. On the other, academic initiatives were obviously not the sole cause of that change. Rather, academics moved in the same direction as public pressures—toward more American content and, to a lesser extent, toward reorganization of American knowledge of international affairs and world history. During and just after the war, several states introduced more extensive compulsory requirements. Pennsylvania mandated eighteen months minimum of American history instead of twelve,[48] while New Jersey legislated for two years in 1945.[49]

In terms of the educational objectives behind the content studied, the war served as a modestly conservative check to prewar tendencies. As one former student of John Hicks wrote in 1942 from Lincoln, Nebraska: "The war has saved history in Lincoln High School from becoming some sort of stuff based on life experience. Now there is no time to bother about progressive education." Hicks himself realized that the pressure to know more about the nation and its political values was irresistible. Hicks told George Mowry, of the University of North Carolina, "It looks to me as if we are in for a boom in American history."[50]

Regarding the actual content of history in the curriculum, the effect was not to stymie prewar pressures, however, but to crystallize longer-term changes. From the 1930s to the 1950s, a noticeable expansion in the amount of time devoted to American history occurred across the nation, before many of the wartime curriculum reforms could have taken full effect. Between 1933–34 and 1946–47, "a great increase" occurred "in the percentage of pupils registered in the Social Studies who were taking United States history, from 16 to 24 percent in grades 9–12, and from 35.5 to 50.7 in grades 7–8." According to the Federal Security Administration, course offerings in U.S. history rose from 33.7 to 53.3 percent of the social studies total.[51] These changes continued after 1945 under the impact of wartime curriculum debates. By the mid-1950s, history was "by far the leading social study" in the eighth, eleventh, and twelfth grades and was a close second in the seventh grade. A decade later, William H. Cartwright observed the still strongly cemented role of American history and predicted it could not be challenged.[52] Stress upon American topics had come, however, at the expense of European and world history in some school systems. "Enrolments in world and modern history declined markedly and the course disappeared from some programs," Wesley reported in 1950. He despairingly concluded that "legislative fiat" had "sentenced American boys and girls for the atomic age to close their eyes to the rest of the world."[53]

* * *

Amid the tumult of curriculum reform, it was easy for historians to lose sight of these patterns of change and continuity that their historical training ought to have made them best able to judge. They harbored exaggerated fears of their discipline's collapse and failed to appreciate the larger forces that were constraining and shaping their own achievements. In short, they succumbed too easily to the jeremiad mentality. Educationalists drew attention, with more astuteness, to these structural shifts. Federal Security Administration figures compiled by educationalist Howard Anderson in 1946–47 suggested that when historians depicted their discipline as in continuous decline in the schools, their alarmism lacked evidence.[54] History was in a stronger position than any other social science in the 1940s. Some of that evidence was statistical, but logical reasoning supported the statistics. History was all-inclusive and therefore suitable for interdisciplinary social studies programs. The demand of social studies, not just for description, but for causal explanations led naturally in the direction of history.[55]

If earlier proposals of the 1930s to change the curriculum are not as dangerous in retrospect as they seemed, the way changes were absorbed within schools was not radical either. In reality, history's survival was helped by an inbuilt inertia in the process of curriculum building.[56] Every report, including Wesley's, faced entrenched teacher habits, competing curriculum demands, poor teacher training, and logistical difficulties such as shortages of suitable texts. As textbook publishers Ginn and Company observed, "the public school program" was a "relatively conservative one" and the "recommendations of experts" entered the "rank and file of schools very slowly." No program could be "turned overnight."[57] Roger Shugg, of Alfred Knopf, concurred that curriculum reports exercised influence through "generally indirect" channels.[58] Moreover, state examinations board requirements restricted rapid change in some areas, for example, in New York.[59] Added to this were problems of pressure groups where local public opinion prevented a special area of study from being undertaken. "When the pressure groups come in the door," Tyler Kepner reported, "the curriculum from above goes out the window."[60]

Inertia was also evident in textbook content. In the 1920s, Frederick Jackson Turner complained about the astonishing time it took to get new viewpoints into common texts.[61] Nearly thirty years later, John Hope Franklin could still complain at the "appallingly slow rate" at which new approaches on African American slavery were assimilated and diffused.[62] Revisionist academic accounts of the era of Reconstruction written in the 1950s and 1960s similarly changed course materials in that field very slowly.[63]

Nor did history's entrenched position in the school social studies curriculum guarantee good teaching or satisfactory knowledge of either American or world history. Two consistent findings in reports from Dawson's in 1924 to Wesley's in 1944 were the poor quality of teacher training and the lack of student engagement with history, particularly American.[64] Mandating U.S. history did not raise student interest and probably hindered it. Numerous surveys showed that U.S. history was disliked by students because they had to repeat it in two or three different grades, and that history in general was one of the most, if not the most, disliked of all subjects because of a high factual content and poor teaching.[65] A Columbia graduate and schoolteacher told Nevins in 1942 that American history was dull compared to European and came across as a bundle of inassimilable facts about matters as dry as "the tariff." She and her friends flocked to European history when in high school and resented U.S. history's compulsory status.[66]

Curriculum inertia preserved history's entrenched place but simultaneously made the teaching of that history more unmanageable. The tendency toward overloaded content was stunningly illustrated in textbooks. Cartwright observed in 1954 that, "because of lengthened courses and lengthened textbooks," the change to social, intellectual, and economic topics had "not been at the expense of the amount of attention given to political history."[67] If John Hope Franklin could complain with some justice about the neglect of and distortions concerning African Americans, the typical textbook writer's response was to incorporate modified passages within the same narrative.[68] Donald Michelson, a teacher educator, confirmed that for world history the situation was worse because typically everything had to be crammed into one course and one year's study. World history textbooks were "characterized by their oppressive bulk" as early as the 1940s.[69]

Reliance on such texts reflected the status and structure of the teaching profession. Poor teacher training and overburdened teachers with little time for preparation stood out as common complaints.[70] After a year's exchange in the United States in 1948, British observer Peter Hill deplored the heavy use of textbooks that came from these circumstances. Teachers and school boards placed "far more reliance on the *ipsissima verba* of the text-book" than in Britain. Indeed, American history texts, "those fat volumes with their multitudinous illustrations, their careful sub-headings, detailed biographies, exercises, questions, and accompanying 'work-books,'" were in Hill's view "dangerously elaborate." American experts had "long complained about the extent to which teachers and pupils rely solely on them." Such methods encouraged, not analytical skills, but rote learning, since the structure of texts was "overwhelmingly concerned" to provide knowledge of facts rather than to stimulate analysis.[71]

★ ★ ★

Hill's observations provided comparative insights backing up the claims that history's position was strong on the outside but had a soft underbelly. He summed up the state of history teaching, showing its strengths and weaknesses while putting into perspective the more extreme claims of decline. Contra Nevins and the *New York Times*, Hill did not think Americans lacked attention to their own past in school curricula. Rather, "the American" was "too zealous about his past." The schools offered "too much national history," since a majority of students had already studied American history for three years before entering college. Not that Hill opposed national history. On the contrary, he found the United States to be exemplary in the use of history for civic instruction in democratic values. In comparison, Britain had in Hill's opinion "too little" of its own national history taught in schools.[72]

Hill deftly pointed to the characteristics of American society that conditioned the responses that historians and educators could frame. The U.S. system was, Hill observed, a product of cultural diversity and mass education. With "large and compact minority groups of recent immigrant stock and its racial disunity," the United States had of necessity sought "a sense of national history as a means of assimilation."[73] Unlike the small elite that attended British secondary schools, the U.S. system catered to a vast audience. Rising school enrollment saw 60.9 percent of students staying on till age seventeen in 1940, compared to 34.6 percent in 1920.[74] Already by 1940, over 79 percent of all potential students aged fourteen to seventeen were in school.[75] The expansion of this mass audience for history between 1920 and 1940 was unmistakable and powered the constant reassessment of school curricula in those years as teachers faced many students with low academic motivation.

The system's heavy reliance on textbooks and demands for factual knowledge reflected mass education and the absence of a national curriculum enforced by the state. This decentralized system contrasted with the British, where Oxbridge and elitism dominated. In the United States, mandating subjects was the right of legislators, a prerogative they often took. This social background conditioned what historians could do to influence school curricula. Hill felt that the United States and its historians had catered well to the great majority, while providing little in the way of advanced and specialized training such as could be found at the British A and O levels system.

What Hill neglected was the vastly different relationship between school and university history teachers in the two countries. This relationship was less favorable in the American case and made the work of historians more difficult. In Britain, the Historical Association was not dominated by academics, as the AHA became during the first decade of the twentieth century. By 1900 the size of the United States and the substantial number of universities had created the critical mass for a separate organization of college teachers. By the 1920s many of these would have doctorates.[76] At the very time that the rise of mass secondary education began in the Progressive years, the AHA was losing its informal bonds with the high schools through the processes of professionalization. After 1910 the NEA began to exert greater and more effective independent influence. After 1924 the NEA ceased to cover universities and became an alliance of school administrators and public school teachers.[77] There resulted after 1945 an almost total professional estrangement. By the early 1960s, of an

estimated 65,000–75,000 history teachers nationwide, only about 300 were AHA members, though 1,200 subscribed to the Service Center for Teachers publications.[78]

In England, the tradition was very different. There the *English Historical Review*, publishing only scholarly work, was not the official organ of the national Historical Association, as was the *American Historical Review* after 1895, but was an independent journal produced at Cambridge University. Instead, the Historical Association published *History*, a journal combining scholarly articles with debates over school teaching. Rather than stress research, the association originally emphasized better relations between teachers and academics.[79] Both were accepted as bona fide historians, and grammar and public school teachers and headmasters served among the officers of the association, a pattern not evident in the United States, where professionalization had gone much further.[80] The result was a more robust advocacy of public outreach in England. *History* and the Historical Association had to think of "ordinary citizens, not of specialists in the study of historical evidence."[81]

This absence of extreme professionalization did not mean the neglect of expert opinion. Key figures in the Historical Association for many years were Professor A. F. Pollard, of the Institute of Historical Research at the University of London, and Professor A. S. Turberville.[82] The latter affirmed that in contemporary history "the guidance of the expert historian" was "much needed for the benefit of the general public." Yet in Britain the category of "expert" included well-trained schoolteachers. The grammar and public schools, in contrast to those in the United States, usually had on their teaching staffs university graduates with honors degrees in history.[83] Dons such as Turberville and G. M. Trevelyan, who themselves had only master's degrees, fitted easily into this pattern.[84]

* * *

In the absence of the institutional cooperation available in England, the AHA had to rely instead on an informal (and unstable) alliance with college education professors and some high school teachers. This cooperation was possible from 1890 to the 1930s because a sizable number of university professors had school teaching backgrounds. Three of the original Committee of Ten of the AHA had such experience, and several of the 1944 committee on American history also had some high school teaching, educational administration, or teachers' college experience. Prominent individual examples still existed of academics who had begun their careers as schoolteachers. Usually these, like Bessie Pierce, retained an interest in the condition of school history. Pierce re-

searched the subject extensively in the 1920s and contributed to the Commission on the Social Studies.[85] Former teachers, like Kansas State (later University of Illinois) historian Fred Shannon, typically worked their way up through
the college and university system while earning the doctorate.[86] Prosperity in
the 1920s temporarily improved the market for academic appointments and
restricted the number of historians with such high school connections. Yet the
depression abruptly reversed that trend; nearly a fivefold increase occurred after 1930 in the number of Ph.D. graduates who took high school positions.
The bleak market for academic history jobs kept alive informal links with the
high schools. It was not uncommon for Ph.D. graduates to begin, by necessity,
their teaching careers in schools, junior colleges, or teachers' colleges.[87]

Some academics believed strongly in the importance of cooperation between universities and high schools. John D. Hicks told a former student in
1943, "Most of our university men would be much better off for some high
school teaching experience."[88] States in the Midwest and Great Plains, such as
Wisconsin and Nebraska, encouraged contact through the "service" orientation of the land grant colleges and universities.[89] Close links existed between
history academics such as Hicks, of Wisconsin, and James Sellers, of the University of Nebraska, and their state history teachers' associations.[90] Moreover,
after Hicks had relocated to Wisconsin, several times Sellers was able to coax
him to return to the state where he had taught in the 1920s to lecture.[91] In 1936
Hicks addressed the fourth annual meeting of the Nebraska State Teachers'
Association on no fewer than three topics: "The First Pres. Roosevelt," "New
Frontiers for Old," and "Frederick Jackson Turner." After moving to the University of California at Berkeley in 1942, Hicks maintained his interest in
teaching and was appalled by its neglect at the university level there. "The effu-
sive comments on my efforts as a teacher," he wrote, "lead me to think that
there is something to the students' opinion that most classes aren't worth attending because the faculty won't do their part." So disgusted was he that he
contemplated a move to the University of California at Los Angeles: "They
haven't as distinguished a faculty down there, but they are friendly, which is
something Berkeley is not, and they still believe that it is not beneath one's dignity to teach school."[92] Even after he became reconciled to Berkeley, Hicks
maintained his commitment to teaching and participated in the Stanford Institute of American History from 1942 to 1948.[93]

A further tie to the schools was the considerable contribution that academic historians made to textbook writing between the two world wars.
Samuel Eliot Morison stressed "an obligation that he [the historian] owes to
the public [in] the writing of textbooks for schools and colleges."[94] Morison
and Henry Steele Commager's *The Growth of the American Republic* was Mori-

son's antidote to dullness among textbooks.[95] Ralph Gabriel at Yale was another prominent scholar who took the time to write textbooks, both college and school. He cooperated with high school teacher Mabel Casner in *Exploring American History* (1931) and lectured at New Haven high schools. Others similarly engaged included Harold Faulkner (Smith College), Arthur Schlesinger, and Merle Curti.[96] Though some academics looked down on school-textbook writing, Stanford's Thomas Bailey defended the genre, in which he was extraordinarily successful: "A man may write a textbook and still be a scholar, even though the book is successful. Why should not scholarship be presented in the form of a synthesis to people who do not have the time or ability to make the synthesis for themselves?"[97] Pecuniary motives were also present, of course. Writing for the high school or other nonacademic audiences could supplement academic income.[98] Historians such as Morison and Commager, the Beards, and Bailey made a great deal of money out of texts. "Mounting royalties are beginning to weigh on my conscience," Bailey admitted in the late 1950s. He was so embarrassed by the amount he made that he donated part of the proceeds to a special Stanford library fund.[99]

Developing textbooks in collaboration with teachers and teacher educators had useful spin-offs, as Gabriel's association with Casner illustrates. The program in social studies planned for Connecticut in the early 1930s threatened history's place. But Gabriel was able to provide Casner with strategic advice. She followed his suggestion that rather than fight the new social studies program she could made "progress" by "trying to 'capture'" it to the benefit of history. Their book *Exploring American History*, with its social and cultural focus, became the intellectual model for her strategy.[100]

The drawback in all of these arrangements was the temporary and informal nature of the ties. They were the result in part of shifting economic conditions rather than the preferences of scholars. Because school teaching was poorly paid and subject to bureaucratic supervision, historians could not regard a high school appointment as much more than a necessity in times of economic hardship—a necessity they would abandon when able to enter university teaching and research. Hicks noted that school teaching often lacked an attractive intellectual environment: "Every university professor who has supervised graduate work knows that he must deal with a steady stream of good people whose sole motive for seeking a Ph.D. degree is to escape from secondary school work."[101]

These ambitions could be fulfilled after the 1940s as they never could before. The audience for graduate and college history rose to create at first a modest, then in the 1960s a dramatic, expansion in the market for historians at the tertiary level. The rising number of undergraduates was important, but even more remarkable was a rapid increase in the number of graduate students who could stock research seminars. For the higher education sector as a whole, graduate numbers by 1970 were between seven and eight times the 1946 levels, compared to a fivefold rise for undergraduates, and history shared in this expansion, with enrollments increasing through the 1960s. The number of history doctorates granted from 1948 to 1957 was more than the number granted for the entire period from 1926 to 1947, and history majors as a percentage of all bachelor degree enrollments had also risen to historically high levels by the 1960s.[102] With over 32 percent of eighteen- to twenty-four-year-olds in higher education in 1970, a large and captive market for history had been created through compulsory courses in U.S. and world history at college level. Historians became as a result less dependent on the high schools for textbook sales. They could now concentrate on monographs or university texts. This market was further enhanced by the paperback revolution, evident by the 1950s. Now cheap additions could be aimed at university students, and more sophisticated source book teaching could be undertaken at universities.[103]

At the same time, ties with teacher educators became fewer and more tenuous. This occurred partly because of the impact of the Nevins/*New York Times* survey, which had been aimed squarely at the Progressive history advocated by most teacher educators. During the war leading figures such as Erling Hunt at Columbia Teachers College resented the implication that they had promoted what Nevins called "social slush" and asserted that teachers' colleges had responded more vigorously than "liberal arts or graduate school faculties" to making the curriculum relevant to the needs of students.[104] After 1945, Hunt continued to object to the conservative turn. But with his influence waning, he gave up the editorship of *Social Education* in 1947 and was increasingly on the defensive as a Progressive in the era of McCarthyism.[105] Key teacher educators who had allied with the historical profession in the interwar years, such as Daniel Knowlton, J. Montgomery Gambrill, and Henry Johnson, had already retired before the war's end. Still others, such as Howard Anderson and Lewis Paul Todd, moved into publishing or administrative positions in the federal government or universities,[106] while Edgar Wesley eventually became disillusioned with the history taught in the schools. This strong defender of history in the 1940s went so far as to advocate the abolition of history courses in a much-noticed article of 1967.[107] The number of such teacher educators specializing in history was always fairly small and had begun to decline by the end of World War II. It became more difficult than in earlier periods to find good educationalists who were trained as historians and had sufficient stature to bridge the gap between the teaching of history and academic scholarship.[108]

Deteriorating relationships with teacher educators were exacerbated in the 1950s by attacks on Progressive education. Some of these attacks were indirectly connected to antileftist pressures, but all reflected a broader academic concern with anti-intellectualism in American life. University of Illinois (later University of Washington) historian Arthur Bestor was at the center of these attempts to destroy the dominant tradition of Progressive education in the schools.[109] At the 1952 Washington AHA meeting, Bestor flayed the secondary schools for lax attitudes and anti-intellectualism.[110] This meeting clearly revealed the new culture of polarization between the schools and colleges, with academics now criticizing from the outside. William Cartwright opposed Bestor at the meeting, expressing regret at "the ending of the cooperation between the American Historical Association and professional educators."[111]

Through circumstances not of his own making, Bestor had more influence at the university level than Cartwright, and he reinforced academic historians' sense of antagonism and suspicion toward their colleagues in the schools. The blunt professor touched a raw nerve among professors facing a flood of enrollments in the colleges and backed up the concerns of influential segments of the American elite who worried about the scientific and technological competitiveness of the United States. The launching of the Soviet Union's first space satellite in 1957 and subsequent embarrassments in space and missile technology reinforced the need to favor the content of knowledge rather than pander to the social role of the schools.[112]

Bestor was, however, an iconoclast better able to stir up alarm than to calmly follow through with the detailed action necessary to build coalitions that could effect change at the school level. He argued selectively and unfairly, alienating those elements within the social studies movement supportive of history and disregarding how much history was taught.[113] Not surprisingly in view of Bestor's tactics, the AHA declined to back his proposals openly and retreated to the support of the Service Center approach. Meanwhile, Bestor took part in the founding of the Council for Basic Education in 1956, where he received support from other historians disturbed by what they saw as the anti-intellectualism of Progressive education. Charter members included a "strong contingent of historians," such as Richard Hofstadter, Ray Billington, Samuel Flagg Bemis, and W. Stull Holt.[114] This organization became a lobby group for the core high school subjects, but it lacked the strong connection with the key professional associations, the MVHA and the AHA, and the networks of influence that those organizations could supply.[115]

It was not the case that academic historians ever lost interest in the question of teaching, however. When Dexter Perkins gave his presidential address to the AHA in 1956, it was titled "We Shall Gladly Teach." The address struck a responsive chord and elicited unprecedented demand for copies from AHA members. Perkins himself was an advocate of the broadest possible approach and understood the need to reach student audiences. But the address dealt with university teaching and the major effect was to stimulate a review of graduate training.[116] Though Perkins would have been disturbed by the situation in which high school links were eroding, academics were freer to ignore the high schools than ever before because the position of history had improved as a result of the cumulative wartime and postwar changes that stiffened compulsory requirements. Academics no longer needed the support of teacher colleagues in the high schools for the survival of history. They could rest comfortably in the knowledge that not only had the United States triumphed in World War II but American history had, too.

Strategically, the focus on national history that was strengthened by the war held dangers as well as advantages for the profession. American history now had a heavy pedagogical burden to bear, as Princeton's Joseph Strayer stated in 1962. Because it was the only social studies subject required in most schools, U.S. history had to "carry most of the load of giving the students essential ideas about the nature of human society."[117] In contrast, efforts to strengthen world history lagged behind, and historians soon became alarmed. The Twentieth Yearbook of the National Council on the Social Studies, published in 1949, was devoted to this theme, and the efforts of scholars such as William H. McNeill and L. S. Stavrianos signaled that academics would not rest content on this score.[118] By the 1960s, the AHA's Committee on Teaching wanted more world history taught: "The domestic history of the United States is fairly well done," the committee admitted, but "the real failure is in the courses dealing with foreign areas and earlier civilizations, and especially in the course in world history." Yet despite repeated attempts, the AHA had trouble getting funding from private corporations and philanthropic organizations to support a proposed study of the school curriculum.[119] The proposals had been left too late. In the 1960s, foundation support turned to the revision of the social studies curriculum and the wholesale attack on the place of history through the New Social Studies.[120]

* * *

This cluster of achievements and failures left the discipline of history vulnerable to the social unrest of the 1960s. The Vietnam War would undermine the focus on the nation-state, with American foreign and domestic policies of Great Society liberalism coming under attack. Until the mid-1960s most historians had supported such policies in the New Deal–Fair Deal tradition. In cementing their position, it might have been helpful if they had retained firmer links with teacher educators and colleagues in the social sciences interested in the schools. But they had not. In a 1963 report for the AHA, W. Stull Holt measured the changes since 1945: "The college and university professors of history value recognitions and honors from their peer group in history far more than any from the teaching world. History, not education, is their profession."[121] Links with the wider teaching profession at the local level were never completely broken, yet the modern pattern had been established. American history's position in the schools remained relatively strong, but academics had ceased to make a case as to why history was an important school subject to preserve. More ominously, they defended their stake in education with diminishing enthusiasm.[122]

Against the shifting and uncertain audiences for the reading of history in the wider community, the institutionalized position of American history teaching in schools and colleges gave some temporary security. Yet historians were now doubly bound to the nation-state. Not only did their teaching interventions stress these links, but historians had become servants of the state. As part of a search for usefulness, they had rushed to defend the nation-state during World War I and World War II. And long before the crisis of relevance in the 1960s, historians in the United States had become strong proponents of applying history to solve social problems. They applied their knowledge and skills to public issues through federal and state governments. Therein lies the hidden past of "public history."

Part 4

PUBLIC HISTORIES

9

Going Public

Public and Applied History, 1890–1930

American historians have long feared that they lacked influence in public life. History was not honored, as it seemed to be in Europe, by political preferment and state power. As Frederick Jackson Turner remarked, Germany's "great public servants" included historians, and England, France, and Italy did not "fail to recognize the union of history and politics." Macaulay, Dilke, Morley, and Bryce were "eminent members of Parliament as well as distinguished historical writers." In the United States, Turner surveyed historians' public influence and found a bleaker record. There, "statesmanship" had been treated as "something of spontaneous generation, a miraculous birth from our republican institutions." Few thought it necessary for political leaders to have "a scientific acquaintance with historical politics or economics."[1] Though these words were uttered in the 1890s, they could be used to describe historians' perception of their political clout one hundred years later. Despite this perception of marginality, American historians did intervene in the production of public historical knowledge and allied their efforts closely to those of the nation-state.

The terms "public history," "applied history," and "policy history" are used to describe these activities.[2] The meanings of these terms have often been subject to dispute, in part because there are two different claims for the beginning of modern public history. Understood as the radical critique and appreciation of historical representations in diverse media from advertising, film, and popular culture to museums and libraries, the modern drive to make academic history in some way more "public" had roots in the 1960s and the New Left.[3] Yet a self-conscious, professionalized field of public history has been more influential and claims a precise but misleading point of departure. This form of public history, more common in the United States than in Britain, coincided with the inception of *The Public Historian*, founded by the late Robert Kelley and others in 1978, and with the creation of the National Council on Public History (NCPH) in 1979.

Whether dated from the NCPH or the radical currents of the 1960s, scholars tend to see public history as something new, marked by the emergence of a cluster of journals, training programs, and professional organizations.[4] Both cynics and sympathetic critics have concluded that the newfound interest in "public history" was one response to a disastrous lack of jobs in academia.[5] In this view, public history was useful because it provided employment to graduates with doctorates in history. In an assessment published in 1980, Michael Kammen noted a rise in the number of "full-time historians" employed in the U.S. government. This shift helped in "countering the job crisis" of that era and provided at the same time a "useful . . . historical perspective."[6] Jobs aside, historians were said to be not much interested in climbing down from their ivory towers. Practitioners consistently reported that academics assigned second-class status to the modern genre of public history.[7] Even when the leading organizations made efforts to bring the two types of history together, as in joint meetings of the NCPH and the Organization of American Historians held every few years in conjunction with the annual Organization of American Historians convention after 1986, relatively few academic historians attended public history sessions. The specialized character of the historical profession perpetuated the gap. Parallel sessions gave little time for the dimly curious to cross subdisciplinary boundaries while maintaining contact with one's immediate peers.[8]

The jobs crisis only partly explains the surge of interest in public history and the development of its key institutional forms. The roots run much deeper. As both William E. Leuchtenburg and David Kyvig have noted, historians have long addressed important public issues. Historians are all in some sense public historians or they are intellectually dead.[9] Some perceptive observers recall historians' involvement in public outreach from the early decades of the twentieth century and recognize that the impressive recent achievements have built upon this tradition.[10] "Part of public history's success stemmed from the fact that it did not start from scratch," observed Julian Zelizer. "Rather, it provided recognition of what many historians had been doing since the founding of the profession in government agencies, archival institutions, historical societies and tourist sites, and museums."[11] Yet no one has explored these legacies or acknowledged just how much modern public history is enmeshed in the larger American tradition of "useful history."[12]

According to many commentators, historians abandoned their responsibility to speak to public issues in the immediate post–World War II period, just as they did in teaching.[13] Peter Stearns and Joel Tarr put it most starkly in 1980: the discipline "made a crucial error about forty years ago. It tragically narrowed its audience to students and other academics." History's "large public audience" had been lost at that time and the profession retreated into "narcissism."[14] That the period from 1930 to 1950 represented the high point of American historians' public involvement cannot be doubted. Why that public involvement was so strong, what forms it took, and why the position changed are the subjects of this chapter. The change was not simply a matter of historians' choosing to narrow their audience. Rather, the academic historians' position was undermined by rival disciplines and, ironically, also by critical changes in the ways that professors sought public usefulness during that period.

The key to interpreting the fluctuations of American academic history's relationship to public history is the role of "the state." Historians at the time of Turner wished to have a public influence that matched that of European colleagues, but one gigantic stumbling block stood in the road. The American state had been weak and divided in the nineteenth century, and the national government was disinclined to aid historical activities well into the twentieth. A constant lament from Scientific historians was the absence of financial support from the federal government for serious historical work. In the 1920s, *American Historical Review* editor John Franklin Jameson and John C. Fitzgerald, acting chief of the Division of Manuscripts in the Library of Congress, both deplored the "meager" U.S. government contribution to history research. It was, charged Jameson, "less than what any of the larger and some of the smaller European countries spend for history."[15] Yet it was not just the failure of the state to preserve the written records of the national government in an accessible national collection that irritated professionals. All aspects of the state's history-making functions were fragmented and ineffective. To be sure, the decentralized nature of history making had its virtues, as observers of twentieth-century dictatorships would concur. But modern-day observers are still struck by the failure of American governments to lend history the support or the prestige of the state. Michael Kammen has argued that national memory has not been state manipulated or directed in the United States but has been produced in civil society—in sharp distinction to the case of some European nations.[16]

This contrast can be overdrawn. State attempts to create and sustain national memory were part of a transnational trend. Nation-state making accelerated in the nineteenth century and again as old multinational empires based mainly in Europe crumbled in the wake of World War I. The expansion of mass electoral politics, mass media, and the tumultuous events of depression and war confirmed the move toward state manipulation of collective memory. In the Soviet Union and Nazi Germany the process was obvious, but democratic countries such as France were also affected.[17] In a different way, American historians used the state extensively and the state used historians to an equal degree. True, contact with the federal state was for most historians episodic during much of the twentieth century, but the New Deal and World Wars I and II produced a profound nationalizing experience within the culture of American academic history. As a result of their experiences in these crucial periods, historians remained attached to the state in a way that shaped their interpretations of the public utility of history and the entire nature of historiography. Before the 1960s, because of this contact between historians and the state, most wrote what Hugh Graham called "regime history."[18] Their work focused on presidents, policies, and legislation. Even most social history remained within these contours. This nation-statist bias served American historians well in their public outreach from the 1920s to the 1960s but faltered badly in the wake of the attacks that the New Left brought to American historiography. From that time, the historians' attitude to the state changed, and the crisis in that relationship has remained as a problem in historians' public mission ever since.

The underrating of the state's role by historians is not a product of historical amnesia but is largely founded on misplaced comparisons with Europe. In the American case, the relatively decentralized and federalized state meant that significant deployment of historians' skills came at different levels and in different ways than in major European countries over the last century. Historians did become involved in government from the turn of the twentieth century, but they worked through local historical societies, city administrations, and state governments at first. Under the federal system this local, state, and regional involvement was a key part of the historical apparatus of state manipulation and promotion of historical memory in the period prior to the 1930s. From the 1930s, far more extensive federal government involvement began to develop.[19] This change promoted a national focus among historians with far-reaching consequences. When the state's history-making activities were closely linked to the local and regional scene, academic historians could remain in touch with identifiable public audiences and exercised a fair degree of public influence. Once the state process of history making became more remote, and more prone to national mass media manipulation, the ability of academics to connect with public audiences through the activities of the state became more problematic.

This complicated set of connections to the building of public memory through the state is the subject of this and the next three chapters. The theme can be divided into two complementary sections. This chapter and the next two focus on the growth of relations with government, particularly the federal government, from before World War I to the 1950s. This phase of historians' public involvement entailed much more in the way of policy history than has hitherto been acknowledged, though their role was by no means mainly policy oriented. Academic historians worked on a variety of projects through the National Park Service, the National Archives, New Deal agencies, the Agriculture Department's history section, and the war efforts in 1917–18 and 1941–45. The involvement with state and local history groups—treated in chapter 12—was different. Here, historians came into close contact with local history and with grassroots efforts to popularize that history in the mid–twentieth century.

Despite the changing relationship between historians and the state, and between academic historians and public history, one thing remained constant: the American historian's public outreach has been the work of experts. American historians spoke of public history as a specialized subdiscipline in the 1970s, whereas British historians preferred to talk about "people's history."[20] The difference highlights the key variable in historians' relationship to the public. The British tradition facilitated popular and working-class recording of their own historical experiences and involved important contributions to this process by trade unions, workers' education, and local history groups, as well as amateur historians.[21] The American tradition became one of *academic* involvement in public activities. Historians attempted, as in other spheres, to make professional history useful. In this way, public history has been an extension of academic history and evidence of the impact of professional discourse across a wide terrain of American history making.

A second theme is the tendency for many initiatives to begin at the margins of the academic profession and to be incorporated within the mainstream as historians sought to extend or prove their relevance at times of economic, political, and military crisis. The flexibility of the profession toward innovations from its margins and to outside influences, and the diversity of its state university system, together with the mix of public and private universities, facilitated moderate change in historical practice. (These same circumstances did not, however, encourage radical change in the profession, its interpretations, or its intellectual approaches that might threaten the social order.) Moreover, the general paradigm of Progressive historiography heavily influenced the work undertaken and yet at the same time was vitally influenced by the conditions of history making that historians encountered. Thus, the role of historians as public figures and as expert intellectuals was always closely tied to the trajectory of the American state. In turn, this continual yet diverse engagement with public life helped to shape the parameters of the scholarship that historians undertook.

* * *

From the earliest days of Scientific History, historians were not quite the ivory tower inhabitants of the conventional caricature. They took part in the cultural and political life of their local communities and contributed to urban Progressive reform. Scientific History's founder in America, Herbert Baxter Adams, not only sought to cultivate local history groups but also promoted the genteel tradition of elite "mugwump" reform while at Johns Hopkins University from 1876. Adams "called attention to many English initiatives in philanthropy and social betterment, encouraging his students to admire the historian *engagé* Arnold Toynbee," who had started the English settlement movement to bring "civilization" to the slums of London. In the 1890s, Adams turned his attention to "current problems in education and social reform," and he produced studies of higher education in the states for the U.S. Bureau of Education. Although Adams failed to develop a viable program of local history in Baltimore, his "civic involvement" in the community cannot be doubted.[22]

More effective and long-lasting roots for the ethic of public service could be found in the Midwest. There, new historical traditions were being invented. State, rather than city, boosterism prevailed, and scholars relied on state patronage and funding to develop expertise. The nexus between state universities and academics energized the service ethic to lengths not seen in the voluntaristic tradition of mugwump reform. In 1910 Turner noted with pride the role in western states of the state university, with its "peculiar power in the directness of its influence upon the whole people." The public universities in such states as Turner's own Wisconsin could, by "training in science, in law, politics, economics and history," supply from the ranks of the masses the "administrators, legislators, judges and experts for commissions" needed to run a democratic society. Open-minded experts could, Turner hoped, "disinterestedly and intelligently mediate between contending interests" and settle the conflicts between capital and labor that divided American society and marked the end of the frontier.[23]

In some cases, this engagement self-consciously took the form of "applied history." An outstanding example was the work of Benjamin Shambaugh

(1871–1940), a professor at the University of Iowa and superintendent of the State Historical Society of Iowa. Under his control the state historical society employed more than two dozen researchers and issued over seven hundred publications covering subjects from documentary sources to popular essays. The Iowa Applied History Series, begun at the time of World War I, was a seven-volume attempt "to bring the light of history to bear upon the solution of current problems of legislation and administration."[24] It dealt with such practical questions as the history of road legislation, workers' compensation, and welfare work.[25] Shambaugh's example was admired, but within historical societies it was not as widely copied as the quest to democratize knowledge of the past. Applied history aided state legislators and government agencies by providing legislative research services but did not provide voters with tangible evidence of taxpayers' money well spent. Museums and traveling history exhibits, pageants, monuments, highway markers, libraries, and archives all did this much better. Only through such public outreach could legislators and state historical society directors justify to voters the expenditure of state money on historical activities. For historians, policy work was also more difficult to do than in some other disciplines. As fields such as economics and public administration developed, they tended to take over the more narrowly utilitarian functions of applied research.

For this reason, the most highly visible examples of engagement in public-policy issues came from political scientists and historical economists rather than from historians per se. It was the marriage of institutional economics and the land grant university tradition of service that produced the most outstanding examples of public-policy-oriented history before World War I. John Rogers Commons was better known as one of the greatest economists of the Progressive Era in the United States. But as part of his contribution to labor and institutional economics, he investigated labor history, editing the ten-volume *A Documentary History of American Industrial Society* (1910–11), as well as writing his four-volume *History of Labour in the United States* (1918–35).[26] Commons also put history and expert policy analysis to action as a member of the first Wisconsin Industrial Commission from 1911 to 1913. Commons "helped prepare most of the legislation that made Wisconsin the laboratory in social and economic reform for other states and the federal government."[27] In his research into "industrial history" he marshaled the talents of the academic historian Ulrich Bonnell Phillips, author of pathbreaking work on the history of slavery, who contributed the first two volumes of the *Documentary History*, on plantation society and the frontier. The series also used the work of the talented labor historian who trained under Commons at Wisconsin, Helen Sumner (Woodbury).[28]

Along with a number of other intellectual radicals, Commons had retreated from a more oppositional stance in regard to capitalism after the
1880s;[29] he did not cease, however, to be an activist and turned his scholarly talents toward the role of the historian as an expert balancing the interests of capital and labor, as Turner had envisaged.[30] Though Commons himself was increasingly handicapped by serious illness prior to his formal retirement from
teaching in 1932, the efforts of the Wisconsin school of labor history that he
established were to be long lasting. Commons and his students demonstrated
the impact on historiography of their form of public intervention and how it
was constituted as expert and specialized service. This impact was far-reaching
and moderately Progressive while marginalizing more radical currents. Commons and his associates pioneered labor history as a conservative enterprise
and launched a school of historiography that had to be confronted by subsequent generations. Their connections with labor in turn meant links with craft
unions and the institutions of the state that supported them.[31] This work favored trade unionism rather than class interpretation and stressed the integra-
tion of American workers into the (capitalistic) American mainstream. It
reinforced American exceptionalism and rationalized the exclusion of large
groups of unorganized workers from material progress. Though new labor
historians in the 1920s began to offer a more complex counterinterpretation of
labor as class conflict, labor historiography continued until the 1960s to be
dominated by Commons's disciples.[32] The formation of the journal *Labor History* in 1960 remained, as one of the journal's founders put it, within this tradition of supporting labor's "leaders [and] organizations" as well as "our balanced two-party system, and an economy based on the profit motive."[33]

Such formative incursions into public policy were encouraged by the fluid
boundaries between social science and history before World War I. Political
science especially focused its agenda upon the concept of the state,[34] and leading political scientists were often indistinguishable from historians. William
Archibald Dunning, founder of the major school of Reconstruction historiography, was a joint professor of history and political philosophy at Columbia.
His colleague John W. Burgess was "primarily a political scientist" but wrote
an extensive three-part history of the United States and believed that history
and political science needed to be studied together. The two disciplines were
for him as inseparable as Dunning believed they were.[35]

Within the discipline of economics, too, prohistorical forces could be detected. Leading American economists Richard T. Ely and John Bates Clark
founded the American Bureau of Industrial Research, which produced *A Documentary History of American Industrial Society* with the financial support of the
Carnegie Institution. Clark and Ely had studied in Germany as students in the

German historical school of economics.[36] Often thought of as the dean of the neoclassical, or "marginalist," school in the United States, Clark nonetheless encouraged economic history as a guide to improving economic theory and its ability to interpret the world. In a suggestive foreword to *A Documentary History,* Clark argued that "America has afforded the richest field for the application of known economic law to the interpretation of history." Conversely, American history offered "the most available means of treating and establishing the correctness of such economic theories."[37]

The type of history that Clark, Ely, and Commons promoted was, however, far from what was traditionally accepted as history in the historical profession.[38] Though in effect Clark advocated a "Scientific" interpretation based on facts, as did most of the American historical profession, he sought to establish that the economic interpretation was scientific. Only among the Progressives who, led by Charles Beard, promoted this economic interpretation of history could a viewpoint congenial to Clark be found. Beard took up this challenge of producing history for the urban industrial age. His landmark *Economic Interpretation of the Constitution* (1913) had obvious relevance to the debates over the Supreme Court's interpretation of Progressive legislation and the introduction of the federal income tax, but he also undertook studies directly linked to public policy. Beard joined in the movement for Progressive urban reform, working for the New York Municipal Research Bureau from 1914. There he became allied to bureau director Edwin Seligman, who sought to apply Progressive principles of economic efficiency to urban politics. Seligman, a Columbia political economist, was also the author of *The Economic Interpretation of History,* a book of essays that influenced Beard's own approach.[39]

Beard's teaching and research for the bureau had an impact on his scholarship and also gave him prestige in public administration that led in the 1920s to service as a consultant in that field in Japan and Yugoslavia. Rather than emerging from an academic environment, Beard's writings were partly, historian Ellen Nore states, "a natural extension of his day-to-day practical involvement in the movement for efficient and humane city government, social justice, and woman suffrage." During this period Beard wrote *American City Government* (1912), a distillation of Progressive reform on urban problems and served as editor of the *National Municipal Review* (1912–14). He was, Clyde Barrow states, "more than a Historian"—at least, it should be added, a "historian" narrowly conceived.[40]

Few, if any other, "historians" could match Beard's diverse talents. In part, the pressure of specialization worked against them. They lacked experience in public policy or the academic expertise in economics, social welfare, or public administration acquired by figures such as Commons and Clark. Students of history more interested in practical implications gravitated for this reason toward the disciplines of economics, politics, and sociology. Beard himself had shifted from the Department of History to a chair in politics at Columbia in 1907, but his loyalties remained with history. The issue was what kind of history.

During and after World War I, Beard increasingly came to be at odds with conservatives in the American Historical Association who resisted the reform of historical practice. But he made clear that the sources of his attack on the Scientific historians went deeper than postwar alienation. Dissatisfaction at the pace of reform toward a more theoretically informed and interpretively realistic discipline contributed to the change in Beard's position. "However great his services in the preservation of national memorials," he put it in 1927, "the historian makes few weighty contributions to political science. In mortal fright lest he should be wrong about something, he shrinks from any interpretation." The flow of words registered Beard's impatience with and contempt for his opponents since "the historian proudly tells us that he has nothing to do with interpretation, that he deals only with indubitable facts."[41] Because of the methodological preferences of Scientific History that Beard identified, and because of the growth in competing disciplines, most historians had little direct opportunity to influence public policy. Though traditions of applied policy research never died completely, history's "principal contribution" to the social order during this period would be "legitimation" of the state through the education system.[42]

American entry into World War I presented a prize opportunity for serious state-oriented legitimation. After 1917 American historians rallied to the service of the state as never before; they saw this work as expiation for insufficient patriotism before the war and as justification for the "scholar's calling."[43] Some, like Samuel B. Harding, professor of European History at Indiana University, worked for the Committee on Public Information (CPI), which produced tendentious propaganda on the righteousness of the Allied cause.[44] By serving the state, scholars believed they would strengthen history. Harding saw the war as an opportunity to shore up the discipline's position as a school subject and in wider public discourse since, he believed, even the "man of affairs" now regarded modern history as vital to the interpretation of current events. Under the direction of Guy Stanton Ford, historians produced pamphlets for the CPI's Division of Civic and Educational Publications. In one notorious case, Jameson and Samuel N. Harper, of the University of Chicago, assessed the wartime propaganda document *The German-Bolshevik Conspiracy* as genuine. The certification of these "manifestly forged documents" showed the extent to which historians abandoned objectivity while professing resolute adherence to that key doctrine of Scientific History. The *War Cyclopedia*, produced by the Division of Civic and Educational Publications and edited by Frederic L. Paxson, Edward S. Corwin, and Samuel B. Harding, had entries by such historical luminaries as Carl Becker, Beard, Sidney B. Fay, and Jameson that sought to remove any remaining doubt that German aggression caused the war.[45]

Through Jameson's initiative, the AHA also established the National Board for Historical Service (NBHS), which was chaired by Evarts B. Greene and whose work was carried out by volunteers. Its main function was to publish pro-Allied materials in the *History Teacher's Magazine* and to advise teachers on the revision of school curricula. The NBHS professedly did not intend to duplicate the "chauvinistic ideas" so "aggressively promoted" by the press and patriotic interest groups. Rather, it would seek, said Greene, to "help in preserving a rational conception of civic education."[46] Its aim was to promote the American nation-state through history education. Yet the fine line between provision of expert knowledge for "civic" purposes and propaganda in pursuit of that cause was frequently crossed.[47]

The aim of aligning history with the state would at the same time shore up the position of history as a discipline against the challenge of the social sciences.[48] In so doing, the CPI and NBHS war work became the greatest single effort to make history popular in American society to that time. James R. Mock and Cedric Larson later claimed, "Probably no man in American history" had "ever before put to press a scholarly work destined for a larger printing" than some of the CPI pamphlets. While it strained credibility to call the pamphlets "scholarly work," the other half of the comment was true—in all, the CPI's history publications under Ford reached 75 million copies. *The War Message and the Facts behind It*, researched by historian William Sterns Davis (University of Minnesota), ran to 2.5 million copies alone.[49]

These facts are well known, and much ink has been spilt in telling them. Less well emphasized has been activism in promotion of a peace settlement. This work did not overturn historians' somewhat complacent and simplistic wartime view that the struggle lay between civilization and barbarism, but critics who have condemned the rush of patriotic blood among the historians of 1917–18 have often missed this other face of wartime activism. James T. Shotwell, a Canadian-born professor of history trained as a medievalist, took leave from Columbia University to work on the war effort in 1917.[50] He helped organize the NBHS and became inaugural chair before giving way to Greene. A strong supporter of the Allied cause, he was soon attracted to President Wilson's efforts to realize a new world order from the calamities of war. He joined Walter Lippman, Edward House, and others in "The Inquiry," a body that Wil-

son had established to study "the major political, economic, legal, and historical questions likely to arise at a future peace conference." Shotwell recruited a
bevy of up-and-coming scholars, such as the young Harvard instructor Samuel
Eliot Morison, and established professors, such as Fay, Dunning, and Charles
Seymour, to aid specialized investigations of the individual nations involved in
the peace settlement, matters of international law, and diplomatic history. Although historians hardly dominated this work (a good deal focused on geography and economics), the project severely qualifies the notion that historians
were involved only in wartime propaganda. Academic reputation and expertise did matter in The Inquiry. The NBHS cooperated in The Inquiry's research
work, using Shotwell as the conduit. Along with others scholars such as Morison, the Columbia historian followed Wilson to Paris as adviser to the American Peace Commission in 1919. There Shotwell assisted in the organization of
the International Labour Office.[51]

Nor did Shotwell stop when the diplomacy had finished. As Harold Josephson has stated, in the interwar period he sought to "keep alive the Wilsonian vision." The massive *Economic and Social History of the World War* undertaken for
the Carnegie Endowment for International Peace was his major achievement.
Taking seventeen years to edit the 152 volumes, Shotwell "sought to determine the precise impact of modern war upon advanced societies."[52] In the
meantime, he became director of the Carnegie Institution's Division of Economics and History in 1924 and worked through this position to promote
world peace. Functionally, Shotwell had almost ceased being a historian and
had become an early practitioner of the fledgling field of international relations. Fittingly, in 1938 he was named Bryce Professor of the History of International Relations at Columbia. So great was the demand for his brand of useful history that he was rarely available for ordinary teaching after 1917. As
Richard Hofstadter dryly remarked in his survey of Columbia's Department
of History, Shotwell's reputation "in the larger world of affairs" had "never
been an unmixed blessing" from "the Department's point of view."[53] Shotwell
would have viewed the matter differently. He regarded his career as both "an
exploration of the mind and the task of statesmanship" and still retained links
with Columbia.[54] Like Beard and Robinson, his teachers and colleagues,
Shotwell had embraced a broad and expansive Progressivism and sought to
promote its relevance to the modern world under the banner of useful history.

Not only did historians aid diplomacy as well as war. In the aftermath of
war, the failure of the United States to join the League of Nations, the release
of new European diplomatic documents on the war, and the collapse of
efforts to attain a "just" peace prompted some highly vocal scholars to repudiate their pro-Allied views with the conviction of a religious conversion. Harry

Elmer Barnes, of Smith College, led the charge to repent.[55] The impact of this controversy on historical interpretation of the European war and on the ideal of scholarly objectivity is well known, but the effects on historical practice have been neglected. Together with the retrenchment of the wartime bureaucracy undertaken for financial and political reasons, the debunking of the war effort distanced historians temporarily from the state.[56] Historians now lacked the ability to find either jobs or status through the state. Especially discredited was the work that historians had already done for the federal government.

For this reason, continuity with prewar Progressivism at the state level was important. Despite the colorful and well-publicized cases of propaganda work during World War I, historians had not given up entirely on much more prosaic public service in the states. There, historical work on public policy continued and provided an important link between state-based Progressivism from the turn of the century and the New Deal. The Commons school and the larger Wisconsin tradition of public service influenced certain historians and economists, who began to build upon their work in the 1910s and 1920s by inventing the field of agricultural history.

In the early twenty-first century, agricultural history is merely a respected but rather obscure subdiscipline. Its role as a source of policy analysis and nonacademic employment for historians has been lost, its innovative and cross-disciplinary character forgotten. This work had its origins in the tradition of public service by universities and in the Turner school of historiography. Within the historical discipline, Ulrich B. Phillips's study for the Commons project on the history of labor (1910) presented the most important early contribution and was followed by his *American Negro Slavery* (1918).[57] However, the genealogy of agricultural history can be traced chiefly through policy-oriented agricultural economists at the University of Wisconsin.

Before World War I, Turner's frontier thesis prompted Wisconsin economist Richard T. Ely to encourage students to explore the frontier from the perspective of agricultural history. Henry C. Taylor, a little-known agricultural economist, took up the challenge, beginning a history of land tenure as part of a project in economic history for the Carnegie Institution, which decided in 1904 to fund a series of studies on American agriculture. Taylor did research for the volume on northern agriculture that was eventually published in a revised version by Percy Bidwell and John I. Falconer in 1925.[58] As professor of agricultural economics at Wisconsin from 1908 to 1919, Taylor's influence was felt mainly through his students and institutional connections. He pushed Falconer toward agricultural history, as well as Lewis C. Gray. The latter was Taylor's most influential student in terms of American historiography and was the author of the *History of Agriculture in the Southern United States to 1860*.[59]

Robert W. Fogel and Stanley Engerman have called this pioneering work an "indispensable source" for the history of slavery.[60]

Taylor did not merely direct agricultural history research; he shaped policies and institutions as well. In 1916 he took charge of the agricultural history section of the Carnegie Institution and then moved directly into government service as chief of the Office of Farm Management in the U.S. Department of Agriculture (USDA) from 1919 to 1921, where he helped organized the Bureau of Agricultural Economics. The historical work of the new bureau was placed in the Division of Statistical and Historical Research, headed by Taylor's student O. C. Stine, who steered it during its close cooperation with historians, which lasted until Stine's retirement in 1951.[61]

Only after World War I did conventional academic historians enter this field in any major way. Turner did not specifically mention "agricultural" history as a field in his frontier thesis in 1893. Not until his presidential address to the AHA in 1909 did he declare, "The whole subject of American agriculture viewed in relation to the economic, political, and social life of the nation" had "important contributions to make" to historiography.[62] Until Louis B. Schmidt, of Iowa State College, outlined "the economic history of American agriculture as a field of study" in 1916, no prospectus for the subdiscipline existed.[63] Within three years, academics and USDA officials cooperated to form an Agricultural History Society, and by 1920, they agreed upon institutional ties between the USDA and the AHA. In return for affiliation, the latter offered to publish for the society a 300-page section each year as part of the AHA annual reports. Nonetheless, the Agricultural History Society soon embarked on its own ambitious research and publishing program blending policy and history.

No better era existed for the expansion of this field than the twenties. The race to produce enough grain for the war effort abruptly ended, leaving plummeting prices and farmers in economic distress in many states. Political discontent ensued, as it had in the 1890s. Seizing the moment, the founders of the Agricultural History Society stressed the value that their work could have for governments. Academics acting as experts would provide impartial advice, put sudden shifts in prices, crops, pest species, and other social and economic problems of agriculture in perspective, and suggest policy alternatives. For Nils Olsen, secretary-treasurer of the Agricultural History Society, "Students of agricultural conditions" were "looking more and more to history for guidance in the solution of present problems." The society envisaged work on price movements, the tariff, and the problem of marketing agricultural surpluses in the wake of the glut and rural depression. Such "outstanding issues" should be viewed, he believed, "in the light of experience" rather than theory. For this purpose, Olsen declared history more useful than abstract economics. He found significant the "marked demand for material on the historical background of these and other agricultural problems."[64] Among other things, the Agricultural History Society would be a clearinghouse of information, an objective that raised the desirability of a journal separate from the AHA's *Annual Reports*.

Agricultural historians lobbied government at the highest levels. Herbert Kellar, of the McCormick Library in Chicago and president of the Agricultural History Society, boldly informed Secretary of Agriculture Henry C. Wallace in 1922 that the "continuation and expansion of this interest in the history of the agricultural development of the country" would help in formulating an agricultural policy for the country.[65] Wallace agreed, but cautioned that USDA work would, "necessarily, be confined to the larger movements in agricultural history."[66] Department official O. C. Stine used the model of contract university research, as in his Rural Life Project, to obtain such policy advice. In turn, policy involvement would help change academic history, Kellar believed. Agricultural policy research would "mean, sooner or later, the entire rewriting of American history."[67] The field would become more realistic in the way that Turner and Beard had hoped.

This close connection with a government sponsor had the drawback of political pressure. When in 1927 the AHA planned a session entitled "Suggestions for an Agricultural Policy for the United States" for its annual convention, Kellar had to parry political interference. Stine objected that the session might "be superficial and more of the character of economic theory than historical analysis." While the doughty Kellar retorted that "the subject of the program" was not "any of their concern," he promised the USDA that discussion would be "non-partisan." Despite this bluster, no separate session on agriculture was held. Instead, as a compromise, the University of Chicago's William E. Dodd spoke on the "drift of American agriculture" from prosperity to depression during and after World War I at the Agricultural History Society dinner held in conjunction with the AHA meeting.[68]

Though the society founded its own journal in 1927, *Agricultural History*, edited by Stine, it maintained links with the mainstream historical profession. The appointment to the USDA of Everett Edwards in 1927 enhanced the role of academic history in the projects of the department. Although he never completed his Ph.D., Edwards had been trained at Harvard under Frederick Merk, who in turn had studied with Turner at Wisconsin. As editor of *Agricultural History* after 1931, Edwards zealously "spread the Turner thesis." He also taught the idea through a course given at American University as part of the USDA Graduate School[69] and wrote historiographical studies of Turner,

Phillips, and Turner disciple Joseph Schafer.[70] During the 1930s Edwards stressed the relationship between the USDA and the universities and gave scholars rooms in which to work at the department, guided their research, and supplied office assistance. He "always felt that his ties were," historian colleague Wayne Rasmussen observed, "closer to the university community than they were to the Department of Agriculture."[71]

The 1930s was a decade of agricultural upheaval due to drought, dust bowls, and New Deal measures of reform. With agricultural topics at the fore in politics, the path was clear for the emergence of the subdiscipline as a major academic field. John D. Hicks's *The Populist Revolt* (1931) signaled the progress, as did the work of Harry Carman, of Columbia, who edited the Columbia Studies in Agricultural History from 1934.[72] When the Economic History of the United States series was first conceived in the late 1930s, two volumes were to be devoted to agriculture. These, eventually published by Fred A. Shannon and Paul W. Gates, would become standard reference works in the field of American history.[73] This historical work had moved away from policy analysis, but the field did retain paths of communication with the USDA. Agricultural history had a strong input from government employees as late as the end of World War II. Twenty-eight percent of articles in *Agricultural History* from 1929 to 1946 came from this source, compared to 10 percent between 1947 and 1967.[74]

From intellectual fashion in the interwar years, however, agricultural history fragmented after World War II and with it the political and reform links of those years. Academic and USDA interests diverged. The latter concentrated on in-house institutional studies and on practical questions such as price-support legislation. A contributory factor in the decline of active government participation from the 1950s was the closure of the Agricultural History Section of the Agricultural Marketing Service of the USDA when its functions were taken over by the Statistical Services Section in 1954.[75] Matching the government's marginalizing of the broad socioeconomic context of agriculture was the growing neglect of the field within universities from the 1960s. However, Wayne Rasmussen remained in the USDA as a contact with the academic community.[76]

Why was the early dynamism of agricultural history lost? In part, as Americans moved from farm to city, historians lost empathy for the country. But the development of social history post-1960 contributed further to this neglect, when economic history went out of fashion. Topics of enduring public and scholarly interest such as slavery and environmental studies became defined as separate fields rather than linked to agricultural history. Yet the later neglect of this pioneering work in applied history stemmed also from the effects of the depression and World War II, which overwhelmed agricultural history with much more extensive federal government intervention in support of history through the New Deal. Simultaneously, the depression weakened the hold of state Progressivism's institutions in which historians had been involved through expert commissions. This was true of Shambaugh's pioneering applied-history scheme in Iowa, where state programs lost funding. The impetus for further work shifted in the 1930s to nationally directed programs.[77] Those programs are the subject of the next chapter.

10

History Making in the New Deal State

Academics by and large welcomed the New Deal's impact. As in other aspects of American political and economic life, the New Deal greatly stimulated the role of the U.S. government in history making. The bureaucratic Leviathan of government agencies during World War I had been quickly dismantled and with it the capacity for historians to serve the federal state. Now, in the 1930s, unemployment in the millions and the threat to the survival of the economic system itself called forth expertise, spurred interest in American traditions, and opened manifold new opportunities for historians to work in government departments and historical projects. Historians' own employment market sagged along with state budgets, just when a substantial rise in Ph.D. numbers occurred. A severe glut in the number of doctorates existed for the first time in the profession's history. Only the federal state's relief activities could absorb the slack. The single most important of these initiatives came from the National Park Service (NPS). This was not a relief program per se but drew upon relief labor through the Civilian Conservation Corps and other programs.

Like the historical work of the U.S. Department of Agriculture (USDA), park history had roots extending back before the New Deal. Historians' interest in national park issues went back at least as far as the work of Albert Bushnell Hart. Writing in 1898 in the *American Historical Review,* he urged attention to historical preservation. This was eight years before the passage of the National Antiquities Act. Hart praised special societies formed to rescue historical sites, noting the Association for the Preservation of Virginia Antiquities and its work for "the embanking of the remnants of Jamestown Island." "[W]e moderns are so overwhelmed with reading matter," Hart argued, "that we do not fully understand the effect of inscriptions which stand in public view—the literature of the bookless." In a farsighted suggestion, he proclaimed that a "service to history and to patriotism would be to catalogue in each state and city the memorable historical sites." Hart favored the careful preservation of monuments but complained that there were too few good ones like Saint-Gaudens's Shaw Memorial in Boston. As a historian of abolitionism and a resident of New England, Hart took particular pride in this example, dedicated as it was to the abolitionist and Civil War commander of the Fifty-fourth Massachusetts Infantry, Robert Gould Shaw. The memorial was "a really individual and inspiring work of art, which could be set up only for the one man whom it commemorates, and yet through him speaks of the heroism of armies, and raises the moral standard of every man who sees it."[1]

Hart's enthusiasm failed to stir most academics, in part because of the fragmented structure of the profession. The American Historical Association's interest in all histories—not just American—handicapped for generations its involvement in these local matters. Support came mainly from within the upstart Mississippi Valley Historical Association (MVHA). By 1914, the association maintained a Committee on Historical Sites and heard papers and passed motions at the annual meeting on the preservation of landscapes and historical landmarks. Mostly these were delivered either by interested amateurs, by local preservationists in cities where the MVHA annual meetings were held, or by the active group of state historical society people within the MVHA. The existence of the MVHA in fact deflected into a different and more specialized arena the involvement that Hart's commentary might have spurred. But structural impediments do not explain the AHA's neglect entirely.[2]

Academic historians showed little interest in historical preservation over the course of the next thirty years. They concentrated on printed and written sources despite Hart's warnings that they must move beyond that narrow view. Hart himself acknowledged that his inspiration came from Europe, where antiquities legislation existed in a number of places by the 1890s. In Nuremberg, Antwerp, and other cities, he reported, "memorial tablets" marking buildings "everywhere abound." In the United States, historians were more interested in the AHA's work to preserve printed and manuscript documentary evidence under the National Historical Manuscripts Commission, established in 1895. "For the historian," wrote Hart, "the buildings of our ancestors are a lesson and an illustration, but he cares especially for official records of events."[3] Privileging documentary evidence as the foundation of scientific truth, professional historians treated visual evidence as a mere matter of aesthetics. The stimulus to reconsider this neglect of material culture would, as in the case of institutional economists for policy history, come from the historical profession's margins.

Not until the New Deal did circumstances arise for historians to act upon Hart's sentiments. The catalyst was the granting of control over all national historic sites to the NPS. This was part of Horace Albright's drive to develop colonial sites and raise the professionalism of the NPS in historic site management after he became NPS director in 1929. Though the National Antiquities Act had been passed in 1906, responsibility for key historic sites was not centralized, with Civil War and other military battlefields remaining under the Department of War. Albright successfully resisted in the early 1930s a plan for a separate National Historic Preservation Commission that would put, Interior Secretary Harold Ickes argued, "history back into the hands of amateurs."[4] Instead, the NPS got control over all U.S. government historic sites, including military parks and national cemeteries, by an executive order of President Roosevelt in 1933.[5] Albright believed that NPS employees "had to alter their image as simply keepers of natural wonders" to gain credibility with the government and attract more tourists. The NPS initiative also came just after Henry Ford's and the Rockefellers' reconstruction of the Deerfield and Williamsburg sites respectively in the 1920s, thus expressing interest in linking patriotism and history through emphasis upon the artifacts of pioneering days.[6] These private efforts did provide one source of inspiration to extend historic park preservation, but state historical societies' work in the 1920s provided another.

One leading figure at the state level was Theodore Blegen, who worked with the Minnesota Historical Society while a history professor at the University of Minnesota. In 1942–43, Blegen would serve as MVHA president.[7] As Minnesota Historical Society assistant superintendent, Blegen reported in 1928 upon the "encouragement" given by his society and others in the Midwest to "the better administration of public memorials, to the creation of new parks, embracing in some cases areas of special historical interest, and to the proper care of such parks."[8] The marking of highways and other sites had been undertaken in a number of states since before World War I, most notably as recorded in Louise Kellogg's work at the State Historical Society of Wisconsin on Wisconsin historical landmarks.[9]

During the Great Depression, Blegen and his colleagues both influenced and embraced the new national movement. He enthusiastically reported to the MVHA in 1934 that "many emergency work projects centering about historic sites and monuments" had already been undertaken by the NPS. These enterprises had been "rich in such results as landmarks restored, battle areas developed, old roads rebuilt, and historical information systematized." More significantly, an attempt had been made "to work out a national policy for historic sites and monuments." The work commenced under Verne Chatelain, "the energetic and competent park historian."[10] Chatelain was a University of Chicago Ph.D. and history professor from Peru State Teachers College in Nebraska.[11] As chief historian for the NPS (later assistant park superintendent in charge of historic sites), Chatelain directed a "small but growing staff of professional historians" from 1931 to 1936.[12]

Academic historians were of little use in planning this work, Chatelain recalled. "I could not turn to agencies like the American Historical Association and get any good ideas. The best help that I got was from Old World sources, like Great Britain, France, to some extent Germany . . . where historical programs" preserving historic sites had been going on for years. But Chatelain did get more assistance from state historical societies. Chatelain had worked at the Minnesota Historical Society for a year, where he knew Blegen. The latter answered Chatelain's call for unemployed historians to serve the NPS. The work was vital for the NPS, the individuals involved, and the future of public history. As Chatelain recalled, "none of these fellows were getting any jobs in the regular historical fields in those days."[13]

The NPS created an unprecedented demand for trained historians. According to Chatelain, "we almost had to invent historians, the pressures became so great." Some 500 historical workers were appointed, including positions as "commanders" of Civilian Conservation Corps camps, as well as "administrative and technical personnel" for Public Works Administration (PWA) and Works Progress/Projects Administration (WPA) programs. This was the "largest influx of historians in the history of the country working in the federal service."[14] These "historians" (some had degrees in political science) were mostly graduate students or recently minted M.A. or Ph.D. graduates without work. A number of the historians employed went on to academic jobs, but many stayed in government positions in the service or shifted to the National Archives.[15]

Incorporating the ideas of Progressive history, Chatelain possessed an ambitious and strikingly contemporary view of his mission—despite the fact that many of the historic sites he administered were chosen for their military significance alone. Joseph C. Robert, a Duke University historian working for him in North Carolina, reported favorably on Chatelain as "very broad in his interest." He wanted "the sections worked up not from just a military point of view" but to show "the broader social and economic story of the piedmont region."[16] At the NPS, historians worked on projects identifying and evaluating historic sites and researching and supervising the marking of historic roads and trails, as well as on the provision of service buildings and museums.[17] Alvin P. Stauffer, a student of Arthur Schlesinger, investigated requests for the creation of historic sites coming from patriotic groups or congressmen. The aim was to discover if the sites really did have historic significance.[18]

Chatelain worked hard to impose professional historical standards. In helping to draft the Act to Provide for the Preservation of Historic American Sites, Buildings, Objects, and Antiquities of National Significance (the historic sites act of 1935), he made sure that an advisory board would represent the views of professional historians, including the AHA. He wanted advice from "experts." Those of his staff who had trained as graduate students or had doctorates pushed the agenda of professional historiography. In reporting on the Lincoln birthplace in Hodgenville, Kentucky, Stauffer impressed upon the NPS the importance of not being "indifferent to historical scholarship." He warned that their work would "suffer in the eye of historians" if they uncritically accepted amateur assessments.[19]

Though Chatelain himself left the NPS in 1936 to join the Carnegie Institution as director of the St. Augustine Restoration Program in Florida,[20] the NPS had institutionalized his work. It continued through his successor, Ronald Lee, a history graduate student at the University of Chicago, who remained head of the Historic Sites Branch until becoming assistant national parks director in 1951. Even more than Chatelain, Lee became pivotal in the promotion of history in the NPS and "encouraged a spirit of cooperation between his staff and the academic community."[21]

Academics began to take notice of the NPS work and developed cooperative programs that have long been forgotten. But these interests originated in and were always strongest in regional, state, and local history societies, not the AHA.[22] For official contact with the preservation movement, AHA participation was important, as it appointed the official professional representative on the historic sites act's National Parks Advisory Board of Trustees. The AHA chose historians working in the NPS to represent the nation's academics but did not make any appointment until 1940. Certainly, the relevance of public and policy history to academic work impressed AHA members who came into contact with the NPS's work. "More emphasis should be given in our colleges and universities," the AHA representative reported during World War II, "to historic sites as source materials of history." But the AHA took no policy initiative, preoccupied as it was with the war and its aftermath.[23]

In contrast, the *Mississippi Valley Historical Review* (*MVHR*) and the *Journal of Southern History* published regular news items in the 1930s on preservation projects; the MVHA conferences included papers on park service matters; and universities and state historical societies provided cooperative labor. The *MVHR* carried relevant papers and notices, including an article on the exploitation of timber resources in the public domain by NPS historian Roy E. Appleman; a history of the creation of Yellowstone National Park by western historian W. Turrentine Jackson; and an NPS position paper by Stauffer and Charles W. Porter describing NPS historical areas as "providing the outdoor or laboratory course for the study of American history."[24] Meanwhile, southern historians' interest was spurred by Coordinating Superintendent B. Floyd Flickinger, a former faculty member at William and Mary College.[25] As superintendent of Colonial National Historical Park, he campaigned for Virginia, North Carolina, and South Carolina Revolutionary battlefield sites to be organized by the NPS "for a more effective presentation of the military campaigns of that war." Along with the historical plan, the NPS formulated a development plan in 1936 that included museums, field instruction, and a guide service.[26] Academics at a number of universities cooperated in these local preservation efforts. At the University of Pittsburgh, in 1939–40, historians directed research for the NPS's plans to restore Fort Duquesne (Fort Pitt), at the headwaters of the Ohio River. Studies included reviewing French and English military papers and all deeds and abstracts covering buildings and street development.[27]

While most academics showed only marginal interest in the content of NPS work, they greeted the New Deal relief work as a boon to historical research. Not only did their students sometimes find employment; several New Deal projects surveyed or collected documentary evidence that would be useful in academic history. At the start of the Roosevelt administration, in 1933–34, the Civil Works Administration (CWA) and the Federal Emergency Relief Administration offered short-term relief projects that employed historians. In Oklahoma the CWA helped arrange manuscript materials on state history that Professor Edward Everett Dale had assembled. State historical societies undertook a variety of such work to accession records. In Pennsylvania, the state library began a "vast project" on state, county, and municipal archives, newspapers, and manuscripts with labor from the CWA. Thirty-two workers were employed at the Colorado Historical Society and ninety-six in Minnesota.[28]

The biggest project was a larger version of this work: the WPA's Historical Records Survey (HRS) of 1935–39. A survey of state and local archives and other historical materials, the project was established at the end of 1935 under the energetic leadership of Luther Evans, a former political science professor.[29] The HRS undertook inventories of public records of towns, counties, and states and then tackled the listing of private manuscripts in some three thousand counties across the country. Among the miscellaneous programs were portrait and newspaper inventories and microfilming of records.[30] At its peak, the HRS employed four thousand white-collar workers and constituted the most extensive program of government support of research in American history undertaken to that time.[31]

The HRS had its origins in a trial project in Cleveland begun by Case Western Reserve historian Robert C. Binkley. In addition to extensive scholarly publication on European history, Binkley developed interests in record management and collection from time spent as a librarian at the Hoover War Library in Stanford in the 1920s. A "pioneer in advocating use of unemployed white-collar workers on the W.P.A. project of preserving local historical records,"[32] Binkley worked through the AHA's Committee on Historical Source Materials to cooperate with Evans, who took up the idea as a nationwide program for relief work.[33] Evans also received support from other respected and influential figures within the AHA and MVHA. Most, like Herbert Kellar and Solon Buck, worked in archives jobs or in museums and local historical associations, at a time when such people were still represented within the leading professional historical bodies. But university historians also had good reason to support these projects. The influence of the Progressive historians was felt especially through Binkley in Ohio and through Arthur Schlesinger, who served alongside his fellow Harvard historian Paul Buck as adviser to the survey in Massachusetts.[34] The state supervisors came from backgrounds as history doctoral or master's degree holders with AHA membership and in some cases experience teaching in universities, but they typically worked in local and state history. They included Lester J. Cappon (Virginia), Christopher Crittenden (North Carolina), Blegen (Minnesota), and Milo Quaife (Michigan). Under their control were many white-collar workers, some of whom were "untrained and uninterested" rather than qualified academics. The project had no way of getting a sufficient number of trained archivists or doctoral degree holders in history for this massive task, which continued under federal funding till 1939.[35]

With the winding down of New Deal support from 1939, Evans arranged for state agencies to continue the HRS into the war years. Julian P. Boyd, of Princeton University (formerly director of the Historical Society of Pennsylvania), wrote a glowing testimony in 1943 when he said of the survey: "It advances our knowledge of the sources of American history at least a century ahead of the normal processes by which scholars and librarians had sort [sic] laboriously and by individual efforts to bring such information to light." Significantly, Boyd felt that interest in history in the wider public had been spurred through the work of the thousands who passed through the program.[36]

For academic historians, the New Deal meant a substantial injection of federal funding into the infrastructure of historical research. The HRS was by no means the only government program that benefited history in this way. From the academic perspective, more important was the creation of the National Archives in 1934. The AHA had lobbied for such action since 1901 through its Public Archives Commission (1900), and John Franklin Jameson supplied leadership to the movement after his arrival in Washington in 1905. The commission was primarily concerned with surveying state records and promoting uniformity of standards in their treatment, but it also stimulated the "professionalization of archivists" through the annual Conference of Archivists established as an AHA affiliate in 1909. Long-term AHA executive secretary Waldo Leland joined Jameson in promoting archives. With Claude H. Van Tyne, he completed the *Guide to the Archives of the Government of the United States in Washington* in 1904, the first of an AHA series in the field.[37]

Even more pressing an issue in Jameson's view than the need for surveys of records or better-trained personnel was the absence of a building to house the records of the national government. Especially scandalous were the incoherent policies of acquisition and preservation of dusty, decaying records scattered across a myriad of agencies. Jameson became a part-time political advocate for the cause of a national archives repository.[38] He emphasized that not only major European countries but also other, less wealthy and populous states such as Mexico and Cuba had national archives, whereas the United States had none.[39] Jameson cultivated congressmen and senators, and developed an alliance with the American Library Association and patriotic groups. Though plans were drawn up as a result of federal legislation in 1913, it was 1926 before work commenced, and it was not until 1934 that the National Archives Act passed and the building opened.[40]

The AHA was particularly influential in shaping the staff profile of the new authority. Nowhere was this clearer than in the choice of the first National Archivist. R. D. W. Connor, Kenan Professor of History at the University of North Carolina since 1921 and formerly secretary of the North Carolina Historical Commission was Jameson's choice. Significantly, Connor "accepted the views expressed by Leland a generation earlier in emphasizing historical training as the primary qualification of an archivist." When Connor left the job in 1941, AHA Executive Council member and treasurer Solon Buck replaced him, and the pattern of influence continued. As a result of AHA pressure and Connor's policies, a "large proportion of the archivists first employed by the

National Archives held graduate degrees in history." Thirty-five history doctoral degree holders had been employed in this institution by 1940–41, a figure
that researchers rated as promising for future employment. Archives work
was a sought-after job. Unlike regionally located relief work, the location of
the National Archives in Washington gave the young and aspiring historian access to abundant record collections for research.[41]

Not only were historians well represented in the new organization; they
also served as members of the Society of American Archivists, formed in 1936,
and as advisers in the shaping of archives policy and practice. Samuel Flagg
Bemis, the prestigious Yale University diplomatic historian, authored the first
society report, "The Training of Archivists in the United States," in 1939. He
recommended the Ph.D. in American history as the preferred qualification,
and this recommendation continued to influence the education of archivists
well into the post–World War II years. Even when specialist archives programs
emerged in the 1950s, they stressed the importance of history and were often
run by trained historians turned archivists and librarians.[42]

The voices of historians were also strongly heard in the policies that the national and state archives adopted and within the new archives association. In
the 1930s the younger historians vigorously championed the development of
new programs and technologies for record collection and delivery of services.
These scholars favored, in the light of the New Deal, democratization of
learning and took their cue from Progressive history. Nowhere was this view
more evident than in the work of Binkley. He stressed the opportunities that
the New Deal programs presented and hailed as truly democratic the opening
of the National Archives to the general public, claiming that "even the most
amateur genealogist should be allowed to browse through old legal records."
The public archives of a community revealed by the HRS could become "a
kind of local encyclopaedia" used, for example, by teachers and Social Security
claimants. Such access would, in Binkley's Progressive vision, make the public
more concerned with and aware of the need for historical preservation.[43]

Of even greater interest to academic historians was the territorial papers
act, a program predating the New Deal but coming to fruition during the Roosevelt years. In 1925 Congress responded to extensive lobbying by the AHA
and state historical societies and authorized the collection of records concerning the early history of the federal territories.[44] Jameson had long supported
this project. "There was," he wrote in 1912, "no portion of the archival papers
of the federal government which is more sought for by historical investigators," especially for the western historical societies' work. But these papers
could not be found in Washington "without special guidance" and were spread
across several agencies.[45] Because the administration of territories was in the

hands of the Department of State until 1873, the project was located there. Preliminary efforts halted when Congress failed to appropriate funds in 1928, but the following year the work recommenced and, in 1931, Clarence Carter took a reduced salary from his position at Miami University of Ohio to carry on this, for him, labor of love in the State Department over the course of the next twenty years. There he remained until 1950, when his work moved to the National Archives. Carter's election as MVHA president in 1937–38 and his presidential address were occasions to highlight the link between professional historians and the state.[46]

Yet the federal state still proved reluctant to provide the ample financial aid that historians believed this and similar projects warranted. Though the first three volumes of the *Territorial Papers* appeared in 1934, the slow progress implied almost a blank check for historical research that congressmen would never write. As Representative J. Walter Lambeth, of North Carolina, told Duke professor William Kenneth Boyd with some irritation in 1937, 125,000 dollars had already been spent and yet the work was "only one-fourth complete." In Lambeth's simple calculation, the final cost to the taxpayer would be at least half a million dollars.[47] The project was in peril of stalling completely.

The AHA protested at congressional indifference, but in Carter's view, academics themselves had backslid. They had failed to maintain the intercommunity coalitions that alone could demonstrate the broad public utility of the project to a parsimonious Congress. Somehow historians thought that with the passage of an act, the job was done.[48] Carter advised that the only way to move Congress was a new and coordinated lobbying campaign, orchestrated by Carter himself, that saw state historical societies, university history departments, and the AHA urging further appropriations. In 1937 Schlesinger and Boyd worked in tandem to achieve this goal by lobbying senators and congressmen.[49] The campaign's success in gaining an extension of funding showed the value of the cooperation that Carter recommended. Historical societies bombarded Congress with letters and petitions, and prominent amateur George Fort Milton testified that the papers were "of value not only to professional historians but also to many unprofessionals [*sic*] who are keenly interest in our national origins."[50]

While the *Territorial Papers* concerned vital archival materials that historians traditionally used, the benefits of the Federal Writers' Project (FWP) were not so readily apparent to scholars.[51] With its focus on the creative arts, the FWP diverged from the collection of documents that Scientific History prized and was more innovative in its intention to tap rising popular interest in American traditions. The collection of narratives of ex-slaves begun in 1936 was one of these projects. Ultimately of great benefit to historiography, it attracted lit-

tle interest at the time from academics, who regarded these records as untrust-
worthy because they were based on oral sources.[52] Librarians, folklorists, and
African American historians were the more important promoters and users of
the series.[53] The earliest interviews of African American slaves illustrated the
innovative role of scholars marginal to the history profession. Again, the roots
of such work went back before the New Deal but found impetus from depression era relief programs. John B. Cade worked in the Extension Department of
Southern University in rural Louisiana. While teaching the history of slavery
there in 1929, "he conceived the idea of securing views of the institution from
living ex-slaves and ex-slave owners." He published his research in the *Journal of
Negro History* in 1935.[54] Cade's oral history work was impressionistic, but
Lawrence Reddick, an African American and an associate editor of the *Journal
of Negro History*, conducted a more extensive Federal Emergency Relief Administration project interviewing 250 ex-slaves while teaching at Kentucky State
College in 1934. By the time the FWP took over the work in 1936, interviews
of ex-slaves "had been extended to eighteen states."[55] But the Washington-
based administrators of the WPA were not impressed by the quality and
coordination of this early work and did not use it as a model. With the rising
interest in folklore as a specialized form of academic study, the chief influence
over the full WPA project came from folklorists John Lomax and Benjamin
Botkin and the poet and literary historian J. Sterling Brown, of Howard University. Yet these three did influence a wider profession in which Progressive
historians were eager to expand the scope of history.[56] Botkin was given space
within the AHA's annual program in 1939 to explain the importance of the
new sources as part of the wider search for the innovative "cultural approach
to history."[57]

A parallel case was the FWP's series of historic guidebooks to the American
states. As a reviewer noted, these were full of "tiny facts that prick the tragic
generalizations of our historians."[58] For critics such as Robert Cantwell, writing in the *New Republic* in 1939, the guides to the towns and cities represented
"the first effort to write American history in terms of its communities."[59] Yet
the academic response was "the professional snobbery of the historian" that
prevented "recognition" of the FWP's work as valuable documentation of the
past.[60]

If many historians neglected these sources and programs in part because
their discourse of objectivity precluded consideration, they also neglected
them because the emphasis was on the generic category of *writers*, not scholars, and there was no guarantee that any historians, let alone unemployed academic ones, would be involved. State officials included Bertrand Wainger, who
was director of the FWP in New York and a professor at Union College with

specializations in American cultural and state history. But his institutional affiliation was primarily in literature.[61] Destined to become much better known among historians, however, was Ray Allen Billington, state director for Massachusetts. He hired Bert Loewenberg, later of Sarah Lawrence College, as an assistant director. Both had been doctoral students in history at Harvard and had Arthur Schlesinger as their mentor. Loewenberg had to supervise for the FWP an elaborate project on the state historical guide for Massachusetts.[62]

★ ★ ★

One key result of the work that new Ph.D.'s undertook in the depression agencies was to make historians more aware of their economic and political relationship to the federal state. Their attachment to the state was solidified, whether they were employed historians recommending their students for work or unemployed ones seeking jobs. This situation gave academics a stronger sense of the importance of nonacademic work, just as it would in the 1970s when a self-conscious public history movement arose. Samuel Bemis told one graduate student in 1934, "Too many first class Ph.D.'s are being graduated, who cannot be placed anywhere in positions which will give them a living." In these circumstances, the "job becomes a matter of the first importance."[63]

On a superficial level, the employment impact of the New Deal upon historians was positive. When William B. Hesseltine and Louis Kaplan surveyed patterns of historical specialization, employment, and research in 1942, they applauded the new job opportunities. They could not but be aware of the "impact of the depression upon college budgets." Many historians had gone into government positions as a result of the poor economic circumstances. By the time World War II broke out, "considerable numbers" worked for the NPS and the HRS, as well as the National Archives. Though only "a few" found work in the USDA and as private archivists for companies such as railroad corporations, Hesseltine and Kaplan concluded that the expansion of archival positions, including "the prospect that the National Archives will establish branches to care for the field records of Federal agencies," might "solve the placement problem."[64]

Yet this assessment was too sanguine. For one thing, New Deal work was uneven in its impact. Hiring practices favored the Northeast and the South. Easterners and particularly southerners controlled key congressional committees, and this encouraged regional links with professional historians. Harvard's Schlesinger and Duke's Boyd, for instance, were influential in getting jobs for their students, and Schlesinger served as a consultant for Harold Ickes in the NPS's choice of an assistant director.[65] This regional dominance of appointments irritated applicants in other parts of the country. The losers tended to blame the AHA, and their experiences reinforced the old division in the historical profession between the MVHA and its older sister body. Thomas Martin, a former history graduate student at Stanford, lost out to the southerner Connor for the position as National Archivist despite support from his Stanford mentors, Edgar Robinson and Thomas Bailey.[66] When Martin testified to the importance of academic patronage within the National Archives and displayed an animus toward the selection process, he did not simply blame the political machinations of congressmen. Jameson and the AHA's eastern establishment had exerted what Martin believed was an undue influence over the National Archives' appointments. A fair "quota" of easterners had already been filled due to Jameson's recommending "sons of the friends of his youth and of his later college and university days." Martin felt that the question of AHA patronage was "quite serious enough" to justify a "determined stand on the part of Western members." He predicted: "If the West lies down and lets this Eastern clique entrench themselves in the $200,000 (more or less) patronage of the National Archives, retain the prestige of having named the Archivist, and control the National Historical Publications Commission (created in the National Archives Act), it will have to eat out of Eastern hands for another generation."[67]

Blatantly political patronage and the need to favor local constituencies were also potent factors in employment. This reality of Washington life alienated some would-be scholars who, like Joseph C. Robert (later at Ohio State), found it demeaning to grovel to congressmen for support.[68] This political interference was felt especially in the NPS, with Chatelain urging qualified historians seeking jobs to provide an avalanche of political recommendations from senators and others with political connections in Washington. The ability of New Deal projects to provide work for academics was not just limited by political patronage, however. In the emergency relief work, local people in each state or county had preference. In Chattanooga, for example, Civilian Conservation Corps camps employed only Tennessee locals on work for the NPS in planning and placing history markers on battlefields.[69]

For those set on an academic career, government work had many frustrations after they secured a position. The focus on administration—and sometimes mindless detail—numbed many a young academic aspirant.[70] Robert found himself in Guilford Court House, North Carolina, month after month "balled up in the red-tape" of working on a park service project. Even permanent work for the government Robert declared to be "avowedly temporary" if an academic offer came up.[71] The situation was worse for those Boyd protégés like Eugene Owen at the Agricultural Adjustment Administration, who had their Ph.D.'s and yet worked in totally unrelated fields. For Owen, clerical duties were "not such as to give any opportunity for research, nor is there any future in the position. And when the office day ends," he reported, "there is very little time for the writing in which I have become interested."[72]

The impact of New Deal programs on historians was mixed, as these examples indicated. A government job was second best to an academic one. As Arthur Schlesinger student Ned Meaney put it in 1937, his National Archives post was inadequate to his ambitions: "I aim to keep myself professionally 'alive' as much as possible during the next few years" and then "transfer to the college field."[73] Alvin Stauffer found his NPS work "not particularly interesting from the standpoint of a historian." He had to do "short investigations of various subjects, mostly military, few of which involve worthwhile research," in addition to handling "much correspondence."[74] The example of Herschel Landru, a student of Samuel Bemis at George Washington University, seemed atypical. He reported in 1933 that he was happy in federal employment. "One can perform as great a service in the Park educational program as ever one can in the University."[75] But the next year Landru proved to be no exception at all when he tried to reenter graduate school.[76] Only Bemis's blunt advice that the chances of an academic job were slim kept him in his position.[77]

Even where the jobs were intellectually rewarding, the records collected were frequently of limited appeal to academics, with the HRS series available mostly in mimeographed form through a limited distribution.[78] Ten times as much material, including "inventories of county records and transcriptions and abstracts of source materials," was collected as published. Moreover, a post–World War II survey showed that among thirty-five young academic historians canvassed for their views, few used the HRS records, because their research did not involve local history. The latter was out of fashion among academic historians in the fifties.[79]

More positive effects were felt by scholars already established in academic positions in the 1930s. The experience of working with New Dealers, finding work for students, and profiting from the records that the New Deal produced made for a growing and solid connection between historians and the liberal-Democratic state.[80] Schlesinger, who had been first a socialist then a Progressive, became a staunch New Dealer, and in a pro-Roosevelt book, *The New Deal in Action*, proclaimed that "no earlier administration" had "so frankly devoted its energies to broad humanitarian purposes."[81] Schlesinger's activism led him to support Roosevelt's judiciary reform and to lobby politicians on behalf of the Supreme Court changes, writing senators that "as a student of American history, I am convinced that the present crisis justifies the measure."[82]

More common than cheerleading for Roosevelt, however, was endorsement of the results of his administration's policies for the discipline. For Schlesinger, Roosevelt was not merely good for America; he was good for historians. No other administration was likely to do more.[83] More circumspectly, the AHA Council acknowledged the importance of New Deal efforts to improve access to historical sources, and it promoted cooperation with federal agencies through the Committee on Historical Source Materials, chaired by Kellar. Binkley served as chair of the key subcommittee in the group, working on access to newspaper sources. Praising the HRS for "the competence and thoroughness of its work," he went so far as to predict an organic link between cultural production and the state, to the benefit of history, scholars, and the American people. In the archival field, relief labor might become a "permanent feature of American cultural economy."[84]

Despite such optimism, the impact of the New Deal alone could not weld American historians to a strong nation-state and its bureaucratic apparatus. The programs were too much contested and contingent upon the political climate for that. Rather, the cumulative effect of those events of the 1930s and the impact of World War II proved decisive. Within just a few years the use of historians as expert advisers and their mass employment writing war histories dwarfed the work of the 1930s. World War I had not achieved such a comprehensive effect because American involvement was too brief, because the role of the United States as a world power remained ambivalent, because historians had reacted in the interwar years against patriotic excess, and because in World War I working for the government required propagandist skills rather than expertise. The steady development of expertise begun in the state governments before World War I, extended by the USDA and later the NPS, proved critical in the long run in rendering academics a legitimate part of government history making. With far greater opportunities available for the use of historians' specialist training as researchers and writers, World War II would complete the job that the depression could not fully accomplish.

11

States of War

World War II, the Cold War, and Remaking History

In September 1942, the president of the American Historical Association wrote a stirring manifesto on historians and war. Published in the *New Republic*, Arthur Schlesinger's "War and Peace in American History" proclaimed history "an important ally of statecraft." Its function was "greatly to enlarge the range of our experience by letting us see how our forerunners met similar difficulties."[1] Schlesinger's call to arms was quite different from Jameson's version delivered to American historians when he was editor of the *American Historical Review (AHR)* in 1917. Jameson had hoped that "public opinion in America" would become "enlightened, homogenous, and powerful" by becoming "informed in the facts and lessons of history." The scholar had to come out from "his cloistered retirement" and to use his knowledge "for the information of the public."[2] In practice, the circumstances of 1917 meant advocacy and propaganda as much as it did "information." Now, in 1942, the emphasis shifted to research skills.[3] Schlesinger envisaged historians as allied to statecraft with all of its implications of advising policymakers and recording history in the making. Schlesinger did not refer to the precedent of "The Inquiry," led by James T. Shotwell, though the use of expertise foreshadowed there was integral to what the Harvard historian intended. Schlesinger also wished to deploy academic know-how in a more democratic direction than ever before by making the comprehensive recording of contemporary war history a general feature of government policy.

To understand Schlesinger's ambitious schemes, his public statement has to be read alongside his private war memorandum in September 1941 to poet and Librarian of Congress Archibald MacLeish. There Schlesinger suggested practical steps historians could take to aid the war effort. A historian or archivist should "be attached to every important wartime agency, who would not only see to it that the routine records are preserved, but that additional ones are created." Every appointee would "make his own memoranda at staff meetings," record data "which might throw light on the behind the scenes workings of the organization," and "encourage officials to discuss their problems with him."[4] Through MacLeish, Schlesinger's views were aired at the highest ranks of government. Federal officials such as Harold Smith, chief of the Bureau of the Budget, were sympathetic to the need for better record keeping if not a full-blown historical program, and on 4 March 1942 the president issued a directive that followed the Schlesinger line. As the *AHR* editor Guy Stanton Ford noted, "For the first time during a major crisis the government has made extensive provision for the recording and writing of national war history."[5]

This order and its execution indicated a high degree of self-consciousness about the war effort and the state's changing place within history making. It was not intended to be a narrow record-keeping exercise. As Vanderbilt University's William Binkley stated, "the historian was being accepted on a frankly utilitarian basis by practical-minded officials who would have rejected him if his application had been made on the basis of preserving records for purely historic purposes."[6] Roosevelt made clear that he wanted more than a "correct record of war administration." He asked the Bureau of the Budget to "cover the field more intensively" using "whatever scholarly labor" was necessary to produce "an accurate and objective account of our present experience."[7] On this basis, fifty-four government agencies established historical programs, employing "hundreds of historians," and many more were called into agencies such as the Priorities Division of the Office of Production Management to assist in current operations and to preserve permanent records.[8]

Roosevelt had asked for a federal advisory Committee on Records of War Administration within the Bureau of the Budget, composed of representatives of appropriate learned societies and those of government agencies. The committee's numbers came disproportionately from AHA members and their sympathizers. Guy Stanton Ford represented the AHA, but also appointed were Schlesinger and Solon Buck, the latter representing the National Archives. From the American Council of Learned Societies, former AHA secretary Waldo Leland served as chair. The committee's job was "to stimulate the major war agencies to maintain records of how they are discharging their wartime duties" and "to advise the special research staff within the Bureau of the Budget in the making of current analyses of administrative problems in major policy fields of the war effort."[9] That dual function did not quite satisfy the historians. Led by Schlesinger, the historians battled government agencies that wished to emphasize purely immediate concerns and pushed within the committee for the broader view. Schlesinger and his allies emphasized again and again the "historical function as the main purpose of the project, as originally directed by the President."[10] Their demands for the committee to sponsor a broader war history created tensions with the social scientists, led by Pendleton Herring, of Harvard, the executive secretary of the committee, whose focus was on administrative matters. The location of the committee within the Bureau of the Budget did not help the historians' cause either. Historians wanted the nongovernmental activities of the war recorded and agitated for a National War History Commission as a separately funded government agency, but political pressures prevented positive action. However, Schlesinger did succeed in getting established, with Social Science Research Council support, a nongovernment Committee on War Studies in September 1943 to complement the military histories.[11] An official history of the nonmilitary agencies was never completed, unlike in Britain. Infighting between social scientists and historians over the objectives and congressional parsimony and other political machinations were the reasons. In the meantime, however, an unprecedented amount of historical activity occurred within the agencies as historians observed the war, wrote draft reports, and put their expertise to work for immediate mobilization purposes.[12]

The effort made scholars such as William Binkley feel useful. Not only had the government accepted the importance of "the writing of history," but it had decreed that the work should be done by "professional historians," and the effects were unprecedented in their extent. By 1945, at least 50 percent of professional historians aged twenty-five to forty had "engaged in some type of war-history activity." They had participated in "the most adequately subsidized cooperative historical project of all time."[13] Some had civilian jobs, though these tended to go to academics with expertise in fields such as economics. In history, training in statistics, labor history, or sociology provided advantages. Thus, the able interdisciplinary historian Caroline Ware headed the program planning unit in the consumer division of the Office of Price Administration from 1941 to 1942 but then went back to an academic job;[14] J. Carlyle Sitterson, of the University of North Carolina, put his knowledge of economic history and the sugar industry to work as a policy analyst in the War Production Board from 1944 to 1946;[15] while future labor historian Irving Bernstein worked at the Bureau of Labor Statistics. More traditional were those working in the field of "information"—this was self-consciously distinguished from the propaganda that dominated in World War I. Arthur Schlesinger Jr. served in the Office of War Information (OWI) until 1943, a position that his father claimed was due to his desire to aid the war effort.[16]

Working in the military and administrative branches did not produce the same negative reaction to the intellectual value or prestige of the task as some relief work done under the New Deal agencies did. Bernstein's job in the Division of Historical Studies of Wartime Problems of the Bureau of Labor Statistics was satisfying. He studied rent control, the conversion of the automobile industry to war production, resource conservation policies, and World War I parallels and precedents to inform future policy in World War II. Bernstein had six to seven research staff working on the problem of automobile production in the post-1918 world and completed forty-seven papers for distribution. His reports were sent to those war agencies facing "similar problems today." With industrial mobilization well under way, he was then directed to look at the issue of demobilization. American policymakers were looking ahead—by looking back. Bernstein told Arthur Schlesinger Sr.: "The work has been very satisfactory. It has permitted me to make a small contribution to the war effort and has offered an opportunity to study in the fascinating fields of war economics and World War history."[17]

Yet there were discontents. The home front was not, Schlesinger Jr. has reminded us, the perfectly united place where all worked for victory.[18] The physically able often preferred to serve in the military. Future University of California professor Henry May wanted to join the army because he was "made a bit restless by the war's being so far away." He found it "a relief to be drafted."[19] The University of Rochester's Blake McKelvey looked forward to being drafted, too. He could not find "any activity" that seemed "to provide any very useful service."[20] Schlesinger Jr. himself resigned his OWI job over a dispute about advertising propaganda—what Schlesinger called the "Ballyhoo method" against "the strategy of truth"—and got a position in the Office of Strategic Services (OSS).[21]

The best-known war activities of historians were performed in the Department of State and the intelligence service. As one scholar has remarked, "The list of historians who worked for the OSS reads like a *Who's Who* of the profession."[22] Historians had special expertise in foreign languages and cultures, and these were much in demand from 1942 to 1945. Economic historian Shepard B. Clough, of Columbia, served in the State Department,[23] while William L. Langer headed the Research and Analysis Branch of the OSS. After the war Langer went on to help establish the Office of National Estimates in the Central Intelligence Agency. With Everett Gleason, the Harvard medievalist, Langer also wrote the semiofficial U.S. government version of wartime diplomacy, *The World Crisis and American Foreign Policy.*[24] In the OSS work, such postwar luminaries as Raymond Sontag and H. Stuart Hughes joined them. Also working for the OSS was Conyers Read, who "set up and recruited a staff for the British empire section of the division of research and analysis" and authored a history of the spy service with colleagues, but the study was declared "classified" and never published.[25] Though the experience proved highly significant, there were limits to the capacity of the intelligence operations to draw upon the historical profession in these ways. Much of the OSS work went to historians in non-American fields because their special expertise in foreign languages and cultures was at a premium.

For Americanists, the war itself provided the most extensive opportunities for service as historians through the development of war histories. To be sure, the genre was not entirely unprecedented. The army and navy had established historical sections in World War I, and Frederic Paxson's multivolume work on World War I, *American Democracy and the World War,* had been begun there.[26] Yet both the army and the navy had their historical activities curtailed heavily by postwar budget cuts. During the interwar years these historical sections, reorganized in 1921, survived but did not prosper. The Army Historical Section was made a branch of the Army War College, while the navy established the Office of Naval Records and Library, headed by Dudley Knox from 1921 to 1946. Both concentrated on preservation of existing material and adjusted relatively slowly to new demands for the collection and surveying of records after 1940. The army did not publish its American Expeditionary Force history until after World War II had started, and by that time the navy still had no comprehensive history of World War I.[27]

Once war engulfed the United States in 1941, the work of these defense agencies expanded rapidly, but it also became divided administratively and conceptually. Two main types of historical work were done thereafter: the gathering of archival material for longer-term histories and documentary collections and on-the-spot histories of military engagements and administrative changes. (Historians also briefed their superiors with policy papers indicating the implications of their historical work.) During the war, both the army and the navy split their historical work into two sections. The Office of Naval Records and Library concentrated on archival work, while operational histories were written within Naval Intelligence. In 1944 an Office of Naval History was formed to coordinate "the preparation of histories and narratives" on the war. After the war these divisions were merged into the Naval Historical Center. The Army Historical Branch in the Intelligence Division of the General Staff was established in 1942 as a response to FDR's executive order, with Walter Wright as chief historian and Lieutenant Colonel John T. Kemper as military chief of the organization. This unit worked on operational histories while the older Army War College Historical Section collected documents and prepared background papers on "pressing issues facing the General Staff" and recorded "a chronology of wartime events."[28]

The U.S. Army Air Force Historical Division differed from both the Army and the Navy cases because it was not formed until 1942—as the direct result of FDR's order. Then, however, it underwent rapid expansion, with some fifty historians hired to work in the division headquarters, as well as additional staff in the field.[29] By 1944, the Air Force was producing one operational history every ten days, each of them reviewed by Guy Stanton Ford and a group of prominent civilian historian consultants. Historians based with units in action overseas produced monthly reports and collected supporting documents. The operational historians were brought back to Baltimore at the end of the war to collate, rewrite, and "polish" the histories. Meanwhile, the Air Force Archives were reorganized. In charge were Lieutenant Colonel Bayard Still (Duke University) and Fulmer Mood (University of California). All of this material ended up in the National Archives after being reviewed in the Historical Division; a committee of advisers, including John Allen Krout (Columbia University) and Richard Newhall (Williams College), then planned a comprehensive air force history.[30] The army also commissioned many professional historians. Eighty-one were being sought during 1943 alone, and the army instructed all battalions and regiments to keep histories of their own activities. As one military man reported, "there is going to be a considerable up-swing now in historical activity among all the various combat units."[31] Among those academically trained scholars used were southern historian Bell Wiley and Europeanist Robert R. Palmer.[32]

The navy's commitment similarly expanded. For archives work, Knox successfully recruited *American Mercury* editor Walter Muir Whitehill—then assistant director of Peabody Museum at Salem and an authority on maritime history—to deal with the collection of records. Other recruits included Richard Leopold, an assistant professor of history at Harvard, who was "credited with establishing the classification and filing system for the operational archives." Equally important was the navy's second major line of historical work—producing operational histories. There were "more than 150 assigned officers in the fleet and ashore who devoted some of their time to historical reports and projects." These officers included such future professional leaders as Carl Bridenbaugh, John M. Blum, Elting Morison, and Rodman W. Paul.[33]

For most scholars this work involved what David Potter called "abrupt retooling."[34] Academics whose explanatory devices favored longer-term forces or whose subjects were domestic political or social history found themselves pitched straight into narrative analysis of immediate military events. C. Vann Woodward, an up-and-coming historian of the New South's racial and political history, gravitated to Naval Intelligence, writing classified accounts of Pacific battles. Of the three military history books that he wrote, two were destined for naval personnel only, though the third, *The Battle for Leyte Gulf,* reached the public through Macmillan in 1947. And a tour de force it was. A historian who had previously only researched southern history had to write, as Potter put it, "expertly of Japanese admirals, naval strategy, the fire power of fighting ships, and complexities of navigation amid the islands of the Philippine archipelago."[35]

While operational histories and the gathering of archival material continued to be the major focus of the armed forces historical work throughout the war, each service eventually published narratives based on the data collected. Reunited after 1945, the army's Historical Division began preparation of a projected eighty-one-volume *U.S. Army in World War II* under the direction of Kent Roberts Greenfield. Though Greenfield did not become chief historian until 1946, he had wartime army service as a lieutenant colonel in the Historical Section and before that served as chair of history at Johns Hopkins University.[36] In the case of the U.S. Army Air Force, the seven-volume air force history was edited by Wesley Frank Craven (Princeton) and James Cate (Chicago)[37] and utilized the talent of many of the officer-historians, such as Duke University's Richard L. Watson and Arthur B. Ferguson, both of whom had written operational histories during the war. These academics and former officers received extra payments from the air force for their part-time work as consultants.[38]

The navy's work was much better known and celebrated due to the stature of its official historian. Samuel Eliot Morison lobbied his way into the official position of historian for the U.S. Navy after being initially rejected for a job with the Office of Naval Records and Library in 1942. He pulled strings within the coterie of Roosevelt's advisers and exploited his reputation as a well-known naval scholar. As a result Morison was commissioned as a lieutenant commander and, man of action that he was, relished "the business of snapping history on the run."[39]

Morison did not work in the Intelligence Section and was not under the control of Knox, but like historians in the Intelligence Section such as Woodward he wrote immediate accounts of the war that he called "history hot off the griddle." This approach meant that he must view the battles and join as much as possible in the action. Morison recalled that he would "participate in an operation, then settle down at some naval base, read all the action reports," and write "a preliminary draft, file it for future use, and then shove off on another operation."[40] Such running commentary was not necessarily reliable. Morison watched the Battle of Kolombangara in the Solomon Islands in July 1943 on the bridge of a battleship with Admiral Ainsworth, but his observation of the numbers of ships sunk proved to be wrong in the light of postwar checking with Japanese records.[41]

Understandably, combat officers in some operational fields resisted the assigning of historical officers. Air force operational historians found that, as one put it, "[i]t was a tough assignment to be dubbed 'hysterical officers' and to carry through on low priority status an academic enterprise in the midst of war."[42] When naval historians went out with the fleets, they were expected to, as it were, "pull their weight." Admiral Chester Nimitz initially sent John H. Kemble, of Claremont College, to a fleet public-relations job but later reassigned him to the tactical analysis section, where he read and prepared reports of each battle, culled dispatches, and made monthly reports. Even Morison was initially greeted with suspicion, but, as author of *Admiral of the Ocean Sea,* his path was smoother than most. On one occasion, Admiral Ernest J. King asked: "Did you write this book about Columbus?" When the answer was affirmative, King shook his hand and boomed: "Welcome aboard."[43]

The other major area of opportunity was involvement in the teaching of American and other histories to the troops. As in World War I, historians taught GIs in regular college offerings and in a variety of special courses created in cooperation with the army. Similar programs operated in the navy and air force. At the University of California, John D. Hicks reported teaching many army basic engineers and premeteorology air corps students in special courses, and navy and marine men "in our regular classes."[44] From Maine to Maryland to Wisconsin and California, the pattern was repeated. Kenneth Stampp taught American history to soldiers in the Army Specialized Training Program at the University of Maryland. By 1943 "a large part of my students," he recalled, probably 25 percent by his estimate, "were G.I.s." Some historians, including the University of Wisconsin's William B. Hesseltine, went to the U.S. military base at Shrivenham, England, where American professors conducted classes.[45] In those cases, academics were required to wear military uniform when teaching. Ralph Gabriel was particularly active in organizing Yale colleagues to give lectures to the troops at the Windsor Locks Air Base in Connecticut, work he justified mainly as a "patriotic contribution."[46] An army orientation course for the First Army Corps based in New England also included contributions from Harvard's Perry Miller.[47] These were not just lectures on American history. They had strong political and ideological content, as well as supplying cultural and geographical background for the troops on topics such

as "Life in a Totalitarian State." Academics also lectured to government policymakers, in Samuel Bemis's case to the Army War College on U.S. foreign
policy and its strategic options.[48] In a similar vein, Edward Mead Earle, of
Princeton, wrote the article "American Security: Its Changing Conditions"
and lectured on strategy to Washington bureaucrats.[49]

The most influential war contribution came, however, at the request of
Ben Lear, general of the Second Army. He solicited from Gabriel a course on
American history to be delivered to the troops in sections by army personnel,
with accompanying course materials. Lear thought the troops needed "a better understanding of current affairs" so they would know why they were fighting.[50] An army officer told Gabriel: "Our officers' board rehearsed your first
lecture yesterday and were most enthusiastic not only about its content but
about the way in which you put words naturally into the mouth of the lec-
turer."[51] Soon after the war began, the War Department produced its own
mandated history syllabus for troops in all army divisions. Though this was a
less-intensive course, it incorporated many of the details and concepts of
Gabriel's pioneering effort.[52]

Some elements within the army did not like what they saw as the strain of
pacifism among pre-1939 American historians. One blunt and cantankerous
colonel, G. S. McCullough, told his friend John D. Hicks, perhaps partly in jest,
that he hoped the army would "insist upon the teaching of American History"
to its troops. "However, they may insist upon a more virile and more patriotic
presentation than you educators have used for the past twenty years."[53] Army
people wrote, nonetheless, in generous praise of the work done by historians
such as Gabriel and Thomas Bailey.[54] This may have been because these historians had tailored their views to the new world-historical situation and repudiated ideas of nonintervention. They had come to the aid of the nation-state.
Bailey was employed to lecture to the air corps orientation course at Air Force
Basic Flying School at Moffett Field in California and for the Bureau of Public
Relations of the War Department in an orientation course.[55] His "Our National Effort, 1939–1941," affirmed the importance of the military and attacked
isolationism. George Washington's "crossing the Delaware in the dead of winter to surprise and destroy a formidable body of the enemy, at Trenton," had
important lessons for Bailey. "[O]ften," he argued, "we have gained safety only
by destroying the source of our enemies' power."[56] Except among a minority
of historians, isolation was out and intervention in. This was true whether the
message came from foreign policy experts such as Bailey or from social, cultural, and political historians such as Hicks and Gabriel. Said Schlesinger, "collective security is the best safeguard of American security." America's fate was
"to be inevitably involved in Europe's recurrent struggles."[57]

Textbooks and monographs also portrayed the new outlook. After he prepared "American History and the Constitution" for the Second Army, Gabriel received requests for copies of the war lectures from the Department of War, the National Association of Manufacturers, and trade union officials alike.[58] Soon, Appleton-Century wanted to publish the series, which became *Main Currents in American History* (1942).[59] Gabriel's war lectures were also closely tied to and stimulated sales of his *The Course of American Democratic Thought* (1942), a book widely seen within the colleges as appropriate to teach American war aims because of its framework of idealism and focus on the moral values of American democracy.[60] Others self-consciously shaped new texts in the light of war. For the army and navy courses that Hicks taught at Berkeley, he used his *A Short History of American Democracy* (1943), a book written "with Army and Navy specifications in mind" because it included certain international topics, such as "material on Communism, Nazi-ism, Fascism, etc., not usually found in texts on American history."[61] The war also boosted sales of some histories written before the war because they were used by the military, such as Hicks's *Federal Union*. Houghton Mifflin anticipated four thousand extra sales of this book because of military insistence on the teaching of American history.[62]

Despite the chastening experience of 1917–19, the nation's major historical association officially joined in the new war effort, too. The War Department commissioned the AHA in 1943 to prepare a series of pamphlets on war and postwar issues for use by the troops at home and abroad. Designed not for courses but for informal discussion groups, these topics for "G.I. roundtables" were to be organized within four general categories: America's allies, foreign affairs, national affairs, and personal and community affairs.[63] The request for the pamphlet series came in response to media criticism that American troops were ignorant of foreign conditions and not interested in contemporary politics. Though some scholars warned Guy Stanton Ford, AHA executive secretary at the time, about government interference in the production of these tracts, the AHA accepted the commission, and Theodore Blegen, president of the Mississippi Valley Historical Association (MVHA), was appointed director of the Historical Service Board in Washington.[64]

Federal authorities apparently chose the leading professional organization for this task because both history and historians were held in high regard. If true, this represented a high point in the collaboration between the state and the historians. The War Department claimed that it chose the AHA over other bodies (such as the Social Science Research Council, the American Council of Learned Societies, and the American Council on Education) because it had "the advantage in the first place with respect to the historical approach—the soundest approach that can be made." But professional status backed disciplinary prestige. Not only was the AHA one of the oldest professional organizations, but despite the relativist controversies of the 1930s, the AHA was "noted for its disinterestedness and impartiality by both the public and Congress."[65]

Not every historian joined in the wartime enthusiasm, however. A sizable group feared either state aggrandizement or wartime propagandistic excess on the part of historians—or both. Addressing a group of social studies teachers, Merle Curti urged them to serve the larger national purpose "by recalling in how many instances patriotism has been merely a cloak for the maintenance of a status quo."[66] Some on the left sat the war out entirely. Kenneth Stampp, reflecting his socialist sympathies rather than his German American roots, remained suspicious of involvement in a European conflict. In a talk at the Indiana Historical Society based partly on his dissertation on the Civil War just completed in 1942, he "reminded some of the older men about how some historians had behaved during World War I." They became "Four Minute Men and ran around spreading war propaganda." Stampp advised his listeners to "keep on teaching history—and teach good history." They ought not to become "agents of the government."[67] The most noted antiwar historian was Charles Beard, who became increasingly disenchanted with U.S. foreign policy. Beard worried that the AHA's official involvement in the writing of war pamphlets would repeat the mistakes of World War I,[68] but his central concern was the accretion of government power and the denial of citizens' rights that the growth of the state entailed. The war powers of the president, Beard stated, were "the unexplored and dark continent of American government."[69] Yet this was not the majority view, as the diminished reputation of Beard's antistatist work after World War II would show.

For most historians, the threat that the wartime power of the state posed for professional autonomy could be met by expertise. As MVHA president at the war's end, William Binkley summed up the consensus. If the war had prolonged prewar debates over historical activism, it also provided a resolution. Relativism could be held at bay by the changing nature of historical practice itself. Binkley praised the wartime use of historians as experts rather than as propagandists—in their published histories as well as in the courses they taught and the service they rendered government bureaucracies. He predicted the emergence of a new generation that would transcend the conflicts over objectivity of the 1930s by combining specialization and service to the nation. From their ranks would come "the leaders of the historical profession of tomorrow."[70] In short, the war had given historians new confidence about their methods and their professionalism.

Whether the resort to historians as experts produced equivalent long-term shifts in the content of historiography is more debatable. To be sure, the volume of military topics studied in the war and immediate postwar years rose markedly. The massive published histories—101 volumes in the key series from the three major services—and the extremely widespread wartime training of historians in military matters made military history a more prestigious option as a specialization for a time. In fact, military history was ranked a creditable fourth, behind only diplomatic, cultural and intellectual, and state and local history, among respondents to a 1952 survey, and well ahead of religious, economic, agricultural, and other prominent fields. But it is doubtful if the effects of war were lasting. New graduate students surveyed at the same time favored intellectual history.[71]

More military history was taught in the 1950s than in the 1920s and 1930s, the height of antiwar sentiment. Some scholars who served in the war, like John Kemble, of Claremont, later specialized in maritime history and served as office-bearers for the Naval Institute and other naval history organizations. Morison's fifteen-volume *History of United States Naval Operations in World War II* took twenty years after the war to complete but, he believed, was "generally regarded as my most important work."[72] Yet military affairs remained marginal within the major universities. It tended to be taught after the war by specialists in such places as Duke University but was confined mostly to the prestigious but specialized military schools. Among the most prominent practitioners of military history was Forrest C. Pogue (later the author of a four-volume biography of General George C. Marshall), who worked for the Army's Historical Division before taking a post at Murray State University in Kentucky in 1954. Oddly, the historians who had served in the U.S. Army Air Force in World War II, such as Richard Watson at Duke, did not teach military history as such, though they did write military history for the Craven and Cate series and included military/technological change within their general courses.[73]

For some, the war's opportunities for government employment marked a shift in intellectual priorities so pronounced that they did not return to civilian duties. The former Johns Hopkins professor Kent Greenfield reported that like most of his colleagues he had paid "little or no attention to military interest" in either his teaching or his studies in the interwar years. "[D]isposed to pacifism" and lukewarm in regard to U.S. intervention in world wars, Greenfield was nevertheless among those who rose to the challenge when the government sought "the 'technical' assistance of historians on a scale and to an extent never before approached."[74] Thus was created "a nucleus of highly competent military historians—something the United States never had before."[75]

While larger numbers of historians wrote military history after the war, far more who had been in the military returned, like C. Vann Woodward, to their civilian work. For these, the war had no direct effect on their later historiographical contributions. Woodward declared *The Battle for Leyte Gulf* a rigorous exercise in the use of historical evidence and "an important part" of his "education as a historian." But he believed that it was "of no real lasting consequence" and "led to no further work in the field."[76] As his colleague David Potter remarked, the book was "almost purely narrative, and reveals little of [Woodward's] historical philosophy."[77]

Though military history remained a subordinate stream in American historiography, war had a more indirect and subtle influence. Wartime changes in the intellectual climate checked the rise of social and economic history. A preoccupation in the teaching and writing of American history with national political history and with wider issues of security, strategy, and diplomacy intensified in the 1940s and remained central to American historiography until the mid-1960s. AHA conventions in the late 1940s and early 1950s featured far more attention to diplomatic history, as well as military and strategic matters, than in the 1930s. Textbooks reflected a stronger focus on American national development, detected in titles such as John Morton Blum et al.'s *The National Experience*.[78] Historians argued among themselves over consensus and conflict interpretations, but as Arthur Mann observed, "most writers of American history belong to the liberal intelligentsia." Kennedy, Stevenson, and, before them, Truman and FDR were their heroes.[79] These writers' works ranged from the little known, such as Air Force historian Richard Watson's work eventually published as *The Development of National Power*, wherein he surveyed the sweeping changes that World War I wrought in American life in terms of foreign policy and war mobilization, to former OSS and OWI employee Arthur Schlesinger Jr.'s multivolume history of the New Deal, through to the foreign policy histories of prominent OSS figures William Langer and Everett Gleason, as well as the textbooks and diplomatic histories of Thomas Bailey and Samuel Bemis.[80]

War made some historians more mindful of the need to emphasize political, diplomatic, and military matters. Samuel Morison explained in his AHA presidential address in 1950 that social history must remain subservient to "political and constitutional history." These "must always be the skeleton on which any other kind of history is hung" and were vital to stopping "the decay of liberty." Within this ideological context of the Cold War, Morison argued that military history could not be ignored, because it had been "an inescapable aspect of the human story." Military history served as part of Morison's assault on Beard, whose "detestation" of armed conflict led him to denounce American entry into World War II. In Morison's view, the antiwar historians of the

1930s bore the blame for appeasement because they failed to teach that "war does accomplish something, that war is better than servitude."[81]

The war and the continued employment of historians on government projects afterward had a still more subtle effect. By shifting the balance further in favor of very recent history and American, rather than non-American, topics, the war reinforced the intellectual objectives of Progressive historians to make history more socially and politically useful. In the postwar years, AHA annual meetings gave special attention to the writing of contemporary history, and courses and publications in this field expanded noticeably.[82] The Office of the Secretary of Defense historian R. W. Winnacker believed that those writing war-generated military histories were "carrying on a 'noble experiment' in contemporary history."[83] For Kent Greenfield, the innovative character of government-related history programs in promoting the study of recent American history gave an excellent reason to remain where the action was rather than return to academia. Contemporary history also helped to free academic historians from the fetish of the archived document. As Morison put it, "I no longer have the reverence for documents that I once had, or the distrust of oral sources that I was once taught."[84] In the long run that shift would be intellectually liberating for social history, but for the moment it was put to the service of the state.

For some historians, service to the state was twisted to mean support of Cold War political and ideological objectives. This was taking the usefulness of history to an extreme. Conyers Read conveyed his deep belief in historians' public roles in his AHA presidential address in 1949. Both his prewar activism on behalf of useful history and the wartime experience contributed to his call for colleagues to enlist in the Cold War to disseminate pro-American views. In a "divided world," Read could see "no alternative" to "the advocacy of one form of social control as against another." By no means all historians agreed with this tack. Some reported that they were embarrassed by Read's open partisanship and believed it a perversion of the useful-history concept. But there was less objection recorded to Morison's call for a "sanely" conservative history made just a year later.[85] Moreover, some historians who winced at Read's blatant political intervention themselves ignored, like Merle Curti, historical evidence when it proved embarrassing to U.S. foreign policy in the 1950s.[86] Thomas Bailey, who opposed Read's election as AHA president, nevertheless delivered such Cold War lectures as "The Political Significance of the United States in the World (the Long War against Communism)"[87] in prominent public forums in California. Even liberals like John Hicks had their professional judgment affected by what others called the Communist "menace."

Most prominently, "vital center" liberal Arthur Schlesinger Jr. crusaded against Communism with gusto while defending domestic liberal reform.[88]

More than these political and ideological affinities with state policies, the economic and intellectual benefits of government cooperation remained firmly on the minds of historians in the postwar years. As Raymond Sontag, of Berkeley, remarked, graduate seminars would be thinly populated indeed if all students insisted on becoming professors.[89] There were simply not enough university jobs, and Sontag believed that historians must recognize this fact. Convinced that the state's relationship to the historical profession had changed irrevocably, the AHA program organizers gave unprecedented publicity at annual meetings to the role of the federal government in history making. Howard Lamar's official report of the 1951 AHA meeting in New York remarked upon "the presence of so many federal historians and members of the armed services who attended the sessions." For Lamar, this indicated that "the historian's talents are being used by the government in understanding contemporary problems and in shaping policy."[90] Similar in tone were the comments of Harvard University's David Owen in reporting a session on the federal government and historians for the 1949 annual meeting: "the general opinion of those on the panel and of numerous speakers from the floor seemed to be that programs such as those of the National Park Service, the National Archives, [and] the Army Historical Division . . . represent substantial accomplishments [and evidence of] the extensive interest of the government in historical activity." Yet, Owen conceded, the meeting had revealed "unsolved problems" that could "seriously jeopardize the successful conduct of historical activity in the federal government."[91] What, for instance, should the academic qualifications of appointees in government service be? Academics wished their government colleagues to set the same professional standards and have the same qualifications as themselves.[92] Yet positions were not uncommonly filled with nonhistorians.[93] The AHA wished to impose standards of expertise and professionalism on the wider process of history making. To those who said that historians should not sully their hands with such work, Sontag argued that "the government needs historians" and that, if professionals did not meet the demand, "nonprofessionals will take over."[94]

To achieve these aims, supporters of public outreach led by Read pushed successfully for an Ad Hoc Committee on the Historian and the Federal Government at the December 1949 AHA meeting. This was composed of five government official, including Greenfield and Constance McLaughlin Green (historian of the Research and Development Board, Department of Defense) and six academic historians. Charged with improving scholarly cooperation with the government,[95] the Ad Hoc Committee, chaired by Read, undertook a survey of the whole professional/government relationship and pointed to the growth of federal employment as a significant part of the historians' job market. After the war, approximately a hundred professional historians remained in government service writing war histories, seventy to eighty were employed in the National Park Service, and others were scattered across a range of government departments and agencies.[96]

The Ad Hoc Committee focused on the critical appraisal of history within government. It claimed success in improving programs by "boring from within" through influence on professional historians already working in Washington. The committee also explored ways in which topics for graduate student dissertations could be chosen in cooperation with federal departments and agencies such as the Department of State.[97] Upon recommendation of the committee, liaison with the federal government was formalized in late 1952 through the establishment of a permanent AHA committee.[98] With Wood Gray (George Washington University) as chair and Greenfield, Green, Jeanette Nichols, Richard Newhall, Dexter Perkins, and Executive Secretary Boyd Shafer as members, this committee lobbied for changes in recruitment regulations, access to archives, and the federal historical publications program.[99] In requesting these changes the AHA responded to more than the legacy of World War II. The new reality of continuous fear of the outbreak of war reinforced the role of historians in the government.

When Cold War gave way to hot war in the Korean conflict in 1950, interest in government historical work had surged again. President Truman issued an executive order indicating that government agencies would be acting as they had during World War II: "I am directing that a Federal historical program be instituted, with a primary purpose of recording the activities which the Federal Government is undertaking to meet the menace of communist aggression."[100] Truman asked AHA president Morison for help in defining "the objectives of the program, obtaining qualified historians," and ensuring that the government's work "meets the high standards of the historical profession."[101] The AHA Ad Hoc Committee on the Historian and the Federal Government readily agreed, reporting that the AHA wanted to be "as useful as possible to government historians responsible for the preparation of accurate and objective historical research."[102]

Yet academic and government aims soon diverged. Political interference in the appointment process was one concern, heightened by the advent of the Eisenhower administration in 1953. Republicans wished to break the New Deal bureaucracy, and, to the extent that historians had become identified with that bureaucracy, they too became targets. Academics especially deplored the element of political patronage that threatened government appointments. With the election of Eisenhower, the AHA had to mobilize support for maintaining the nonpartisan character of the position of Archivist of the United States. The AHA successfully threw its aid behind the incumbent, Wayne C. Grover, and, with the help of state historical societies and sympathetic government bureaucrats, staved off the challenge to the nonpolitical character of the appointment.[103]

The conflicts also involved the differing intellectual objectives of academics and bureaucrats. Academics cared most about access to and preservation of records and about the "objectivity" of research done under government sponsorship. In contrast, bureaucrats tired of the academic desire to produce exhaustive research and emphasized the need to meet government's short-term goals while leaving the production of more objective, long-range histories to academics. As Winnacker put it, "the immediate objective in this effort to write contemporary history" was not "historical analysis per se, but making historical analysis useful to the agency which employs the historian." The government historian working in a current historical program, he reported, "frequently must choose between a preliminary report and a thorough historical analysis. It is proper that he decides in favor of the former," hoping "that future research will cover the existing lacunas."[104]

Historians within government were pulled by conflicting loyalties and interests. Stifled by government red tape and political scrutiny, they also wished to meet the standards of doctoral training. Paul Scheips, who worked in the Signal Corps Historical Division in Washington, wrote a candid memorandum in 1953 documenting the incipient hostility on Capitol Hill and in government bureaucracies to historians in government service. Claiming that politicians were wary of the political and practical suitability of academics, Scheips spoke of "troglodytes both outside of and within the Government who oppose history as either some kind of a costly academic frill or as a program in any event to be viewed with great suspicion." Government historians also faced possible criticism from their university colleagues, who had little idea of the practical pressures upon government employees. Scheips taxed academic historians because of their focus on the advantages that government historical work could provide them rather than on the adaptation of historical skills to analysis of government problems. "I get the impression that the tendency is to overemphasize the matter of positions for historians and to underemphasize the value to the Government of a sound historical program."[105]

Little different in the early 1950s were attitudes in the State Department. There the Division of Historical Policy Research was among the programs most visible to and valued by academic historians.[106] In 1953 historian Donald

M. Dozer, a departmental analyst who came from the University of Maryland, wrote: "Historical studies have been allowed to fall into low esteem in the State Department." Dozer especially attacked the tendency to use academics for pure research and the failure to analyze policy using historical precedents. The production of "long monographs," he recommended, "ought to be discouraged as being more suitable for private researchers and as requiring too much time of Departmental historians."[107]

For their part, some academics continued to regard government-sponsored history with suspicion. The Ad Hoc Committee noted the importance of critical reviews of official publications and of historical reports written for use within the government. They conceded that the "danger still exists that official history will not be adequate or honest history."[108] This reflected unease over the objectivity question and the hostility of some academics to the biases in those studies that favored government policy. Langer and Gleason had access to privileged State Department documents while researching recent American foreign policy, but revisionists did not.[109] Denying Charles Beard access to classified material on the coming of World War II had animated more than that scholar. His friends carried on the struggle after his death in 1948.[110] A particularly vigorous and well-noted attack came at the AHA meeting in 1952 from Beard ally Howard K. Beale. As Beale put it, "there is the government historian paid by the government to write its history, and the semiofficial historian screened and given special facilities by the government. There is serious question whether much of the mass output of detailed history of all branches of the armed services, produced at colossal cost to the taxpayer, can be justified by the intrinsic importance of the product." Where the work reflected partial or privileged access to sources, its value was minimal. This judgment, Beale believed, was fair "even where the historians write what the government wants because they honestly share the government's view."[111] This critique presaged later debates of the 1980s on "client" influences over public history and on the role of historians as public-policy advocates.[112]

Other scholars, such as Arthur Schlesinger Jr., straddled the fence on this issue. "Unreasonable demands by scholars for premature publication might," he replied to Beale, "cause government officials to refrain from putting their more confidential views in writing." But he affirmed historians' efforts "to maintain full freedom of thought and to prevent the calamities of censorship and of official distortion of the historical record."[113] Schlesinger's line was closer to that adopted by the AHA, which admitted the dangers but looked positively on moves to write balanced and "objective" history within government. The Ad Hoc Committee "encouraged and applauded" Greenfield in applying those standards to the army war history program. The committee also expressed gratification to learn that "careful policy appraisal of historical precedents is playing an increasingly important part in policy decisions."[114]

The Ad Hoc Committee did not know it at the time, but this controversy over the role of historians in support of the state occurred at the end of a twenty-year period of expansion in federal government employment of historians. The Office of the Secretary of Defense under Winnacker was the last of the Department of Defense military history offices to be established (in 1949). Though the Atomic Energy Agency appointed Richard Hewlett in 1957 as its official historian, this was an exception.[115] Most of the small federal history offices established in government agencies dated from the 1960s and the 1970s.[116] The 1950s presented a period of consolidation and even loss of momentum, with little hiring after 1953.[117]

The end of the Korean War signaled an end to expansion, but equally important was the imposition of a Civil Service Commission register in 1950. This register made security of tenure available to historians coming from outside government but also made it more difficult for many agencies to get the historians they wanted and hindered the easy flow of academics that had occurred during and after World War II.[118] In its report in 1952 the Ad Hoc Committee called for immediate measures "to solve the crucially important, and yet totally unresolved problem of persuading the Civil Service Commission to revise its present procedures in recruiting historians."[119] In 1955 the AHA was still lobbying unsuccessfully for changes to these conditions that stymied federal historians' employment.[120]

Political circumstances had changed, too. Big government was under attack, at least rhetorically, and liberal-minded historians fell foul of Republican Party vendettas, especially those led by Senator Joseph McCarthy. The AHA had allegedly committed the sin of supporting the New Deal. Charging "an 'interlock' among the foundations and 'accessory agencies,'" the staff of the House Committee on Tax Exempt Foundations implied that the Commission on the Social Studies was "part of a conspiracy" that had recommended "the end of laissez faire."[121] The AHA Committee on the Historian and the Federal Government (succeeding the Ad Hoc Committee in December 1952) found it necessary to devote much of its time during 1953–54 not to advocating improved standards of historical research in government or lobbying for more federal programs but to "defend[ing] historical and related programs" against political attacks.[122]

The political persecution reflected, many historians believed, a climate of renewed anti-intellectualism that threatened their relations not only with government but also with a wider public. At the nexus between these two threats,

politicians seemed to present the most danger for the new alliance of historians with the federal state. Paul Scheips reported Washington's distrust of intellectuals in the Eisenhower years: "I have it from a government historian
with years of the broadest kind of experience that some members of Congress
view historians only a little less contemptuously than economists." Government historians urged that contemporary history be renamed "record distillation" in the light of this "anti-intellectual climate."[123]

Academics reacted in diverse ways to the climate of political repression,
anti-intellectualism, and misunderstanding of historical work. Some, stung by
the critics, focused on their relationships with a wider public by a renewed
campaign to improve history in the schools. State and local historians, for their
part, continued to strive to write history in a way more in tune with popular
audiences.[124] Boyd Shafer, AHA executive secretary, took a more academic
tack appropriate to his position, vowing to combat hostility from legislators
by improving public understanding of the importance of the historical profession. Referring in 1955 to "increasing attacks these past years on 'intellectuals'" that "have led us to examine again our basic objectives," Shafer noted
that historians had begun to think once more "how we might more effectively
popularize the value of history and historical study" without "cheapening and
vulgarizing" the discipline.[125] But Shafer recognized the diversity of the profession and its responses. Not everybody wished to popularize history, and
Shafer knew that public links could be built in many ways.

Faced with these outside pressures, American historians became seriously
interested in the social history and social role of intellectuals as a separate
group detached from social classes.[126] In this move, they followed in part the
work of sociologists such as Talcott Parsons and Edward Shils,[127] but the
wider social science discussion reflected the same ideological context: a climate of political hostility toward intellectuals and pressures on funding at the
same time that the universities became a location for the bulk of the nation's
intellectual activity.

Historians' interventions in public-policy debates had, some now argued,
obscured historical truth and besmirched the profession in the process. These
critics came from many points in the political spectrum. Reflecting his origins
in 1930s-style Progressive history, Merle Curti agreed that historians should
still contribute to public-policy debates, but in a critical and independent way.
In a barely concealed reaction to Conyers Read, he cautioned in 1952 against
"using our craft to support a currently held policy" and questioned "any position which calls for a return to the patriotic affirmations without due regard to
our critical functions."[128] Three years later he stressed the reverse danger coming from immense pressures placed upon intellectuals, the political hostility to

their intervention in policy debates, and the understandable reaction to seek refuge in specialization.[129] Conservative versions of the "treason of the intellectuals" thesis, first formulated by French scholar Julien Benda decades earlier, also appeared. Columbia University's Jacques Barzun claimed that "the greatest danger to the democratic State" was probably "the contamination of its policies by Intellect."[130] He reminded readers of the "orgy of intellectualism" that accompanied Fascism and Communism's totalitarian excesses.[131]

Tied to this criticism of policy intervention was the repudiation of Progressive history and its philosophical relativism.[132] The reaction against Beard's attacks on Roosevelt's foreign policy in the 1940s justified historians' detachment from advocacy. Beard and some of his allies had abandoned, Oscar Handlin noted later, "all effort at factual accuracy" in their interpretations of the origins of that conflict.[133] Though the ideal of the public intellectual persisted in the work of historians such as Richard Hofstadter and C. Vann Woodward, they operated in a new and ironic key, detached from the social institutions that had sustained earlier generations.[134]

* * *

Even though historians maturing in the age of Eisenhower warned against too close an involvement in public policy and reaffirmed the fundamentally academic nature of their craft, the growth of the American state could not be denied or undone. Historians' involvement in policymaking, begun in the 1930s and 1940s, did not cease and in the 1960s would expand again. Eventually, in 1979, the Society for History in the Federal Government would be established. Affiliated with the AHA, it developed the institutional links between historians in government and in academia that the Ad Hoc Committee had pioneered. The momentous events of the depression and war had helped create a substantial place for historians within government. Many of the wartime historians who had staffed the OSS continued to advise policymakers, just as historians such as Thomas Bailey did in the case of the State Department. Immediately after World War II, Bailey's *Diplomatic History of the American People* won the "highest praise" at the State Department as worthy of the library "of every foreign service post."[135]

Cold War activism tying historians to American foreign policy was, however, nowhere more clearly demonstrated than in the case of Yale's Samuel Bemis. Bemis lectured to the Air War College in the 1950s, served on the advisory committee of scholars on the army history of the war, and cultivated close relations with State Department officer Carlton Savage, executive secretary of the Policy Planning Committee from 1947 to 1962 and a former Bemis student. Consulted repeatedly for his views on "international developments" throughout the 1950s and early 1960s,[136] Bemis volunteered interventionist and strongly anti-Communist opinions on Cuban-American relations, Vietnam, and the Cold War.[137] He lobbied Ambassador Henry Cabot Lodge on how to counter Soviet propaganda at the United Nations in 1958[138] and hinted that the United States should have attacked Cuba immediately after Fidel Castro revealed himself as a Communist. Bemis's AHA presidential address in 1961, "American Foreign Policy and the Blessings of Liberty," measured American foreign policy in terms of the "fundamental purposes and values of our life as a nation," which were reflected in American liberalism and democracy.[139] President John Kennedy, himself a member of the AHA, praised the address even though he jokingly noted that Bemis was a Republican, and Secretary of State Dean Rusk reportedly used it in preparing his own remarks in a speech he gave to the AHA on American foreign policy at the same annual meeting.[140]

Bemis, like many other historians, had in the 1940s exchanged an alliance with the public through the New Deal for the increasingly bureaucratic wartime state and its Cold War successor. That move gave historians a place in policymaking and in the writing of government history, as well as employment for some of their students. But historians' links with wider audiences had suffered. They were now, through a combination of their focus on their expertise, their preferment in government, and their reaction against the pseudo-populist conservatism of the McCarthy period, drifting apart from public audiences in a way quite foreign to the years before 1941.

This reliance on the state left historians precariously placed in terms of public influence. If intellectual and social changes cast them adrift from government, their public prestige would diminish substantially. The profession remained vulnerable to an attack from within by historians who would criticize both the elitism of scholars and their involvement in state policies regarded as unacceptable in wider society or among their colleagues. World War II had been thought "the best of wars," Howard Zinn has remarked, but during the Vietnam War historians' support for the state would face a challenge to their practice that would undermine the tradition of policy history and force the revival of public history in a broader, more populist, and radical spirit.[141]

In the 1930s it had been possible to write for the public through federal government work. Historians could easily embrace public causes in a way that closely conformed with their intellectual objectives. World War II underlined this socially useful role and tied it to the American victory over Fascist dictators. Now, these academic and public interests diverged. A closer alliance with local and state history might have kept academics in touch with popular interests, but they had loosened ties with that field. The tensions between local and academic historians and the attempts of some academics to reach a wider public through the state and local history movement constitute the second and equally important area of historians' relations with the state in American history.

12

The State, the Local, and the National

Connecting and Disconnecting with Public Audiences

"In the pageant of the arts and sciences, the local historian does not figure brightly. He is tolerated only as a poor relation of the mighty scholars who chronicle the deeds of parliaments and armies, for it seems clear that since the whole is greater than the part, he who writes of one small section cannot be as great as he who writes of nations and the world."[1] So stated Dixon Ryan Fox, of Columbia University, in 1923 when he attended the annual Conference of State and Local Historical Societies sponsored by the American Historical Association. As a friend of Charles Beard and Arthur Schlesinger, Fox was an enthusiast for the New History. He was also a strong supporter of local history and a councilor of the New York State Historical Society. Ironically, as a partisan for popular involvement, he tended to exaggerate academic resistance to his claims. In fact, Fox was part of a widespread effort from the 1890s to the 1940s seeking to connect academic scholars to local history.

Far from being uninterested, academic historians routinely intervened in state and local history. Fox himself provides evidence of such sympathetic involvement. Yet the way academics intervened produced the resentment that Fox revealed. Scientific historians at the turn of the twentieth century had developed an ambitious project to reform local history by infusing it with the Scientific discourse, linking local events and materials to the production of national history. This meant that local and state history would have a subordinate role—and that local historians would feel inferior. Some, like Fox, noted that academics did not meet the local historians as equals, but they failed to convince the majority of the profession to adopt an alternative approach. The rigidity of academic historians' responses to local history compared unfavorably with the efforts of French and English historians. These succeeded to a greater degree in shaping historical practice from the base up using the materials of local history. Ironically, in democratic America, history was conceived from the top down.

But all was not lost from the perspective of popularizing history. In the 1930s, a countervailing movement with its roots in the professionalization of state and local history arose to contest AHA leadership. Spurred by the circumstances of the depression, the New Deal, and the revival of interest in local and regional traditions, professional historians, mostly operating within state and local history societies, forged a new alliance of popular and professional objectives. At first the new group declared its independence from the AHA and sought outright popularization as its goal. Within twenty years, however, professional and popular objectives within state and local history converged as the popularization drive stalled. One result was to highlight the long-term influence of professional historians in imposing national, Scientific standards upon the state and local history movement. Under their influence, the latter's practice became more professionalized than in comparable countries. But in the meantime, professional American historiography had become fragmented between nationally and internationally oriented academic history on the one hand and specialized professional historians in state historical societies on the other. Further, professionalization eroded links with amateurs, local history groups, genealogists, and antiquarians. These groups were pushed out of the orbit of academic history almost entirely.[2]

* * *

The project to link state to national history was part of the attempt of American historians to connect to the realities of the state; a system of weak federal and stronger local authority and loyalties encouraged a pragmatic and decentralized reliance on state government support for history. Links developed from the 1890s to the 1930s between academics and state historical societies in the midwestern and western regions, where land grant colleges and universities had been established. Far from neglecting the state, academics attempted to use the federal system to build stronger national loyalties. At the same time they were influenced by Rankean visions of a historical politics located in the state. Scientific History privileged the realms of politics and the nation and the use of written documents to validate this critical history.

Almost from the beginnings of Scientific History in the 1880s, professionals courted state and local history groups and coordinated their activities in the service of national history. Within a broad and ambitious program of documentary collection and publication, local societies and antiquarians were given the grassroots role of acquiring materials for national historical syntheses. The professionals would impose national standards of documentary collection and criticism, coordinate this material, and publish it, disseminating it widely on the national level.

When the AHA was established in 1884, it included a substantial group of amateurs. Some of these were gentlemen writers or politicians of note, but many were obscure figures affiliated with the state and local historical societies. Not until the 1890s did the new generation of professionally trained Ph.D.'s located in the universities begin to control the association. They took a greater, though not dominant, position at that time but did not forget the important role of amateurs. Contacts were coordinated through the AHA's National Historical Manuscripts Commission (NHMC), founded in 1895; the Carnegie Institution's Bureau of Historical Research (1903) and its publications; and the Conference of State and Local Historical Societies, established in 1904 as a loose affiliate of the AHA, with its officials appointed by the association.[3]

Academics viewed this exercise as one of "cooperation." Many were sensitive to the concerns of local and state groups and urged that grassroots evidence of social and economic history be drawn into any national synthesis.[4] But the discourse of Scientific History circumscribed an interactive cooperation by privileging professional practice. Formally trained and valuing their qualifications as providing them with knowledge and power, academic historians wished to lead amateurs in a certain direction and were relatively closed to the potentially valuable insights that local historians could add in the form of sources other than literary ones and cultural and social perspectives on history peculiar to place. Rather, documents were privileged, and national themes imposed.

Especially important in the AHA's program was the NHMC, which set out to publish documents of American history that would provide the foundation upon which Scientific History could be erected. Chaired by *American Historical Review* editor John Franklin Jameson, the NHMC quickly sought out individuals and groups already collecting and publishing manuscripts in a flurry of activity in many states.[5] Jameson argued that the NHMC should be concerned with manuscripts of national significance but admitted that "the line between the local and the general is hard to draw" and realized that the Mississippi Valley region, where much of the new historical society activity of the 1890s was centered, would be critical to his plans.[6] The network of local contacts built up by Jameson and his successors over the next few years formed the basis of official cooperation between the state and local groups in the Conference of State and Local Historical Societies (usually referred to from its beginning as simply the Conference of Historical Societies).

Jameson resigned his NHMC post in 1899, but the work continued under Reuben Thwaites, the Wisconsin Historical Society superintendent and a supporter of close links between amateurs, local historical societies, and professional historians. In 1905 Jameson himself took the important role of coordinating American historical research as director of the Carnegie Bureau in Washington. Here he extended his cultivation of many community history groups, particularly where he saw the opportunity to extend the influence of the AHA and achieve a broader coverage of the topics of American history in his bibliographical and archival projects.[7] At the AHA's annual meeting in 1905 he dwelt on his desire to be "useful to state and local history societies and to promote co-operation among them."[8] The Carnegie Institution promised the preparation of lists of documents from French, Spanish, and British archives, all of which would "help keep societies, especially those of the West, from duplicating each other's work in the printing of material or the procuring of transcripts."[9]

To Jameson, the first important task in the construction of a national American history was the gathering of diplomatic, political, and military facts of relevance to the history of the early American colonies and Republic. Because the United States had inherited a landmass contested by European empires, this quest involved both national and international action, with records to be collected in imperial archives as well as locally. This dual-fronted drive for documents enhanced the importance of academic historians as coordinators who could secure the reciprocal services of local enthusiasts wanting copies of foreign sources relevant to their states' colonial histories.[10]

In this work, Jameson and his colleagues had a clear hierarchy that placed local history at the bottom in terms of its ultimate utility for the building of the nation. These local groups gathered raw materials for processing and assembly in the workshops of the trained technicians, the professional historians. Jameson insisted that the Carnegie work must focus on production of documents "so selected that the money expended will help the widest possible circle of those who shall be pursuing the next highest stages—the writing of monographs and of general histories."[11] In a similar vein, he urged the American Antiquarian Society in Worcester, Massachusetts, to broaden its scope and become what it was always intended to be by "name and aspiration," that is, "a national, as distinct from a local, society."[12]

This hierarchical view also had gender aspects. "Scientific History," as studied in the doctoral seminars, was masculinist in orientation and practiced largely by men.[13] In contrast, amateur historical societies gave a much greater role to women. This was particularly true in the small local societies, whose work professionals depicted as the "harmless pastime of eccentric spinsters."[14] Local work was often considered women's province, though the women concerned, like Louise Kellogg of the State Historical Society of Wisconsin, might sometimes be trained professionals.[15] In Harvard historian Albert Bushnell Hart's formulation, historical societies offered a possible safety valve of employment for "some of those graduates of women's colleges, whose preparation seems wider than their later opportunities."[16] Whether they were men or women, Jameson regarded most local historians as antiquarians who had nothing substantive to tell professionals. At worst, they were deadweight. Thus, he described the situation of the amateur groups in New England: "Their historical societies seem . . . becalmed at present, even a prey to ship worms—meaning genealogists, who turn their old timbers into sawdust."[17]

The first generation of academic historians in the 1880s would, through the "germ theory," interpret the evidence collected in this hierarchical effort. This approach sought the roots of the evolution of local communities in their European origins. American national history's distinctive features, however, became increasingly important as a competing theme by the turn of the century. Frederick Jackson Turner had a crucial role in supplying a new interpretation to explain American development and relate the local to the national. According to the frontier thesis, American nationalism had been forged in westward expansion. As one disciple, Solon Buck, remarked in the 1920s, the "largely antiquarian focus" of local history had under Turner's influence been altered by "emphasis on the importance of the frontier, of sectionalism, and of social and economic forces in the development of the American people."[18]

In attempting to seize control of the discourse of history in the United States, academics had distinct advantages due to the flowering of late-nineteenth-century historical consciousness that largely coincided with the rise of professional historiography. Especially aiding the academics was the unevenness in the growth of this consciousness. They confronted a historical society "movement" that was fragmented by region, approach, and values. The eastern historical societies were well entrenched, reasonably well endowed, and run by nonacademics as in some European countries. These, however, had more in common with the professionals than with genealogists and local historians in that region and were part of the nonprofessional group admitted from the start to the councils of the AHA. The South was very different. There academic history made little headway until the 1920s, with popular consciousness of history driven by southern patriotic and hereditary societies, especially the Daughters of the Confederacy. In a number of states, such as Florida, Kentucky, Tennessee, and West Virginia, the local and state groups stagnated in the period before World War I.[19] Furthermore, veterans groups censured academics when they strayed from the shibboleths of the Confederacy's Lost Cause. In North Carolina, Trinity College was the site of John Spencer Bassett's 1903 attack on "racial demagoguery." His affirmation of the character of Booker T. Washington won him opprobrium among orthodox southerners.[20] Most southern-born academics participated in the celebration of Confederate memory—or they left the region, as Bassett did in 1906.[21] A start was made toward professionalization through the Alabama Department of Archives and History (1901), the Mississippi State Department of Archives and History (1902), and the North Carolina Historical Commission (1903), but not until the 1930s did circumstances allow consistent professional growth to be achieved in the (southern) state historical society movement.

The Midwest supplied the third regional variation, but the one most amenable to professional influence. There, historical consciousness was changing rapidly. The frontier period had ended and communities began to take stock of their experience of westward settlement. This process was aided by centenaries and semicentenaries of the American exploration and settlement and of the organization of midwestern areas as territories and then as states within the Union. Because western societies did not have the resources of the older eastern ones, however, they were more open to an alliance with academics and the state.

Sectional differences worked to the advantage of those academics wishing to use a national strategy to control amateur history in its local manifestations. Here, the divisiveness of the Civil War and Reconstruction had exposed the weakness of the American Union. Racial animosity, along with sectional tensions, needed to be contained. In the South, much historical opinion served to exacerbate North-South and racial divisions and so make national reconciliation more difficult. Academic historians therefore concentrated on their role in a healing process as advocates of a supposedly impartial Scientific History. After the reporter of the AHA convention session on southern history in New York in 1909 heard W. E. B. Du Bois speak on the benefits of Reconstruction (along with W. A. Dunning and U. B. Phillips), he remarked with measured distaste that "the discussion which followed consisted largely of the conventional and non-historical discourses to which the topic too easily gives rise." Academic historians saw themselves as representing cosmopolitan impartiality against the rancorous debates of nineteenth-century American divisions over slavery, even though the practical outcome was a "consensus" that was "racist" as well as nationalist.[22]

Unable to change the South directly, academic historians looked to the Midwest to supply cement for the Union, linking north and south. In the areas that were crucial to the national coordination of history under academic leadership, the professors' cause was tied to that of the state universities and state historical societies. During the Progressive Era, these midwestern states were interested in taking control of local history to provide better funding and coordination for the amateurs who had started it. This drive was inspired by Progressive Era ideas of positive government, especially in Wisconsin but also in Iowa, Illinois, and Minnesota. Natural allies of the Scientific historians, these state societies worked cooperatively to implement the AHA agenda.

The period from 1890 to 1914 was an opportune time for such cooperation, though the relationship was to be fraught with tension, misunderstandings, and false expectations. Booming local interest in history stimulated in part by the "closing" of the frontier was evident in Michigan and Wisconsin in the 1880s and 1890s. But the desire to preserve the past extended into the 1920s in such states as Oklahoma and Nevada. Local history representatives often cited the end of "pioneer" days as a factor in their efforts. According to the Oklahoma Historical Society: "The landscape is fast changing. Forests are yielding their charms to the cereal queen, and prairies are gathering to them the foliage of the deserted forest. . . . To preserve views of the primitive, and landscapes as they change; of people, etc., has been one of the cardinals in our efforts."[23] The Nevada Historical Society emphasized that Indian tribes were "fast disappearing" and white settlement was "rapidly getting beyond the pioneer period."[24] The AHA took heart from this surge of local interest. Indeed, Jameson and his colleagues found the Midwest and Great Plains regions to be the centers most responsive to requests for active involvement in the search for documents. New England and the Mid-Atlantic states, where most academic history was based, were already better documented, and professional historians had easier access to sources. Though Jameson was a corresponding member of the Massachusetts Historical Society, he complained that many of the societies in New England were lethargic and at times uncooperative with his supervisory efforts—small wonder, because they were better established than those farther west and had less need of outside help.[25]

On the general scope of American historical inquiry, amateurs and antiquarians respected professional authority. They tacitly and often explicitly conceded that local and state historiography was inferior to that of the academics. While professionals made strenuous critiques of antiquarianism, equally damning comments came from nonacademic historians themselves. James Trustlow Adams complained of the need for "tickling the vanity of the living generation" in local historical work,[26] while Worthington C. Ford, representing the Massachusetts Historical Society, pointed out at the AHA annual meeting in 1909 the "lack of discretion, judgment, or knowledge, and careless editing often displayed" by local groups. This patrician scholar disparaged the work of genealogists and antiquarians and "the preponderance of articles of merely family or personal interest."[27] In the South and West, amateurs likewise deferred to the professionals on larger issues of historiography. Alexander Lawton, vice-president of the Central of Georgia Railway Company, did service for the Georgia Historical Society and regularly read the *American Historical Review.* Even though this gave him a sense of a "high standard of historical work," he declined an offer by Professor Allen Johnson to prepare sketches of Georgians for the *Dictionary of American Biography.* "I have neither the patience nor the time nor the skill to come up to it," he admitted in 1927. But he did help Johnson get competent scholars to do the work for the *Dictionary* in Georgia.[28]

Nevertheless, amateurs had much experience on which to draw, and they did not hesitate to offer local expertise, including that on the methodology of history. Community groups were sometimes more innovative in their use of sources and methods than professionals were. Jameson wrote the Oklahoma Historical Society requesting news of manuscript collections, but for the period of Oklahoma's European history, the society believed that the request was misplaced. The European phase was already accessible: "Every phase of our first coming to this land and stewardship" was on "record in the public print." The society preferred to chart historic changes in the land by acquiring sketches and paintings as well as by recording and preserving other visual and oral evidence. "Special efforts have been made," the society's secretary M. P. Campbell reported, in "the form of recollections or reminiscences of first days by earliest settlers" while this type of informant "still lives to tell these unpublished experiences."[29] A focus on environment, personal experience, material culture, and memory was common in the local societies in other states, too. Marking graves and other historic sites and collecting oral history and assorted memorabilia reflected local enthusiasts' commitment to the history of their own communities. The Michigan Pioneer and Historical Society sought to "gather up the fragments" so that "nothing is lost" and predicted that "all classes of information relating to our State will have their interest and value."[30]

Academic historians did not simply dismiss such materials as trivia, provided their significance could be interpreted and broadened by an appropriate professional. Turner's frontier thesis, heavily grounded in the local history materials of the Wisconsin State Historical Society and his own memories of the frontier transformation, was an important example of the incorporation of grassroots history into a professionalized explanation of the West that enlarged the scope and significance of national history.[31] Yet interest in amateur projects stopped precisely there at the absorption of new ideas. Financial help for local, amateur work was a different matter, and so too were power relations. Disputes over money soon interfered with hopes of a joint enterprise; there was much misunderstanding about the extent of AHA largesse. Local historians wanted financial help from the national historical association and deferred to it in matters of scholarly interpretation. But there was criticism, too. L. Belle Hamlin of the Historical and Philosophical Society of Ohio attacked the Carnegie Institution's Bureau of Historical Research for its failure to distribute AHA publications to historical societies for free. Hamlin explained that local historians sought AHA guidance and inspiration, but different priorities regarding the importance of communicating with the general public and spreading a more democratic conception of history lay behind her criticisms: "Our little local historical society, with all of its poverty, shows a more liberal spirit and a greater desire to extend to the reading public an additional knowledge of American history" than did Jameson and his colleagues.[32] Other local historians criticized Jameson's bureau and the AHA for mean responses in disputes over the allocation of money to local societies. Jameson frequently had to explain that his funds were far from limitless. To make the best use of scarce resources, the bureau had, he argued, to concentrate on record collection that would have the widest impact. Diplomatic, political, and military facts of relevance to the emergent United States took precedence, hence the need to follow the NHMC program for collecting sources in archives abroad.[33]

Power was also at issue. Local and state history enthusiasts attacked their marginalization in the AHA's committees and councils.[34] These amateurs asserted their practical knowledge of local history and of the methods conducive to collection of records. There and in matters of the organization of the local historical societies, they chafed at the AHA's control and attacked the unwillingness of the academics to take their advice seriously. Especially vocal was Clarence Burton, a well-to-do lawyer who ran his own Burton Library of Historical Research in Detroit and served as Michigan Pioneer and Historical Society president.[35] Burton assisted the AHA in the collection of documents for the NHMC and sank thousands of dollars of his own money in the project. He joined in the work of the Conference of Historical Societies but soon criticized the AHA as "quite unwilling to admit a layman to any voice in the man-

agement of the Association." Jameson disputed this and cited cases of nonprofessionals on the AHA executive prior to 1906, but Burton sensed the underlying trend of the relationship.[36]

Burton and others joining the AHA felt intimidated by the professionals.
As Burton stated of the 1904 annual meeting, "I feel like a cat in a strange gar-
ret, going to Chicago to meet the professors and students and historians. . . . I
am only a laboring man, full of the work that brings the daily dollar, and only
with an occasional hour to spend in study."[37] Because of the AHA's failure to
take notice of the needs of such historians, by 1914 attendance by amateurs at
the Conference of Historical Societies had dropped off markedly. Discontent
coincided with the abortive attempt in 1915 by academic members of the
AHA to reform the association. The rebellion proved to be a "tempest in Clio's
teacup" that produced, according to the episode's chief chronicler, moderate
reforms in the AHA's structure, democratizing its processes. However, local
history discontent connected to this disturbance should not be dismissed as
the work of "bush leaguers."[38] Key local society representatives chafed at the
academics' neglect of the conference, and the AHA had to make concessions
by establishing a new "semi-autonomous" affiliation in 1916.[39] Yet this conces-
sion did little to restore confidence. After 1923, the conference languished
again, with relatively few societies paying affiliation dues and local societies remaining unresponsive to calls for information from the AHA. For their part,
academics responded dismissively to this decline in local and state history involvement.[40] Jameson told an English correspondent that the local groups
could be largely ignored as a serious force on the grounds of their demonstrated lack of interest in the AHA. The "semi-autonomous" conference was
"not a strictly constituted body" and "membership and attendance" were "ca-
sual."[41]

The emerging tension between local history and academic historians was
partly mitigated for a time by the rise of the patriotic and hereditary societies.
Much of the amateur enthusiasm for history in the early decades of the twentieth century went, not to the historical societies directly, but into patriotic and
genealogical groups such as the Sons of the American Revolution.[42] Sensing
their rising numbers and political influence, the AHA attempted to draw these
societies into its orbit.[43] Contrary to the assumption that academics increasingly ignored amateurs, patriotic and genealogical societies were included in
the program of the AHA on several occasions between 1911 and 1923. Their
work was praised in reports of the annual meetings, and representatives of the
patriotic groups were added to the Executive of the Conference of Historical
Societies and later to the AHA's Committee on Hereditary Societies, created in
1920.[44] The 1922 AHA annual meeting in New Haven featured addresses by

Dixon Ryan Fox for the AHA and by leaders of the Daughters of the American Revolution. An entire section of the AHA *Annual Report* was devoted to the work of the Connecticut groups. This temporary alliance occurred despite the fact that the hereditary societies expressed a profound political conservatism and deep commitment to the Americanization of immigrants.[45]

Notwithstanding this flirtation, the AHA's relationship with patriotic and hereditary societies soured quickly in the mid-1920s. Especially important in disillusioning the academics was the onset of textbook warfare in the 1920s. Though the issue primarily concerned the profession's relations with schools, the strains were also felt upon the AHA's wider popularization drive.[46] With patriotic societies such as the Sons of the American Revolution charging pro-British and anti-American bias in textbooks written by prominent professionals, relations with academics were bound to suffer. These attacks called into question the value of any alliance with patriotic groups.[47] Also poisoning the AHA's response to the hereditary and patriotic societies was the suspect nature of the commercial ventures to which they contributed because these might compete with the academics' aspirations to control the general field of American history and might bring the AHA, by implication, into scholarly and public disrepute. Businessman Frank Allaben had first attracted the Daughters of the American Revolution and other similar groups to a "National Historical Society" (later renamed the "American Historical Society") in 1915–16, much to the discomfort of Jameson's circle. Jameson feared that the publication of its *Journal of American History* was likely to be confused by unsuspecting local groups with the work of the *American Historical Review (AHR)*. These fears resurfaced in the mid-1920s. Jameson and A. R. Newsome, of the University of North Carolina, accused the American Historical Society of exploiting the good name and reputation of the AHA for lucrative commercial gain.[48]

The AHA's detachment from nonacademic history groups by the late 1920s threatened a power vacuum at the state history level. Yet despite discontents at their neglect, amateurs lacked a clear alternative view of how historiography could be organized. From the 1890s to the 1920s, power and prestige lay with the rising professionals and their claims to history as a science. For one thing, local and state societies were divided among themselves throughout this period.[49] As Jameson observed, any society that remained under the control of antiquarians could not seriously challenge the AHA, since it was "naturally constrained by the very force of its local interest from effective cooperation."[50] The vast gap between well-endowed, patrician-dominated institutions of the Northeast and more democratic ones in the West demonstrated the disunity in the local and state history movement that the AHA could effectively use to promote the interests of academic history.

The state historians had, moreover, no agreed model of independent historical effort to put in place of cooperation with academics at the national level; some state historians, notably Thomas Owen of the Alabama Department of Archives and History, argued for the state governments having control of archival collection, yet Warren Upham of the Minnesota Historical Society disagreed. The independent state historical societies should do the work of collecting, but with appropriations from government. If the work were directly under the control of the state, Upham argued, there was a "danger of being subjected to political influence."[51] Lack of an agreed alternative meant that the obvious rumblings of discontent over inferior status did not amount to a serious movement for secession. The AHA-appointed secretary of the Conference of Historical Societies, Augustus Shearer, had noted criticism during World War I but did not detect "any desire to separate from the A.H.A."[52]

Also delaying a revolt against academic history was the emergence in 1907 of the Mississippi Valley Historical Association.[53] The MVHA constituted a regional challenge to the dominance of the older professional body, whose power lay in the universities of the Northeast, but it served also as a crucial mediator between the AHA and local and state historians. In the region where the most vital work was being done before 1930 in state and local history, the MVHA provided a new source of contact between academics and state societies. This new intermediary body extended academic influence while negating the possibility of total dominance of historical production by the AHA itself and showing that the historical profession was broader than the AHA.[54]

Jameson and his allies hoped to use the MVHA as a complementary professional association to extend the influence of Scientific History. "[S]cientifically trained men" would "find it possible, by a little exertion, to control the new movement,"[55] he hoped. Such a result was possible because he and his university colleagues were already busy sending their graduates to work in the state historical societies and were reaping benefits through new allies for the enterprise of Scientific History. Especially important was the new association's vice-president, Clarence W. Alvord, of the University of Illinois, who assured Jameson that the Executive Committee contained a majority in favor of "scholarly work" and hoped that "the better trained men" would "control the state societies." Astutely, he argued that the MVHA could neutralize tension over amateur/professional divisions. By bringing the "two classes closer together" to promote "mutual confidence," the new association could take up the subject of documentary collections in European archives with more popular support than the AHA could muster.[56] To maintain the primacy of professional objectives, Alvord had the statement describing the MVHA mission as being to "popularize" history struck from the constitution at its first meeting in October 1907.[57]

Nevertheless, the new association included nonacademic influences in its early days and maintained a strongly regional focus. The first president was Alabaman archivist Thomas Owen, while Clarence Paine, the secretary, was an amateur associated with Great Plains promoter J. Sterling Morton in the production of a history of Nebraska. The MVHA constitution stated its purpose as "to promote historical study and research and to secure cooperation between the historical societies and the departments of history of the Mississippi Valley." With its first annual meeting coinciding with that of the American Library Association in Minneapolis in 1908, the new group emphasized links with archival, historical society, and library work in addition to academic history.[58]

After 1914, the association's new journal, the *Mississippi Valley Historical Review* (*MVHR*), was hailed by Jameson as an agent of professionalization despite initial consternation that it might trespass on his work,[59] but the *MVHR* still maintained important links with local and state societies. The new venture had a number of leading historical societies as guarantors, including those of Nebraska, Wisconsin, Minnesota, and Illinois, along with the Mississippi State Department of Archives and History. Each year until 1920, it included extensive reports on the activities of historical societies,[60] and a strong regional focus remained in its treatment of subject matter throughout the interwar years.

This regional distinctiveness was underlined by the role of Clara Paine, who served as the association's corresponding secretary from 1916 to 1952. Taking over when her husband died, Paine not only organized the business side of the MVHA; a local historian and registrar of the Colonial Dames of America in Nebraska,[61] she dealt with the presidents of the association on policy matters and advised on the nomination of the future presidents and members of committees. As John D. Hicks remarked in 1936, "To her, . . . more than to . . . any historian, is due the continued success of the Association."[62] Paine also opposed vigorously the loss of the association's regional identity and campaigned successfully against the adoption of a less parochial name. Not until 1944 was an effort made, led by Paul Angle, of the Illinois State Historical Society, to change the name to one which might reflect the growing importance of national American history in the work of its now predominantly academic membership. At the annual meeting in St. Louis, Paine lobbied successfully against Angle, and in her report of the meeting, she suppressed the details of his recommendations. Paine's supporters, such as James Sellers (University of Nebraska), argued that the MVHA should be true to those like her who had underwritten the association financially in its lean years during the 1930s depression.[63]

Because it remained a regional organization, the MVHA's professional leaders could more easily identify with and cooperate with state historians and societies. This circumstance mitigated conflicts between historical societies and academics and indirectly functioned to deflect criticism of the AHA. Yet in practice the MVHA's academic activities from the 1920s were firmly controlled by university-based professionals and reflected academic research priorities.

Paradoxically, not until professionals fully replaced amateurs at the state level was a challenge to AHA control likely. The change came from within the state and local societies. Contemporaneously with the struggle between the national academic elite and amateurs, the state and local history movement itself was being transformed in ways that Alvord had anticipated. Experts in local and state history arose to dispute academic history's dominance. By the 1930s these professionals, often trained Ph.D.'s and archivists themselves, chose a separate path of development and made scathing attacks on the AHA. The irony was that it was these same professionals who were at first guided and stimulated by the AHA to systematize local and state history. To an increasing extent, the men who led the state-sponsored societies—and they usually were men—supported Scientific History. An early example was Milo Quaife, who took the State Historical Society of Wisconsin from its semiprofessional leadership under Reuben Thwaites to full professionalization. Quaife had earned a Ph.D. from the University of Chicago in 1908, but in 1914, after a short teaching career, he became superintendent of the State Historical Society of Wisconsin and from 1920 to 1922 was editor of the *Wisconsin Magazine of History*. As managing editor of the *MVHR* from 1924 to 1930 and MVHA president in 1919, Quaife was closely tied to the emerging professional ethos in American history.[64]

At about the time that Quaife's career was on the rise, amateur influence in many state societies was in eclipse. It diminished sharply but unevenly, aided by the retirement and death of enthusiastic leaders, whose work was gradually taken over by the states. In a typical example of the erosion of the voluntaristic tradition and its replacement by one of state functionaries, Clarence Burton's Michigan Pioneer and Historical Society was subsumed after 1913 into the Michigan Historical Commission.[65] This shift reflected growing attempts to manipulate historical memory and channel patriotism into officially sanctioned state institutions.[66] The newly professionalized societies founded journals such as Quaife's *Wisconsin Magazine of History* (1917) and updated older ones. Therein a trend could be detected away from emphasis on antiquarian collection to publication of research, and from antiquarian to professional control.

As professionals took control of state and local history, resentment against the AHA resurfaced in the 1930s. Critical was the quickening of interest in state history and archival preservation in the American South. No less important, the New Deal rekindled enthusiasm for "Americana," particularly the preservation of the artifacts of local communities. That interest in "grassroots history" could not have come at a more propitious time.[67] Professionals who found academic employment difficult to obtain during the depression swelled the ranks of the local and state history movement. Though often trained as historians, they worked instead in state libraries and archives. There they developed new loyalties to the state scene and chafed at the attitudes of the nationally oriented academic historians.

*   *   *

The depression's immediate impact was to force more coordinated approaches to the problems of state and local history. Legislative cuts to budgets threatened historical agencies in Missouri, Illinois, North Dakota, and other states in the early 1930s and fueled demands for a vigorous organization that could promote history's interests within the federal and state governments. The stock market crash and dwindling private philanthropy for the first time gave the state-supported agencies of the West and the privately endowed ones of the East common economic interests in overcoming the divisions that the AHA had previously managed. The AHA seemed to lack both the vigor and the will to represent those interests in the national arena, let alone on the state scene.[68] Particularly after 1935, however, the New Deal's programs of enhanced government intervention created positive opportunities for a new professional group to assert leadership over local history—to establish a grassroots history "movement" led by experts but legitimated in terms of popular need.

The new professionals were far more serious competitors for public influence than the amateurs had been. Their training, together with state legislative requirements, encouraged these activists to focus not only on local history but also on techniques of record preservation and public presentation rather than history research. Moreover, local political pressures forced them to take account of popular demands. Christopher Crittenden, head of the North Carolina Department of Archives and History, claimed that academic history had become not only too specialized but also "too highly professionalized." Most

AHA members were college professors and their interests were different from those of the general public. Not so his fellow state and local historians. He announced in 1938: "Many of us who are engaged in historical work need to cooperate actively with the public." He would do this by producing "a first-class readable history of every state" and a history "of every county."[69]

To achieve this popular outreach, Crittenden broadened the scope of history well beyond the written texts that concerned most academic practitioners. He focused as much on care of graves, historic houses, and monuments as on documents and argued that more could be learned about these ways of commemorating the past and conveying its significance from the National Park Service than from academic historians. Crittenden also offered an instrumentalist interpretation of history and its audiences that drew upon the surging interest in popular American traditions. The audience was of key importance, not whether the history was accurate. The aim was to serve the public, he proclaimed, and if "the masses fail properly to appreciate what we are trying to do," the "fault is mainly our own."[70] Crittenden's views reflected a questioning of objectivity fueled by the academic debates over relativism in the 1930s, but in turn these debates were conditioned by the economic and political circumstances that encouraged populist and utilitarian approaches.[71]

Although the rhetoric was democratic and oriented toward regional pride, Crittenden envisaged a crucial place for experts in the new public-oriented history. Most definitely, his attention to wider audiences did not mean that amateurs should rule. Calling for "a broad, ambitious, and expensive program of historical work," he invoked the model of states such as Oklahoma where "active and efficient historical organizations" were now "controlled by specialists" in local and state history and in archival preservation. He wanted more, not fewer, professional historical journals and trained doctorates to staff the libraries, archives, and historical societies, but he also felt that these experts could not move in their interpretation and interests too far out of step with the public.[72]

The new professionals had allies among academics such as Arthur Schlesinger and Roy F. Nichols.[73] Yet most academic support came from younger scholars forced to accept nonuniversity or marginal college positions. Experience in the 1930s depression made such people more inclined to look at history from "the bottom up."[74] The New Deal and the influence of Progressive history worked in the same direction. With the growth of these populist interests, the 1939 and 1940 AHA conventions featured important sessions on local history, oral traditions, and urban history. "As long as historians were content to write political and diplomatic history, examination of local divergences was not essential," Gerald Capers argued in a 1939 session on local history. But "the story of how Americans have lived as individuals and communities can be told only on the basis of local history." This special session chaired by Constance McLaughlin Green indicated, the *AHR* editors suggested, "an advance toward placing local historical research in the position it should hold as the basic discipline of American social history."[75]

Supportive academically trained historians often worked at the local level in archives or libraries, though sometimes they straddled the divide between academia and local history. One such was Lester Cappon, a Harvard Ph.D., library archivist, and assistant professor at the University of Virginia.[76] A prominent supporter of state and local history, he was nevertheless very dismissive of "the static regime of the antiquarian" prevalent in parts of the South, compared to the "modern historical scholarship" that emerged in the North in the 1880s. In Virginia, local records were still not consolidated as late as the 1930s. Historical journals were "confined almost entirely to the recital of well-known episodes in military and political annals, to genealogies in which the begat and the begotten were little more than lists of names, and to miscellaneous documents in need of an editor."[77] What the South needed in Cappon's view was a "virile crop of historians" (the gendered choice of the term was significant in itself) exhibiting the traits of "the critical scholar." Far from simply championing localities and amateurs, the new practitioners focused on greater state control of local history and more rigorous professionalization.[78]

Whether based in universities or state and local history employment, these activists hoped that public interest and professional expertise could be blended under their leadership through the historical preservation movement. This potential was illustrated in the involvement of the national government in the development of historic parks and monuments.[79] State and local historians regarded New Deal efforts at producing a tangible history through archaeology as critical to their own project. The preservation movement would aid efforts to provide a professionalized service to the public in the presentation of stories about the American states' and nation's pasts.[80]

This chance to work with grassroots preservation was not the only alternative attraction to cooperation with academics. The immediate occasion of the rupture with the AHA was the development of archiving as a separate profession. The opening of the National Archives in Washington in 1934 and the establishment of the Society of American Archivists in 1936 spurred archivists to develop their professional goals.[81] Julian P. Boyd, librarian of the Historical Society of Pennsylvania, noted the new movement for archival preservation in the local and state historical societies: "There are thousands of problems calling for co-operative solution by these societies—in publishing, in methods of gathering materials, in the exchange of duplicates and extraneous material, in the administration of libraries with attendant special problems, in the matter of gaining public support and finances, and in the enormously complicated field of preserving, by means of micro-photography, materials for research."[82] In Boyd's view, the presentation of history to the general public and the solution of professional problems in information services could never be dealt with satisfactorily in the academically dominated AHA.

The separation of professional archivists from academics was especially apparent in the South, where leadership came from Crittenden. His rise to importance reflected the development in the 1920s and 1930s of southern efforts to improve historical societies, to match the earlier midwestern achievements. "The time is ripe," Crittenden stated in 1939, "for the creation of a better co-ordinated, more closely knit organization" than the Conference of Historical Societies. "What can be accomplished . . . is clearly shown by the successful movement culminating in the formation of the Society of American Archivists."[83] Like many others, he castigated the AHA's indifference toward local history observed over several years.[84]

From Crittenden, Boyd, and their allies came the idea of creating a separate state and local history association. In 1935 the AHA had attempted half-heartedly to maintain the existing relationship by introducing a new plan for affiliating the local societies with the AHA. Yet this initiative was strenuously opposed within the Conference of Historical Societies.[85] Boyd "wholly disagree[d]" with any institutional link to an "indifferent" parent organization such as the AHA had proved to be. According to Boyd, the AHA Conference could "never achieve an important influence so long as it [was] dependent upon a parent body whose major interests lie, not in the field of administration of these organizations that house materials for research, but in the field of research itself."[86] A planning conference of the state and local history groups in 1940 saw most of the participants siding with Crittenden and Boyd. Some speakers argued that meetings of the group should no longer even be held at the same time as the AHA meeting. Ernst Posner provided inspiration for such a stance from abroad. He had been a state archivist in Berlin but had fled Nazi Germany and had become professor of archival administration at American University. Posner encouraged the formation of a state and local history group similar to that in his homeland, the National Federation of German Associations for the Study of History and Antiquity (Gesamtverein der Deutschen Geschichts- und Altertumsvereine), founded in 1852. It combined genealogists, folklorists, archaeologists, antiquarians, and local historians in a society independent of academics, received subsidies "from the Reich, and . . . the big estates," and attached its meetings to the annual conference of the society of archivists. Though delegates expressed "much interest" in Posner's proposal, the German example was a dubious one in the international climate of 1940 and the key parallels did not exist.[87] The federal government and business would not support such an organization in the United States. Rather, the American movement represented an attempt by experts in the local and state fields to democratize history making. Yet the Conference heeded Posner's broader call for independence from the AHA and, on the German model, a closer alliance with archivists and librarians. Spurred by a genuine interest in making history relevant to the general public, the American Association for State and Local History (AASLH), established as a result of this meeting, immediately set about that task. The Committee to Publicize American History was established, with Crittenden as chair.[88] *State and Local History News*, founded in 1941, took over the role of reporting grassroots history previously performed by the *MVHR*. By and large, the AHA did not seriously contest this split, because its main priorities had long been with national and international history.

★ ★ ★

The paths of academic and state and local history had now substantially diverged. Until the late 1950s, "popularization" would be the chief theme in local and state history work. But the going was not easy. The new program's major achievement was the inception of *American Heritage* in 1947. The AASLH originally intended this quarterly to "deal exclusively with the teaching of local, community history in our schools, historical societies, museums and similar agencies."[89] A more ambitious and glossy version relaunched by the AASLH in 1949 signaled a determination to market the magazine more widely to the literate public. But the national marketing strategy and the inclusion of more general, less place-specific items moved away from local and state history, leaving grassroots activists to complement this national approach with more modest, state-based programs to extend popular influence. There, too, glossy magazine formats often replaced the scholarly orientation of the state historical society periodicals, as in the case of *Montana: The Magazine of Western History*.[90] No longer content to rely on traditional dissemination through libraries and archives, the more innovative states also tried ambitious programs of outreach through other means during the 1950s. "Historymobiles" in Wisconsin, Florida, and Indiana spread the message to local communities that history mattered.[91] These museums in motion paralleled on a state level the Freedom Train program of the National Archives, which took the documents of American constitutional and political history on a railroad exhibit around the country from 1947 to 1949.[92] Meanwhile, pamphlets and conferences of the AASLH promoted an ideological focus on patriotism and "Americanism" as a way of achieving popular appeal.

In the 1940s and 1950s, state historians openly admitted that they required stronger political and financial support from their legislatures, and this dictated to some degree a more patriotic approach to the past. "[T]ax-supported institutions," declared the AASLH's president Clifford Lord, urgently needed to "rally greater public interest and support for their programs."[93] But patriotism also came to be viewed more positively than a knee-jerk response to the demands of legislators. It was a necessity in the Cold War struggle, a way of identifying the locality with the nation. In an AASLH statement, "Making Our Heritage Live" by Sylvester K. Stevens, Clifford Lord, and Albert B. Corey, the Cold War orientation and the search for "Americanism" was made clear. Stevens, especially, found in local history "an Anchor for our Faith in America."[94]

Patriotic Americanism was inherent in the AASLH program from the beginning. In the 1930s Crittenden had urged state historical societies not to diverge too far from their publics and from their political patrons in the state legislatures. This North Carolinian not only emphasized that the public was always right but also drew the corollary of the need to bend to the political and social demands of particular groups within the local publics in states that were prepared to provide money and legislative support for historical research. Public historians, he had argued, must actively cultivate "patriotic societies" and reject the views of academics "prejudiced" against such groups. These amateurs could help historians in passing "desirable legislation."[95]

After World War II, however, the novelty of Crittenden's stance was blunted. Academics themselves displayed patriotic enthusiasm, which brought them into closer ideological, if not organizational, alignment with the AASLH. The latter, after all, did little more than reaffirm the conservative and instrumental stance of Conyers Read and Samuel Eliot Morison on global and national political issues that they had taken in their presidential addresses to the AHA in 1949 and 1950.[96] The parting of the ways between professional and amateur historians should not, therefore, be exaggerated.

A common commitment to American patriotism was not the only shared value. As part of a rapprochement, in the 1950s leaders of the state history movement developed second thoughts about their single-minded quest for popularization.[97] Running *American Heritage* as the flagship of popularization soon became an administrative and financial drain for the AASLH, and so it entered into an arrangement whereby the magazine was effectively taken over in 1954 by Allan Nevins's Society of American Historians and the Parton Publishing Group.[98] Two effects flowed from this takeover. There was much resentment within the AASLH with what former editor Earle Newton charged was "a sell-out" to Nevins's group.[99] This resentment soured the popularization drive, which now seemed tarnished with commercialism and triviality.[100] On the other hand, the AASLH benefited financially from the new orientation of the magazine, which went on to financial success. With the funds that its 15 percent stake in the project produced, the association was able to discharge the debts accumulated by the sole venture from 1947 and, ironically, to redirect its attention to the issue of professionalizing local history.

The AASLH used this advantageous situation to effect a change that some influential members already desired. Lord was one who saw an opportunity to return the AASLH to its local and state history roots and to reemphasize professionalism. He believed that the group had "a real job to do" in "raising standards" within local and state history. He urged "fewer political" and more "professional appointments, higher standards and higher salaries." Rather than the "trickery and gadgetry which has been so much a part of the program of the association in recent years," content and purposefulness impressed Lord as the way of the future.[101] In effect, Lord and his colleagues believed that the AASLH had already "done enough toward popularization." By 1957, the association had examined the costs and benefits of popularization in a special committee on long-range planning. Significantly, its chairman was the original architect of the association's drive to make history popular twenty years before. Christopher Crittenden conceded that "our membership will probably consist mainly of professionals (while at the same time not barring but actually welcoming any interested laymen who may wish to join)." His report amounted to a full confession that professionalization must once again take precedence over popularization.[102]

That the AASHL could not sustain *American Heritage* beyond 1954 without the input of business interests is a salutary reminder of the perils and limits of popularization strategies. Public enthusiasm for the types of history traditionally championed at the state and local level should not be exaggerated. As early as the 1920s Jameson astutely observed that the numbers of enthusiastic workers in many local societies had fallen, particularly in the East, and that it was no longer possible to rely on amateurs for support in the search for records. Even the Massachusetts Historical Society had "a much smaller amount of working force than it had fifty years ago," Jameson stated.[103] Local societies were partly alienated by professionalization at the state level, which discouraged the genealogical emphasis energizing nineteenth-century local history.[104] The shift of the AASLH back to professionalization by 1960 was in part related to the erosion of popular interest in what the state societies had to offer, not just resentment at the loss of control over *American Heritage*. In Michigan, a Historical Commission official reported the decline in grassroots history measured in the numbers of people attending meetings and in the number of active societies. In that state there were at least fifty groups in the 1920s but most of these were defunct by 1950 and others had atrophied. Typical was the Grand Traverse Historical Society. "The five or six elderly people who belong to this organization . . . prefer to consider themselves an exclusive group having meetings two or three times a year at which members discuss the history of their families or of the region along the old pioneer reminiscence line."[105] Yet it was not just the passing of the older type of collector/antiquarian that mattered.

Postwar economic and social change made worrying inroads on America's sense of locality. In 1957, Columbia University historian Louis M. Hacker analyzed changing patterns of local loyalties in an address to an AASLH conference. Geographic mobility, the large and growing size of anonymous metropolitan areas, and the economic and social power of the federal government weakened "attachment" to place, he believed. The state governments, too, were "becoming less significant" in economic welfare. Local historians reacted indignantly to Hacker's arguments, yet their defense consisted in discussing how the state-based professional organizations of historians could curb the trend and encourage local history from the top down.[106]

This erosion of purely local, amateur historiography reflected the hegemony of the state history movement, its professional leadership, and the increasingly national orientation of that leadership. Local history for the most part now had to be interpreted through the national story and by state historians who took custody of local history.[107] This "national approach" contributed, along with the renewed emphasis upon professional standards and delivery of services to researchers, to a partial rapprochement between the AASLH and the academic historians. By the early 1960s, Walter Muir Whitehill had concluded a major review, *The Independent Historical Societies* (1962), that was sympathetic to professionalism and cooperation with academics. He observed with satisfaction that the "members of the parent and daughter associations" (the AHA and the AASLH) were once more "speaking the same language and understanding one another."[108]

Nevertheless, the split within professional historiography after 1940 did contribute to a further fragmentation of American history and a diminution of potential academic outreach in post–World War II America. Divorced from the economic need to make history "popular" in the community by the greater availability of university careers and lacking institutional, intellectual, and methodological connections to local history, academic historians had facilitated the emergence of the recognizably contemporary split between local history audiences and academics. Not that the separation can be attributed solely to the aloofness of academics; state and local historians forged their autonomous association in the context of achieving their own professional status. It was no longer a case of amateur versus professional but of the competing interests of different professional groups, which reflected the growing organizational focus of American life. Moreover, by encouraging transformation of the state societies in the first place, and by supplying academically trained historians to these institutions, the professors helped steer the state and local history movement away from antiquarianism and secured it for professional control.

* * *

Looking back over the twists and turns of academic relations with state and local history since the 1890s reveals one profound professional impact. The missionaries for Scientific History working at the state level helped create a new genealogy for national history. Crucial to this process was the distancing of American history from what came before the arrival of Anglo settlement. Local historians felt the need to stress a clear break with the Indian past and, in different ways, with French and Spanish settlement. Scientific historians worked within the state historical societies to achieve these aims, with much of the work accomplished by the 1920s, in the formative phase of the relationship.

Using the canons of evidence and privileging written documents, Scientific History's allies in the local and state history societies silenced vernacular readings of white-Indian relations and denounced views of the Indian past based on oral sources, legends, and myths. A secondary consideration was to downplay the contribution of Europeans who preceded Anglo occupation, because these mixed more freely with the "savage" Indians than Anglos did later. Accepting the evolutionary theory of civilization, Scientific History sought to relegate American Indian cultures to the stage of prehistory. American Indians should be studied as something past, retrievable through the techniques of the allied science of archaeology. Indeed, through the Wisconsin Archaeological Society, that work was organizationally and methodologically separate. It was just not "history."

Indian stories were treated as "romance"—representing a tragic and colorful but bygone era. This removed Indians from history into myth and tradition.[109] As early as 1900, Reuben Thwaites collected Indian stories with this agenda in mind, noting that there were "in the published annals of Wisconsin too few Indian legends, such as lend a poetic glamour to the history of many other States."[110] Historical society officials in Iowa and Minnesota also encouraged pageantry parades where local historical groups could express the "history and romance" of Indian tribes while demonstrating also the ephemeral nature of French and Indian settlement. These pageants typically "recounted the entire history" of a locality but constructed it as the progress of a community "from barbarism to civilization."[111]

The same officials denigrated amateur work that rehabilitated the historical significance and roles of Indians in the era of white contact. As superintendent of the Wisconsin State Historical Society after 1914, Milo Quaife took on this role as chief censor. He attacked writers such as Louise Houghton, author of *Our Debt to the Red Man* (1918), for "unscholarly use of historical materials and zealous devotion to a preconceived theory." She was, according to Quaife, "a passionate advocate of the Indian" who threw together "with little logical sequence incidents and facts designed to show the French and Indian strain in our population in the best possible light." In contrast to such amateur accounts, Quaife praised those with the imprimatur of state historical societies. Thomas Teakle's *The Spirit Lake Massacre* received approval because it depicted sympathetically the roles of whites in an 1857 incident that served "to clear the red man from Iowa" and thus opened the territory to "civilized development."[112]

Quaife's successor went even further in the celebration of European progress. From 1920, Superintendent Joseph Schafer pushed his ambitious project to depict the entire history of Wisconsin as the assertion of land improvement under Anglo-Americans. This, the Domesday Book project, dominated the society's work in the 1920s. Best remembered as an unflinching follower of the frontier thesis, Schafer sought to identify "the makers of all Wisconsin farms, since these were the most characteristic pioneers." On the basis of accurate information about them he proceeded to "study the process of civilization building on the foundations they laid." Schafer planned to interest ordinary people in the local history of their communities by publishing original settlement plats, in the hopes of finding a market among interested residents. The plats would be "real works of art," with "the topographical features of the township wrought into them." Schafer envisaged a popular market among landowners but also hoped that the documents would "lay a new basis for the study of western history." They would carry the original American surveyors' descriptions of the land "in its wild state" to help students in "reconstructing primitive conditions."[113] These views were similar to those of purely academic historians. Edward Potts Cheyney began the first volume of the American Nation series, *The European Background of American History,* by stating in his preface: "The history of America is a branch of that of Europe. . . . From the time of the settlement forward, the only population of

America that has counted in history has been of European origin."[114] That the views of academics and the state history movement's leaders were similar should not surprise. Both were a product of Scientific History.

* * *

By drawing a line between history and prehistory in this way—between fact and romance—professional historians denied American history great depth compared to European, and historical consciousness was thereby shaped indelibly. Note the contrast between the assertion of settlement discontinuity in the United States and the British local history movement's easier acknowledgment of its entire human past. For example, W. J. Harte commented, with respect to the town of Exeter, that there has never been a time since "the dawn of history when this hill has not been inhabited." In Exeter, he announced, "we live in the atmosphere of a long historic past, and we are proud of it."[115]

Distinctive institutional features of British academic culture gave a larger, separate space to amateur groups.[116] Two very old and dominant English universities, the absence of state universities and state archives from which to colonize local history with professionals, and a tradition of history training for civil service rather than for academic careers all allowed the field to remain open to interested nonprofessionals. The development of worker education extension activities at Ruskin College—which Charles Beard contributed to at the turn of the twentieth century—provided further examples of the vitality of alternatives to the American pattern of professional domination. Beard was not able to reproduce the Ruskin College environment in the United States, though he did try with some success to aid worker education in the 1920s.[117] Meanwhile, local history prospered in Britain, with a good deal of cooperation between amateurs and professionals. As late as the 1960s, the Cambridge Group for Population Studies, for example, relied heavily "on the painstaking researches of an army of local amateurs to produce their massive overview of English demographic trends over three centuries." Adult education units and extramural departments within the tertiary education sector nurtured local work until incorporated in mainstream history departments in universities in recent decades. Even in the 1990s, the *Local Historian,* the journal of the British Association for Local History, still partly targeted interested amateurs. To be sure, this local history tradition had come under attack by the 1980s with the restructuring of British higher education, but academic historians with an interest in the field still struggled to avoid a "damaging amateur-professional split."[118]

British conditions gave amateurs some space at the local level, but this had drawbacks because it allowed the survival of a "narrow" and more "antiquarian" view of local history than in France. It was precisely this "parochial" approach that the British Association for Local History sought to supplant in the 1990s with one "clearly indebted" to the *Annales* tradition of "local and regional studies."[119] France's different path shows advantages of professionalization when infused into local history in a different way. There, professionals gradually came to ascendancy, as in the United States, but local influences fed into national historical projects in a more reciprocal and mutually beneficial form. This relationship was previewed in an influential work of Marc Bloch's, *L'Île-de-France* (1913). There Bloch surveyed the local historical production that was the foundation of his own early work. The book is paradigmatic of the subsequent development of *Annales* scholarship in the way Bloch probed beyond official political and administrative boundaries and valued sources other than conventional historical documents. Like Jameson, Bloch understood the importance of cooperation with local historical societies possessing valuable records and resources. Both Bloch and Jameson wanted local historical societies to investigate social and economic processes rather than concentrate on genealogy.[120] Yet Bloch was more attentive to regional variation and to the problematic nature of national and provincial boundaries, since in France these had changed so often over time. Bloch was interested in the national story, to which he hoped local history could contribute, but he did not attempt to fit the latter into a national administrative and political framework. Rather, he advocated using local materials to develop a synthesis of cultural, economic, and social histories. Bloch was more inclined than Jameson to look favorably on the work of local societies and sought to encourage nonprofessionals to contribute to wider debates by focusing on topics that were geographically circumscribed but which broached wider themes. There were "perhaps too many" biographies of villages, he observed, but too few studies of "rural society."[121] Nevertheless, his attitude toward the local histories was remarkably favorable. "Historians are sometimes unjust to local societies," Bloch insisted. "Certain irregularities . . . which make them the despair of bibliographers, and more than this, the uneven quality of the work that they publish, has often caused us to forget the priceless services they have rendered and still render continuously to historical studies."[122]

Several conditions shaped French responses. One, shared with Britain, was the preexisting institutionalization of amateur traditions, and hence the importance of cooperating with these groups rather than simply supplanting them. Many of the regional societies were well established by the mid–nineteenth century, a position reinforced by "a real renaissance of [local] history study" after 1870. Groups such as the Société de l'Histoire de Paris et de l'Île-de-France (1874) included in their number historians who were to become leading scholars of the day, for example, *Revue Historique* editor Gabriel Monod. They gathered information on "inscriptions and documents from the archives" and "archaeological information."[123] Bloch felt it necessary to encourage these influential groups rather than to delegate subordinate tasks to them. In the United States, westward expansion meant that Jameson and his allies could use the newly developed western societies to outflank the older eastern amateurs in the interests of professional control.

Another difference lay in tactical capacities to incorporate popular history into a national story without risking divisiveness. The French had no need to draw a sharp line between the regional cultures of the ancien régime and the republican nation-state. The "ancien régimes" of the United States—stretching back to the Amerindian cultures and Euramerican empires—proved riskier propositions to incorporate. Equally important, divisive regional conflicts within the United States since the Revolution threatened state structures profoundly. The constitutional and racial revolution of the Civil War era that created the foundations of the modern American nation-state could not easily find its genealogy in the incorporation of that diverse history. American historians needed to transcend local racial and constitutional stories in order to build a national history. Popular historical consciousness associated with sectional and racial divisions had to be controlled in the interests of republican unity, while in France, popular forces could be mobilized in the defense of revolutionary traditions against threats to the Republic from 1870 through to the 1940s. Bloch was an ardent nationalist as well as an advocate of both local and comparative history and characteristically argued that the Revolution could be better understood as the product of conditions in an ancien régime that varied markedly in regional circumstances.[124]

A third condition was French success in creating a historical discourse that was not fragmented spatially. To a lesser degree than in the American case, where federalism prevailed, history was not divided by administrative state divisions.[125] There were exceptions to the American pattern, of course. One of the most outstanding historians of the Progressive Era provided the most intriguing possibility. Frederick Jackson Turner's *The Significance of Sections in American History* offered a parallel to Bloch's and Fernand Braudel's views of the importance of geographical forces studied regionally. Developed in the 1920s in a series of essays, Turner's work on sections stressed geographical, rather than administrative, divisions. Published posthumously, its impact was limited in comparison with the *Annales* school or Turner's earlier work on the frontier. Though the latter was an environmental interpretation, Turner used the frontier process as an ex post facto explanation for national trends and shared characteristics.[126]

Although in France professionals gained influence through the *Annales* school after World War II, they had drawn heavily upon local materials to produce their paradigm. In contrast, U.S. academics imposed on the local scene, seeking to duplicate their Scientific History in a new arena. The result was a fragmentation avoided in France, where elite historians retained prestige in public discourse despite a recent extension of jeremiads over specialization and professionalization to that country.[127] Though historiography is increasingly internationalized and historical practice has converged to a considerable extent, legacies remain in differing historiographical traditions and in the differing ways that patterns of professionalization and specialization are experienced. Within each of these diverse national historiographies, professionals tended to gain greater control over local and state historical groups, but in different ways, to different degrees, and with different results. In the case of the United States, professionalized history gained a wide public utility through its influence on state and local history practice, though its successes have entailed drawbacks in the partial estrangement of academics from local history audiences. These effects continued to haunt the profession in discussions over the state of American history's public audiences and academic responses in the 1990s.

The Forgotten

From the Fifties to the New Left and Beyond

In the wake of the New Left, the complex character of the fifties receded for a time from memory. It became the dreaded era in which intellectual torpor, anti-Communism, and consensus took over. For historians' public engagement, too, the decade has seemed a turning point, but it was never so simple. Indeed, in some ways, these years presented a high point of diverse outreach among the inheritors of the liberal Progressive tradition. Public intellectuals continued to be a prominent feature of academic life in general, and the history profession shared in the fruits of several decades of public activity. Arthur Schlesinger Jr. was the most visible figure—Pulitzer Prize winner, essayist in *Saturday Review, Atlantic, Partisan Review,* and *New Republic,* and occasional television commentator, too.[1] Becoming President Kennedy's assistant in 1961, Schlesinger attained some political, as well as intellectual, prominence. There were always rivals, but few were as active as he was from the time of *The Vital Center* (1949) through to the Kennedy campaign.[2]

Among those rivals, several deserve mention. Equally liberal was Henry Steele Commager, who became increasingly important in the 1950s and 1960s as an essayist who reflected historically on public issues from the state of the nation's schools to the corrosive effects of both television and McCarthyism.[3] Eric Goldman and Oscar Handlin won major prizes for popular works on, respectively, liberalism and the immigrant experience, and they and

Kenneth Stampp (on slavery) and C. Vann Woodward (on the New South) intervened in public debates using their historical knowledge as background to comment on current controversies. Woodward's *Strange Career of Jim Crow* (1955) spoke directly to the issue of segregation. John Hope Franklin and Woodward prepared monographs on the history of segregation for the *Brown v. Board of Education* litigation of 1954; these were used in the plaintiff's legal brief, though sociological evidence was considered more valuable by the lawyers.[4]

The cohort of scholars shaped by the postwar experience are known as consensus historians, but there was much more diversity and dissent than that label allows. Woodward, Commager, and Schlesinger championed liberalism against conservatism. Some maintained the Progressive economic interpretation, for example, Merrill Jensen, who wrote on the Revolution in terms that were more explicitly Beardian than consensual.[5] Not until the mid-1950s was there a significant shift from the Progressive view. Nor were older inheritors of that tradition, such as Merle Curti, a spent force. As AHA president in 1954, Curti called on his colleagues to maintain public engagement.[6] Most historians did not desert public debates and continued to side with the FDR-Truman tradition. Representative figures such as Schlesinger and Nevins were politically active and supported Adlai Stevenson before moving on to Kennedy in 1960.[7]

The public impact of these historians was shaped, not by sheer idealism or political willpower, but by new historical conditions. For one thing, the "ivory tower" itself was changing. The growing prestige of the major universities as centers of specialized knowledge facilitated new relations between historians and audiences. In 1953 a *Saturday Review* contributor observed that "many of the ideas, much of the information, and a large part of the attitudes of the intelligent American man in the street a generation hence are being developed on the campuses of colleges and universities today."[8] American intellectuals in this context became newly conscious of the universities' potential importance as sources of scientific and economic power and as sites for cultural criticism, a fact reflected in reports of inquiries into higher education.[9]

Equally important were changes in the publishing industry that helped to disseminate ideas. These changes promoted a wider appeal for academic writings, but not the general audiences or the democratic appeal that earlier generations had courted. Relations between historians and their audiences shifted more than before to favor the role of the historian as expert commentator. Some historians could appear, like Schlesinger and Goldman, on television, but publishing continued to provide the key platform for their work. Here there was both continuity and change. *Saturday Review, Partisan Review,* and the *New York Times Book Review* provided outlets for essayists such as Commager. For book publishing, three developments stand out. The first was the growth of a small number of prestigious commercial presses that defied the trends of the 1940s and maintained academic connections; the second was the rise of the university presses to national prominence; and the third was the paperback revolution. Some of the most prestigious of the nation's commercial publishers continued to promote the work of historians. Most notable was Harper and Row through the New American Nation Series. Edited by Commager and Richard B. Morris, this project boasted twenty-two completed volumes by 1963 out of a projected forty-seven and marshaled the work of some of the best academic historians.[10] Aside from this quasi-collective and standardized enterprise, a surprising number of prominent historians still produced at least a part of their individual output through commercial publishing houses. Handlin wrote for Little, Brown; Schlesinger for Houghton Mifflin; and Goldman, Richard Hofstadter, and Stampp for Knopf, which gave them the broader outlets of Random House and Vintage Books.

These were exceptional figures, however. The prospects for such publication were diminishing for the majority, as Dixon Wecter already showed to be the case in the late 1940s.[11] The elite who succeeded found other academics resentful of their achievements. As Goldman, one of the most successful authors, wrote after publication of his *Rendezvous with Destiny* for Knopf, "Nowadays in the academic profession, if somebody comes along and manages to get some attention to their work in the commercial press, apparently they become fair game for the frustrations of a lot of people." "Sniping" about commercial success was hardly new among academics, but Goldman believed that a "kind of defeatism" in one "wing of the academic profession" had intensified these sentiments.[12] For this reason, much more important in the reconfiguration of academic relations with their audiences was the university press as a phenomenon of growing intellectual and social significance in the 1950s.[13] Readers were, as a publisher observed in 1960, becoming "acquainted with new and varied lists of university press titles. In recent years the academies have exhibited an increasing trend to publish books that may be said to possess 'generalized special interest,' as well as scholarly monographs and reprints of documents not easily available."[14] In the second half of the 1950s, the university presses defied earlier predictions of narrowness and tackled the paperback market through special imprints. Cornell began in 1955 with its Great Seal Books, and then such presses as Chicago (Phoenix Books) and Oxford (Galaxy Books) followed. Moreover, commercial publishing houses began issuing paperback reprints of university press titles.[15]

The term "generalized special interest" indicated both the strengths and the limitations of the appeal. The paperbacks of university historians reached a (substantial) niche audience created by higher education. After initially seeking more general audiences for the new product, in the mid-1950s publishers discovered that "one of the largest segments" of demand was "the college market."[16] Both commercial and academic publishers drew thereafter on the rising numbers of college students and college-trained people in the sale of humanities titles.[17] For Oxford's Galaxy Books half the sales were in universities.[18] This specialized audience, however, could in exceptional cases be the platform for a book of much wider appeal when the topic hit the mark of contemporary political concern. An excellent example of the way university presses adapted and were able to project academic works upon a wider public was Woodward's Oxford University Press title of 1955, *The Strange Career of Jim Crow*. Reissued as a Galaxy paperback in 1957, *Strange Career* moved beyond the small academic clientele whom Woodward thought he was addressing; because of the great controversies over segregation from 1955 to 1965, the book reached a "vast, amorphous audience" and made Woodward's "public, as distinct from his professional reputation."[19]

If the paperback revolution, serious commercial publishers, the rise of university presses, and the beginning of television created new opportunities for historians to broaden their message, the message itself began to change, too. The enhanced, specialized contexts of production encouraged a new form of public intellectualism among elite historians. Historians' public engagement began to take different forms, forms that disturbed the bearers of the Progressive tradition. Most notable was an incipient detachment from the institutions of mass culture. Public outreach would in future be measured by heightened intellectual activity among a cultured elite, in which prestigious historians would comment with critical distance upon popular culture and the social movements associated with it. Academic historians with ambitions to be public intellectuals now focused on criticism of American society's political conformism and cultural blandness; they expressed distaste at the tyranny of the anti-intellectuals and recoiled from the political hysteria surrounding McCarthyism.[20] Richard Hofstadter "conceived in response to the political and intellectual condition of the 1950s" a study of anti-intellectualism in American life.[21] In his pathbreaking *The Liberal Tradition in America*, Louis Hartz found American political culture ideologically impoverished, while Schlesinger declared the intellectual "on the run" in American society after the Eisenhower victory.[22] An advocate of writing for a wider public, he worried for the rest of the decade that his colleagues had "succumbed to the homogenizing atmosphere of the age of Eisenhower" and abandoned broader engagement. Yet Schlesinger himself wrote with disdain of the popular culture of 1950s religious revivalism and criticized rising public interest in heritage as the historical equivalent of a Billy Graham revival.[23]

The paradox was that elitist types, aloof from 1950s popular culture, could at the same time be culturally significant figures—public intellectuals with high media recognition. Possibly the most representative example of the new dispensation, as well as the most talented, was Hofstadter. His first book that was aimed at a wide audience—*The American Political Tradition* (1948)—eventually reached over one million sales thanks to college adoptions.[24] Hofstadter also wrote a successful two-volume college text and, courtesy of the growing paperback revolution, his hardbacks published through Knopf became the paperback Vintage Books that sold all over the country in such unlikely locations as drugstores by the 1960s. Frequently the subject of press interviews and comment, his prodigious production, his graceful style, and the pertinence of his work to contemporary problems made him almost a cult figure. In the *New York Times Book Review* in 1955, Denis Brogan announced Hofstadter's status: "It is not often that a work of original scholarship is also a work of great topical importance." Hofstadter, Brogan argued, had examined, criticized, and replaced "some of the most popular stereotypes of recent American history, but his historical investigation has a high degree of contemporary utility." He had rethought the American past for liberals "while ignoring the tradition that serious books must be dull."[25]

Like his predecessors Beard and Nevins, Hofstadter sought to bridge the market between the popular and the scholarly without vulgarizing history, but he rejected those who, like Beard, became "entirely the publicist." Hofstadter aimed his work at "the general high grade intellectual public."[26] Like Beard he sought to address contemporary problems from a radical liberal position. Until the mid-1950s he was greatly influenced by—and in intellectual debt to—Beard, yet he had by that time departed from the Progressive tradition. Not only did he differ in his assessment of the economic interpretation of history, but he also broke from the Progressives in his position as an intellectual vis-à-vis institutions and movements for social change. He was much more the specialized and detached intellectual, secure in the university, dismissive of popular movements, and eschewing direct engagement with the machinery of government and social change.[27] His alienation was in part a reaction against McCarthyism and its excesses, considering his background as a one-time Communist in the late 1930s.[28] This experience influenced his historical interpretations. He praised the role of experts in the New Deal but dismissed the ephemeral character of much of the earlier American reform tradition in his *American Political Tradition* and *Age of Reform*.[29]

Hofstadter's intellectual detachment did not prevent him from endorsing

the expert public interventions of his colleagues. He defended the position
that one test of "intellectual responsibility might be the social usability of a
body of ideas."[30] As Leon Fink observes of the wider intellectual community,
post-Progressive historians "generally accommodated themselves to the 'process democracy' of elite rule and a passive public."[31] This made them advocates of expertise. Social realities rooted in concrete historical practice encouraged such endorsement. Despite his preference for the intellectual, Hofstadter
could not deny the important roles that historians played as expert advisers to
governments and (sometimes) corporations in the postwar world. He recognized that historical practice was diverse and that many historians were engaged in a variety of public activities—a situation which blurred the hard and
fast division between the historian as intellectual and as specialized expert. He
admitted that many fitted on either side at various times in their careers. His
attention to this matter was also connected to his desire to mediate between
the social sciences and history and make the expertise of the social scientist
available to enrich scholarship in a way that would put emphasis, not upon
complete coverage of a topic, but upon innovative interpretation. Hofstadter
saw this suspension of history between the literary arts and the social sciences
as advantageous. It allowed the historian to move easily between government
and the academy, giving opportunities "to have valuable interchanges with
many kinds of intellectual and practical activity, with politics and public
affairs, with journalism and mass media, with literature and criticism, with science, philosophy, and art, and with the social sciences."[32]

This pluralist compromise was unstable, however. In the 1960s, Hofstadter
began to despair of the possibility of bringing the roles of expert adviser and
intellectual observer together in fruitful cooperation. His own discipline was
tougher to fit into the category of policy-oriented knowledge than most of the
social sciences were. When asked to serve on a White House panel in 1964, he
replied that he could not see what skills or resources he could bring to help
frame policy analysis.[33] This rejection of history as policy was a theme he
affirmed in The Progressive Historians in 1968. "Unlike economics and sociology, history is not, in the jargon of our time, a policy science." Rather than "de-
ploring this as a limitation, we may seize upon it as a luxury."[34] As for the
broader cultural prospect, he even began to doubt the possibilities of melding
critical intellect with power altogether.[35]

The change in Hofstadter's views in the mid-1960s was brought about by
the New Left, but the Vietnam War provided the vital context. Within a few
short years the government/academic cooperation that Hofstadter had acknowledged would come under severe challenge as the practice of historians
and their values changed dramatically. Before he died in 1970 Hofstadter felt

the full force of the critique against existing historical practice that the New Left launched. In the reaction that followed against the dominant historiography, some others who were prominent in the 1950s did not fare as well intellectually as Hofstadter. But like him, they seemed to move away from direct involvement in the idea of a useful history at precisely the time that the New Left began to espouse it. In the process, many of the heirs of the older liberal Progressive tradition became the discredited, or even the forgotten.

* * *

Historical fashions change, and with them go the fates of historians. We write about the past. Most of us hope that our research has enduring value. Yet our work often fades rapidly after we pass from the scene, to be discarded in the search for new interpretations, new debates. We become the forgotten. One such historian left behind by the tides of history was Eric Goldman. He provides an example of an academic whose career coincided with the high tide of the liberal democratic state's expansion that saw historians engage with public life from the 1890s to the 1950s. No one scholar could possibly epitomize the trajectory of public engagement that I have been describing in this book. Many were more impressive as scholars. But Goldman comes close to representing the later stages of these tendencies and their fate in the turbulent decades of the 1960s. In the 1950s Goldman was a prominent figure, but by the 1970s he was almost ignored and his reputation had gone into steep decline. His work did not address the questions that historians found most engaging and thus, in graduate school, did not excite the younger generation.

Goldman was born in Washington, DC, in 1915, the city whose political life would form the basis of his enduring intellectual interests. He took his doctorate at Johns Hopkins, then taught there before moving to Princeton in 1942, where he eventually became Rollins Professor of History and remained until retirement in 1985. Goldman wrote as he believed. American reform was his main theme, particularly the urban, liberal New Deal tradition. In 1952 he published *Rendezvous with Destiny,* which celebrated the modern reform tradition and was awarded the Bancroft Prize for distinguished American history. An heir to the Progressives, he also championed their interest in contemporary history. Thus, in 1956 he published *The Crucial Decade: America, 1945–55.*[36]

As a young man in the 1930s, Goldman disparaged the idea of the cloistered intellectual life. He championed those who, like Charles Beard, responded to the urgent demands for reform. At the ripe age of twenty-one, Goldman wrote "Historians and the Ivory Tower," a defense of Beard's relativistic proposition that as the social climate changes, so too does written history.[37] Befitting his interest in history's public significance, Goldman became a staff writer on national affairs for *Time* magazine during World War II. In the postwar years, he wrote general histories of national political life. Allan Nevins's campaign to raise the standards of popular history appealed to him. He wrote for *American Heritage* and from 1962 to 1969 served as president of the Society of American Historians. Nor did Goldman ignore student audiences. He taught a popular U.S. history course at Princeton and in 1947, with Erling Hunt and Frederic Lane, completed *The World's History,* a high school text.[38] Television attracted him, too. As Goldman rose within the profession, the new medium was emerging as a powerful social force, and Goldman was right there as an advocate. He served as moderator of *The Open Mind,* an NBC show that won Emmy Awards in 1962 and 1966. Later, he worked as a commentator on CBS.[39]

Goldman served the nation-state as assiduously as he served the public. In 1953–54 he lectured for the State Department in Europe and, in 1956, in India. Though he had long written about politics and power, Goldman was thrust into political prominence only with the assassination of President Kennedy. Lyndon Johnson did not have the links with the liberal intelligentsia that Kennedy had cultivated. When Johnson sought someone to fill the role that Arthur Schlesinger Jr. had played for Kennedy, he settled on Goldman. Attached to the White House staff as "special consultant" from 1964 to 1966, Goldman's brief was to liaise with the intellectual community and thereby gain "fresh, new imaginative ideas" from the "nation's scholars and specialists." He would synthesize such input and suggest policies. Though Goldman resigned in 1966 over many policy differences with Johnson and had no misconception of his limited role in the White House, he attempted to provide historical perspective to Johnson's vision for the "Great Society." In 1969 he published *The Tragedy of Lyndon Johnson,* his account of that much-troubled administration.[40]

Goldman's achievements (and those of the more intellectually formidable Schlesinger) cannot be divorced from the alliance of historians and the nation-state cemented in the 1940s and 1950s. In this sense, Goldman was clearly a social product. Historians such as Samuel Flagg Bemis and Thomas Bailey advised the Department of State, war histories were written by academics such as Samuel Eliot Morison, and through the Committee on the Historian and the Federal Government the AHA had developed a strong interest in placing historians in the federal bureaucracy as consultants and employees. More controversially, some presidents of the AHA had, from Conyers Read in the late 1940s to Bemis in the early 1960s, championed American foreign policy and defense of the free world in the struggle against "totalitarianism." The state had also provided well for historians by mandating the special importance of their discipline within the social studies. Historians of the United States, especially, had benefited from the greater emphasis within university and school curricula placed upon knowledge of the history of the nation-state.

Officials in the Organization of American Historians valued the contacts with high officials implied by Goldman's position and that of Schlesinger. To *Journal of American History* editor Martin Ridge, appointments of historians to the White House staff seemed evidence of public "status"—a position that Frederick Jackson Turner could not see academics attaining in American political life in the 1890s.[41] No longer could it be said that historians languished without public voice. No longer could it be argued that political leaders lacked the opportunity of "a scientific acquaintance with historical politics or economics."[42] Goldman was right there in the White House to provide historical perspective. Goldman was among the beneficiaries of the improved position of history as a discipline in the 1950s and early 1960s. But quickly his influence was gone. Neither the *American Historical Review* nor the *Journal of American History* reviewed *The Tragedy of Lyndon Johnson,* and some reviewers in the wider quality press offered snide assessments.[43] Similarly, Schlesinger faced criticism for his earlier role in the White House and obfuscation of Kennedy's foreign policies.

Both suffered because of the Vietnam War and the accompanying civil unrest. The racial and social conflicts of the 1960s chipped away and then fragmented the liberal pluralist vision based on political and economic reform.[44] The war also sparked the reassertion of serious questioning of the direction of American social and racial policies, and dissent flourished. Within history, contrary interpretations had never been entirely smothered in the "consensus" of the 1950s, but now those historians who had celebrated American reform and sided with the policies of the liberal state came under attack. As Robin Winks, who himself had served in the State Department as a cultural attaché, observed, until the 1960s "it had always been regarded as legitimate for a member of the academy to work temporarily in government." But the "trauma of the sixties" erased that memory and put historians and government into opposing camps.[45] For stalwarts of the older view of government/academic links, like Goldman mentor W. Stull Holt, the years from 1968 to 1978 became the "miserable decade."[46]

As is well known, radicals repudiated the liberal historians of the 1950s for their consensus views. Those who had played down conflict in American history came to represent all historians of that era. The "consensus" construct reflected the Left's determined opposition to the established elite of historians.[47] For some of these critics, social and labor history offered a way to account for the civil unrest and to explain how and why the United States had got into the mess that it was in. Historians needed to get back to the people, many in the New Left insisted. The past must be studied from the bottom up. Diverse radical dissent as well as liberal reform had to be recognized.

From a different angle came another criticism of the liberal historians that fed into the developing critique of 1950s orthodoxy. The journal *Studies on the Left* (founded in 1959) included articles by historians who wrote in an identifiably Marxist or Marxist-derived context. This group of historians included members of the "corporate liberal school" such as James Weinstein, as well as members of the "Williams school," which was devoted to analysis of U.S. foreign policy and was established by William Appleman Williams.[48] Gabriel Kolko's *The Triumph of Conservatism* (1963) and Weinstein's work on corporate liberalism identified early Progressive reform as consolidating the modern Leviathan of the liberal state that New Left critics faced in their struggles against the Vietnam War and racism.[49]

The underlying theme in the New Left's attack was the implication of historians in the agenda of the state. The New Left attacked the state and the alliance between historians and the federal government. People like Schlesinger had "put history at the service of power," in New Left historian Jesse Lemisch's view.[50] As Howard Zinn saw it, a few prominent "court" historians such as Schlesinger and John Roche had sold out. More specific criticisms came from Noam Chomsky, who accused Schlesinger of lying about the Bay of Pigs incident and engaging in history as "colossal cynicism."[51]

Ironically, this complicity in the "warfare state" came as part of a search for relevance, a search whose objectives were close to those of the New Left. Liberal historians had become tainted by their very success at making history useful. The call for a return to a history from the bottom up was accompanied by the critique that in the 1940s and 1950s academic historians had become prisoners of a very political and conservative view of the world. Conyers Read provided an excellent example. His radio work was an attempt to widen the appeal and communication of scholarly history, but in the 1960s this achievement was forgotten. Instead, his AHA address of 1949 became emblematic of the dangers of mixing intellect and power. The Beardian advocate of public and responsive outreach to interpret the momentous events of the 1930s had in the Cold War become the bearer of embarrassing demands that historians enlist in that ideological struggle. These claims were easy for New Left historians to denounce; doing so helped them to define and develop their own version of relevant history.

When the New Left called for a return to activism, defenders of professional historiography muddied the waters further by affirming historical objectivity. They consolidated the cult of detachment that had already been observed in the 1950s. Irwin Unger's widely read critique of the New Left called for "pure history." So too did David Donald trumpet history for its own sake, and Oscar Handlin began formulating his *Truth in History,* whose message was respect for objectivity and disdain for policy-oriented historians. These responses were misleading. The de facto activism of the 1950s historical profession was partly obscured and distorted by this knee-jerk reaction to the New Left.[52]

To radicals like Staughton Lynd, these calls for truth were irrelevant to social needs. For Lynd, "the times" no longer permitted the indulgence of the detached intellectuals who could "restrict themselves to cloistered thought." It was time to "venture into the arena where political parties, and workingmen, and young people do their things seeking to clarify that experience which becomes ours as well, speaking truth to power from the vantage point of that process of struggle."[53] Lynd's call implicitly conceded the lineage of intellectual detachment that Unger and others claimed.

Yet the contrast between the pure historiography of mainstream historians and the committed, uncloistered radicals that Lynd projected was untenable. Even those prominent historians who urged intellectual detachment in the 1950s and 1960s had, in fact, practiced social and political activism through their historical writing. Handlin, for example, was involved in the support of various Jewish American causes and of the Center for the Study of Liberty. In the 1960s he was an "outspoken" supporter of American policies in Vietnam.[54] As Maldwyn Jones observed, "present-mindedness" was to "give form to most of what Handlin wrote from 1954 onward."[55] Such historians had not retreated to an ivory tower. Jesse Lemisch concluded no less in his essay "Present-Mindedness Revisited," delivered to the AHA convention in 1969. Many had asserted strongly the need to maintain public relevance for history—but they had done so by serving the nation-state and its foreign policies.[56]

Lemisch disagreed with Lynd, but he shared the view that the New Left could project an alternative form of public outreach, one that would not focus on elites or reinforce their power but rather would embrace all the people.[57] Lemisch believed that by studying objective realities scholarship could contribute to the picture of dissent and radicalism and thus help shatter the idea of a liberal consensus. Though they differed in their accounts of how New Left history should regard scholarly activism from the perspective of public audiences, both Lemisch and Lynd attacked the allegiance of the intellectuals to state-oriented history.

New Left historians also sought to broaden the predominantly political and economic agenda of the older historiography. Infused with the New Left slogan "The Personal Is Political," radical feminist and antiracist demands were reflected in the journal *Radical America* by the early 1970s.[58] The new history "from the bottom up" quickly embraced new social trends, at first feminism, civil rights, and the study of African American culture. Other specialist interests followed. Ironically, the "pure" historians became complicit in this attack on the study of economics and politics because they encouraged the professional tendency to disengage from activism—traditions that before the 1960s had centered on liberal reform of a political and economic kind.[59]

A striking case of the erosion of the older syntheses was labor history, whose strength traditionally lay in its analysis of and links with craft and industrial unions. While the attempt to embrace gender, cultural, and racial issues was essential for the broadening of labor historiography, it led to antagonism between conventional union-based history and the New Left. In a sweeping review of the new labor history published in 1972, Robert H. Zieger remained sympathetic to the older approach. He complained that "the emerging labor history" constituted an "attack upon mainstream unionism" and had weakened the consensus established by the "labor-economist historians," yet provided no new synthesis. Meanwhile, "technology diminished the manual laboring force," thus marginalizing the object of analysis of labor history as a whole. Given these circumstances, the New Left could not hope for much aid from organized labor except at the local level through personal contacts.[60]

The new social history that emerged from these fractious and complicated debates was not entirely new, but the retreat from the state was. The social history of the 1930s had drawn inspiration from the expanded activism of the American state, and historical research and employment developed in alliance with New Deal agencies. The role of government was vitally important to the discovery of popular culture and radical movements at that time. By the 1970s, younger historians wished to rediscover the history of society, but they reframed social history to focus more on the personal, the nonpolitical, and the noninstitutional. They turned to social history and neglected conventional political and economic content.

The new public history was also shaped by the battles of the 1960s. In the 1940s and 1950s, the alliance of historians and government was very much how public history was framed. Here were the antecedents of modern policy history. Yet in the 1960s and after, policy history failed to flourish despite the need for critical analysis of the state, and public history was conceived more as a response to grassroots desires than as an alliance with business or government. One wing, influenced by new radical approaches to social history, made connections with the working-class and minority social protests through importation of the British History Workshop movement idea, analyzed popular culture, studied mainstream film and television, and even spurred the making of alternative film genres.[61] This impulse included the early work of the *Radical History Review* (founded in 1975). At the same time, more traditional connections with state historical societies and universities were reasserted, and the new public history became effectively professionalized as a subdiscipline. This process was aided by the patterns of available funding.

Although the New Left history disparaged direct links with the federal government, the new social history emerging from the New Left became more dependent upon government grants. The establishment of the National Endowment for the Humanities (NEH) in 1965 gave academics a role in public history projects, since academic consultants were required under the law's funding procedures. However, this did not mean the same attachment between government and historians that certain Progressive state governments, such as Wisconsin, and the New Deal and wartime agencies had forged. These earlier traditions had involved state employees and created research projects directly reliant on government funding and administered by state and federal agencies. In the NEH, academic historians' private activities were subsidized and a certain kind of "elitism and scholasticism" was thereby encouraged.[62]

Many of the traditional alliances that history had developed in and out of the federal government were now disparaged. In (justly) accusing existing American history for racial and sexist bias, the New Left indirectly attacked the white majority and ethnics who felt included in the existing social order. Once again the task for American historians became, as it had been in the 1920s, how to incorporate the new insights of historical studies and their specialized, research-oriented agendas with older views of the American creed. This set the context for the contemporary debate. By the 1980s "diversity" had become central to professional history's agenda and yet at the same time posed new fragmentary pressures that lay behind widespread political attacks on multiculturalism.

* * *

The danger in abandoning the older historical traditions was throwing the baby out with the bathwater. The achievements of the wider cohort of academic historians shaping historical practice to the 1950s were not inconsiderable. Nor could their ideological allegiances be equated with "consensus" history. The overriding concern of professional historians had been to make history useful. On some occasions the effects were flawed, but other attempts offered hope for the future. The promise of some of these approaches was sometimes obscured in the 1960s and beyond. Contemporary debates revisit these arguments without being more than dimly aware of the precedents and the battles fought before, and without awareness of the structural conditions that shaped and are today shaping responses to such questions.

Historians often forget that the inheritance of these histories still affects us. The impact of these earlier generations is not recognized because it is so intrinsic to our practice that its outlines are almost invisible. For example, American history is far more given to the study of the recent past and contemporary events than it was before the rise of Progressive history, which also promoted the study of American history in schools. All this, and more, was a product of the historical practice studied in this book. The impacts were also interpretive and methodological. The Progressives pioneered the use of new source materials, particularly of oral history as used in the WPA narratives of the 1930s. The new social history with its focus on history from the bottom up was also pioneered in the 1930s, though its achievements were obscured by the impact of World War II in enhancing the study of diplomatic and military history and by the closer alliance of historians with the state.[63]

Such threads of continuity with earlier historical practice must be recognized. Public history provides another prominent example. This is not to assert a Whiggish brief for the unilinear development of modern public history and its distant origins in the historical practice of the first half of the twentieth century. Change must be recognized. Yet recent involvement of historians in public and applied fields did have elements of continuity with traditions of local activism that went back to the formation of the Conference of Historical Societies within the AHA in 1904, the applied-history initiatives of Benjamin Shambaugh, and the myriad of projects sponsored by the Department of Agriculture and by the New Deal. Nor did the work of historians within federal agencies cease simply because historical fashions had shifted in the 1960s. The National Park Service, the Department of Defense, and other federal agencies build upon beginnings made in the 1930s and 1940s.[64]

A further area of continuity concerns the patterns of innovation that earlier historians had displayed in dealing with mass media communication of history. Though devalued after the demise of the film and radio initiatives of the 1920s to the 1940s, these contacts also began to be rebuilt in the 1960s and beyond.[65] Historians began to reconnect with modern media, especially film. Beginning in 1959, the AHA formed a television committee and sought to find ways of harnessing film to collegiate education without sacrificing classroom teaching.[66] A major AHA project from 1967 to 1970 saw historians editing feature films for classroom use;[67] and from 1967, prominent historians such as William H. McNeill spoke on the use of film in history at the AHA conventions in sessions specially devoted to new media.[68] The first serious studies of film history by academic historians—notably Robert Sklar's research that produced *Movie-Made America* a few years later—came at the same time.[69] From the Historians' Film Committee, founded in 1970, came a group of researchers who published a newsletter that became the journal *Film and History*.[70] While the growth of the Public Broadcasting Service (PBS) network after 1969, provisions for the use of historian consultants for documentary films funded by the NEH, and expansion of cable television in the 1980s would spur further cinematic interests in the 1990s, historians did not suddenly rediscover film then. They were already doing so in this period of transition in the 1960s.

Even for history teaching, the profession's neglect since the mid-1950s should not be exaggerated. A minority always remained concerned with schools, but the formation of the AHA Teaching Division in 1974 and the report of Richard Kirkendall on history enrollments for the Organization of American Historians published in 1975 signaled a turning point. It was principally, however, the decline of college-level history majors as a proportion of the enlarged college cohort in the late 1960s and early 1970s as sociology and psychology surged ahead that brought home the threat to history as a discipline and started reengagement with the schools.[71]

One would expect such elements of continuity in public outreach—and more than the contemporary debate reveals—because historical practice has always been a social product, influenced by long-term historical forces. In the United States, it has developed within a particular intellectual setting and in response to external political, social, and cultural pressures, not just the internal forces of professional discourse. It is equally important to recognize that historical practice has undergone several waves of change in response to perceived crises that occurred from the 1890s to the 1990s. In each of these waves historians have sought to deal with questions of popularization and overspecialization and to move beyond elitist constraints to incorporate new social movements and conditions.

These waves of change reveal a model of historical practice. A succession of technology revolutions changed audiences for history. At each new development, new technologies raised anxieties about the roles of academics and popular history making, just as the Internet does at the beginning of the twenty-first century. Prior to the 1960s, the impact of these technological changes was absorbed and to some extent contained. Historical practice was reformed, but it was not changed in revolutionary ways.

A key factor in explaining the patterns of influence that historians exerted—and their limits—is the structure of the profession. The decentralized and competitive university system played a role but so too did diversity and complexity within professional institutions. The profession was not

monolithic, a feature that discouraged revolutionary change in historical practice and made cohesive action often difficult but that also served as a strength.
The diffusion of power between the AHA and the MVHA extended professional influence by allowing the MVHA to mediate between the AHA and the
local and state history groups and teachers. Also part of this complex pattern
was a third tier—the local and state societies that became professionalized
themselves, a development which, however, marginalized amateurs and local
history groups.

This study has sought to put in perspective contemporary criticisms of
American professional historiographical traditions. Historical objectivity was
an important goal of historians, but it was not their only concern. The disciplinary discourse never put history in a rigid straightjacket. Scientific History was
challenged by Progressives, who sought with some effect to reconnect with
wider audiences; combat excessive specialization; apply history to the pressing
social problems after 1900 through government agencies and policies; and
make the teaching of history more relevant to the lives of the more democratized schools after 1920. Attempts were also made to revive state and local history and put it on a more professional and yet more "popular" basis.

One might take a comforting message from this review of the history of
historical practice. The earlier occurrence of similar jeremiads indicates a misplaced rhetoric of anxiety within the profession over long periods of time.
This anxiety reflected the aspirations of historians toward a universal historical problematic that would meet the challenge of specialization and extend
the political and social position of historians within the academy and the wider
society. Although the tradition of the jeremiad has repeatedly distorted the position of American historiography, it would be a mistake to derive a purely positive message of restored confidence in professionalism from this record. One
must identify the features that were useful in those earlier traditions but that
remain absent or underemphasized in modern historiography.

A distinctive intellectual content was vital in extending professional historiography's influence. This agenda remains worthy of attention on several
fronts. The most impressive feature was the engagement with economic history and its connections to politics—in effect, this interest served as a treatment of the state, though a relatively nontheoretical one, uninfluenced by
Marxism. Since the mid-1960s this older politico-economic tradition has been
increasingly neglected in favor of social history, then cultural history and cultural theory. The rise in the 1970s of the new economic history and its methods of econometrics seemed somewhat forbidding or dubious to many historians, and its reliance on abstract models of economic theory did not impress

them either. In the polarized academic climate that resulted, the wider area of the politics of the economy tended to get lost on both sides.[72]

Although some scholars work on the history of the American state—usually in political science or sociology—and on economic history, these topics have only on rare occasions since the 1960s been convincingly integrated into broader debates about American history, which have tended to revolve around cultural and social history. The example of the Progressive paradigm and its influence suggest a need to make each of these topics central to the reconstruction of more general frameworks of American historiography.

A related theme is the question of synthesis. The achievements of US historiography were closely linked with traditions of narrative synthesis that flourished before the 1950s. The role of the Progressive paradigm in providing a comprehensive structure for public outreach from the turn of the century has been demonstrated in this study. In the interwar years, especially, narratives structured around the Progressive interpretation supplied a general framework within which teaching, research, and outreach in the fields of state and applied history, and publishing for wider audiences, could be deployed. The power of this interpretive framework reached its zenith in the Beards' *Rise of American Civilization* and *America in Midpassage* but was also seen in cooperative historical projects and in many college and school textbooks. Even the more politically conservative Samuel Eliot Morison located his work within the "Jackson to FDR" reform tradition, thus acknowledging the hegemony of this interpretation in the first half of the twentieth century.[73] Before World War II, Allen Nevins was also subject to the same intellectual influence incorporating the social and economic history of the American people within liberal democratic progress.[74]

These narratives have been fondly recalled in an age of specialization since the 1970s, yet discontinuity must also be appreciated. Special conditions allowed the Progressives' historical syntheses to counter diversity. Compelling narratives that underpinned a shared research and outreach project were facilitated by the trajectory of the nation-state, which coincided with the agenda of professionalizing historical discourse. State-based Progressivism encouraged the fertile environment of applied, state, and local history that informed the work of Turner, agricultural historians, and many others. The narratives produced by Beard and his followers in the 1930s did not emerge out of thin air either. They developed in the context of an evolving historical practice. They were themselves the product of institutional structures and of political and intellectual circumstances that shaped a historiography that valued public intervention and that shared a coherent agenda of political and economic reform to provide a guiding path for research and teaching. Since the 1950s, research, teaching, and outreach agendas have become more specialized, and there is less communication between them than before that time. This book has described and explained how those changes came about. Thus, the material circumstances that would encourage an overarching paradigm have been partly missing since that time. Yet traditions and links were never entirely lost, and there were signs of change in the 1990s in the efforts of the organizers of historical conferences, editors of journals, and leaders of professional organizations to seek once more the broader implications of their work—efforts that recalled earlier achievements. That work involves synthesizing the democratic potential of the newer forms of specialized history with the older focus on the public institutional networks of the Progressives.[75]

At the same time, cautionary aspects of this tale must be recalled. Whether dealing with federal government agencies, textbooks, films, radio, school curricula, or historical societies, historians seeking larger audiences confronted uncomfortable realities. Powerful interests, lobby groups, and fractious and diverse constituencies far removed from the tenor of academic interpretation impinged upon their activities. Attempts to court genealogical and patriotic societies, for example, produced friction and disillusionment. Academic historians faced opposition because of their critical perspectives on the past long before the current culture wars. But the unpalatable alternative to analytical and critical approaches was retrogression to a patriotic historiography such as had dominated American popular culture in the nineteenth century—and one that reflected dominant classes and races.

* * *

In all, the record presents a mixed picture of continuity and change, of achievement and failure. In the light of this complex legacy, any common assumptions concerning professional historical "decline," fragmentation, and disengagement have to be severely qualified. Neither professionalization nor the discourse of history and its quest for objectivity automatically or inexorably widened the distance of academics from their audiences. In the early and middle decades of the twentieth century, academic historians were able to forge wider links, in some cases despite—in others because of—their professional discourse. There was much more variety and variability in historians' responses to public issues than is usually understood. Historians shaped a more professionalized practice and were partly successful in spreading the influence of this practice to specific but changing audiences. But these gains came at costs. American history gained heightened political significance; it became an intensely contested field, more closely tied to the state, understood as a set of political institutions of governance and control, and to political and national history.

American historiography remains contested and controversial; yet in the contemporary debates there is much continuity with—and much to learn from—the period from the 1890s to the 1950s. In those decades American historians forged their strong traditions. They helped to create useful histories. Today, historians concerned that their discipline has lost its intellectual way cannot simply copy their work, which was done in different circumstances. But these earlier efforts merit reflection, respect, criticism, and perhaps emulation at another time of perceived crisis for history.

NOTES

Prologue

1. "As a Historian's Fame Grows, So Do Questions on Methods," *NYT,* 11 January 2002, A1, A19.

2. Roger Rosenblatt, "Essay: A Writer's Mind," *NewsHour with Jim Lehrer,* 17 January 2002, http://www.pbs.org/newshour/essays/jan-june02/writers _1-17.html (accessed 29 September 2002); CNN, 7:45 P.M. (Pacific daylight time), 10 January 2002. For the History Channel, see Brian Taves, "The History Channel and the Challenge of Historical Programming," in Gary R. Edgerton and Peter C. Rollins, eds., *Television Histories: Shaping Collective Memory in the Media Age* (Lexington: University Press of Kentucky, 1999), 261–81.

3. Kenneth T. Jackson, "The Power of History: The Weakness of a Profession," *JAH,* 88 (March 2002), 1299–1314.

4. Robert Townsend, "History and the Future of Scholarly Publishing," *Perspectives,* October 2003, 35.

5. Sharon Strover, "United States: Cable Television," http://www.museum .tv/ archives/etv/U/htmlU/unitedstatesc/unitedstatesc.htm (accessed 14 June 2004); Taves, "History Channel," 261–81.

6. Ian Tyrrell, *The Absent Marx: Class Analysis and Liberal History in Twentieth-Century America* (Westport, CT: Greenwood Press, 1986), chaps. 1–2.

7. Michael Kammen, *Mystic Chords of Memory: The Transformation of Tradition in American Culture* (New York: Knopf, 1991).

8. Peter Novick, *That Noble Dream: The "Objectivity Question" and the American Historical Profession* (New York: Cambridge University Press, 1988).

9. John Bodnar, *Remaking America: Public Memory, Commemoration, and Patriotism in the Twentieth Century* (Princeton: Princeton University Press,

1992), 251; David Glassberg, *American Historical Pageantry: The Uses of Tradition in the Early Twentieth Century* (Chapel Hill: University of North Carolina Press, 1990); David W. Blight, *Race and Reunion: The Civil War in American Memory* (Cambridge: Belknap Press, Harvard University Press, 2001); Gaines Foster, *Ghosts of the Confederacy: Defeat, the Lost Cause, and the Emergence of the New South, 1865 to 1913* (New York: Oxford University Press, 1986); "The Practice of American History: A Special Issue," *JAH*, 81 (December 1994).

10. John Bodnar, ed., *Bonds of Affection: Americans Define Their Patriotism* (Princeton: Princeton University Press, 1996); Roy Rosenzweig and David Thelen, *The Presence of the Past: Popular Uses of History in American Life* (New York: Columbia University Press, 1998); John R. Gillis, ed., *Commemorations: The Politics of National Identity* (Princeton: Princeton University Press, 1994).

11. Gary Nash, Charlotte E. Crabtree, and Ross E. Dunn, *History on Trial: Culture Wars and the Teaching of the Past* (New York: Knopf, 1998); Jonathan Zimmerman, *Whose America? Culture Wars in the Public Schools* (Cambridge: Harvard University Press, 2002).

12. Ellen Fitzpatrick, *History's Memory: Writing America's Past, 1880–1980* (Cambridge: Harvard University Press, 2002).

13. Edgerton and Rollins, *Television Histories.* On applied history, see Rebecca Conrad, *Benjamin Shambaugh and the Intellectual Foundations of Public History* (Iowa City: University of Iowa Press, 2002).

14. Antonio Gramsci, "The Formation of Intellectuals," in Gramsci, *The Modern Prince and Other Writings* (New York: International Publishers, 1957), 118–25. There is an expanding literature helping to track shifts in the roles of public intellectuals. See Russell Jacoby, *The Last Intellectuals: American Culture in the Age of Academe* (New York: Basic Books, 1987); Thomas Bender, *New York Intellect: A History of Intellectual Life in New York City, from 1750 to the Beginnings of Our Own Time* (New York: Alfred A. Knopf, 1987), chap. 8; Leon Fink, *Progressive Intellectuals and the Dilemma of Democratic Commitment* (Cambridge: Harvard University Press, 1997); Leon Fink, Stephen T. Leonard, and Donald M. Reid, eds., *Intellectuals and Public Life: Between Radicalism and Reform* (Ithaca: Cornell University Press, 1996); Richard A. Posner, *Public Intellectuals: A Study of Decline* (Cambridge: Harvard University Press, 2001); Thomas Bender, *Intellect and Public Life: Essays on the Social History of Academic Intellectuals in the United States* (Baltimore: Johns Hopkins University Press, 1993); Tevi Troy, *Intellectuals and the American Presidency: Philosophers, Jesters, or Technicians?* (Lanham, MD: Rowman and Littlefield, 2002).

Chapter One

1. *NYT,* 8 May 1998, http://www.polisci.ucla.edu/faculty/trachtenberg/histsoc/nyt.html; Elizabeth Fox-Genovese and Elizabeth Lasch-Quinn, eds., *Reconstructing History: The Emergence of a New Historical Society* (New York: Routledge, 1999). The Historical Society also publishes its own *Journal of the Historical Society* and maintains a Web site. See http://www.bu.edu/historic/journal.html.

2. Allan Bloom, *The Closing of the American Mind* (New York: Simon and Schuster, 1987); E. D. Hirsch, *Cultural Literacy: What Every American Needs to Know* (Boston: Houghton Mifflin, 1987).

3. Arthur M. Schlesinger Jr., *The Disuniting of America* (New York: W. W. Norton, 1992), 127, 137–38.

4. Ibid., 99, 123, 127.

5. *Time*, 3 February 1992, 82, 85.

6. See Stephen J. Summerhill and John Alexander Williams, *Sinking Columbus: Contested History, Cultural Politics, and Mythmaking during the Quincentenary* (Gainesville: University Press of Florida, 2000).

7. *Time*, 7 October 1991, 52.

8. Kirkpatrick Sale, *The Conquest of Paradise: Christopher Columbus and the Columbian Legacy* (1990; repr., London: Hodder and Staughton, 1991); *Time*, 3 Feb. 1992, 86.

9. Summerhill and Williams, *Sinking Columbus*, 119.

10. W. H. McNeill, "Why Study History? Three Historians Respond," in Paul Gagnon and the Bradley Commission on History in Schools, *Historical Literacy: The Case for History in American Education* (Boston: Houghton Mifflin, 1989), 107.

11. C. Vann Woodward, "A Short History of American History," *NYTBR*, 8 August 1982, reprinted in Woodward, *The Future of the Past* (New York: Oxford University Press, 1989), 320.

12. Eugene Genovese and Elizabeth Fox-Genovese, "The Political Crisis of Social History," *Journal of Social History*, 10 (Winter 1976), 205–20; Lawrence Stone, "The Revival of Narrative: Reflections on a New Old History," *Past and Present*, no. 85 (November 1979), 3–24; Woodward, "Short History," 320–21.

13. Thomas Bender, "Wholes and Parts: The Need for Synthesis in American History," *JAH*, 73 (June 1986), 120–36; David Thelen, ed., "A Round Table: Synthesis in American History," *JAH*, 74 (June 1987), 108–30.

14. Eric H. Monkkonen, "The Dangers of Synthesis," *AHR*, 91 (October 1986), 1148. Monkkonen's position reflected, it should be noted, that of the then-prestigious social science history, whose practitioners believed these disciplinary trends were inevitable.

15. Gertrude Himmelfarb, *The New History and the Old: Critical Essays and Reappraisals* (Cambridge: Belknap Press, Harvard University Press, 1987); Joan Scott, review in *AHR*, 92 (October 1987), 699–700; Wayne Urban, review in *JAH*, 75 (December 1988), 869–74.

16. Peter Novick, *That Noble Dream: The "Objectivity Question" and the American Historical Profession* (New York: Cambridge University Press, 1988), chap. 16.

17. See, e.g., Thomas L. Haskell, "Objectivity Is Not Neutrality: Rhetoric vs. Practice in Peter Novick's *That Noble Dream*," *History and Theory*, 29, no. 2 (1990), 153–57; James T. Kloppenberg, "Objectivity and Historicism: A Century of American Historical Writing," *AHR*, 94 (October 1989), 1011–30. Alan Megill called for "a critical pluralism, for standards of evaluation appropriate to the forms of knowledge being sought." See Alan Megill, "Recounting the Past: 'Description,' Explanation, and Narrative in Historiography," *AHR*, 94 (June 1989), 627–53, quotation at 653.

18. Richard W. Fox, "Public Culture and the Problem of Synthesis," *JAH*, 74 (June 1987), 115.

19. Darrett Rutman, "Comment," *AHR*, 84 (December 1979), 1324.

20. Russell Jacoby, *The Last Intellectuals: American Culture in the Age of Academe* (New York: Basic Books, 1987).

21. Elizabeth Lasch-Quinn, "Democracy in the Ivory Tower? Toward the Restoration

of an Intellectual Community," in Fox-Genovese and Lasch-Quinn, *Reconstructing History,* 28, 29, 30.

22. Theodore Hamerow, "The Bureaucratization of History," *AHR,* 94 (June 1989), 654–60, quotation at 656.

23. Louis R. Harlan, "The Future of the American Historical Association," *AHR, 95* (February 1990), 3, 5.

24. Roy Rosenzweig and David Thelen, *The Presence of the Past: Popular Uses of History in American Life* (New York: Columbia University Press, 1998); Michael Frisch, "American History and the Structure of Collective Memory: A Modest Exercise in Empirical Iconography," in Frisch, *A Shared Authority: Essays on the Craft and Meaning of Oral and Public History* (Albany: State University of New York Press, 1990), 29–54; Susan Porter Benson, Stephen Brier, and Roy Rosenzweig, eds., *Presenting the Past: Essays on History and the Public* (Philadelphia: Temple University Press, 1980).

25. Joyce Appleby, Lynn Hunt, and Margaret Jacob, *Telling the Truth about History* (New York: Norton, 1994); Richard Evans, *In Defence of History* (London: Granta, 1997).

26. Patrick Joyce, "The Return of History: Postmodernism and the Politics of Academic History," *Past and Present,* no. 158 (February 1996), 207–35.

27. Haskell, "Objectivity Is Not Neutrality," 153–57; Appleby, Hunt, and Jacob, *Telling the Truth about History;* Joyce Appleby, "One Good Turn Deserves Another: Moving beyond the Linguistic: A Response to David Harlan," *AHR,* 94 (December 1989), 1326–33; David Hollinger, "The Return of the Prodigal: The Persistence of Historical Knowing," *AHR,* 94 (June 1989), 610–21, esp. 611. For a review of the literature and an attempt to mediate the many contending positions, see Robert F. Berkhofer Jr., *Beyond the Great Story: History as Text and Discourse* (Cambridge: Belknap Press, Harvard University Press, 1995).

28. Robert Archibald, review in *AHR,* 105 (April 2000), 511–12; symposium on *The Presence of the Past,* in *Public Historian,* 22 (Winter 2000), 15–44.

29. Otis Graham, "Dealing Ourselves Back In: Professional Historians and the Public," *Public Historian,* 22 (Winter 2000), 27–29.

30. Michael Kammen, "Carl Becker Redivivus; Or, Is Everyone Really a Historian?" *History and Theory,* 39 (May 2000), 230–42, quotation at 239.

31. Ronald Grele, "Clio on the Road to Damascus: A National Survey of History as Activity and Experience," *Public Historian,* 22 (Winter 2000), 31–34.

32. Gary Nash, Charlotte E. Crabtree, and Ross E. Dunn, *History on Trial: Culture Wars and the Teaching of the Past* (New York: Knopf, 1998), 158.

33. Michael Wallace, "Culture War, History Front," in Tom Engelhardt and Edward T. Linenthal, eds., *History Wars: The "Enola Gay" and Other Battles for the American Past* (New York: Henry Holt, 1996), 181.

34. Edward T. Linenthal, "Anatomy of a Controversy," in ibid., 52.

35. Tom Engelhardt and Edward T. Linenthal, "Introduction: History under Siege," in ibid., 5.

36. Richard Kohn, "History and the Culture Wars: The Case of the Smithsonian Institution's *Enola Gay* Exhibition," *JAH,* 82 (December 1995), 1036.

37. Victor Davis Hanson, "The Dilemmas of the Contemporary Military Historian," in Fox-Genovese and Lasch-Quinn, *Reconstructing History,* 194.

38. Kohn, "History and the Culture Wars," 1062–63. For Thomas Woods the lesson was the need for historians to represent the views of veterans' groups in the historians' diverse interpretations. See Thomas A. Woods, "Museums and the Public: Doing History Together," *JAH*, 82 (December 1995), 1111–15. *Journal of American History* editor David Thelen believed that historians must engage veterans' groups in a conversation. See David Thelen, "History after the *Enola Gay* Controversy," *JAH*, 82 (December 1995), 1034.

39. Engelhardt and Linenthal, "Introduction," 5.

40. Sean Wilentz, "Clio Banished? Battles over History in the Schools," in Fox-Genovese and Lasch-Quinn, *Reconstructing History*, 283.

41. Michael A. Bellesiles, *Arming America: The Origins of a National Gun Culture* (New York: Knopf, 2000); Western Missouri Shooters Alliance, http://www.wmsa.net/bellesiles.htm (accessed 6 August 2002); Kimberley Strassel, "Academic Accountability," *Wall Street Journal*, 6 June 2002, http://www.opinionjournal.com/columnists/kstrassel/?id.110001806 (accessed 6 August 2002); see also Tanya Metaksa, "Arming America: A Recognized Fraud," FrontPageMagazine.com, 5 March 2002, http://www.frontpagemag.com/Articles/ (accessed 16 October 2002).

42. Strassel, "Academic Accountability." These complicated relationships were further illustrated in the connections developing after 2000 between Senator Robert Byrd and the American Historical Association. The latter awarded Byrd a special lifetime achievement award in 2004. Since passage of the bill in 2001 in which Congress approved Byrd's Teaching American History grant program, "vast amounts of federal money" had been "flowing into history education," much to the approval of academics. See "History, Democracy, and Citizenship: The Debate over History's Role in Teaching Citizenship and Patriotism," Organization of American Historians Report, http://www.oah.org/reports/tradhist.html. Yet this funding centered on American history, not all fields, and on precollegiate education. Moreover, the subsequent George W. Bush initiative to promote the teaching of American history was welcomed by professionals, but Bush chose a well-known nonacademic, David McCullough, to accompany him during the announcement. The Organization of American Historians found it "deeply disturbing" that the chief professional organizations were not invited to participate in the "formulation of the presidential initiative." Ira Berlin and Lee W. Formwalt, "White House Initiative on American History," http://www.oah.org/pubs/nl/nov02/initiatives.html (accessed 3 June 2004).

43. Bloom, *Closing of the American Mind;* Hirsch, *Cultural Literacy.*

44. Sam Hillard cited in Karen J. Winkler, "New Breed of Scholar Works the Territory That Lies between History and Geography," *Chronicle of Higher Education*, 33, no. 4 (1986), 6–7.

45. Sheldon Stryker, "Editor's Comments," *American Sociological Review*, 47 (February 1982), iii.

46. Herbert J. Gans, "Sociology in America: The Discipline and the Public," *American Sociological Review*, 54 (February 1989), 1–16, quotation at 6.

47. Tony Becher, "Historians on History," *Studies in Higher Education*, 14, no. 3 (1989), 268, 272.

48. Robert Kelley, Communication, *AHR*, 93 (February 1988), 284.

49. Simon Schama, "History and the Imagination of Our Hearts," *Guardian Weekly*, 6 October 1991, 22. See also Harlan, "Future of the American Historical Association," 3, 5.

50. David Cannadine, "The State of British History," *Times Literary Supplement,* 10 October 1986, 1139.

51. Georges Duby, *History Continues* (Chicago: University of Chicago Press, 1994), 109.

52. Stephen Alomes, "The Nature of Australian Studies," *Journal of Australian Studies,* no. 30 (September 1991), 14.

Chapter Two

1. Quotation from Lucy Salmon to Evarts B. Greene, 15 December 1917, box 251, Appointments, 1916–17 file, AHA Papers, LC; see also Salmon to Greene, 16 December 1916, ibid.

2. Charles McLean Andrews, "Some Recent Aspects of Institutional Study," *Yale Review,* 1 (February 1893), 393.

3. William Milligan Sloane, "History and Democracy," *AHR,* 1 (October 1895), 3, 9, 16–19, quotation at 9.

4. Quotations from Lucy Salmon to Evarts B. Greene, 15 December 1917, box 251, Appointments, 1916–17 file, AHA Papers; see also Salmon to Greene, 16 December 1916, ibid.

5. Andrews, "Some Recent Aspects of Institutional Study," 392, 393, 409.

6. Sloane, "History and Democracy," 3, 16–19.

7. John Franklin Jameson, "A New American Historical Journal" [1918], reprinted in Morey D. Rothberg and Jacqueline Goggin, eds., *John Franklin Jameson and the Development of Humanistic Scholarship in America,* vol. 1, *Selected Essays* (Athens: University of Georgia Press, 1993), 335–37, quotation at 336.

8. John Franklin Jameson's metaphor is mentioned in John Higham et al., *History: The Development of Historical Studies in the United States* (Englewood Cliffs, NJ: Prentice-Hall, 1965), 25.

9. Jameson, "New American Historical Journal," 335.

10. Ibid.; Morey D. Rothberg, " 'To Set a Standard of Workmanship and Compel Men to Adhere to It': John Franklin Jameson as Editor of the *American Historical Review,*" *AHR,* 89 (October 1984), 961.

11. Jameson, "New American Historical Journal," 336.

12. Joseph Schafer to John Franklin Jameson, 24 March 1925, box 126, file 1492, John Franklin Jameson Papers, LC.

13. "Report of the Meeting of the American Historical Association at New Orleans," *AHR,* 9 (April 1904), 451. Fear of religious sectarianism within the profession may also have contributed to the disbanding of the Church History section: Secretary of the Conference of Historical Societies, Augustus Shearer, to AHA, undated [1917], box 471, Conference of Historical Societies file, AHA Papers.

14. Jameson to Clarence Alvord, 10 November 1916, box 113, file 1155, Jameson Papers.

15. Jameson to Woodson, 17 May 1916, box 55, file 124, ibid.

16. August Meier and Elliott Rudwick, *Black History and the Historical Profession: 1915–1960* (Urbana: University of Illinois Press, 1986), 35, 28.

17. Jameson, "New American Historical Journal," 336, quotation at 335. See also Jameson to Woodson, 24 June 1916, box 55, file 124, Jameson Papers.

18. David D. Van Tassel and James A. Tinsley, "Historical Organizations as Aids to History," in W. Hesseltine and Donald R. McNeil, eds., *In Support of Clio: Essays in Memory of Herbert A. Kellar* (Madison: State Historical Society of Wisconsin, 1958), 139.

19. "Suggested Objectives and Policies of the Industrial History Society" [11 February 1940], box 104, file 10, Herbert Kellar Papers, SHSW, Madison, WI.

20. Van Tassel and Tinsley, "Historical Organizations as Aids to History," 140.

21. Herbert Kellar, "The Historian and Life," *MVHR*, 34 (June 1947), 25, 29; Van Tassel and Tinsley, "Historical Organizations as Aids to History," 139.

22. "How the Public Received the *Journal of Negro History*," *Journal of Negro History*, 1 (April 1916), 225–32, quotation at 230.

23. Julie Des Jardins, *Women and the Historical Enterprise in America: Gender, Race, and the Politics of Memory, 1880–1945* (Chapel Hill: University of North Carolina Press, 2003), 219–25; see also Ellen Fitzpatrick, *History's Memory: Writing America's Past, 1880–1980* (Cambridge: Harvard University Press, 2002).

24. U. B. Phillips [1904], quoted in Merton E. Dillon, *Ulrich Bonnell Phillips: Historian of the Old South* (Baton Rouge: Louisiana State University Press, 1985), 54.

25. Charles Beard, *A Charter for the Social Sciences* (New York: Charles Scribner's Sons, 1932), 19.

26. Arthur Schlesinger Sr., "History," in Wilson Gee, ed., *Research in the Social Sciences: Its Fundamental Methods and Objectives* (New York: Macmillan, 1927), 215.

27. Kellar, "The Historian and Life," 25.

28. Fitzpatrick, *History's Memory*, esp. 182–83; Vera Shlakman, *Economic History of a Factory Town: A Study of Chicopee, Massachusetts* (1934; repr., New York: Octagon Books, 1969); Norman Ware, *The Industrial Worker, 1840–1860: The Reaction of American Industrial Society to the Advance of the Industrial Revolution* (1924; repr., Chicago: Quadrangle Books, 1964).

29. The first clear stirring against the institutional economists' domination came in the work of Henry David. See the report of the AHA annual meeting in Jesse D. Clarkson, "Escape to the Present," *AHR*, 46 (April 1941), 545, 547; Henry David, *History of the Haymarket Affair* (New York: Farrar and Reinhart, 1936).

30. Louis B. Schmidt, "The Economic History of American Agriculture as a Field of Study," *MVHR*, 3 (June 1916), 39–49; Louis B. Schmidt, "An Unworked Field in Mississippi Valley History," *Iowa Journal of History and Politics*, 21 (January 1923), 94–111.

31. Nils Olsen to J. F. Jameson, 25 May 1921, box 46, file 25, Jameson Papers; Lyman Carrier to Jameson, 15 February 1921, ibid.; Program of the Annual Meeting of the Agricultural History Society, 1923, ibid.; Jameson to Joseph Schafer, 25 March 1926, box 126, file 1492, ibid.; O. C. Stine to P. W. Washington, 26 April 1929, box 80, Agricultural History Society file, AHA Papers.

32. "Proposal to Form an Industrial History Society," 6 December 1939, box 104, file 6, Kellar Papers; Herbert Heaton, "Recent Developments in Economic History," *AHR*, 47 (July 1942), 725–27.

33. Dexter Perkins, "Aids to Historical Research and Publication," *AHR*, 34 (January

1929), 275–80; Richard D. Younger, "Foundations and the Study of History," in Hesseltine and McNeil, *In Support of Clio*, 111–16; William B. Hesseltine and Louis Kaplan, "Doctors of Philosophy in History: A Statistical Study," *AHR*, 47 (July 1942), 772–73.

34. John U. Nef, "Historians and Social Scientists: Both Have a Contribution," *SRL*, 16 September 1944, 16. See also John U. Nef, *Search for Meaning: The Autobiography of a Non-conformist* (Washington, DC: Public Affairs Press, 1973).

35. Frederick Jackson Turner, *The Significance of Sections in American History* (1932; repr., Gloucester, MA: Peter Smith, 1959). For New England, see Gregory M. Pfitzer, *Samuel Eliot Morison's Historical World: In Quest of a New Parkman* (Boston: Northeastern University Press, 1991), xix, 138–40. There was a modestly prosouthern tone in much professional historical writing on the South and revisionist accounts of the Civil War era in the 1930s. See Don E. Fehrenbacher, "Division and Reunion," in John Higham, ed., *The Reconstruction of American History* (New York: Harper and Row, 1962), 112; Thomas Pressly, *Americans Interpret Their Civil War* (1954; repr., New York: Free Press, 1962), 283–84. For southern history's vernacular traditions, see David W. Blight, *Race and Reunion: The Civil War in American Memory* (Cambridge: Belknap Press, Harvard University Press, 2001).

36. Ellen Fitzpatrick, "Caroline F. Ware and the Cultural Approach to History," *American Quarterly*, 43 (June 1991), 175; Fitzpatrick, *History's Memory*, 185–87.

37. Clarkson, "Escape to the Present," 545, 547.

38. The Editors, "Educating Clio," *AHR* 45 (April 1940), 516; the Editors, "History and Historians at Chicago," *AHR*, 44 (April 1939), 481.

39. Charles Beard, "Written History as an Act of Faith," *AHR*, 39 (January 1934), 21–24.

40. Caroline F. Ware, ed., *The Cultural Approach to History* (New York: Columbia University Press, 1940), 6. See also Fitzpatrick, "Caroline F. Ware and the Cultural Approach to History," 175.

41. *NR*, 8 January 1936, 260, quotation at 261; see also *NR*, 2 August 1939, 365; W. E. B. Du Bois, "Stealing a Continent," *NR*, 24 June 1936, 210; Edgar Johnson, "American Mosaic," *NR*, 3 March 1937, 115–16.

42. B. Lamar Johnson, "Needed: A Doctor's Degree for General Education," *Journal of Higher Education*, 10 (February 1939), 75–78.

43. John C. Granbery, "The Ph.D. Superstition," *Journal of the National Education Association*, 26 (December 1937), 305.

44. A. Howard Meneely, "Graduate Training in History," *SE*, 5 (January 1941), 31, 32.

45. Guy S. Ford to Waldo Leland, 25 May 1943, box 133, American Council of Learned Societies file, AHA Papers.

46. Theodore Blegen, "Our Widening Province," *MVHR*, 31 (June 1944), 18.

47. The Editors, "The Association at Providence," *AHR*, 42 (April 1937), 421.

48. Ibid.; William E. Lingelbach, ed., *Approaches to American Social History* (New York: D. Appleton and Co., 1937).

49. The Editors, "Association at Providence," 423.

50. Howard Mumford Jones, "What's the Matter with Literary Scholarship?" *SRL*, 18 March 1939, 3.

51. Allan Nevins, *The Gateway to History* (New York: D. Appleton and Co., 1938), 366.

52. Robert L. Schuyler, "Some Historical Idols," *Political Science Quarterly,* 47 (March 1932), 7, 16; Clarkson, "Escape to the Present," 559; Solon Buck to R. L. Schuyler, 3 April 1941, box 19, file Sa–Se, Solon Buck Papers, LC.

53. Hesseltine and Kaplan, "Doctors of Philosophy in History," 765–800; William L. Sachse, "Echoes from Chicago," *AHR,* 47 (April 1942), quotation at 487.

54. Guy Stanton Ford, "Tomorrow and Higher Education," p. 12, address at the Second Alumnae Institute of Government and Higher Education, University of Minnesota, 6 May 1944, box 144, G.S.F. Speeches file, AHA Papers.

55. Robert A. McCaughey, *International Studies and Academic Enterprise: A Chapter in the Enclosure of American Learning* (New York: Columbia University Press, 1984).

56. Richard H. Shryock, "American Historiography: A Critical Analysis and a Program," *Proceedings of the American Philosophical Society,* 87 (July 1943), 46; Robert S. Lynd, *Knowledge for What? The Place of Social Science in American Culture* (Princeton: Princeton University Press, 1939), 138.

57. Merle Curti to Thomas Bailey, 12 September 1944, box 3, file 8, Thomas Bailey Papers, Department of Special Collections, Stanford University Libraries.

58. Ware, *Cultural Approach to History,* 10, 13–14.

59. R. R. Palmer, "Report of the Sixty-third Annual Meeting," *AHR,* 54 (April 1949), 739.

60. Richard Huber, "A Theory of American Studies," *SE,* 18 (October 1954), 267.

61. For a leading example, see Henry Nash Smith, *Virgin Land: The American West as Symbol and Myth* (Cambridge: Harvard University Press, 1950).

62. Allen F. Davis, "The Politics of American Studies," *American Quarterly,* 42 (September 1990), 353–74, esp. 356.

63. J. F. Wellemeyer Jr., "Survey of United States Historians, 1952, and a Forecast," *AHR,* 61 (January 1956), 343; Dexter Perkins, John Snell, and the Committee on Graduate Education of the American Historical Association, *The Education of Historians in the United States* (New York: McGraw-Hill, 1962), 29–31, 142; McCaughey, *International Studies and Academic Enterprise.*

64. Carl Becker, *The Heavenly City of the Eighteenth-Century Philosophers* (New Haven: Yale University Press, 1932); Carl Becker, *Modern History: The Rise of a Democratic, Scientific, and Industrial Civilization* (New York: Silver Burdett, 1931).

65. *"What Is the Good of History?" Selected Letters of Carl L. Becker, 1900–1945,* ed. Michael Kammen (Ithaca: Cornell University Press, 1973), 115n.

66. Carlton J. H. Hayes, "The American Frontier—Frontier of What?" *AHR,* 51 (January 1946), 202.

67. Perkins, Snell, and Committee on Graduate Education of the American Historical Association, *Education of Historians,* 20, 29–31.

68. By 1985, John Higham could describe history in the United States as "a house in which the inhabitants are leaning out of many open windows gaily chattering with the neighbors while the doors between the rooms stay closed." Higham, "Paleface and Redskin in American Historiography: A Comment," *Journal of Interdisciplinary History,* 16 (Summer 1985), 111–12.

69. Louise Carroll Wade, "Assistance Available for Post-doctoral Historical Research

and Publication," *AHR*, 62 (April 1957), 570–93; Younger, "Foundations and the Study of History," 120–24; George L. Anderson, "Mechanical Aids in Historical Research," in Hesseltine and McNeil, *In Support of Clio*, 91.

70. Perkins, Snell, and the Committee on Graduate Education of the American Historical Association, *Education of Historians*, 29–31, quotation at 142.

71. Boyd C. Shafer, "The Year's Business, 1957," *AHR*, 63 (April 1958), 838.

72. George Barr Carson Jr. (director, Service Center for Teachers of History) to Clifford Lord (director, State Historical Society of Wisconsin), 21 December 1956, box 7, file 1, SHSW-NOC, Madison, WI; Dexter Perkins, "We Shall Gladly Teach," *AHR*, 62 (January 1957), 291–309.

73. Arthur M. Schlesinger Jr., "Probing the American Experience" [1958], reprinted in Arthur M. Schlesinger Jr., *The Politics of Hope* (London: Eyre and Spottiswoode, 1964), 49. See also W. Stull Holt, *The Historical Profession in the United States* (Washington, DC: AHA, 1963), 21. In 1953, Holt declared that scholarly training could "produce technicians but not the rich, wise minds from which alone great history can be written." Holt, "Historical Scholarship in the United States" [1953], in Holt, *Historical Scholarship in the United States and Other Essays* (Seattle: University of Washington Press, 1967), 62–63, 37–38.

74. Fitzpatrick, *History's Memory*, epilogue.

75. C. Vann Woodward drew attention in 1982 to the "fragmentation of the profession into highly specialized fields" in a way which suggested that the problem was unprecedented. Woodward, "A Short History of American History," *NYTBR*, 8 August 1982, reprinted in Woodward, *The Future of the Past* (New York: Oxford University Press, 1989), 320.

76. Schlesinger, "Probing the American Experience," 49, 51.

77. Andrews, "Some Recent Aspects of Institutional Study," 381–410.

78. G. D. Lillibridge, "History in the Public Schools," *SE*, 22 (March 1958), 8.

Chapter Three

1. Allan Nevins, *The Gateway to History* (New York: D. Appleton and Co., 1938), iv, iii.

2. Allan Nevins, "What's the Matter with History?" *SRL*, 4 February 1939, 3, 4, 16.

3. William Langer in *NYHT*, 18 September 1938, in Allan Nevins Ephemera, Columbia University Archives.

4. John Spencer Bassett, "The Present State of Historical Writing," in Jean J. Jusserand et al., *The Writing of History* (New York: Charles Scribner's Sons, 1926), 94–95, 101, 99.

5. Wilbur C. Abbott, "The Influence of Graduate Instruction on Historical Writing," in Jusserand et al., *Writing of History*, 37–38.

6. Arthur Schlesinger Sr., "History," in Wilson Gee, ed., *Research in the Social Sciences: Its Fundamental Methods and Objectives* (New York: Macmillan, 1929), 225.

7. "The State of History Writing and Publishing," *PW*, 24 July 1926, 251.

8. XYZ, "Books Are Doomed," *SRL*, 16 January 1932, 464. See also editorial, *SRL*, 14 March 1936, 8.

9. "A Lament for History," *Atlantic Monthly*, 115 (March 1915), 430; James Trustlow Adams, "Morituri Te Salutamus," *SRL*, 27 April 1929, 952–53.

10. Ray Allen Billington, "Allan Nevins, Historian: A Personal Reminiscence," in Ray Allen Billington, comp., *Allan Nevins on History* (New York: Charles Scribner's Sons, 1975), x.

11. "Reading on the Farm," *PW,* 1 December 1928, 2273.

12. Letter to editor, *SRL,* 19 October 1935, 9.

13. Editorial, *SRL,* 14 March 1936, 8; Charles Lee, *The Hidden Public: The Story of the Book-of-the-Month Club* (Garden City, NY: Doubleday and Co., 1958), 30–32.

14. Sanford Cobb, "College Graduates *Do* Read—Some!" *PW,* 26 May 1934, 1917.

15. Janice A. Radway, *A Feeling for Books: The Book-of-the-Month Club, Literary Taste, and Middle-Class Desire* (Chapel Hill: University of North Carolina Press, 1997), 297–300; Joan Shelly Rubin, *The Making of Middlebrow Culture* (Chapel Hill: University of North Carolina Press, 1992), xii–xvi.

16. Radway, *A Feeling for Books,* 298–99.

17. Rubin, *Making of Middlebrow Culture,* 105, 121; Henry Seidel Canby, "Literature in a Democracy," *Century Magazine,* 99 (January 1920), 400–401.

18. Rubin, *Making of Middlebrow Culture,* 105.

19. Henry Wysham Lanier, "The Public Taste for Standard Literature," *PW,* 9 March 1929, 1207, 1208, 1216.

20. Allan Nevins, "Annals of American Culture," *SRL,* 8 October 1927, 167.

21. The *New York Herald Tribune's* equivalent arrived in 1925. *PW,* 4 March 1939, 966.

22. John Tebbel, *A History of Book Publishing in the United States,* vol. 3, *The Golden Age between the Two Wars, 1920–1940* (New York: R. R. Bowker, 1978), 5; John Tebbel, *A History of Book Publishing in the United States,* vol. 4, *The Great Change, 1940–1980* (New York: R. R. Bowker, 1981), 182; *NR,* 1 October 1930, 177.

23. Frederick Jackson Turner, "Since the Foundation [of Clark University (1889)]," in Turner, *The Significance of Sections in American History* (1932; repr., Gloucester, MA: Peter Smith, 1959), 212; Nevins, "Annals of American Culture," 166; Thomas Bender, *New York Intellect: A History of Intellectual Life in New York City, from 1750 to the Beginnings of Our Own Time* (New York: Alfred A. Knopf, 1987), 207.

24. Walden Fawcett, "Census Reveals Book Publishing Trends," *PW,* 16 May 1925, 1620.

25. Editorial, *SRL,* 14 March 1936, 8.

26. "News of the Week: Title Output Off Ten Percent," *PW,* 1 January 1934, 44.

27. Frederick Lewis Allen, "Best-Sellers, 1900–1935: The Trend of Popular Reading Taste since the Turn of the Century," *SRL,* 7 December 1935, 24.

28. Michael Kammen, *Mystic Chords of Memory: The Transformation of Tradition in American Culture* (New York: Alfred Knopf, 1991), 462.

29. See, e.g., Georg Lukács, *The Historical Novel,* trans. Hannah Mitchell and Stanley Mitchell (London: Merlin Press, 1962); Herbert Butterfield, *The Historical Novel: An Essay* (Cambridge: Cambridge University Press, 1924).

30. "The Historical Novel," *PW,* 23 Aug. 1924, 594; *PW,* 6 November 1937, 1827.

31. Kenneth L. Roberts, *Arundel, Being the Recollections of Steven Nason of Arundel, in the Province of Maine* (Garden City, NY: Doubleday, Doran, and Co., 1930); Hervey Allen, *An-*

thony Adverse (New York: Farrar and Rinehart, 1933); Margaret Mitchell, *Gone with the Wind* (New York: Macmillan, 1936).

32. Priscilla Murolo, "History in the Fast Lane: Howard Fast and the Historical Novel," in Susan P. Benson, Stephen Brier, and Roy Rosenzweig, eds., *Presenting the Past: Essays on History and the Public* (Philadelphia: Temple University Press, 1986), 56; Louis Adamic, "What the Proletarian Reads," *SRL*, 1 December 1934, 321.

33. Editorial, *SRL*, 14 March 1936, 8.

34. Arthur Vernon Tourtellot, "History and the Historical Novel: Where Fact and Fancy Meet and Part," *SRL*, 24 August 1940, 3, 16.

35. Hewitt H. Howland, "An Historical Revival," *PW*, 9 June 1934, 2134, 2137.

36. "Books into Movies," *PW*, 8 September 1934, 753–54.

37. David Van Tassel, "From Learned Society to Professional Organization: The American Historical Association, 1884–1900," *AHR*, 89 (October 1984), 954, 952. Peter Novick briefly discusses this argument about the relationship between professional and amateur historiography in *That Noble Dream: The "Objectivity Question" and the American Historical Profession* (New York: Cambridge University Press, 1988), 47–50. John Higham et al., *History: The Development of Historical Studies in the United States* (Englewood-Cliffs, NJ: Prentice-Hall, 1965), 20, mark 1907 as the point of transition, but Novick rates the transition as incomplete in 1907.

38. Henry Nash Smith to Wallace Stegner, 19 December 1972, Correspondence, box 2, file 9, 1945–72, Henry Nash Smith Papers, Bancroft Library, University of California, Berkeley.

39. Bruce Catton quoted in Roy Rosenzweig, "Marketing the Past: American Heritage and Popular History in the United States," in Benson, Brier, and Rosenzweig, *Presenting the Past*, 32.

40. Wallace Stegner, *The Uneasy Chair: A Biography of Bernard DeVoto* (Garden City, NJ: Doubleday, 1973), 7.

41. Henry F. Pringle, *Theodore Roosevelt: A Biography* (New York: Blue Ribbon Books, 1931).

42. Allan Nevins, "Down to Normalcy," *SRL*, 9 November 1935, 5; Mark Sullivan, *Our Times, 1900–1925*, 6 vols. (New York: C. Scribner's Sons, 1926–35).

43. "The Pulitzer Prize Winners," *SRL*, 7 May 1938, 10; Marquis James, *Andrew Jackson: Portrait of a President* (Indianapolis: Bobbs-Merrill, 1937).

44. Allen, "Best-Sellers, 1900–1935," 26; Frederick Lewis Allen, *Only Yesterday: An Informal History of the Nineteen-twenties* (New York: Harper and Bros., 1931); Geoffrey Parsons, "As We Were," *SRL*, 12 December 1931, 363–64. Parsons was chief editorial writer for the *Herald-Tribune* and author of *The Stream of History* (New York: Scribner, 1929), 364.

45. Carl Sandberg, *Abraham Lincoln: The War Years* (New York: Harcourt, Brace, and Co., 1939).

46. "The Pulitzer Awards," *SRL*, 11 May 1940, 13.

47. Walter Millis, *Road to War: America, 1914–1917* (Boston: Houghton Mifflin, 1935); Walter Millis, *The Martial Spirit: A Study of Our War with Spain* (Boston: Houghton Mifflin, 1931); *NR*, 8 May 1935, 372.

48. David E. Kyvig, "History as Present Politics: Claude Bowers' *The Tragic Era*," *Indi-*

ana Magazine of History, 73, no. 1 (1977), 25; Claude Bowers, *The Tragic Era: The Revolution after Lincoln* (Boston: Houghton Mifflin, 1929); Claude Bowers, *My Life: The Memoirs of Claude Bowers* (New York: Simon and Schuster, 1962).

49. Nevins to Freeman, 4 November 1948, box 91, Douglas Southall Freeman Papers, Rare Book and Manuscript Collection, Alderman Library, University of Virginia. For Freeman, see David S. Johnson, *Douglas Southall Freeman* (Gretna, LA: Pelican Publishing Co., 2002). For Agar (1897–1980), see *Who Was Who in America,* 7:4.

50. George F. Milton, "History as a Major Sport," *SRL,* 1 June 1935, 3, 4.

51. DeVoto to [Mr.] Banker, 13 April 1948, box 4, file 67, Bernard DeVoto Papers, Department of Special Collections, Stanford University Libraries.

52. Henry Pringle to Committee on Admissions, The Century Association, 6 August 1943, box 1, file Commager, Henry Pringle Papers, LC.

53. Louis Adamic, *Dynamite: The Story of Class Violence in America* (New York: Viking, 1931); Louis Adamic, *The Native's Return: An American Immigrant visits Yugoslavia and Discovers His Old Country* (1934; repr., Westport, CT: Greenwood Press, 1975); Adamic, "What the Proletarian Reads," 321; Matthew Josephson, review of *Hamilton Fish,* by Allan Nevins (New York: Dodd, Mead, 1936), *NR,* 20 January 1937, 362; David Shi, *Matthew Josephson: Bourgeois Bohemian* (New Haven: Yale University Press, 1981), 176.

54. Darlene C. Hine, introduction to Henrietta Buckmaster, *Let My People Go: The Story of the Underground Railroad and the Growth of the Abolition Movement,* ed. Darlene C. Hine (Columbia: University of South Carolina Press, 1992), x.

55. For local history, see chap. 12 below.

56. Bonnie G. Smith, *The Gender of History: Men, Women, and Historical Practice* (Cambridge: Harvard University Press, 1998), chap. 6; Jacqueline Goggin, "Challenging Sexual Discrimination in the Historical Profession," *AHR,* 97 (June 1992), 769–802.

57. James Trustlow Adams, "Puritan Women," *SRL,* 21 May 1938, 4. Margaret Bell also wrote *Margaret Fuller: A Biography* (New York: C. Boni, 1930). Buckmaster to Herbert Aptheker, 5 December 1938, box 1, file 3, Herbert Aptheker Papers, Department of Special Collections, Stanford University Libraries. See also Hine, introduction, x; Barbara Abrash, Glenna Matthews, and Anita R. May, "Angie Debo: A Study in Inspiration," *Organization of American Historians Newsletter,* 17 (February 1989), 22; Shirley Leckie, *Angie Debo: Pioneering Historian* (Norman: University of Oklahoma Press, 2000).

58. Paul S. Boyer, "Constance Lindsay Skinner," *NAW,* 3:295–96.

59. Nevins, "What's the Matter with History?" 16. Nevins named only two other women among prominent amateurs: Constance Skinner and Mary Beard.

60. See Shelley Rubin, *Constance Rourke and American Culture* (Chapel Hill: University of North Carolina Press, 1980); Kenneth S. Lynn, "Constance Mayfield Rourke," *NAW,* 3:199–200.

61. See, e.g., Louise Houghton, *Our Debt to the Red Man* (Boston: Stratford Co., 1918), reviewed in "The Wider Field," *Wisconsin Magazine of History,* 2, no. 3 (1918–19), 387.

62. Leckie, *Angie Debo.*

63. Adams to Nevins, 20 September 1925, James Trustlow Adams Papers, Rare Books and Manuscripts, Butler Library, Columbia University. On the academics, see Marcus W. Jernegan, "Productivity of Doctors of Philosophy in History," *AHR,* 33 (October 1927), 1–22.

64. James A. Hodges, "George Fort Milton and the Art of History," *History Teacher,* 18 (February 1985), 251–52.

65. Turner, "Since the Foundation [of Clark University (1889)]," 212.

66. Hodges, "George Fort Milton and the Art of History," 252–54.

67. John Franklin Jameson, "The Present State of Historical Writing" [1910], reprinted in Morey D. Rothberg and Jacqueline Goggin, eds., *John Franklin Jameson and the Development of Humanistic Scholarship in America,* vol. 1, *Selected Essays* (Athens: University of Georgia Press, 1993), 299. Jameson noted, however, in 1902 that the share of historical production by academics was rising, with professionals producing half the output ("The Influence of Universities upon Historical Writing," in ibid., 269).

68. Milton to Ferris Greenslat, 3 July 1934, box 16, George Fort Milton Papers, LC.

69. Cf. Russell Nye, "History and Literature: Branches of the Same Tree," in John Braeman, ed., *Essays on History and Literature* (Columbus: Ohio State University Press, 1966), 126.

70. Jameson, "Influence of Universities," 273.

71. Albert Bushnell Hart, "Imagination in History," *AHR,* 15 (January 1910), 248.

72. William Milligan Sloane, "History and Democracy," *AHR,* 1 (October 1895), 21, 19.

73. William Milligan Sloane, "The Substance and Vision of History," *AHR,* 17 (January 1912), 241.

74. See, e.g., Max Farrand, "The Quality of Distinction," *AHR,* 46 (April 1941), 518. Imagination needed to be present in all good history, Farrand averred, but always restrained by facts. In this the novelist failed and "invariably lapses into woeful mistakes."

75. Sim T. Carman to Guy Stanton Ford, 31 December 1940, box 123, file "General 1941," AHA Papers, LC; Ford to S. T. Carman, 9 January 1941 (quotations), ibid.

76. Theodore Clarke Smith, "The Writing of American History in America from 1884 to 1934," *AHR,* 40 (April 1935), 447.

77. Ibid.; Arthur M. Schlesinger, "Amateur History," *SRL,* 19 December 1936, 3, 14. Samuel Eliot Morison criticized the writings of "journalist-historians"; see Gregory M. Pfitzer, *Samuel Eliot Morison's Historical World: In Quest of a New Parkman* (Boston: Northeastern University Press, 1991), xix, 138–40. See also Arthur C. Cole, "Dividing a Nation," *SRL,* 13 October 1934, 203; Henry Nash Smith to Wallace Stegner, 19 December 1972, Correspondence, box 2, file 9, 1945–72, Smith Papers; Crane Brinton, "Materials of History," *SRL,* 10 September 1938, 11; Farrand, "Quality of Distinction," 517; Max Lerner, "Midpassage—Toward What?" *NR,* 14 June 1939, 164.

78. On William B. Munro, see Robert Glasgow to Gabriel, 17 September 1921, series IV, box 21, file 359, Ralph Gabriel Papers, Yale University Library. Cf. Michael Kammen, *Selvages and Biases: The Fabric of History in American Culture* (Ithaca: Cornell University Press, 1987), 92.

79. Kammen, *Mystic Chords,* 376.

80. Brinton, "Materials of History," 11.

81. Even where, as in George Fort Milton's case, amateur historians dealt with southern themes or wrote from a prosouthern viewpoint, they addressed national issues such as the Civil War and Reconstruction. Moreover, academics reviewed more often than in later

decades for the leading newspapers and periodicals. See "Pity the Poor Scholars," *SRL*, 13 September 1930, 117.

82. Oscar Handlin, *Truth in History* (Cambridge: Belknap Press, Harvard University Press, 1979), 379–82.

83. Kammen, *Selvages and Biases*, 91; Adams to M. A. De Wolfe Howe, 21 October 1929, in Allan Nevins, *James Trustlow Adams: Historian of the American Dream* (Urbana: University of Illinois Press, 1968), 183; Adams to Nevins, 20 September 1925, Adams Papers.

84. James Trustlow Adams, "History and the Lower Criticism," *Atlantic Monthly*, September 1923, 311, 316.

85. "The State of History Writing and Publishing," *PW*, 24 July 1926, 251.

86. Parsons, "As We Were," 364, 363.

87. Jameson, "Influence of Universities," 270.

88. Adams to M. A. De Wolfe Howe, 21 October 1929, in Nevins, *James Trustlow Adams*, 182.

89. Quoted in Hodges, "George Fort Milton and the Art of History," 259.

90. See Allan Nevins Papers, boxes 48–49, passim, in Rare Books and Manuscripts, Butler Library, Columbia University; Nevins, *James Trustlow Adams*, 182. See also, e.g., Nathan Goodman to George Stevens, 9 February 1939, box 49, Nevins Papers.

91. Farrand, "Quality of Distinction," 518.

92. George F. Milton to Hicks, 16 December 1933, box 13, John D. Hicks Papers, Bancroft Library, University of California, Berkeley. Chattanooga had hosted the MVHA three years before. Milton claimed that "quite a number of people here would esteem it a distinct honor to have the American Historical Association hold its sessions in our midst." See also Milton to Hicks, 14 October 1935,ibid.

93. Milton to Hicks, 26 April 1938, ibid.

94. Milton to Beatrice Rothschild, 24 April 1944, box 27, file April 1944, Milton Papers.

95. Earl L. Bell to Gabriel, 24 July 1941, series I, box 6, file 97, Gabriel Papers.

96. Robert Wolf to Arthur M. Schlesinger, 28 July 1928, box 3, Arthur M. Schlesinger Papers, Harvard University Archives. Though "not an historian," he claimed to be "sufficiently acquainted with the techniques of research" to write the book.

97. Schlesinger to Wolf, 7 August 1928, ibid.

98. Editorial, "Writing American History," *SRL*, 6 November 1937, 8; Samuel Eliot Morison and Henry Steele Commager, *The Growth of the American Republic*, 2nd ed., 2 vols. (New York: Oxford University Press, 1937). See also Henrik Van Loon to Arthur M. Schlesinger, 19 January 1926, box 3, Schlesinger Papers.

99. Boyer, "Constance Skinner," 296.

100. See the oral history conducted in 1996 by Ann Lage: *Kenneth M. Stampp, Historian of Slavery, the Civil War, and Reconstruction, University of California, Berkeley, 1946–1983* (Berkeley: Regional Oral History Office, Bancroft Library, University of California, 1998), 259. See also Kyvig, "History as Present Politics," 21, 31.

101. Robert Glasgow to Gabriel, 17 September 1921, series IV, box 21, file 359, Gabriel Papers.

102. Richard L. Watson Jr., "The Chronicles of America," *South Atlantic Quarterly*, 50 (January 1951), 109–21, esp. 110.

103. Allen Johnson quoted in Gabriel to A. H. Brook, 30 November 1928, series I, box 1, file 3, Gabriel Papers.

104. Carl Becker, *The Eve of the Revolution: A Chronicle of the Breach with England*, Chronicles of America, vol. 21 (New Haven: Yale University Press, 1918); William E. Dodd, *The Cotton Kingdom: A Chronicle of the Old South*, Chronicles of America, vol. 27 (New Haven: Yale University Press, 1918); Carl Fish, *The Path of Empire: A Chronicle of the United States as a World Power*, Chronicles of America, vol. 46 (New Haven: Yale University Press, 1919); Charles McLean Andrews, *Colonial Folkways: A Chronicle of American Life in the Reign of the Georges*, Chronicles of America, vol. 9 (New Haven: Yale University Press, 1919); Charles McLean Andrews, *The Fathers of New England: A Chronicle of the Puritan Commonwealths*, Chronicles of America, vol. 6 (New Haven: Yale University Press, 1919).

105. Evarts B. Greene, review in *AHR* 25 (January 1920), 295.

106. St. George L. Sioussat, review in *AHR*, 25 (April 1920), 556.

107. George Parmly Day, "The Story of the Chronicles of America," *Ohio History Teachers' Journal*, no. 33 (March 1924), 432, 427.

108. *New York Tribune*, quoted in ibid., 426.

109. *North American Review*, quoted in ibid, 425.

110. D. R. Anderson, review of *Pioneers of the Old Southwest: A Chronicle of the Dark and Bloody Ground*, by Constance Rourke, Chronicles of America, vol. 18 (New Haven: Yale University Press, 1919), *AHR*, 26 (October 1920), 113.

111. Evarts Greene, review in *AHR*, 25 (January 1920), 295.

112. "In the Bookmarket," *PW*, 14 December 1929, 2756–57.

113. The fifteen-volume Pageant of America series was edited by Ralph Henry Gabriel and published by Yale University Press from 1925 to 1929.

114. Krout, "The Making of the 'Pageant of America,'" *HO*, 22 (March 1931), 103; on Gabriel, see Robert A. Skotheim, *American Intellectual Histories and Historians* (Princeton: Princeton University Press, 1966), 212–44.

115. Lotta A. Clark to F. E. Spaulding, 10 November 1924, series IV, box 21, file 364, Gabriel Papers. On pageants, see David Glassberg, *American Historical Pageantry: The Uses of Tradition in the Early Twentieth Century* (Chapel Hill: University of North Carolina Press, 1990).

116. Gabriel to A. H. Brook, 30 November 1928, series I, box 3, file 1, Gabriel Papers.

117. Dixon Ryan Fox to A. H. Brook, 2 October 1924, series IV, box 21, file 363, ibid. On the amateur tradition of pictorial histories, see Gregory M. Pfitzer, *Picturing the Past: Illustrated Histories and the American Imagination, 1840–1900* (Washington, DC: Smithsonian Institution Press, 2002), 236.

118. Gabriel to Brook, 30 November 1928, series I, box 3, file 1, Gabriel Papers.

119. Herbert Askwith to Mr. Firman, Yale University Press, 15 October 1928, ibid.

120. On the power of the United Daughters of the Confederacy in textbook controversies, see David W. Blight, *Race and Reunion: The Civil War in American Memory* (Cambridge: Belknap Press, Harvard University Press, 2001), 278–82.

121. Krout, "Making of the 'Pageant of America,'" 104.

122. John Allen Krout, *Annals of American Sport,* Pageant of America, vol. 15 (New Haven: Yale University Press, 1929); Krout, "Making of the 'Pageant of America,'" 103–4, 106.

123. Herbert Askwith to Mr. Firman, Yale University Press, 15 October 1928, series I, box 3, file 1, Gabriel Papers.

124. *Pittsburgh Press,* 25 August 1928, series I, box 2, file 19, ibid.; *Boston Post* editorial, 3 June 1927, series IV, box 21, file 367, ibid.

125. Editorial, "The Second Step," *SRL,* 5 February 1938, 8.

126. L. H. Gipson to E. A. Schirner, 12 December 1926, series IV, box 21, file 366, Gabriel Papers.

127. Richard H. Shryock to Gabriel, 22 April 1927, series IV, box 21, file 367, ibid.

128. Charles S. Brody to Yale University Press, 27 June 1930, series IV, box 21, file 353, ibid. See also Arthur Schlesinger Jr., *A Life in the Twentieth Century: Innocent Beginnings, 1917–1950* (Boston: Houghton Mifflin, 2000), 67.

129. R. S. Smoker to Brook, 20 October 1928, series I, box 1, file 3, Gabriel Papers; Brook to Gabriel, 2 January 1934, series I, box 4, file 68, ibid.

130. Lotta A. Clark to F. E. Spaulding, 10 November 1924, series IV, box 21, file 364, ibid. For some schools, however, the reading matter was, teachers reported, "too advanced and too condensed." See M. E. Blanchard to R. S. Smoker, 17 January 1929, series I, box 1, file 3, ibid.

131. Arthur M. Schlesinger, "Points of View in Historical Writing," *PW,* 14 January 1928, 145–48.

132. See Handlin, *Truth in History,* 72; Schlesinger Jr., *A Life in the Twentieth Century,* 43–46; Novick, *That Noble Dream,* 179. William E. Lingelbach, ed., *Approaches to American Social History* (New York: D. Appleton and Co., 1937), provides illuminating assessments delivered at the AHA annual meeting in 1936. See also Charles Beard, review of *The Rise of the City, 1878–1898,* by Arthur M. Schlesinger, History of American Life, vol. 10 (New York: Macmillan, 1933), *AHR,* 38 (July 1933), 780.

133. The Editors, "The Association at Providence," *AHR,* 42 (April 1937), 423, 422.

134. Lucian Lamm and Daniel M. Feins, "Charles A. Beard," *SS,* 5 (April 1941), 263–68; Hubert Herring, "Charles A. Beard, Free Lance among Historians," *Harper's Magazine,* May 1939, 643; Maurice Blinkoff, "The Influence of Charles A. Beard upon American Historiography," *University of Buffalo Studies,* 12 (May 1936), 31, 36, 38, 75.

135. Charles and Mary Beard, *America in Midpassage* (New York: Macmillan, 1939); Lerner, "Midpassage—Toward What?" 164.

136. Albert Jay Nock, "A Model History," *SRL,* 9 July 1927, 957; see also Ellen Nore, *Charles Beard: An Intellectual Biography* (Carbondale: Southern Illinois University Press, 1983), chap. 9.

Chapter Four

1. Allan Nevins, *The Gateway to History* (New York: D. Appleton and Co., 1938) 268; Allan Nevins, "Recent Progress of American Social History," *Journal of Economic and Business*

(New York: Charles Scribner's Sons, 1975), 118–20.

2. Allan Nevins, *James Trustlow Adams: Historian of the American Dream* (Urbana: University of Illinois Press, 1968), 40; Allan Nevins, "American Life," *SRL*, 4 March 1933, 464; Allan Nevins, "Recent Progress of American Social History," 121–22; Nevins, *Gateway to History*, 271.

3. Robert Middlekauf, "Telling the Story of the Civil War: Allan Nevins as a Narrative Historian," *Huntington Library Quarterly*, 56 (Winter 1993), 71–72.

4. Conyers Read to Dexter Perkins, 3 March, 1939, box 86, file 1933–41, AHA Papers, LC.

5. See Levering Tyson and Josephine MacLatchy, eds., *Education on the Air and Radio and Education, 1935: Proceedings of the Sixth Annual Institutes for Education by Radio Combined with the Fifth Annual Advisory Assembly of the National Advisory Council on Radio in Education* (Chicago: University of Chicago Press, 1935), 158, 160, 162.

6. Conyers Read to James P. Baxter III, 14 September 1938, box 86, file 1935–39, AHA Papers.

7. For a different view, see Michael Kammen, *Mystic Chords of Memory: The Transformation of Tradition in American Culture* (New York: Alfred Knopf, 1991), 541. See also Peter Novick, *That Noble Dream: The "Objectivity Question" and the American Historical Profession* (New York: Cambridge University Press, 1988), 195.

8. Conyers Read to Nevins, 13 October 1938, box 48, file 1, Allan Nevins Papers, Rare Books and Manuscripts, Butler Library, Columbia University.

9. Read to Nevins, 24 March 1938, box 48, file 3, Nevins Papers.

10. Novick, *That Noble Dream*, 195.

11. *Annual Report of the American Historical Association for the Year 1935*, vol. 1, *Proceedings, 1933, 1934, and 1935* (Washington, DC: Government Printing Office, 1938), 145; "Reference to a Popular Magazine of History," box 2, file 1938, Jan.–June, Solon Buck Papers, LC.

12. William L. Langer to Nevins, 17 March 1938, box 48, file 2, Nevins Papers; Spencer Brodney to Arthur M. Schlesinger, 5 May 1937; and Brodney to Schlesinger, 22 May 1937, box 12, Arthur M. Schlesinger Papers, Harvard University Archives.

13. Dexter Perkins to Conyers Read, 14 February 1936, box 86, file 1933–41, AHA Papers.

14. Solon Buck to Conyers Read, 16 January, 1939, box 3, file 1939 Jan.–June, Buck Papers; Fred Shannon to Nevins, 21 February 1939, box 49, file 3, Nevins Papers.

15. Allan Nevins, "What's the Matter with History?" *SRL*, 4 February 1939, 3, 4, 16.

16. Ibid., 16.

17. Ibid.

18. Conyers Read to Nevins, 27 February 1939, box 49, file 3, Nevins Papers.

19. Solon Buck to Nevins, 1 March 1939, ibid. University of Chicago historian Bessie Louise Pierce also refused to join the new society for similar reasons, even though not "in any way opposed to the popularization of history." Pierce to John Allen Krout, 31 August 1939, enclosed in Pierce to John D. Hicks, 5 September 1939, box 10, John D. Hicks Papers, Bancroft Library, University of California, Berkeley.

20. Allan Nevins, "Clio's Mansions," *SRL*, 20 January 1940, 9.

21. Allan Nevins, "Not Capulets, Not Montagues," *AHR*, 65 (January 1960), 253–70.

22. John Allen Krout form letter, August 1943, Douglas Southall Freeman Papers, box 51, Rare Book and Manuscript Collection, Alderman Library, University of Virginia.

23. John Krout to Fellows of the [SAH] Society, 10 April 1943, box 15, file "Society of American Historians," Freeman Papers; Conyers Read to Nevins, 16 June 1943, box 57, file "Correspondence of Allan Nevins 1943," Nevins Papers.

24. Roy Rosenzweig, "Marketing the Past: *American Heritage* and Popular History in the United States," in Susan P. Benson, Stephen Brier, and Roy Rosenzweig, eds., *Presenting the Past: Essays on History and the Public* (Philadelphia: Temple University Press, 1986), 25.

25. Ibid., 26, 27; *NYTBR*, 17 October 1954, 27.

26. Rosenzweig, "Marketing the Past," 28.

27. *NYTBR*, 17 October 1954, 27.

28. Rosenzweig, "Marketing the Past," 29.

29. Rudolph Clemen, *The Historian as Literary Artist: The First Francis Parkman Awards Dinner, . . . 1957*, box 6, file 9, SHSW-NOC, Madison, WI; John A. Garraty to Merle Curti, 9 May 1960, box 39, file 2, Merle Curti Papers, SHSW.

30. Rudolph Clemen to Eric Goldman, 5 December 1958; and Society of American Historians, Inc., Report of the Executive Vice-President, 25 April 1960, box 45, file 8, Eric F. Goldman Papers, LC.

31. W. Stull Holt, *Historical Scholarship in the United States and Other Essays* (Seattle: University of Washington Press, 1967), 64–72.

32. Ray Dovell to Bernard DeVoto, 21 February 1946, box 13, file 257, Bernard DeVoto Papers, Department of Special Collections, Stanford University Libraries.

33. Stewart Holbrook to DeVoto, 21 July 1947, box 13, file 264, ibid.

34. [Houghton Mifflin representative] to DeVoto, 10 September 1947, box 13, file 260, ibid. For a later period see Eric H. Monkkonen, "The Dangers of Synthesis," *AHR*, 91 (October 1986), 1148.

35. Wallace Stegner, *The Uneasy Chair: A Biography of Bernard DeVoto* (Garden City, NJ: Doubleday, 1973), 316–17; Dovell to DeVoto, 15 April 1947, box 13, file 258, DeVoto Papers.

36. Flyer in box 63, file 1947, Nevins Papers; see also Dovell to DeVoto, n.d., box 13, file 257, DeVoto Papers.

37. Dovell to DeVoto, n.d., box 13, file 257, DeVoto Papers.

38. Dovell to DeVoto, 9 January 1948, box 13, file 261, ibid.

39. Dovell to DeVoto, [February?] 1946, box 13, file 257, ibid.

40. Arthur M. Schlesinger Jr., *The Politics of Hope* (London: Eyre and Spottiswoode, 1964), 51. Schlesinger tended to support academic titles: Roy Nichols's *Disruption of American Democracy* may have been "a bit scholarly and detailed for some readers," but "it is a rich and ample analysis which repays the kind of study it demands." Enclosure, Arthur M. Schlesinger Jr., review of Nichols, *Disruption of American Democracy*, with Dovell to DeVoto, 8 October 1947, box 13, file 260, DeVoto Papers.

41. "Bulletin, Special and Confidential," DeVoto to [Board of Editors], 21 October 1947, box 3, file 59, DeVoto Papers.

42. Holbrook to DeVoto, 20 December 1946, box 13, file 263, ibid.

43. Stewart Holbrook to DeVoto, 17 December 1947, box 13, file 264, ibid.

44. Holbrook to DeVoto, 22 January 1949, ibid.

45. *NYT,* 13 November 1937, 20.

46. Dumas Malone to Ray Dovell, 25 November 1957, series RG21/7.831, box 3, file "History Book Club 1954–58," Dumas Malone Papers, Rare Book and Manuscript Collection, Alderman Library, University of Virginia.

47. Malone to Dovell, 1 August 1956, ibid.

48. Dovell to Malone, Walter Millis, and Louis B. Wright, 4 November 1957; Malone to Dovell, 25 November 1957, ibid.

49. Based on personal observation as a member of the HBC in the 1970s.

50. Kammen, *Mystic Chords,* 537; *American Heritage* successfully appealed to this politics of nostalgia. It sought to "highlight your heritage, your sense of roots and place" (*NYTBR,* 17 October 1954, 27).

51. Schlesinger, *Politics of Hope,* 49.

52. Daniel Bell, "Modernity and Mass Society: On the Varieties of Cultural Experience," in Arthur M. Schlesinger Jr. and Morton White, eds., *Paths of American Thought* (Boston: Houghton Mifflin, 1963), 416.

53. "Effect of Television on Reading Is Estimated in Recent Surveys," *PW,* 21 April 1951, 1707–9.

54. Bell, "Modernity and Mass Society," 426.

55. Frank Luther Mott, *American Journalism: A History,* 3rd ed. (New York: Macmillan, 1962), 863–65.

56. *PW,* 8 January 1949, 116; and annual surveys of book production in *PW.* History went from 804 of 10,600 titles in 1939 (7.56 percent) to 527 of 10,892 (4.83 percent) in 1949.

57. "American Book Publication, 1951," *PW,* 19 January 1952, 221.

58. Dixon Wecter, "What Can University Presses Teach Professors?" *PW,* 10 July 1948, 115; "Means, Extremes, Percentages, and Averages," *PW,* 21 May 1949, 2049.

59. "Means, Extremes, Percentages, and Averages," 2051.

60. Victor Reynolds, "Looking Forward," *Saturday Review,* 4 April 1953, 26.

61. Wecter, "What Can University Presses Teach Professors?" 114, 115.

62. W. Stull Holt, *The Historical Profession in the United States* (Washington, DC: AHA, 1963), 22. See epilogue, below, for an extended discussion.

63. Barbara Tuchman, *Practising History: Selected Essays* (London: Papermac, 1983), 56–57; on George Dangerfield (1904–87), see *Current Biography, 1953,* 142–44.

64. David Cannadine, *G. M. Trevelyan: A Life in History* (New York: W. W. Norton, 1992); *The Historical Association, 1906–1956* (London: Historical Association, 1955), 50–51. On Nevins, see Middlekauf, "Telling the Story of the Civil War," 67–81.

65. Rosemary Jann, "From Amateur to Professional: The Case of the Oxbridge Histo-

rians," *Journal of British Studies*, 22 (Spring 1983), 122–47; F. M. Powicke, "English Local Historical Societies," *Canadian Historical Review*, 13 (September 1932), 257–63.

66. *The Historical Association, 1906–1956*, esp. 50–51; Cannadine, *Trevelyan*.

Chapter Five

1. For the pros and cons see Robert Brent Toplin, "Reel History: A Special Issue," *Perspectives*, 37 (April 1999), 1, 8–52; Robert Brent Toplin, "Film and History: The State of the Union," ibid., 9; Philip M. Taylor, "Television: The First Flawed Rough Drafts of History," in Gary R. Edgerton and Peter C. Rollins, eds., *Television Histories: Shaping Collective Memory in the Media Age* (Lexington: University Press of Kentucky, 1999), 144. While mentioning that "Yale University historians had, in the 1920s, participated in the creation of historian vignettes on film for use in primary and secondary schools," Gerald Herman states that before the "last thirty years" "most historians" insisted on the "marginality" of film and television "to their concerns, to their training, to their individualized methods of work." Gerald Herman, "Chemical and Electronic Media in the Public History Movement," *Public Historian*, 21 (Summer 1999), 113. Gary Edgerton, "Mediating Thomas Jefferson," in Edgerton and Rollins, *Television Histories*, 170–71, dates historians' interest from the early 1970s and states that "majority interest" never reached "critical mass" until the mid-1980s (pp. 170–71). For historians' treatment of individual historical pictures, see Mark C. Carnes et al., *Past Imperfect: History according to the Movies* (New York: Henry Holt, 1995). On film history, see also Robert Brent Toplin, *History by Hollywood: The Use and Abuse of the American Past* (Urbana: University of Illinois Press, 1996).

2. Robert Rosenstone, *Visions of the Past: The Challenge of Film to Our Idea of History* (Cambridge: Harvard University Press, 1995), 49.

3. Ibid., 2. Rosenstone criticizes historians for their naivety not only about film's accuracy but also about the power politics of mainstream film (p. 46).

4. Michael T. Isenberg, *War on Film: The American Cinema and World War I, 1914–1941* (Rutherford, NJ: Fairleigh Dickinson University Press, 1981), 26; Edgerton, "Mediating Thomas Jefferson," 171.

5. Peter Novick, *That Noble Dream: The Objectivity Question and the American Historical Profession* (New York: Cambridge University Press, 1988), 194; Rosenstone, *Visions of the Past*, 2.

6. D. W. Griffith quoted in Isenberg, *War on Film*, 31.

7. See Everett Carter, "Cultural History Written with Lightning: The Significance of *The Birth of a Nation*," in Peter C. Rollins, ed., *Hollywood as Historian: American Film in a Cultural Context* (Lexington: University Press of Kentucky, 1983), 9–20; Leon F. Litwack, "*The Birth of a Nation*," in Carnes et al., *Past Imperfect*, 136–41; John Hope Franklin, "*Birth of a Nation*—Propaganda as History," *Massachusetts Review*, 20 (Autumn 1979), 417–34.

8. Robert Sklar, *Movie-Made America: A Cultural History of American Movies* (New York: Random House, 1975); Lary May, *Screening out the Past: The Birth of Mass Culture and the Motion Picture Industry* (New York: Oxford University Press, 1980).

9. Edgar Dale, *The Content of Motion Pictures* (New York: Macmillan, 1935).

10. Henry James Forman, *Our Movie-Made Children* (New York: Macmillan, 1933), chap. 3.

11. Mrs. William [Camilla?] Cavalier to Edgar Robinson, 8 April 1935; R. D. Davies to Robinson, 20 February 1935; and Cavalier and Mr. Allen Widdenham to Robinson, 30 January 1935, box 7, file 54, Edgar Eugene Robinson Papers, Department of Special Collections, Stanford University Libraries; *Program for Local chapters . . . and some important facts relating to Block Booking and Blind Selling* (n.p.: n.d. [1935]); Forman, *Our Movie-Made Children,* chap. 3; Sklar, *Movie-Made America,* 128–35.

12. See, e.g., Charles Beard, *The Nature of the Social Sciences in Relation to Objectives of Instruction* (New York: Charles Scribner's Sons, 1934), 140, 141.

13. *NYT,* 10 July 1925, 17.

14. "Moving Pictures as an Aid in Teaching," *Indiana Magazine of History,* 9 (June 1913), 120.

15. Frederick Jackson Turner, *The Significance of Sections in American History* (New York: Henry Holt, 1932), 214.

16. Dixon Ryan Fox, "Patriotism on the Screen: The Use of the 'Chronicles of America Motion Pictures' in Americanization," *Ohio History Teachers' Journal,* no. 34 (May 1924), 456; Walter Benjamin, "The Work of Art in an Age of Mechanical Reproduction," in Walter Benjamin, *Illuminations,* ed. Hannah Arendt, trans. Harry Zohn (New York: Schocken Books, 1969), 217–51.

17. George Parmly Day, "The Story of the Chronicles of America," *Ohio History Teachers' Journal,* no. 33 (March 1924), 432; Nathaniel Stephenson, "The Chronicles of America in Motion Pictures," ibid., 433; W. T. Waugh, "History in Moving Pictures," *History,* 11 (January 1927), 326.

18. Glasgow to Ralph Gabriel, 17 September 1921, series IV, box 21, file 359, Ralph Gabriel Papers, Yale University Library.

19. Max Farrand, "The Quality of Distinction," *AHR,* 46 (April 1941), 515.

20. Stephenson (1867–1935) was a former newspaperman who taught at the College of Charleston (1902–22) and at Scripps College (1927–35). *Who Was Who in America,* 1:1178; obituary, *MVHR,* 22 (June 1935), 157.

21. Stephenson to Robinson, 14 January 1925, box 3, Robinson Papers; Schafer to Farrand, 9 June 1924, box 2, file 7; and Schafer to Farrand, 4 June 1924, box 2, file 7, Joseph Schafer Papers, SHSW, Madison, WI; Donald Mattheisen, "Filming U.S. History during the 1920s: The Chronicles of America Photoplays," *Historian,* 54, no. 4 (1992), 634.

22. Daniel C. Knowlton and J. Warren Tilton, *Motion Pictures in History Teaching: A Study of the Chronicles of America Photoplays as an Aid in Seventh Grade Instruction* (New Haven: Yale University Press, 1929), 6.

23. John Franklin Jameson, "The Meeting of the American Historical Association at Columbus," *AHR,* 29 (April 1924), 426.

24. Fox, "Patriotism on the Screen," 461.

25. Dixon Ryan Fox, "Chronicles of America Photoplays," *PW,* 22 November 1924, 1700.

26. A. E. Bacon (Yale University Press Film Service) to Edgar E. Robinson, with Robinson to Payson Treat, 19 November 1925, box 3, file 18, Robinson Papers; Robinson to Treat, 29 October 1925, ibid.

27. Waugh, "History in Moving Pictures," 324–29.

28. *NYT,* 30 September 1923, 6; Mattheisen, "Filming U.S. History," 636.

29. Waugh, "History in Moving Pictures," 326.

30. Robert S. Lynd and Helen Merrell Lynd, *Middletown: A Study in American Culture* (New York: Harcourt, Brace, and World, 1929), 265. Adults said they were "too grown up for such things" (p. 200).

31. *PW*, 22 November 1924, 1700.

32. See, e.g., "The Chronicles of America Photoplays News Bulletin," 23 January 1928, box 789, AHA Papers, LC.

33. *Vitalizing the Teaching of the State and Federal Constitutions* (October 1928) [Lincoln, NE: n.p., 1928], in file for 1929, box 13, John D. Hicks Papers, Bancroft Library, University of California, Berkeley.

34. Knowlton and Tilton, *Motion Pictures in History Teaching*, 93.

35. Catherine B. Firth, "The Use of Films in the Teaching of History: Some Comments on Two Reports," *History*, 17 (July 1932), 128–42. These reports were Knowlton and Tilton's *Motion Pictures in History Teaching* and Frances Consitt's *The Value of Films in History Teaching* (n.p.: Bell, 1931).

36. Mattheisen, "Filming U.S. History," 627–640.

37. Stephenson, "Chronicles of America in Motion Pictures," 437, 435.

38. Stephenson to Robinson, 17 June 1925, box 3, file 18, Robinson Papers.

39. Robinson to Stephenson, 6 July 1925, ibid.

40. *Detroit Times*, 24 June 1931; and *Detroit Saturday Night*, 11 April 1931, series IV, box 21, file 354; *New York Sun*, 11 April 1931, series IV, box 21, file 357, Gabriel Papers.

41. Stephenson to Robinson, 15 June 1925, box 3, file 18, Robinson Papers.

42. Waugh, "History in Moving Pictures," 326–27.

43. Fox, "Patriotism on the Screen," 457–58.

44. Irene Sewall to Yale University Press Film Service, 14 February 1928, series IV, box 22, file 368, Gabriel Papers.

45. Cf. Mattheisen, "Filming U.S. History," 639.

46. Lawton to Brook, 3 June 1927, series IV, box 21, file 367, Gabriel Papers. On the lobbying effort of the UDC, see David W. Blight, *Race and Reunion: The Civil War in American Memory* (Cambridge: Belknap Press, Harvard University Press, 2001), 278–82.

47. Blight, *Race and Reunion*, 278–82.

48. *The Report of the President-General to the 36th Annual Convention of the United Daughters of the Confederacy, 1929, Biloxi, Mississippi* (n.p., 1929), 4, in series I, box 1, file 8, Gabriel Papers.

49. A. H. Brook to Gabriel, 17 February 1940, report from M. Jacob Joslow, Ludlow, Mass., series I, box 4, file 81, Gabriel Papers; Edgar Robinson to Stephenson, 6 July 1925, box 3, file 18, Robinson Papers.

50. H. A. Wise (Southwestern Missouri State Teachers' College) to A. H. Brook, 25 November 1932, series I, box 2, file 37, Gabriel Papers; Firth, "Use of Films in the Teaching of History," 140; Norman Donaldson to Robinson, 9 April 1925, box 3, file 18, Robinson Papers. Grace Hotchkiss, "The Use of the Motion Picture as a Technique of Instruction," *SS* (January 1937), 9, noted that most schools still did not have a specialized motion picture room and there were relatively few movies suitable for 16-millimeter projectors.

51. See Douglas Gomery, *The Hollywood Studio System* (Basingstoke: Macmillan, 1986).

52. Henry Johnson, *The Other Side of Main Street: A History Teacher from Sauk County* (New York: Columbia University Press, 1943), 235–36.

53. Erling Hunt, "Scholars' History versus School History," *SS*, 26 (December 1935), 516.

54. "Final Report and Recommendations of the Committee on History to the College Entrance Examination Board," *SS*, 27 (December 1936), 546; Hunt, "Scholars' History versus School History," 516.

55. T. M. Beard, "Co-operation in University Stations," in Josephine H. MacLatchy, ed., *Education on the Air: Third Yearbook of the Institute for Education by Radio* (Columbus: Ohio State University, 1932), 28.

56. "Books into Movies," *PW*, 8 September 1934, 753.

57. Allan Nevins to Evarts B. Greene, 17 February 1939, box 4, Allan Nevins Papers, Rare Books and Manuscripts, Butler Library, Columbia University.

58. Edgar Wesley, *American History in Schools and Colleges: The Report of the Committee on American History in Schools and Colleges of the American Historical Association, the Mississippi Valley Historical Association, the National Council for the Social Studies; Edgar B. Wesley, Director* (New York: Macmillan, 1944), 50.

59. Hamilton Basso added that Burton Hendrick's *Statesmen of the Lost Cause: Jefferson Davis and His Cabinet* (Boston: Little, Brown and Co., 1939) might serve as a "cooling corrective." *NR*, 5 February 1940, 185.

60. *Anti-Negro Propaganda in High School Textbooks* (New York: NAACP, 1939), 8–9, in box 1, file 4, Herbert Aptheker Papers, Department of Special Collections, Stanford University Libraries.

61. W. E. B. Du Bois, *Dusk of Dawn: An Essay toward an Autobiography of a Race Concept* (New York: Harcourt, Brace, and Co., 1940), 239–40; Thomas Cripps, "The Negro Reaction to the Motion Picture *Birth of a Nation*," *Historian*, 25 (May 1963), 244–62; Thomas Cripps, *Slow Fade to Black: The Negro in American Film, 1900–1942* (New York: Oxford University Press, 1977); Blight, *Race and Reunion*, 393–97.

62. Harvey Wish, review of *Magic Shadows: The Story of the Origin of Motion Pictures*, by Martin Quigley Jr. (Washington, DC: Georgetown University Press, 1948), *MVHR*, 35 (June 1948), 138–39.

63. Charles Beard and Mary Beard, *The Rise of American Civilization*, vol. 2 (New York: Macmillan, 1927), 777.

64. Charles Beard and Mary Beard, *America in Midpassage* (New York: Macmillan, 1939), 595–601, quotations at 592 and 593.

65. George S. Counts, *Report of the Commission on the Social Studies*, part 9, *The Social Foundations of Education* (New York: Charles Scribner's Sons, 1934), 299, quotation at 297.

66. Charles Beard, *A Charter for the Social Sciences* (New York: Charles Scribner's Sons, 1932), 62, 64; see also Commission on the Social Studies, *Conclusions and Recommendations of the Commission* (New York: Charles Scribner's Sons, 1934), 22; and Beard, *Nature of the Social Sciences*, 141.

67. Edward Countryman, "John Ford's *Drums along the Mohawk*: The Making of an

American Myth," in Susan P. Benson, Stephen Brier, and Roy Rosenzweig, eds., *Presenting the Past: Essays on History and the Public* (Philadelphia: Temple University Press, 1986), 87–102; Eric Breitbart, "The Painted Mirror," in ibid., 117.

68. Margaret F. Thorp, *America at the Movies* (New Haven: Yale University Press, 1939); Ellis, review of Thorp, *MVHR*, 26 (March 1940), 645.

69. Counts, *Social Foundations of Education*, 299.

70. Du Bois, *Dusk of Dawn*, 239–40; David Levering Lewis, *W. E. B. DuBois: Biography of a Race, 1868–1919* (New York: Henry Holt and Co., 1993), 506–9.

71. Wesley, *American History in Schools and Colleges*, 50.

72. Rosalie Stewart to Nevins, 12 April 1939, box 48, Nevins Papers; William James Fadiman to Nevins, 16 February 1939, ibid.

73. Nevins to Evarts B. Greene, 17 February 1939, box 4, Nevins Papers. The "direct harm" that mass media did was "seldom great," and "the worst inflictions of the mass media seldom sink in far." Allan Nevins, "Not Capulets, Not Montagues," in Ray Allen Billington, comp., *Allan Nevins on History* (New York: Charles Scribner's Sons, 1975), 23.

74. "Teachers' Section," *MVHR*, 31 (March 1945), 439; ibid., 34 (June 1947), 161–62.

75. Thorp, *America at the Movies*, 165–66; T. R. Adam, *Motion Pictures in Adult Education* (New York: American Association for Adult Education, 1940), 45–46; Erik Barnouw, *Documentary: A History of Non-feature Film* (New York: Oxford University Press, 1974), 113–21; Peter C. Rollins and Harris J. Elder, "Environmental History in Two New Deal Documentaries: *The Plow that Broke the Plains* and *The River*," *Film and History*, 4 (1974), 1–7.

76. Dorothy Arbaugh, "Morion Pictures and the Future Historian," *American Archivist*, 2 (April 1939), 106–14.

77. Jesse D. Clarkson, "Educating Clio," *AHR*, 46 (April 1941), 510.

78. Beard and Beard, *Midpassage*, 595, 598–99, quotation at 616.

79. Jason R. Glass, "Oral History of Bradford Perkins," http://www-personal .unimich.edu/~amnornes/Glass.html (accessed 28 May 2004). For the Why We Fight series, see Benjamin L. Alpers, "This Is the Army: Imagining a Democratic Military in World War II," *JAH*, 85 (June 1998), 153–57; Thomas W. Bohn, *An Historical and Descriptive Analysis of the "Why We Fight" Series* (New York: Arno Press, 1977), 103–5; William T. Murphy, "John Ford and the Wartime Documentary," *Film and History*, 6, no. 1 (1976), 1–9; Clayton R. Koppes and Gregory D. Black, "What to Show the World: The Office of War Information and Hollywood, 1942–1945," *JAH*, 64 (June 1977), 87–105.

80. Arthur M. Schlesinger Jr., *A Life in the Twentieth Century: Innocent Beginnings, 1917–1950* (Boston: Houghton Mifflin, 2000), 150–51; Siegfried Kracauer, *From Caligari to Hitler* (1947), cited in ibid., 154.

81. John D. Hicks to Fredric March, 27 July 1939, box 10, Correspondence, 1939, Hicks Papers; Nevins, "Not Capulets, Not Montagues," 23.

82. E.g., Everett Carter, "Cultural History Written with Lightning: The Significance of *The Birth of a Nation*," *American Quarterly*, 12 (Autumn 1960), 347–57; Margaret Thorp, "The Motion Picture and the Novel," *American Quarterly*, 3 (Autumn 1951), 195–203.

83. Clayton Ellsworth, "Clio and the Camera," *MVHR*, 31 (March 1945), 579–84.

84. Carl Bridenbaugh, "The Neglected First Half of American History," *AHR*, 53 (April 1948), 514.

85. Irene F. Cypher, "Perspective for Learning—through Filmstrips," *EdScreen and AVGuide,* 36 (February 1957), 72–73.

Chapter Six

1. Key sources on radio include Erik Barnouw, *The Golden Web: A History of Broadcasting in the United States,* vol. 2 (New York: Oxford University Press, 1968); Susan J. Douglas, *Listening In: Radio and the American Imagination* (London: Time, 1999); Robert McChesney, *Telecommunications, Mass Media, and Democracy: The Battle for the Control of U.S. Broadcasting, 1928–1935* (New York: Oxford University Press, 1993); Susan Smulyan, *Selling Radio: The Commercialization of American Broadcasting, 1920–1934* (Washington, DC: Smithsonian Institution Press, 1994); Douglas B. Craig, *Fireside Politics: Radio and Political Culture in the United States, 1920–1940s* (Baltimore: Johns Hopkins University Press, 2000); Hugh R. Slotten, *Radio and Television Regulation* (Baltimore: Johns Hopkins University Press, 2000); Michele Hilmes and Jason Loviglio, eds., *Radio Reader: Essays in the Cultural History of Radio* (London: Routledge, 2002).

2. Edgar Wesley, *American History in Schools and Colleges: The Report of the Committee on American History in Schools and Colleges of the American Historical Association, the Mississippi Valley Historical Association, the National Council for the Social Studies; Edgar B. Wesley, Director* (New York: Macmillan, 1944), 50.

3. Frederick Jackson Turner, *The Significance of Sections in American History* (New York: Henry Holt, 1932), 214.

4. Erik Barnouw, *A Tower in Babel: A History of Broadcasting in the United States,* vol. 1 (New York: Oxford University Press, 1966); Barnouw, *Golden Web.*

5. "Proceedings of the Fourth Annual Assembly of the National Advisory Council on Radio in Education, Inc., . . . 1934," in Levering Tyson, ed., *Radio and Education: Proceedings of the Fourth Annual Assembly of the National Advisory Council on Radio in Education, Inc., 1934* (Chicago: University of Chicago Press, 1934), 1–106.

6. Mrs. Harold Vincent Milligan, "Women Organize to Listen," in Levering Tyson and Josephine MacLatchy, eds., *Education on the Air and Radio and Education, 1935: Proceedings of the Sixth Annual Institutes for Education by Radio, Combined with the Fifth Annual Advisory Assembly of the National Advisory Council on Radio in Education* (Chicago: University of Chicago Press, 1935), 183–91, quotations at 190.

7. Craig, *Fireside Politics,* 212–13; Barnouw, *Tower in Babel,* 261.

8. Introduction, Tyson and MacLatchy, *Education on the Air,* v.

9. Kate Lacey, "Radio in the Great Depression: Promotional Culture, Public Service, and Propaganda," in Hilmes and Loviglio, *Radio Reader,* 26.

10. Theodore Blegen, "State Historical Agencies and the Public," *Minnesota History Bulletin,* 9 (June 1928), 129.

11. *State and Local History News,* 1 (July 1942), 1; *NYT,* 9 August 1942, II: 5.

12. Josephine H. MacLatchy, ed., *Education on the Air: Second Yearbook of the Institute for Education by Radio* (Columbus: Ohio State University, 1931), 133.

13. H. B. McCarty to John D. Hicks, 28 August 1933, box 13, John D. Hicks Papers, Bancroft Library, University of California, Berkeley. WHA also broadcast Wisconsin history as part of the Wisconsin College of the Air; *MVHR* 29 (December 1942), 472;

Mrs. E. M. Shuart [*sic*] to Radio Station WHA Madison, 27 February 1942, box 10, Hicks Papers.

14. William B. Hesseltine to Hicks, 23 September 1942, box 10, Hicks Papers.

15. Hattie S. Parrott, "The North Carolina Radio School," in *Education on the Air: Fourth Yearbook of the Institute for Education by Radio* (Columbus: Ohio State University, 1933), 139, 141.

16. Joseph F. Wright, "Significant Activities of the Radio Station at the University of Illinois," in MacLatchy, *Education on the Air: Second Yearbook,* 109.

17. E. M. Shuart to Radio Station WHA Madison, 27 February 1942, box 10, Hicks Papers; Josephine H. MacLatchy, ed., *Education on the Air: Eighth Yearbook of the Institute for Education by Radio* (Columbus: Ohio State University, 1937), 73, 77.

18. *State and Local History News,* 1 (July 1942), 1.

19. Josephine H. MacLatchy, ed., *Education on the Air: Tenth Yearbook of the Institute for Education by Radio* (Columbus: Ohio State University, 1939), 370.

20. Parrott, "North Carolina Radio School," 139, 141.

21. Tracy Ferris Tyler, *An Appraisal of Radio Broadcasting in the Land-Grant Colleges and State Universities* (Washington, DC: National Committee on Education by Radio, 1933); Craig, *Fireside Politics,* 212.

22. The AHA annual report for 1940 listed Braun as "Read." See also the earlier *Annual Report of the American Historical Association for the Year 1938* (Washington, DC: Government Printing Office, 1939), xxii, which lists Braun's address as Read's. Throughout, for the sake of clarity, I shall call her Braun.

23. Evelyn Plummer Braun, "Broadcasting History: The Story of 'The Story behind the Headlines,'" *Bulletin of the Association for State and Local History,* 1, no. 7 (October 1943), 161.

24. Elizabeth Yates Webb, "A Broadcasting Venture in Mass Education," in Tyson, *Radio and Education: Proceedings of the Fourth Annual Assembly,* 201.

25. Braun to S. Howard Evans, 4 April 1938, box 64, file 42, National Broadcasting Company Papers, SHSW, Madison, WI.

26. John Allen Krout, "History," in Levering Tyson, ed., *Radio and Education: Proceedings of the Second Annual Assembly of National Advisory Council on Radio in Education, Inc., 1932* (Chicago: University of Chicago Press, 1932), 73–74.

27. Levering Tyson, ed., *Radio and Education: Proceedings of the First Annual Assembly of the National Advisory Council on Radio in Education, Inc., 1931* (Chicago: University of Chicago Press, 1931), 217, 218.

28. Payson Smith to A. B. Hart, 3 February 1931, box 21, file "Radio," Albert Bushnell Hart Papers, Harvard University Archives.

29. Braun, "Broadcasting History," 175.

30. Webb, "Broadcasting Venture," 200.

31. Ibid., 295, 200, 201, 202; Conyers Read, "Problems of Program Organization," in Tyson and MacLatchy, *Education on the Air and Radio and Education, 1935,* 159.

32. Braun, "Broadcasting History," 169, 174–75.

33. Webb, "Broadcasting Venture," 202, 204.

34. Braun, "Broadcasting History," 172.

35. Bruce Lenthall, "Critical Reception: Public Intellectuals Decry Depression-Era Radio, Mass Culture, and Modern America," in Hilmes and Loviglio, *Radio Reader*, 41–51; Charles Beard and Mary Beard, *America in Midpassage* (New York: Macmillan, 1939), 920–21.

36. T. R. Adam, *Motion Pictures in Adult Education* (New York: American Association for Adult Education, 1940), 67.

37. Phillips Bradley, "The Story behind the Headlines—an Experiment in Education for Democracy," *Bulletin of "The Story behind the Headlines,"* 2, no. 1 (18 October 1938), 16.

38. Webb, "Broadcasting Venture," 200; Read, "Problems of Program Organization," 158–59; "XYZ," *SRL*, 16 January 1932, 464; Read to James R. Angell, 10 January 1938, box 64, file 42, NBC Papers.

39. Columbia University Bureau of Applied Social Research, *Radio Listening in America: The People Look at Radio—Again* (New York: Prentice Hall, 1948), 1.

40. Paul Lazarsfeld, "The Effect of Radio on Public Opinion," in Douglas Waples, ed., *Print, Radio, and Film in a Democracy* (Chicago: University of Chicago Press, 1942), 72–73; Paul Lazarsfeld, comments in "Broadcasts for General Education: Report of a Work-Study Group," in MacLatchy, *Education on the Air: Tenth Yearbook,* 142–43.

41. Webb, "Broadcasting Venture," 194, 210, 200.

42. John Allen Krout, "Report of the Committee on History," in Tyson, *Radio in Education: Proceedings of the First Annual Assembly,* 218.

43. Webb, "Broadcasting Venture," 194.

44. Ibid. (final quotation); Braun, "Broadcasting History," 165.

45. Webb, "Broadcasting Venture," 213.

46. Read, "Problems of Program Organization," 162, 158; Webb, "Broadcasting Venture," 194.

47. Eric Hobsbawm, *The Age of Extremes: The Short Twentieth Century, 1914–1991* (London: Abacus, 1995), 196.

48. Braun, "Broadcasting History," 164, 170.

49. Cesar Saerchinger, "Broadcasting News as History," in Josephine H. MacLatchy, ed., *Education on the Air: Ninth Yearbook of the Institute for Education by Radio* (Columbus: Ohio State University, 1938), 175, 169.

50. "Report of the Executive Secretary for 1947 with Summary of Reports of Standing Committees," box 153, file "Council—December meeting 1947," AHA Papers, LC; "Report of the Executive Secretary and Managing Editor for 1948," box 163, file "Business Meeting—1948," ibid.

51. Braun, "Broadcasting History," 175, 176, 178.

52. Conyers Read to Members of the Executive Committee, AHA, 20 April 1938, box 2, file 1938 Jan.–June, Solon Buck Papers, LC.

53. "Of Radio and History," *Bulletin of "The Story behind the Headlines,"* 1, no. 1 (8 March 1938), 19.

54. Read to James R. Angell, 25 July 1938, box 58, file 38, NBC Papers; Guy Stanton Ford to Members of the Committee on Committees, 24 November 1947, box 153, file "Committee on Committees 1947," AHA Papers.

55. "Minutes of the Meeting of the Executive Committee of the American Historical Association," 6 March 1938, box 86, file 1935–39, AHA Papers; Braun "Broadcasting History," 163.

56. Braun, "Broadcasting History," 179.

57. Braun to Edmond S. Meany, 2 April 1937, box 81, file 1935–39, AHA Papers.

58. Braun to Dexter Perkins, 6 December 1937, box 81, file 1935–39, ibid.

59. Braun, "Broadcasting History," 181.

60. Read to James R. Angell, 10 February 1938, box 64, file 42, NBC Papers.

61. Flyer, "The Story behind the Headlines," box 3, file 1939—July–December, Buck Papers; editor's foreword to ". . . *Rendezvous with Destiny": An NBC Documentary Recording Based on Radio Addresses of Franklin D. Roosevelt* (n.p.: [1946]); Braun to Guy Stanton Ford, 5 May 1946, box 122, file "Radio Committee," AHA Papers.

62. Braun, "Broadcasting History," 183.

63. *Radio Daily,* 7 March 1938, box 64, file 42, NBC Papers.

64. Braun, "Broadcasting History," 183.

65. "England's Foreign Policy," reprinted in MacLatchy, ed., *Ninth Yearbook,* 305–10.

66. [Conyers Read], "A Matter of Emphasis," *Bulletin of "The Story behind the Headlines,"* 1, no. 5 (5 April 1938), 16.

67. Elizabeth Yates Webb, "Can We Keep Our Heads?" *Bulletin of "The Story behind the Headlines,"* 1, no. 8 (26 April 1938), 15–19.

68. "Report of the Executive Secretary on the Activities of the American Historical Association during the Year 1937," p. 14, box 86, file "American History Association, Executive Secretary 1937," AHA Papers.

69. "Report of the Committee of Judges on Awards," in MacLatchy, ed., *Ninth Yearbook,* 220; Braun to Solon Buck, 10 May 1938, box 2, file 1938 Jan.–June, Buck Papers.

70. Franklin Dunham to C. W. Fitch, 10 May 1938, box 64, file 5, NBC Papers.

71. "How Can We Publicize American History?" *State and Local History News,* 2 (September 1943), in box 133, file "American Association of State and Local History," AHA Papers.

72. Committee Reports and Index for Annual Report, 1943, box 139, file "Radio Committee," AHA Papers; James R. Angell to Walter Preston Jr., 30 June 1939, box 72, file 67, NBC Papers.

73. "The Draft of the Report of the Executive Secretary on the Activities of the American Historical Association during the Year 1941," box 124, file "Council and Executive Committee, 1941," AHA Papers.

74. Braun to Dexter Perkins, 21 June 1939, box 139, file "Committee Reports and Index for Annual Report, 1943," AHA Papers; Barnouw, *Golden Web,* 68n, 86, 153; William H. Hartley, "Sight and Sound in Social Studies," *SE,* 5 (March 1941), 224.

75. Conyers Read, "Radio Committee," box 129, file "Radio Committee, 1942," AHA Papers.

76. *The Story behind the Headlines,* mimeographed transcripts, e.g., 20 January 1946, Columbia University Library.

77. James R. Angell to Braun, 22 September 1938, file 42, box 64, NBC Papers.

78. ". . . *Rendezvous with Destiny*"; Braun to Guy Stanton Ford, 5 May 1946, box 122, AHA Papers.

79. Wilmer C. Harris to AHA, 22 April 1946, box 122, file "Radio Committee," AHA Papers.

80. For Thomas Bailey's position, see memorandum from Ella Lunn, Goucher College, to AHA Nominating Committee, 13 August 1942, box 8, file 32, Thomas Bailey Papers, Department of Special Collections, Stanford University Libraries; see also memo from Lunn, 31 August 1942, ibid.

81. Solon Buck to Braun, 3 November 1938, box 2, file 1938 July–Dec., Buck Papers; see also Braun to Buck, 4 November 1938, ibid.

82. Read to Guy Stanton Ford, 16 November 1944, box 141, file "Radio, Committee on, 1944–45," AHA Papers.

83. Ford to Read, 21 November 1944, ibid.

84. William G. Harley (Program Coordinator, National Association of Educational Broadcasters) to Dumas Malone, 21 July 1951, series RG21/7.872, box 10, file "The Jeffersonian Heritage," Dumas Malone Papers, Rare Book and Manuscript Collection, Alderman Library, University of Virginia.

85. Max Savelle to Russell Sanjek, 10 March 1954, box 1, file 1/45, Max Savelle Papers, Department of Special Collections, University of Washington Libraries; Thomas Cochran to Carl Haverlin, 15 March 1954, box 2, file "Factory Comes to New England," Cochran, box 2, *The American Story* Papers, Rare Books and Manuscripts Library, Butler Library, Columbia University; press release, 24 May, n.d., ibid.

86. The audience for such programs on the BBC numbered, according to Eric Hobsbawm, only "a few tens of thousands." Eric J. Hobsbawm, *Interesting Times: A Twentieth-Century Life* (London: Allen Lane, 2002), 176.

87. Oliver P. Newman (Batten, Barton, Durstine and Osborn, Inc.) form letter, box 93, file "Radio Broadcasts," AHA Papers.

88. Hartley, "Sight and Sound in Social Studies," 224.

89. James R. Angell, Walter Lippmann, and Frank Monaghan, "History in This Hour," box 75, file 41, NBC Papers; "Information on *Cavalcade of America*," prepared for Educational Directors of the National Broadcasting Company, box 76, ibid.

90. "Information on *Cavalcade of America*." See also Arthur M. Schlesinger and Dixon Ryan Fox's *The Cavalcade of America, Series 2* (Springfield, MA: Milton Bradley, 1938), noted in *MVHR*, 26 (January 1939), 137.

91. *Annual Report of the American Historical Association for the Year 1935*, vol. 1, *Proceedings, 1933, 1934, 1935* (Washington, DC: Government Printing Office, 1938), 132.

92. Martin Gramm Jr., *The History of "The Cavalcade of America"* (Kearney, NH: Morris Publishing, 1998), unpaginated text.

93. Hartley, "Sight and Sound in Social Studies," 224.

94. Angell, Lippmann, and Monaghan, "History in This Hour," p. 3, in box 75, file 41, NBC Papers.

95. Ibid.; Gramm, *History of the Cavalcade of America*, unpaginated text.

96. Barnouw, *Golden Web*, 89–90.

97. Ibid., 91.

98. "Information on *Cavalcade of America*," 6.

99. Ibid., 3–5, 7–8.

100. See William Hawes, *The American Television Drama: The Experimental Years* (Tuscaloosa: University of Alabama Press, 1986); Frank Sturken, *Live Television: The Golden Age of 1946–58 in New York* (Jefferson, NC: McFarland, 1990).

101. Paul Lazarsfeld, comments in "Broadcasts for General Education: Report of a Work-Study Group," in MacLatchy, *Education on the Air: Tenth Yearbook*, 142–43.

Chapter Seven

1. Allan Nevins, "American History for Americans," *New York Times Magazine*, 3 May 1942, 6, 28.

2. Erling Hunt to Guy Stanton Ford, 13 April 1943, 15 April 1943, and 21 April 1943, box 126, file "American History, Teaching of," AHA Papers, LC; *NYT*, 21 June 1942, 1; Michael Kammen, *Mystic Chords of Memory: The Transformation of Tradition in American Culture* (New York: Knopf, 1991), 663–64, 817 n. 28.

3. *NYT*, 4 April 1943, 1, 32.

4. Diane Ravitch and Chester E. Finn, *What Do Our 17-Year-Olds Know? A Report on the First National Assessment of History and Literature* (New York: Harper and Row, 1987).

5. Louis Harlan, "Social Studies Reform and the Historian," *JAH*, 77 (December 1990), 801–11; David Kennedy, *OAH Newsletter*, May 1990, 13. American diplomatic historian Robert H. Ferrell raised a considerable stir with his outbursts in "History and the Public Schools," *OAH Newsletter*, February 1990, 6: "'Today's college freshmen know almost no American history and . . . they have wasted plenty of my time teaching them the most elementary of facts about it." Others, like Richard Kirkendall, worried about the impact of declining history enrollments on the subject of history. Kirkendall, "The Status of History in the Schools," *JAH*, 62 (September 1975), 557–70. Gary Nash blamed academics for neglecting the teaching of history at the precollegiate level. Gary Nash, Charlotte E. Crabtree, and Ross E. Dunn, *History on Trial: Culture Wars and the Teaching of the Past* (New York: Knopf, 1998), 66–67.

6. Hazel W. Hertzberg, "History and Progressivism: A Century of Reform Proposals," in Paul Gagnon and the Bradley Commission on History in Schools, *Historical Literacy: The Case for History in American Education* (Boston: Houghton Mifflin, 1989), 95.

7. Ibid.; Peter Novick, *That Noble Dream: The "Objectivity Question" and the American Historical Profession* (New York: Cambridge University Press, 1988), 185–93, 368–72, mentions earlier attempts to influence the schools. Nash, Crabtree, and Dunn, *History on Trial*, esp. 66–67. See also W. Stull Holt, *The Historical Profession in the United States* (Washington, DC: AHA, 1963), 14; David Jenness, *Making Sense of Social Studies* (New York: Macmillan, 1990), 102.

8. Kenneth Jackson and Barbara Jackson, "Why the Time Is Right to Reform the History Curriculum," in Gagnon and Bradley Commission, *Historical Literacy*, 11.

9. Carl Becker, review of *The New History and the Social Studies*, by Harry Elmer Barnes, *SRL*, 15 August 1925, 38; Justus D. Doenecke, "Harry Elmer Barnes: Prophet of a Useable Past," *History Teacher*, 8, no. 2 (1975), 265–76; Harry Elmer Barnes, "The Past and Future of History," *HO*, 12 (February 1921), 51.

10. Maurice Blinkoff, "The Influence of Charles A. Beard upon American Historiography," *University of Buffalo Studies*, 12 (May 1936), 31, 36, 38, 75.

11. Ellen Nore, *Charles Beard: An Intellectual Biography* (Carbondale: Southern Illinois University Press, 1983), chap. 7.

12. Jonathan Zimmerman, *Whose America? Culture Wars in the Public Schools* (Cambridge: Harvard University Press, 2002), 21, 26–27, 60, 78, 98.

13. See James Trustlow Adams, "History and the Lower Criticism," *Atlantic Monthly*, September 1923, 308–17; editorial, *NYT*, 29 December 1923, 12.

14. John Franklin Jameson, "The Meeting of the American Historical Association at Columbus," *AHR*, 29 (April 1924), 428; John Franklin Jameson, "The Meeting of the American Historical Association at Washington," *AHR*, 33 (April 1928), 537; Bethany Andreasen, "Treason or Truth: The New York City Textbook Controversy, 1920–1923," *New York History*, 66 (October 1985), 397–419; Jonathan Zimmerman, "'Each "Race" Could Have Its Heroes Sung': Ethnicity and the History Wars in the 1920s," *JAH*, 87 (June 2000), 92–111.

15. Ralph Guinness to Guy Stanton Ford, undated, for December 1947 council meeting, box 153, AHA Papers; Guinness to Ford, 20 October 1947, ibid.; Guinness et al. to Ford, 20 October 1947, ibid.; Ford to Guinness, 15 October 1947, ibid.; Guinness to Ford, 28 December 1946, ibid.; AHA council meeting report, *AHR*, 53 (July 1948), 688.

16. The best existing survey remains Hazel Hertzberg, *Social Studies Reform, 1880–1980* (Boulder, CO: Social Science Education Consortium, 1981). For the post–World War II period, see also Diane Ravitch, *The Troubled Crusade: American Education, 1945–1980* (New York: Basic Books, 1983).

17. Hertzberg, "History and Progressivism," 74; National Education Association, Committee of Ten on Secondary School Studies, *Report of the Committee on Secondary School Studies* (Washington, DC: Government Printing Office, 1893); Theodore R. Sizer, *Secondary Schools at the Turn of the Century* (New Haven: Yale University Press, 1964). For teaching practice, see Larry Cuban, *How Teachers Taught: Constancy and Change in American Classrooms, 1880–1990*, 2nd ed. (New York: Teachers College Press, 1993).

18. See correspondence and report of the Committee of Five, e.g., Andrew C. McLaughlin to Charles Homer Haskins, 5 December 1907, box 460, file "Committee of Five," AHA Papers; B. S. Hurlbut to Haskins, 18 November 1907, ibid.; *The Study of History in Secondary Schools: Report to the American Historical Association by a Committee of Five: Andrew C. McLaughlin, chairman* . . . (New York: Macmillan, 1911); American Historical Association, Committee of Seven, *The Study of History in Schools* (New York: Macmillan, 1899).

19. Sizer, *Secondary Schools at the Turn of the Century*, 48, 199; *The Statistical History of the United States: From Colonial Times to the Present*, with introduction and user's guide by Ben J. Wattenberg (New York: Basic Books, 1976), 383.

20. John Franklin Jameson, "The Meeting of the American Historical Association at Cleveland," *AHR*, 25 (April 1920), 373.

21. National Education Association, *The Social Studies in Secondary Education: A Six-Year Program Adapted Both to the 6-3-3 and the 8-4 Plans of Organization* (Washington, DC: Government Printing Office, 1916); "Report of the Committee on Social Studies of the Commission on the Reorganization of Secondary Education of the National Education Association," *History Teacher's Magazine*, 8 (January 1917), 4–25; Daniel Knowlton, "A Decade of Committee Activity," *HO*, 10 (December 1919), 499.

22. "Report of the Committee on Social Studies of the Commission on the Reorganization of Secondary Education of the National Education Association," 4–26; see also Luther V. Hendricks, *James Harvey Robinson: Teacher of History* (New York: King's Crown Press, 1946).

23. Quotation in Carol S. Gruber, *Mars and Minerva: World War I and the Uses of the Higher Learning in America* (Baton Rouge: Louisiana State University Press, 1975), 131.

24. Ibid., 131–35; "Report of Committee on History and Education for Citizenship," part 4, "Syllabus for Modern History in Tenth Grade," prepared by Daniel Knowlton, *HO*, 12 (May 1921), 165–89; for Knowlton, see *Who Was Who in America*, 5:404; "A Report of Progress," Supplement to *HO*, 10 (June 1919), 350. On Johnson and other teacher educator allies, see Charles Homer Haskins to Evarts B. Greene, 21 December 1916, box 252, file "Committee on Appointments," AHA Papers.

25. "Conference on the Report of the Committee on History and Education for Citizenship in the Schools," *HO*, 11 (March 1920), 111. The final report is "Report of Committee on History and Education for Citizenship," *HO*, 12 (March 1921), 87–96.

26. "Report of the Secretary and Papers Read at the Conference on the Report of the Committee on History and Education for Citizenship in the Schools," *HO*, 11 (February 1920), 73–89.

27. "Proceedings of the Thirty-fifth Annual Meeting of the American Historical Association," *Annual Report of the American Historical Association for the Year 1920*, vol. 1 (Washington, DC: Government Printing Office, 1925), 102, 106; Edgar Dawson, "Efforts toward Reorganization," *HO*, 20 (December 1929), 373; Edgar Dawson, "The History Inquiry," *HO*, 15 (June 1924), 249.

28. Leon C. Marshall, *Social Studies in Secondary Schools* (Chicago: University of Chicago Press, 1922), quoted in Dawson, "History Inquiry," Report of the Director, 250.

29. Charles A. Ellwood, "Sociology and the Social Studies, with Special Reference to History," *HO*, 14 (December 1923), 349–50.

30. "A National Council for the Social Studies," *HO*, 12 (April 1921), 190; "Annual Meeting, National Council for the Social Studies," *HO*, 13 (April 1922), 137, 139; "The Progress of the National Council for the Social Studies," *HO*, 14 (December 1923), 343–46.

31. John Spencer Bassett to Arthur M. Schlesinger, 22 August 1924, box 2, Arthur M. Schlesinger Papers, Harvard University Archives.

32. Jameson, "Meeting of the American Historical Association at Columbus," 427; Dawson, "History Inquiry," 250.

33. N. Ray Hiner, "Professions in Process: Changing Relations among Social Scientists, Historians, and Educators, 1880–1920," *History Teacher*, 6, no. 2 (1973), 218; see also Hendricks, *James Harvey Robinson*, 47–63.

34. Arthur M. Schlesinger to John Spencer Bassett, 18 December 1922, box 2, Schlesinger Papers.

35. Carl Becker to Henry Johnson, 24 October 1922, ibid.

36. In the interwar years Dewey himself became increasingly critical of too utilitarian an education, however. Robert Westbrook, *John Dewey and American Democracy* (Ithaca: Cornell University Press, 1991), 500–510.

37. August C. Krey, "Social Studies in the Colleges, 1909 to 1929," *HO*, 20 (September

1929), 319–21; J. Montgomery Gambrill, "The New World History," *HO,* 18 (October 1927), 265–66; Symposium on "Problems of Teaching History in College," especially Arthur H. Noyes, "Freshman History Instruction at Ohio State University," *HO,* 21 (April 1930), 153–55; Witt Bowden, "The Problem of the Better Student in the College Introductory Course in History," *HO,* 21 (April 1930), 157; "Conference on College Course in American History, New Haven, December 28, 1922," *HO,* 14 (March 1923), 93–98; Gilbert Allardyce, "The Rise and Fall of the Western Civilization Course," *AHR,* 87 (June 1982), 705–17; Nash, Crabtree, and Dunn, *History on Trial,* 51–52.

38. John Franklin Jameson, "The Meeting of the American Historical Association at Ann Arbor," *AHR,* 31 (April 1926), 436.

39. John Franklin Jameson, "The Meeting of the American Historical Association at Rochester," *AHR,* 32 (April 1927), 448.

40. "History and Other Social Studies in the Schools, Report of a Committee, Submitted to the Council of the American Historical Association, Approved, December 1926," *HO,* 18 (March 1927), 110. The 1925 committee consisted of Bassett, Ford, Ernest Horn, Henry Johnson, William E. Lingelbach, Leon Marshall, Charles E. Merriam, Jesse H. Newlon, and A. C. Krey. See also A. C. Krey, "Thirty Years after the Committee of Seven," *HO,* 20 (February 1929), 65.

41. Novick, *That Noble Dream,* 190.

42. A. C. Krey, "Report of the Investigation of the Social Studies," *HO,* 21 (February 1930), 63–66; Lawrence J. Dennis, *George S. Counts and Charles A. Beard: Collaborators for Change* (Albany: State University of New York Press, 1989), 333–36; Dexter Perkins, "The Meeting of the American Historical Association at Indianapolis," *AHR,* 34 (April 1929), 470.

43. Charles Beard, "The Trend in Social Studies," *HO,* 20 (December 1929), 370.

44. Charles Beard, *The Nature of the Social Sciences in Relation to Objectives of Instruction* (New York: Charles Scribner's Sons, 1934); Harry Elmer Barnes, review of *The Nature of the Social Sciences,* by Charles Beard, *AHR,* 40 (October 1934), 97–99; Nore, *Beard,* 21.

45. Dennis, *George S. Counts and Charles A. Beard,* 102. See Kenneth Edward Gell, "Implications of the Report of the Commission on the Social Studies of the American Historical Association as It Affects the High School Teacher," *SS,* 25 (October 1934), 299; Franklin Bobbitt, review of *Conclusions and Recommendations of the Commission* (New York: Charles Scribner's Sons, 1934), *School Review,* 42 (September 1934), 549; Tyler Kepner, "Comments on *Conclusions and Recommendations,*" *SS,* 25 (November 1934), 348.

46. Erling Hunt, "Conclusions and Recommendations of the Commission on the Social Studies of the American Historical Association," *SS,* 25 (October 1934), 283. A number of historians wrote individual volumes for the commission and were aligned to one degree or another with the commission. See, e.g., Merle Curti, *Social Ideas of American Educators* (New York: Charles Scribner's Sons, 1935).

47. "History and Other Social Studies in the Schools," 110–13. Krey, "Thirty Years after the Committee of Seven," 65; Hunt, "Conclusions and Recommendations," 282.

48. Edgar Wesley, "A Guide to the Commission Report," *SS,* 27 (November 1936), 438–39.

49. Commission on the Social Studies, *Conclusions and Recommendations of the Commission* (New York: Charles Scribner's Sons, 1934).

50. Quotation from B. H. Bode, "Which Way Democracy?" *SS*, 25 (November 1934), 344; see also Gell, "Implications of the Report of the Commission on the Social Studies," 299; Bobbitt, review of *Conclusions and Recommendations of the Commission*, 549; Kepner, "Comments on *Conclusions and Recommendations*," 348.

51. Editorial, *SS*, 25 (May 1934), 215.

52. Wesley, "Guide to the Commission Report," 448, quotation at 450.

53. Burr W. Phillips, "Some Current Criticisms of the Teaching of History," *HO*, 24 (May 1933), 245–46; Burr W. Phillips to John D. Hicks, 27 March 1942, box 10, John D. Hicks Papers, Bancroft Library, University of California, Berkeley; "Notes and News," *SE*, 1 (February 1937), 133.

54. Michael H. Lucey, "Next Steps," *SS*, 25 (November 1934), 348–49.

55. Vierling Kersey, "*Conclusions and Recommendations:* Report of the Commission on the Social Studies," *SS*, 25 (November 1934), 349.

56. Kepner, "Comments on *Conclusions and Recommendations*," 348.

57. See John S. Valentine, *The College Board and the School Curriculum: A History of the College Board's Influence on the Substance and Standards of American Education, 1900–1980* (New York: College Entrance Examination Board, 1987).

58. *Annual Report of the American Historical Association for the Year 1935*, vol. 1, *Proceedings, 1933, 1934, and 1935* (Washington, DC: Government Printing Office, 1938), 135.

59. Conyers Read, "The Dissenting Opinion of Mr. Tyler Kepner," *SE*, 1 (February 1937), quotation at 92; "Final Report and Recommendations of the Commission on History to the College Entrance Examination Board," *SS*, 27 (December 1936), 548–53; Conyers Read, "A Matter of Emphasis," *Bulletin of "The Story behind the Headlines,"* 1, no. 5 (5 April 1938), 14–18; Conyers Read to Arthur M. Schlesinger, 23 April 1937, box 12, Schlesinger Papers.

60. "Final Report and Recommendations of the Commission on History," 551.

61. Erling Hunt, "The New College Board Exams," *SE*, 2 (September 1938), 382.

62. "Final Report and Recommendations of the Commission on History," 549, quotation at 548.

63. Eugene C. Barker, "The Changing View of the Function of History," *SS*, 29 (April 1938), 149, 154.

64. Conyers Read to P. Cram, 16 April 1937, box 12, Schlesinger Papers.

65. Theodore Clarke Smith, "The Writing of American History in America from 1884 to 1934," *AHR*, 40 (April 1935), 449.

66. Daniel C. Knowlton, letter to editor, *SE*, 1 (March 1937), 156–57.

67. Erling Hunt, "Social Studies: Preparation for College or Life," *SE*, 1 (February 1937), 80; Wesley, "Guide to the Commission Report."

68. Hunt, "Social Studies: Preparation for College or Life," 78.

69. Tyler Kepner, "The Dilemma of the Secondary-School Teacher," *SE*, 1 (February 1937), 86.

70. Ralph B. Guinness, "Education for Democracy," *SS*, 28 (April 1937), 156–57.

71. "The Alternative History Examinations of the College Entrance Examination Board," *SE*, 2 (September 1938), 399–403, esp. 399.

72. See chap. 8. After 1942 the CEEB replaced almost all written, essay-type examinations with new, multiple-choice question tests under the Scholastic Aptitude Test (SAT) system. Additional written examinations, including in American history, continued to be administered, but only for secondary schools that wanted to give them as "terminal school examinations." The war had forced the change, encouraging standardization to accommodate the demands of the armed forces and the need for efficiency and comparability across the education system. Academics were uncomfortable with these tests, as were some high school principals and teachers. Though the change did not affect the structure of the curriculum engineered by Read, indirectly the tests reflected larger shifts in Progressive education threatening historians' own compromise with curriculum reform. Valentine, *The College Board and the School Curriculum,* 51–53.

73. Herbert Donavan, "The New Course in European History in New York City High Schools," *HO,* 24 (April 1933), 186. Louise I. Capen's *Across the Ages* was billed by the American Book Company as an example of the unit plan. The unit plan was praised: "The New Civic History, constructed on an original unit plan, tells vividly the story of man's achievements"; *SE,* 4 (December 1940), 528.

74. "Notes and News," *SE,* 2 (April 1938), 281.

75. Donald Alter, "World History: Surveys or Substance?" *SE,* 4 (October 1940), 422.

76. Phillips, "Some Current Criticisms of the Teaching of History," 244.

77. S. P. McCutcheon, "Eight Year Study—Progressive Education Association: An Introduction," *SE,* 2 (April 1938), 229–32.

78. "Notes and News," *SE,* 2 (January 1938), 51.

79. Ibid.; Leon A. Wilber, "Adapting a World History Course to a New Curriculum Proposal," *SE,* 3 (December 1939), 628–29.

80. G. H. V. Melone, John Burroughs School, Clayton, Missouri, cited in "Notes and News," *SE,* 2 (January 1938), 51.

81. "Notes and News," *SE,* 2 (January 1938), 51.

82. Hertzberg, "History and Progressivism," 91–92.

83. Commission on the Social Studies, *Conclusions and Recommendations,* 11–12.

84. Beard, "A Memorandum from an Old Worker in the Vineyard," *SE,* 2 (September 1938), 383, 384.

85. Beard, *Nature of the Social Sciences,* 68.

86. Beard, "Memorandum from an Old Worker," 384; Charles Beard and Mary Beard, *America in Midpassage* (New York: Macmillan, 1939), 585–646.

87. Beard, "Memorandum from an Old Worker," 383; *NYT,* 9 April 1942, 26; Beard, "A Challenge to Educational Leaders," *Civic Leader,* 10 (28 September 1942), 2–3.

88. Beard, "Memorandum from an Old Worker," 383.

89. *NYT,* 9 April 1942, 26.

Chapter Eight

1. Bessie Louise Pierce, *Public Opinion and the Teaching of History in the United States* (New York: Alfred A. Knopf, 1926).

2. *Western Catholic,* reprinted in *Irish World and American Liberator,* 3 March 1923, 6;

Irish World and American Liberator, 26 May 1923, 3; Jonathan Zimmerman, "'Each "Race" Could Have Its Heroes Sung': Ethnicity and the History Wars in the 1920s," *JAH,* 87 (June 2000), 92–111.

3. *Irish World and American Liberator,* 12 May 1923, 5; Charles Grant Miller, *Treason to American Tradition: The Spirit of Benedict Arnold Reincarnated in United States History Revised in Textbooks* (n.p.: National Society of the Sons of the American Revolution, 1922).

4. Joseph Schafer, "The Sons of the American Revolution and School Histories," *Wisconsin Magazine of History,* 7, no. 1 (1923–24), 105; *San Francisco Examiner,* 14 April 1923.

5. *NYT,* 13 February 1925, 19.

6. See Bethany Andreasen, "Treason or Truth: The New York City Textbook Controversy, 1920–1923," *New York History,* 66 (October 1985), 397–419.

7. Gary Nash, Charlotte E. Crabtree, and Ross E. Dunn, *History on Trial: Culture Wars and the Teaching of the Past* (New York: Knopf, 1998), 31; Zimmerman, "'Each "Race" Could Have Its Heroes Sung,'" 96.

8. John Franklin Jameson, "The Meeting of the American Historical Association at Columbus," *AHR,* 29 (April 1924), 428.

9. John Franklin Jameson, "The Meeting of the American Historical Association at Washington," *AHR,* 33 (April 1928), 537.

10. See *Washington Herald,* 26 November 1935; Carl Becker to editor of the *Washington Herald,* 26 November 1935, in Michael Kammen, ed., *What Is the Good of History? Selected Letters of Carl L. Becker, 1900–1945* (Ithaca: Cornell University Press, 1973), 232–33; Carl Becker, *Modern History: The Rise of a Democratic, Scientific, and Industrial Civilization* (New York: Silver Burdett, 1931).

11. Francis T. Spalding to Conyers Read, 17 January 1941, box 123, file "General, 1941," AHA Papers, LC. See also Ned H. Dearborn to R. L. Schuyler, 6 February 1941, box 122, unmarked file [3], AHA Papers; Conyers Read to Executive Committee, 26 March 1941, ibid.; Schuyler to Read, 31 March 1941, ibid.; Memo. to the Council and the Exec. Committee of the Council of the AHA, 7 April 1941, ibid. Ralph Robey became chief economist for the NAM in 1946. See *DAS,* 1951 ed., 791–92.

12. *NYT,* 23 August 1940, 17.

13. Ibid., 28.

14. *NYT,* 4 April 1943, 1.

15. Hugh Fraser quoted in Allan Nevins, "More American History? A Letter," *SE,* 6 (December 1942), 345.

16. See, e.g., *St. Louis Post-Dispatch,* n.d. [probably 28 June 1942]; *Detroit Free Press,* 28 June 1942; *Baltimore Sun,* 22 June 1942; *Evening Bulletin* (Providence, RI), 6 July 1942, all in CAHSC, box 2, file 4, SHSW, Madison, WI; "Editorial Comment by Hearst Newspapers on American History," box 1, file 7, CAHSC; *Washington Post* clippings, 6, 7, 8 April 1943, in box 126, folder "American History, Teaching of," AHA Papers; *Cleveland Plain-Dealer,* 12 April 1943, quoted in "Statement of Policy of the Committee on American History," box 57, Correspondence 1943, Allan Nevins Papers, Rare Books and Manuscripts Library, Butler Library, Columbia University; Erling Hunt to Guy Stanton Ford, 12 November 1942, box 126, folder "American History, Teaching of," AHA Papers; *Pittsburgh Press,* 26–30 October 1942, quoted in *New York Times,* 11 September 1944, 16.

17. *NYT,* 1 July 1942, 11 (Willkie); 28 June 1942, 31; 30 June 1942, 20 (Pouch).

18. Columbia University Bulletin of Information, [19]43 series, no. 6, 23 January 1943, box 126, file "American History, Teaching of," AHA Papers.

19. Ford to Arthur M. Schlesinger, 12 April 1943, ibid.

20. Guy Stanton Ford to Edgar E. Robinson, 29 April 1943, box 141, untitled file on history teaching, ibid.

21. Ibid.; Guy Stanton Ford to Nellie Neilson, 5 July 1943, box 141, untitled file on history teaching, AHA Papers.

22. See, e.g., Minutes of the Committee on American History in the Schools and Colleges, Committee on American History in the Schools and Colleges (CAHSC) Collection, SHSW; O. F. Ander to Edgar Wesley, 17 April 1943, CAHSC Collection; John D. Hicks to Wesley, 20 July 1943, ibid.; Harold Bradley to Wesley, 27 and 30 August 1943 and 13 and 18 September 1943, ibid.

23. Edgar Wesley, *American History in Schools and Colleges: The Report of the Committee on American History in Schools and Colleges of the American Historical Association, the Mississippi Valley Historical Association, the National Council for the Social Studies; Edgar B. Wesley, Director* (New York: Macmillan, 1944), 87.

24. *NYT,* 17 December 1943, 26; Wesley, *American History in Schools and Colleges, 63–84.*

25. Wesley, *American History in Schools and Colleges,* 89; Caroline F. Ware, ed., *The Cultural Approach to History* (New York: Columbia University Press, 1940), 6; the Editors, "Educating Clio," *AHR,* 45 (April 1940), 516.

26. Cf. Nash, Crabtree, and Dunn, *History on Trial;* Peter Novick, *That Noble Dream: The "Objectivity Question" and the American Historical Profession* (New York: Cambridge University Press, 1988); Hazel W. Hertzberg, "History and Progressivism: A Century of Reform Proposals," in Paul Gagnon and the Bradley Commission on History in Schools, *Historical Literacy: The Case for History in American Education* (Boston: Houghton Mifflin, 1989).

27. Henry Johnson, review of *American History in Schools and Colleges,* by Edgar Wesley, *School and Society,* 59 (8 April 1944), 254–55.

28. James B. Palmer to Edgar Wesley, 2 and 8 November 1950, box 2, file 6, CAHSC Collection; Michael Harper to Wesley, 7 November 1950, ibid.; Robert W. Shugg to Wesley, 8 November 1950, ibid.; Julie K. Walker to Wesley, 8 November 1950, ibid.

29. C. Eden Quainton, acting executive officer, University of Washington History Department, to John D. Hicks, 8 November 1943, box 10, John D. Hicks Papers, Bancroft Library, University of California, Berkeley.

30. *History in the High School and Social Studies in the Elementary School: The Record of an Inquiry Conducted among the Members of the Middle States Council for the Social Studies,* vol. 41 of *Annual Proceedings,* ed. Jeanette P. Nichols, Morris Wolf, and Arthur C. Bining (Philadelphia: n.p., 1944), 63.

31. Fourth of July address to the San Jose Lions Club, in *San Jose Morning Herald,* 19 July 1923, box 2, file 13, Edgar Eugene Robinson Papers, Department of Special Collections, Stanford University Libraries.

32. Stanford Conference of California College and University Teachers of American History, held 27 and 28 August 1942, 6, in box 141, untitled file on history teaching, AHA Papers.

33. Stanford Conference of California College and University Teachers of American History, held 27 and 28 August 1942 (p. 20), box 141, untitled file on history teaching, AHA Papers. Robinson's actions won wide press coverage; *NYT*, 20 September 1942, II: 5; 4 October 1942, II: 5.

34. "Adjustment of the College Curriculum to Wartime Conditions and Needs," box 141, untitled file on history teaching, AHA Papers.

35. Eugene Hugh Byrne quoted in Clarence McClelland, "Should the Study of American History in College Be Made Compulsory?" *School and Society*, 57 (16 January 1943), 67–68; see also Carl Pegg et al., *American Society and the Changing World* (New York: F. S. Crofts and Co., 1942); *SRL*, 3 October 1942, 11; William L. Sachse, "Echoes from Chicago," *AHR*, 47 (April 1942), 482.

36. A. T. Volwiler to Guy Stanton Ford, 27 January 1944, box 134, Committee on American History in Schools and Colleges, file 1944, AHA Papers; *NYT*, 7 February 1945, 1.

37. Allen F. Davis, "The Politics of American Studies," *American Quarterly*, 42 (September 1990), 353–74; Richard H. Shryock, "American Historiography: A Critical Analysis and a Program," *Proceedings of the American Philosophical Society*, 87 (July 1943), 46; *NYT*, 21 April 1946, 29; Ian Tyrrell, "The Challenge of De-provincializing US History in World War Two," in "Internationalizing U.S. History," ed. Dirk Hoerder, special issue, *Amerikastudien/American Studies*, 48 (Spring 2003), 41–59.

38. Boyd Shafer, "The Year's Business, 1955," *AHR*, 51 (April 1956), 801.

39. George Barr Carson Jr. (Director, Service Center for Teachers of History) to Clifford Lord, 21 December 1956, box 7, file 1, SHSW-NOC.

40. Martin P. Andersen (Head, Dept. of the Institutes, UCLA) to John D. Hicks, 5 May 1948, box 14, Hicks Papers; Edgar E. Robinson to Hicks, 30 April 1948, ibid.; Thomas A. Bailey, "The Obligation of the Teacher to Be a Scholar," *SE*, 13 (December 1949), 355–58.

41. Van R. Halsey Jr., "American History: A New High School Course," *SE*, 27 (May 1963), 259, 261.

42. Emlyn Jones to Sol Katz, 6 December 1961, box 2, file 67, W. Stull Holt Papers, Department of Special Collections, University of Washington Libraries; C. Eden Quainton to Hicks, 8 November 1943, box 10, Hicks Papers.

43. Richard L. Watson Jr. to George B. Carson Jr., 22 July 1957, Richard L. Watson Jr. Papers, Series II, Conference on Teaching the Social Studies, 1957–75, Duke University Library; Cartwright and Watson, eds., *Reinterpretation of American History and Culture* (Washington, DC: National Council on the Social Studies, 1973), 4.

44. Thomas A. Bailey, "Revitalizing American History," *SE*, 24 (December 1960), 371–74.

45. John R. Valley, "College Action on Candidates for Advanced Placement in History," *SE*, 23 (November 1959), 330.

46. Elwood G. Campbell, "Status of Advanced Placement American History Courses in Secondary Schools," *SE*, 28 (April 1964), 213.

47. John S. Valentine, *The College Board and the School Curriculum: A History of the College Board's Influence on the Substance and Standards of American Education, 1900–1980* (New York: College Entrance Examination Board, 1987), 86–87.

48. *NYT,* 11 September 1944, 16, quoting *Pittsburgh Press,* 3 September 1944, statement by Dr. W. W. Lantz, superintendent of Allegheny County schools.

49. *NYT,* 3 April 1945, 20.

50. "Emma" to Hicks, [December] 1942, box 10, Hicks Papers; Hicks to George Mowry, 5 August 1943, ibid.

51. *Teaching of United States History in Public High Schools: An Inquiry into Offerings and Registrations, 1946–47,* Federal Security Agency, Bulletin 1949, no. 7 (Washington, DC: Government Printing Office, 1949), 4.

52. William H. Cartwright, "What Is Happening in the Social Studies," *SE,* 18 (February 1954), 77, quotation at 78; William H. Cartwright, "What Is Happening in the Social Studies II," *SE,* 18 (March 1954), 115; William H. Cartwright, "Selection, Organization, Presentation, and Placement of Subject Matter in American History," *SE,* 29 (November 1965), 435; David Jenness, *Making Sense of Social Studies* (New York: Macmillan, 1990), 255–58.

53. Edgar B. Wesley, *Teaching the Social Studies in the High Schools,* 3rd ed. (Boston: Heath, 1950), 112.

54. *Teaching of United States History in Public High Schools, 1946–47,* 4.

55. Erling Hunt, "School History," *SE,* 9 (April 1945), 149.

56. Larry Cuban, *How Teachers Taught: Constancy and Change in American Classrooms, 1880–1990,* 2nd ed. (New York: Teachers College Press, 1993), 1, 112–13, 298–301.

57. James B. Palmer to Wesley, 2 November 1950, box 2, file 6, CAHSC Collection.

58. James B. Palmer to Wesley, 2 and 8 November 1950, ibid. This "drag" in the adaptation of textbooks to scholarship was not new. See Charles Beard, "The Trend in Social Studies," *HO,* 20 (December 1929), 370; Irene T. Butler, "The Textbooks and the New Discoveries, Emphases, and Viewpoints in American History," *HO,* 23 (December 1932), 395–402.

59. Ralph Guinness, "Education for Democracy," *SS,* 28 (April 1937), 156–57.

60. Tyler Kepner, "The Dilemma of the Secondary-School Social-Studies Teacher," *SE,* 1 (February 1937), 86.

61. Frederick Jackson Turner to Arthur M. Schlesinger, 15 April 1922, box 2, Arthur M. Schlesinger Papers, Harvard University Archives.

62. John Hope Franklin, "New Perspectives in American Negro History," *SE,* 14 (May 1950), 196–200, quotation at 200.

63. See the oral history conducted in 1996 by Ann Lage: *Kenneth M. Stampp, Historian of Slavery, the Civil War, and Reconstruction, University of California, Berkeley, 1946–1983* (Berkeley: Regional Oral History Office, Bancroft Library, University of California, 1998), 261; Cartwright, "What Is Happening in the Social Studies," 77.

64. Jameson, "Meeting of the American Historical Association at Columbus," 299–300, 427; John Franklin Jameson, "The Meeting of the American Historical Association at Cleveland," *AHR,* 25 (April 1920), 373; Edgar Dawson, "The History Inquiry," *HO,* 15 (June 1924), 271; "History and Other Social Studies in the Schools, Report of a Committee, Submitted to the Council of the American Historical Association, Approved, December 1926," *HO,* 18 (March 1927), 121; Wesley, *American History in Schools and Colleges,* 94–95.

65. F. B. Bolton, "The Attitude of High School Pupils toward History," *SS,* 28 (May 1937), 217.

66. W. M. Hecker to Allan Nevins, 12 June 1942, box 55, file 1942 (2), Nevins Papers. See also Conference of Junior College Teachers of American History, Stanford University, 27 and 28 November 1942 (p. 5), list of resolutions, attached, unnumbered, box 141, untitled file on history teaching, AHA Papers; Stanford Conference of California College and University Teachers of American History, 27 and 28 August 1942 (p. 11), box 141, untitled file on history teaching, AHA Papers. See, more generally, Frances Fitzgerald, *America Revised: History Schoolbooks in the Twentieth Century* (Boston: Little, Brown, 1979), esp. 189–90.

67. Cartwright, "What Is Happening in the Social Studies II," 115.

68. Franklin, "New Perspectives in American Negro History," 196–200.

69. Donald Michelson, "Teaching World Civilization: An Approach to Education for World Citizenship," *SE*, 12 (March 1948), 113.

70. Franklin, "New Perspectives in American Negro History," 200.

71. Peter Hill, "The Teaching of History: An Anglo-American Contrast," *SE*, 13 (January 1949), 269, reprinted from the *Times* (London), 4 April 1949.

72. Ibid.

73. Ibid.

74. Ridgway F. Shinn Jr., "Geography and History as Integrating Disciplines," *SE*, 28 (November 1964), 396.

75. *The Statistical History of the United States: From Colonial Times to the Present,* with introduction and user's guide by Ben J. Wattenberg (New York: Basic Books, 1976), 372.

76. John Spencer Bassett, preface to Jean Jules Jusserand et al., *The Writing of History* (New York: Scribner's, 1926), viii; Charles W. Colby, "The Craftsmanship of the Historian," in ibid., 85; Marcus W. Jernegan, "Productivity of Doctors of Philosophy in History," *AHR*, 33 (October 1927), 19; William B. Hesseltine and Louis Kaplan, "Doctors of Philosophy in History: A Statistical Study," *AHR*, 47 (July 1942), 782.

77. On the NEA's objectives, see Wayne J. Urban, *Gender, Race, and the National Education Association: Professionalism and Its Limitations* (New York: RoutledgeFalmer, 2000).

78. W. Stull Holt, *The Historical Profession in the United States* (Washington, DC: AHA, 1963), 18.

79. *The Historical Association, 1906–1956* (London: The Association, 1955), 8.

80. "The Board of Education Report on the Teaching of History," reported by C. H. K. Marten, *History,* 9 (April 1924), 34.

81. E. A. Fulton, "The Teaching of Contemporary History," *History,* 13 (July 1928), 110, quotation at 119.

82. On Pollard, see *The Historical Association, 1906–1956,* 20–21. On Turberville, see A. S. Turberville, "History Objective and Subjective," *History,* 17 (January 1933), 292.

83. C. M. Cox and C. H. Greene, "The Teaching of History in the Schools" I.— Berkhamstead, *History,* 5 (January 1921), 204.

84. *The Historical Association, 1906–1956.* Publication of this volume signaled a shift in the alliance between academics and teachers. Thereafter, the pages of the *History* journal had only brief references to teaching and other nonacademic aspects of history.

85. Bessie Louise Pierce, *Citizens' Organizations and the Civic Training of Youth* (New York: Charles Scribner's Sons, 1933).

86. *DAS,* 1951 ed., 847.

87. Hesseltine and Kaplan, "Doctors of Philosophy in History," 789. Junior colleges and high schools showed four- to sixfold increases in the number of teachers with doctoral degrees from 1926 to 1935; *DAS,* 1951 ed., 847; Ann Lage, *Stampp,* 80, 82.

88. John D. Hicks to William H. Herman, 14 June 1943, file January–June 1943, box 10, Hicks Papers.

89. *Nineteenth Annual Conference on the Teaching of History and the Social Sciences . . . May 7, 1938,* box 13, ibid.

90. Irma Costello to John D. Hicks, 21 August 1928, ibid. Hicks was to address the history section of the Nebraska State Teachers' Association in Omaha.

91. James Sellers to John D. Hicks, 5 January 1936, ibid. See also *Fourth Annual Meeting, Nebraska History Teachers' Association, Lincoln, . . . April 23–25, 1936* (n.p., 1936), ibid.

92. John D. Hicks to E. B. Fred (dean, College of Agriculture, University of Wisconsin), 18 December 1942, box 10, ibid.

93. See Edgar E. Robinson to John D. Hicks, 30 April 1948, box 14, ibid. See also Theodore Blegen to Hicks, 20 November 1946, ibid.; John D. Hicks, *My Life with History: An Autobiography* (Lincoln: University of Nebraska Press, 1968).

94. Samuel Eliot Morison, *Vistas of History* (New York: Knopf, 1964), 41–42.

95. Samuel Eliot Morison and Henry Steele Commager, *The Growth of the American Republic* (New York: Oxford University Press, 1930); editorial, "Writing American History," *SRL,* 6 November 1937, 8.

96. Harold Faulkner, Tyler Kepner, and Hall Bartlett, *The American Way of Life: A History* (New York: Harper and Brothers, 1941); Lewis Paul Todd to Merle Curti, 13 April 1947, box 66, file 8, Merle Curti Papers, SHSW; Merle Curti and Lewis Paul Todd, *America's History* (New York: Harcourt, Brace, 1950); Arthur M. Schlesinger, "Survey of High School Texts and Source Books in United States History," *Ohio History Teachers' Journal, Bulletin,* no. 5 (1916); John D. Hicks to George Mowry, 16 November 1953, file "Short History," box 1, Hicks Papers; Hicks to Mowry, 22 July 1953, ibid.

97. Bailey, "Obligation of the Teacher to Be a Scholar," 356.

98. Hicks to Editorial Dept., Macmillan, 16 July 1928, box 13, Hicks Papers. Hicks hoped his source book "might have some appeal to the general reader."

99. Thomas Bailey to Edgar E. Robinson, 23 December 1959, box 5, file 8, and other materials in box 5, file 11, Thomas Bailey Papers, Department of Special Collections, Stanford University Libraries.

100. Mabel Casner to Ralph Gabriel, 14 November 1932, series I, box 2, file 39, Ralph Gabriel Papers, Manuscripts and Archives, Yale University Library.

101. John D. Hicks to Edgar Wesley, 27 August 1943, box 1, file 4, CAHSC Collection.

102. *Statistical History of the United States,* 363; Dexter Perkins, John Snell, and the Committee on Graduate Education of the American Historical Association, *The Education of Historians in the United States* (New York: McGraw-Hill, 1962), 20–21; Richard Kirkendall, "The Status of History in the Schools," *JAH,* 62 (September 1975), 557–70.

103. W. Stull Holt, "Who Reads the Best Histories?" *MVHR,* 40 (March 1954), reprinted in W. Stull Holt, *Historical Scholarship in the United States and Other Essays* (Seattle:

University of Washington Press, 1967), 64–72; Holt, *Historical Profession in the United States*, 22; Thomas Bailey, "Revitalizing American History," 374.

104. Erling Hunt, "American History in Democratic Education," *SE*, 6 (December 1942), 351, quotation at 350.

105. Erling Hunt to Merle Curti, 2 April 1952, box 20, file 5, Merle Curti Papers; Richard Shryock to Erling Hunt, 14 November 1942, Richard Harrison Shryock Papers, Library of the American Philosophical Society, Philadelphia.

106. Howard Anderson served at the U.S. Office of Education from 1946 to 1954 and later as provost of the University of Rochester. *DAS*, 1968 ed., 11.

107. Edgar Wesley, "Let's Abolish History Courses," *Phi Delta Kappan*, 49 (September 1967), 3–8.

108. Howard Anderson to John D. Hicks, 20 January 1944, box 1, file "Teaching of history," box 14, Hicks Papers; Erling Hunt to Hicks, 22 January 1946, ibid.; Frank N. Freeman to Hicks, 21 February 1946, ibid.

109. Lawrence Cremin, *The Transformation of the School: Progressivism in American Education, 1876–1957* (New York: Knopf, 1957), 343–47; Arthur Bestor, *Educational Wastelands: The Retreat from Learning in Our Public Schools* (Urbana: University of Illinois Press, 1953); Arthur Bestor, *The Restoration of Learning: A Program for Redeeming the Unfulfilled Promise of American Education* (New York: Knopf, 1956); Holt, *Historical Profession in the United States*, 14.

110. Sidney Painter, "The Washington Meeting, 1952," *AHR*, 58 (April 1953), 760; Arthur Bestor, "Anti-intellectualism in the Schools," *New Republic*, 19 January 1953, 11–13.

111. Painter, "Washington Meeting," 760.

112. Cremin, *Transformation of the School*, 347–53, analyzes the worsening political climate for Progressive education in the 1950s.

113. See Bestor's voluminous, highly miscellaneous, and even chaotic papers left at the Department of Special Collections, University of Washington Libraries. See, e.g., Bestor to Charles Sellers, 17 January 1966, box 3, file on correspondence (various years); William Cartwright to Bestor, 22 April 1966 and enclosures, in box 5, unfiled correspondence. See also Diane Ravitch, *The Troubled Crusade: American Education, 1945–1980* (New York: Basic Books, 1983), 75–76.

114. Hazel Hertzberg, *Social Studies Reform, 1880–1980* (Boulder, CO: Social Science Education Consortium, 1981), 92; Richard Hofstadter, *Anti-intellectualism in American Life* (New York: Knopf, 1962), 349, 354–58.

115. Hertzberg, *Social Studies Reform*, 89–92.

116. Dexter Perkins, "We Shall Gladly Teach," *AHR*, 62 (January 1957), 291–309; Dexter Perkins and John Snell, *The Education of Historians in the United States* (New York: McGraw-Hill, 1962); Boyd Shafer, "The Year's Business, 1957," *AHR*, 63 (April 1958), 838.

117. Joseph Strayer, "History," in *The Social Studies and the Social Sciences*, sponsored by the American Council of Learned Societies and the National Council for the Social Studies (New York: Harcourt, Brace, and World, 1962), 29, cited in Cartwright, "Selection, Organization, Presentation, and Placement of Subject Matter in American History," 438; see also Lewis Todd, "Opportunities for American History," in Richard E. Thursfield, ed., *Seventeenth Yearbook of the National Council for the Social Studies* (Washington, DC: NCSS, 1946), 8.

118. Edith West, ed., *Improving the Teaching of World History, Twentieth Yearbook of the National Council on the Social Studies* (Washington, DC: NCSS, 1949). L. S. Stavrianos, "New Viewpoints in Teaching World History," *SE,* 37 (March 1962), 131, called for a "new global framework in World History."

119. "Proposal for a Study of World History in the Schools," March 1962, box 692, Committee on Teaching file, AHA Papers; Minutes of the Meeting of the Committee on Teaching, 5 May 1962, box 692, ibid.; W. Stull Holt to Peter Caws (Carnegie Corporation), 9 January 1964, ibid. Also see John M. Thompson to Paul Ward, 3 November 1970, box 721, "World History Project, Indiana University" file, AHA Papers.

120. Hazel Hertzberg, "The Teaching of History," in Michael Kammen, ed., *The Past Before Us: Contemporary Historical Writing in the United States* (Ithaca: Cornell University Press, 1980), 480–81; William T. Lowe, "Where Should History be Taught?" *Clearing House,* 39 (December 1964), 210–13; I. I. Olicker and J. Wolfson, "The Need for Renovating the Teaching of Social Studies," *Clearing House,* 38 (September 1963), 47–49; Wesley, "Let's Abolish History Courses," 3–8. For a review of this trend but sympathetic to history, see Morris Gall, "The Future of History," *SE,* 29 (May 1965), 269.

121. Holt, *Historical Profession in the United States,* 10.

122. Richard L. Watson Jr. to Robert L. Zangrando, 14 July 1966, Richard L. Watson Jr. Papers, Duke University Library; William L. Cartwright and Richard L. Watson Jr., "Historical Study in a Changing Curriculum," in William L. Cartwright and Richard L. Watson, eds., *The Reinterpretation of American History and Culture* (Washington, DC: NCSS, 1973), 12.

Chapter Nine

1. Frederick Jackson Turner, "The Significance of History" [1891], reprinted in John Mack Faragher, *Rereading Frederick Jackson Turner* (New York: Henry Holt, 1994), 24, 25; see also Marcus W. Jernegan, "The Productivity of Doctors of Philosophy in History," *AHR,* 33 (October 1927), 19; Wilbur C. Abbott, "The Influence of Graduate Instruction on Historical Writing," in J. J. Jusserand et al., *The Writing of History* (New York: Charles Scribner's Sons, 1926), 35.

2. Peter Stearns and Joel Tarr, "New, Public Uses for History," *NYT,* 7 June 1980.

3. The focus upon grassroots activism and popular culture was stronger in Britain and can be dated from the work of Raphael Samuel and the History Workshop starting in 1966–67. See also the work of the Birmingham Centre for Contemporary Cultural Studies in Richard Johnson et al., *Making Histories: Studies in History-Writing and Politics* (London: Hutchinson, 1982). For the United States, see the articles in *Radical History Review,* 1 (1973–74); Warren Leon and Roy Rosenzweig, eds., *History Museums in the United States: A Critical Assessment* (Urbana: University of Illinois Press, 1989); Susan Porter Benson, Stephen Brier, and Roy Rosenzweig, eds., *Presenting the Past: Essays on History and the Public* (Philadelphia: Temple University Press, 1980).

4. Peter Novick, *That Noble Dream: The "Objectivity Question" and the American Historical Profession* (New York: Cambridge University Press, 1988), 510, 512; Michael Kammen, "The Historian's Vocation and the State of the Discipline in the United States," in Michael Kammen, ed., *The Past before Us: Contemporary Historical Writing in the United States* (Ithaca: Cornell University Press, 1980), 44–45.

5. G. Wesley Johnson, "The Origins of *The Public Historian* and the National Council on Public History," *Public Historian*, 21 (Summer 1999), 167–68, discusses the perception of a job crisis in the 1970s. See also Novick, *That Noble Dream*, 510–21; Kammen, "Historian's Vocation," 44–45. David E. Kyvig, "Public or Perish: Thoughts on Historians' Responsibilities," *Public Historian*, 13 (Fall 1991), 17, gives a dissenting view.

6. Kammen, "Historian's Vocation," 44.

7. James B. Gardner, "The Redefinition of Historical Scholarship: Calling a Tail a Leg?" *Public Historian*, 20 (Fall 1998), 44.

8. Personal observations of the joint meeting at St. Louis, April 1989.

9. Kyvig, "Public or Perish"; William E. Leuchtenburg, "The Historian and the Public Realm," *AHR*, 97 (February 1992), 1–18.

10. See esp. Rebecca Conrad, *Benjamin Shambaugh and the Intellectual Foundations of Public History* (Iowa City: State University of Iowa Press, 2002).

11. Julian E. Zelizer, "Clio's Lost Tribe: Public Policy History since 1978," *Journal of Policy History*, 12, no. 3 (2000), 371; Arnita Jones, "Public History Now and Then," *Public Historian*, 21 (Summer 1999), 23–24.

12. This is not to deny that modern public history differs from the public involvement of historians prior to the 1960s. While museum, archival, and historic preservation work has continued to build upon earlier achievements, policy analysis has not prospered. See Hugh Davis Graham, "The Stunted Career of Policy History: A Critique and an Agenda," *Public Historian*, 15 (Spring 1993), 15–37.

13. Kyvig, "Public or Perish," 14; Leuchtenburg, "The Historian and the Public Realm," 1; Stearns and Tarr, "New, Public Uses for History."

14. Stearns and Tarr, "New, Public Uses for History."

15. John Franklin Jameson, "The Meeting of the American Historical Association at Washington," *AHR*, 33 (April 1928), 524; see also Allan Nevins, *The Gateway to History* (New York: D. Appleton and Co., 1938), 107.

16. Michael Kammen, *Mystic Chords of Memory: The Transformation of Tradition in American Culture* (New York: Knopf, 1991), 700–701; see also John Bodnar, *Remaking America: Public Memory, Commemoration, and Patriotism in the Twentieth Century* (Princeton: Princeton University Press, 1992), 251.

17. See the chapters in Pierre Nora, director, *Realms of Memory: Rethinking the French Past*, vol. 1, *Conflicts and Divisions*, trans. Arthur Goldhammer (New York: Columbia University Press, 1996), esp. Lawrence D. Kritzman, "Foreword: In Remembrance of Things French," xiii; and Pierre Nora, "From *Lieux de memoire* to *Realms of Memory*," vi–xvii.

18. Graham, "Stunted Career of Policy History," 22.

19. Bodnar, *Remaking America*, 250–51.

20. Raphael Samuel, *People's History and Socialist Theory* (London: Routledge and Kegan Paul, 1981); Paul Thompson, *The Voice of the Past: Oral History* (Oxford: Oxford University Press, 1978). The term "public history" was imported into Britain, Australia, and other countries where its use was unfamiliar. See Priscilla Boniface, "History and the Public in the UK," *Public Historian*, 17 (Spring 1995), 23; Paul Ashton and Paula Hamilton, "Streetwise: Public History in New South Wales," *Public History Review*, nos. 5–6 (1996–97), 9–16.

21. Samuel, *People's History and Socialist Theory*; Thompson, *Voice of the Past*.

22. John Higham, "Herbert Baxter Adams and the Study of Local History," *AHR*, 89 (December 1984), 1225–39, quotations at 1237.

23. Frederick Jackson Turner, "Pioneer Ideals and the State University," in Faragher, *Rereading Frederick Jackson Turner*, 114, 115.

24. Julian P. Boyd, "State and Local Historical Societies in the United States," *AHR*, 40 (October 1934), 31. For Shambaugh's work within the lineage of public history, see Conrad, *Benjamin Shambaugh*.

25. David D. Van Tassel and James A. Tinsley, "Historical Organizations as Aids to History," in W. Hesseltine and Donald R. McNeil, eds., *In Support of Clio: Essays in Memory of Herbert A. Kellar* (Madison: State Historical Society of Wisconsin, 1958), 145; Boyd, "State and Local Historical Societies in the United States"; Benjamin Shambaugh, *Applied History* (Iowa City: State Historical Society of Iowa, 1914); Conrad, *Benjamin Shambaugh*, 82–86.

26. John R. Commons et al., eds., *A Documentary History of American Industrial Society*, 10 vols. (Cleveland: Arthur H. Clark Co., 1910–11); John R. Commons, *History of Labour in the United States*, 4 vols. (New York: Macmillan, 1918–35).

27. Joseph Dorfman, "John R. Commons," in *International Encyclopedia of the Social Sciences*, new ed. (New York: Macmillan, 1968), 22.

28. Ulrich B. Phillips, *Plantation and Frontier*, vols. 1–2 of *A Documentary History of American Industrial Society* (Cleveland: A. H. Clark, 1910); Frederick I. Olson, "Helen Sumner Woodbury," *NAW*, 3:650–52.

29. Dorothy Ross, "Socialism and American Liberalism: Academic Social Thought in the 1880s," *Perspectives in American History*, 11 (1977–78), 5–79; Leon Fink, "Intellectuals versus 'Workers': Academic Requirements and the Creation of History," *AHR*, 96 (April 1991), 406–11.

30. Ellen Fitzpatrick, "Rethinking the Intellectual Origins of American Labor History," *AHR*, 96 (April 1991), esp. 426; Turner, "Pioneer Ideals and the State University," 114–15.

31. Lafayette G. Harter Jr., *John R. Commons: His Assault on Laissez-faire* (Corvallis: Oregon State University Press, 1962), chap. 7.

32. Joseph G. Rayback, *A History of American Labor*, expanded and updated ed. (New York: The Free Press, 1966), 463.

33. Quoted in Robert H. Zieger, "Workers and Scholars: Recent Trends in American Labor Historiography," *Labor History*, 13 (Spring 1972), 247.

34. James Farr, "Political Science and the State," in James Farr and Raymond Seidelman, eds., *Discipline and History: Political Science in the United States* (Ann Arbor: University of Michigan Press, 1993), 64–79.

35. Richard Hofstadter, "The Department of History," in R. Gordon Hoxie et al., *A History of the Faculty of Political Science, Columbia University* (New York: Columbia University Press, 1955), 212.

36. Geoffrey M. Hodgson, *How Economics Forgot History: The Problem of Historical Specificity in Social Science* (London: Routledge, 2001), 138.

37. John Bates Clark, foreword to Phillips, *Plantation and Frontier*, 44.

38. Ibid., 41.

39. Jane S. Dahlberg, *The New York Bureau of Municipal Research: Pioneer in Government Administration* (New York: New York University Press, 1968), 25, 132–34, 232.

40. Ellen Nore, *Charles Beard: An Intellectual Biography* (Carbondale: Southern Illinois University Press, 1983), 38–39, quotation at 38; Clyde W. Barrow, *More than a Historian: The Political and Economic Thought of Charles A. Beard* (New Brunswick, NJ: Transaction Publishers, 2000), 8–9.

41. Charles Beard, "Time, Technology and the Creative Spirit in Political Science," *American Political Science Review,* 21 (February 1927), 1–11, quotation at 6; Charles Beard, "The Frontier in American History," *NR,* 16 February 1921, 350; Nore, *Charles Beard,* 115.

42. Novick, *That Noble Dream,* 69, 70.

43. Frederick Jackson Turner, quoted in ibid., 117. See generally George T. Blakey, *Historians on the Home Front: American Propagandists for the Great War* (Lexington: University Press of Kentucky, 1970); Carol S. Gruber, *Mars and Minerva: World War I and the Uses of the Higher Learning in America* (Baton Rouge: Louisiana State University Press, 1975); Lawrence E. Gelfand, *The Inquiry* (New Haven: Yale University Press, 1963).

44. Gruber, *Mars and Minerva,* 131, 136–37, 144.

45. Novick, *That Noble Dream,* 118n, 124–25; United States Committee on Public Information, *War Cyclopedia: A Handbook for Ready Reference on the Great War,* ed. Frederic L. Paxson, Edward S. Corwin, and Samuel B. Harding (Washington, DC: Government Printing Office, 1918); James R. Mock and Cedric Larson, "When Clio Joined the Colors," *SRL,* 30 September 1939, 16.

46. Evarts B. Greene to James T. Shotwell, 27 September 1918, box 4, file "Shotwell, James T.," Evarts B. Greene Papers, Rare Books and Manuscripts, Butler Library, Columbia University.

47. Gruber, *Mars and Minerva,* 130–31.

48. Novick, *That Noble Dream,* 117.

49. Mock and Larson, "When Clio Joined the Colors," 16, quotation at 13.

50. James T. Shotwell to Greene, 21 September 1918, box 4, file "Shotwell, James T.," Greene Papers.

51. Harold Josephson, "Shotwell, James Thompson," in Warren F. Kimball, ed., *Biographical Dictionary of Internationalists* (Westport, CT: Greenwood Press, 1983), 673; Harold Josephson, *James T. Shotwell and the Rise of Internationalism* (Rutherford, NJ: Fairleigh Dickinson University Press, 1975); Charles DeBenedetti, "Peace Was His Profession: James T. Shotwell and American Internationalism," in Frank J. Merli and Theodore A. Wilson, eds., *Makers of American Diplomacy,* vol. 2 (New York: Scribner, 1974), 81–101; James T. Shotwell, *The Autobiography of James T. Shotwell* (Indianapolis: Bobbs-Merrill, 1961); James T. Shotwell, *At the Paris Peace Conference* (New York: Macmillan, 1937); Gregory M. Pfitzer, *Samuel Eliot Morison's Historical World: In Quest of a New Parkman* (Boston: Northeastern University Press, 1991), 62–65; Gelfand, *The Inquiry,* 53–56.

52. Josephson, "Shotwell, James Thompson," 674.

53. Hofstadter, "Department of History," 230.

54. Shotwell, *Autobiography,* 11. Shotwell remained a historian, publishing studies of U.S. and world history in the 1950s (ibid., 332).

55. Harry Elmer Barnes, *The Genesis of the World War: An Introduction to the Problem of War Guilt* (New York: Knopf, 1926); Novick, *That Noble Dream,* 208–18.

56. Harry Elmer Barnes, "The Past and the Future of History," *HO,* 12 (February 1921), 51.

57. Phillips, *Plantation and Frontier;* Ulrich B. Phillips, *American Negro Slavery: A Survey of the Supply, Employment and Control of Negro Labor as Determined by the Plantation Regime* (New York: D. Appleton and Co., 1918); Merton E. Dillon, *Ulrich Bonnell Phillips: Historian of the Old South* (Baton Rouge: Louisiana State University Press, 1985), 51–52.

58. Percy Bidwell and John I. Falconer, *History of Agriculture in the Northern United States, 1620–1869* (Washington, DC: Carnegie Institution, 1925).

59. Lewis C. Gray, *History of Agriculture in the Southern United States to 1860,* 2 vols. (Washington, DC: Carnegie Institution, 1933).

60. Robert W. Fogel and Stanley Engerman, *Time on the Cross: Evidence and Methods, a Supplement* (Boston: Little, Brown, 1974), 188.

61. Wayne D. Rasmussen, "The Growth of Agricultural History," in Hesseltine and McNeil, *In Support of Clio,* 155.

62. Frederick Jackson Turner, "Social Forces in American History" [1910], reprinted in Faragher, *Rereading Frederick Jackson Turner,* 135. Ray Allen Billington, *Frederick Jackson Turner: Historian, Scholar, Teacher* (New York: Oxford University Press, 1973), 365, describes Turner as a "pioneer" in agricultural history, but he was so only indirectly.

63. Louis B. Schmidt, "The Economic History of American Agriculture as a Field of Study," *MVHR,* 3 (June 1916), 39–49; Louis B. Schmidt, "An Unworked Field in Mississippi Valley History," *Iowa Journal of History and Politics,* 21 (January 1923), 94–111. Schmidt did graduate work at Chicago, Cornell, and Wisconsin. He became professor of history at Iowa State College in 1919. *DAS,* 1951 ed., 829.

64. Nils Olsen to Herbert Kellar, 25 May 1921, box 84, file 1, Herbert Kellar Papers, SHSW.

65. Herbert Kellar to Henry C. Wallace, 4 January 1922, box 84, file 2, ibid.

66. Henry C. Wallace to Kellar, 20 January 1922, ibid.

67. Herbert Kellar to Henry C. Wallace, 4 January 1922, ibid.

68. Herbert Kellar to O. C. Stine, 27 October 1927, box 84, file 7, ibid.; John Franklin Jameson, "The Meeting of the American Historical Association at Washington," *AHR,* 33 (April 1928), 522.

69. Everett Edwards to Arthur M. Schlesinger, 23 January 1928, box 3, Arthur M. Schlesinger Papers, Harvard University Archives; Rasmussen, "Growth of Agricultural History," 161. See also *DAS,* 1951 ed., 258.

70. Rasmussen, "Growth of Agricultural History," 161; Arnita Jones and Wayne D. Rasmussen, "Wayne Rasmussen and the Development of Policy History at the United States Department of Agriculture," *Public Historian,* 14 (Winter 1992), 11–28.

71. Jones and Rasmussen, "Wayne Rasmussen," 19.

72. Rasmussen, "Growth of Agricultural History," 162.

73. Fred A. Shannon, *The Farmer's Last Frontier: Agriculture, 1860–1897,* Economic History of the United States, vol. 5 (New York: Holt, Rinehart, and Winston, 1945); Paul W.

Gates, *The Farmer's Age: Agriculture, 1815–1860*, Economic History of the United States, vol. 3 (New York: Holt, Rinehart, and Winston, 1960).

74. Humphrey Jessel Humphreys, "The Influence of Current Events on the Choice and Treatment of Subjects Published in *Agricultural History* between 1927 and 1966" (unpublished paper, School of History, University of New South Wales, 1986, in possession of I. Tyrrell), 7.

75. *Agricultural History,* 28, no. 3 (1954), 131; Humphreys, "Influence of Current Events," 8.

76. Jones and Rasmussen, "Wayne Rasmussen," 11–28.

77. Conrad, *Benjamin Shambaugh,* 137–38.

Chapter Ten

1. Albert Bushnell Hart, "The Historical Opportunity in America," *AHR,* 4 (October 1898), quotations from 5, 6, 3, 6.

2. See Clarence Paine to Frank Lowden (chair of Committee Advisory to the LaSalle Memorial Association), 16 October 1914, box 1, file "Committee Structure 1914–1915," Organization of American Historians Papers, Indianapolis Special Collections and Archives, Indiana University—Purdue University Library, Indianapolis; "Report of the Committee on Historic Sites," in Milo Quaife, ed., *Proceedings of the Mississippi Valley Historical Association for the Year 1914–1915,* vol. 8 (Cedar Rapids, IA: Torch Press, 1916); Jean McNaughton Stevens, "The Preservation of Landmarks," in Benjamin Shambaugh, ed., *Proceedings of the Mississippi Valley Historical Association for the Year 1913–1914,* vol. 7 (Cedar Rapids, IA: Torch Press, 1914), 79–81; Clara S. Paine, "Minutes of Business Transacted," in *Proceedings of the Mississippi Valley Historical Association for the Year 1916–1917, MVHR* Supplement, vol. 9 (Cedar Rapids, IA: Torch Press, 1918), 241–42.

3. Hart, "Historical Opportunity," 2, 6.

4. John Bodnar, *Remaking America: Public Memory, Commemoration, and Patriotism in the Twentieth Century* (Princeton: Princeton University Press, 1992), 176. See also Harlan D. Unrau and G. Frank Williss, "To Preserve the Nation's Past: The Growth of Historic Preservation in the National Park Service during the 1930s," *Public Historian,* 9 (Spring 1987), 19–49; Barry Mackintosh, "The National Park Service Moves into Historical Interpretation," *Public Historian,* 9 (Spring 1987), 51.

5. Charles B. Hosmer Jr., *Preservation Comes of Age: From Williamsburg to the National Trust, 1926–1949,* 2 vols. (Charlottesville: University Press of Virginia, for Preservation Press, National Trust for Historic Preservation in the United States, 1981), 1:530–31.

6. Bodnar, *Remaking America,* 176; Michael Kammen, *Mystic Chords of Memory: The Transformation of Tradition in American Culture* (New York: Knopf, 1991), 466–67, 469–70.

7. *DAS,* 1951 ed., 80.

8. Theodore Blegen, "State Historical Agencies and the Public," *Minnesota History Bulletin,* 9 (June 1928), 130–31.

9. State Historical Society of Wisconsin, *Proceedings of the Society at Its Seventy-fifth Annual Meeting Held October 20, 1927* (Madison: The Society, 1928), appendix "Highway Markers and Landmarks," box 21, Louise Phelps Kellogg Papers, SHSW; Blegen, "State Historical Agencies," 130.

10. Theodore Blegen, "Some Aspects of Historical Work under the New Deal," *MVHR*, 21 (September 1934), 200.

11. Charles B. Hosmer Jr., "Verne E. Chatelain and the Development of the Branch of History of the National Park Service," *Public Historian*, 16 (Winter 1994), 25–38.

12. Bodnar, *Remaking America*, 177; Hosmer, *Preservation Comes of Age*, 1:513.

13. Hosmer, "Verne E. Chatelain," 33, 36.

14. Ibid., 37, 36.

15. David L. Smiley, "The W.P.A. Historical Records Survey," in W. Hesseltine and Donald R. McNeil, eds., *In Support of Clio: Essays in Memory of Herbert A. Kellar* (Madison: State Historical Society of Wisconsin, 1958), 22; "Historical News and Comments," *MVHR*, 23 (September 1936), 341.

16. Joseph C. Robert to W. K. Boyd, 19 January 1934, box 13, William Kenneth Boyd Papers, Duke University Library.

17. Ibid.; A. P. Stauffer to Arthur M. Schlesinger, n.d. [c. May 1937]; Stauffer to Schlesinger, 10 September 1936, box 12, Arthur M. Schlesinger Papers, Harvard University Archives; C. Leigh Ripley to Boyd, 14 January 1934, box 13, Boyd Papers; Hosmer, "Verne E. Chatelain," 36.

18. A. P. Stauffer to Arthur M. Schlesinger, 10 September 1936, box 12, Schlesinger Papers.

19. Alvin P. Stauffer quoted in Hosmer, *Preservation Comes of Age*, 2:928, 930.

20. "Historical News and Comments," *MVHR*, 24 (June 1937), 148–49; Hosmer, "Verne E. Chatelain," 26. Chatelain's work for the Carnegie Institution led to his *The Defenses of Spanish Florida, 1565 to 1763* (Washington, DC: Carnegie Institution, 1941). During World War II he undertook liaison and administrative work for the Government Printing Office but later returned to academia at the University of Maryland.

21. Hosmer, *Preservation Comes of Age*, 1:606; *DAS*, 1951 ed., 548.

22. Thus, as early as 1932, progress in the work of mapping and photographing Cliff Palace and Spruce Tree House in the Mesa Verde National Park was reported in *MVHR*, 19 (June 1932), 158.

23. "Report of Representative on the National Parks Association Board [*sic*]," in Thomas C. Mendenhall, "Carrying On: Echoes from New York," *AHR*, 49 (April 1944), 586, noted of the National Parks Advisory Board of Trustees that "no matters of relevance" to the AHA were discussed at the board meeting in 1943. See also "The Year's Business," *AHR*, 50 (April 1945), 654.

24. Roy E. Appleman, "Timber Empire from the Public Domain," *MVHR*, 26 (September 1939), 193–208; W. Turrentine Jackson, "The Creation of Yellowstone National Park," *MVHR*, 29 (September 1942), 186–306; Alvin P. Stauffer and Charles W. Porter, "The National Park Service Program of Conservation for Areas and Structures of National Historical Significance," *MVHR*, 30 (June 1943), 48.

25. Edwin C. Bearss, "The National Park Service and Its History Program: 1864–1986—an Overview," *Public Historian*, 9 (Spring 1987), 22.

26. "Historical News and Notices," *Journal of Southern History*, 2 (November 1936), 555.

27. "Historical News and Comments," *MVHR*, 26 (June 1939), 139.

28. Blegen, "Historical Work under the New Deal," 196–198.

29. Robert W. Kidder, "The Historical Records Survey: Activities and Publications," *Library Quarterly*, 13 (April 1943), 136–40; Luther Evans, "The Historical Records Survey," 12, copy in box 105, file 6, Herbert Kellar Papers, SHSW.

30. "The Microfilm Program of the Historical Records Survey," *Journal of Documentary Reproduction*, 1 (1938), 59–62; Kidder, "Historical Records Survey," 147.

31. Evans, "Historical Records Survey," 12; Smiley, "W.P.A. Historical Records Survey," 3–28, esp. 3. As a result of the formation of the National Archives, a separate Survey of Federal Records commenced in 1936, directed by Philip Hamer, formerly a historian at the University of Tennessee. See John D. Hicks to Philip S. Hamer, 20 February 1936, box 13, John D. Hicks Papers, Bancroft Library, University of California, Berkeley; Hamer to Hicks, 19 and 24 February 1936, ibid.; *DAS*, 1951 ed., 375.

32. Obituary, *AHR*, 45 (July 1940), 1008. See also Robert C. Binkley, *Methods of Reproducing Research Materials*, 2nd ed. (Ann Arbor: Edwards Brothers, 1936).

33. Conyers Read, "Historical News," *AHR*, 43 (April 1938), 734.

34. Smiley, "W.P.A. Historical Records Survey," 19; Luther Evans to Arthur M. Schlesinger, 10 December 1936, Schlesinger Papers.

35. Smiley, "W.P.A. Historical Records Survey," 16, 18–19, quotation at 14.

36. Julian P. Boyd quoted in Sargent B. Child (director, WPA HRS) to Florence Kerr (WPA assistant commissioner), 21 May 1943, box 127, file "Bibliography of American Travel, Committee on, 1942," AHA Papers, LC.

37. G. Philip Bauer, "Public Archives in the United States," in Hesseltine and McNeil, *In Support of Clio*, 65; Victor Gondos Jr., *J. Franklin Jameson and the Birth of the National Archives, 1906–1926* (Philadelphia: University of Pennsylvania Press, 1981), 13–14; Claude H. Van Tyne and Waldo Leland, *Guide to the Archives of the Government of the United States in Washington* (Washington, DC: Carnegie Institution of Washington, 1904).

38. Bauer, "Public Archives," 66.

39. John Franklin Jameson, "The Need of a National Archives Building," in Morey D. Rothberg and Jacqueline Goggin, eds., *John Franklin Jameson and the Development of Humanistic Scholarship in America*, vol. 1, *Selected Essays* (Athens: University of Georgia Press, 1993), 318.

40. Gondos, *J. Franklin Jameson*, 174–75.

41. Bauer, "Public Archives," 68.

42. Lester J. Cappon, "The Archival Profession and the Society of American Archivists," *American Archivist*, 15 (July 1952), 195–204; Samuel F. Bemis, "The Training of Archivists in the United States," *American Archivist*, 2 (July 1939), 154–61.

43. Robert C. Binkley, "Strategic Objectives in Archival Policy," *American Archivist*, 2 (July 1939), 163, 165–66.

44. 43 Stat. 1104. See *Territorial Papers of the United States. Message from the President of the United States Transmitting a Report from the Acting Secretary of State Recommending the Enactment of Legislation Authorizing an Additional Appropriation* . . . (Washington, DC: Government Printing Office, 1937), 75th Cong., 1st sess., Senate Doc. 9, in box 14, Boyd Papers.

45. Jameson, "Need of a National Archives Building," 319.

46. Clarence E. Carter, "The United States and Documentary Historical Publication," *MVHR*, 25 (June 1938), 3–22.

47. J. Walter Lambeth to W. K. Boyd, 30 April 1937, box 14, Boyd Papers.

48. Carter, "United States and Documentary Historical Publication," 22.

49. Blegen, "Historical Work under the New Deal," 200–201; Carter, "United States and Documentary Historical Publication," 3–22; Arthur M. Schlesinger to Representative J. Walter Lambeth et al., 28 April 1937, box 12, Schlesinger Papers; Lambeth to W. K. Boyd, 30 April 1937 and Charles S. Sydnor to Cordell Hull, 8 May 1936, in *Territorial Papers of the United States,* p. 15, box 14, Boyd Papers. A Ph.D. from the University of Illinois, Carter served as MVHA president in 1937–38. *DAS,* 1951 ed., 144.

50. George F. Milton to Cordell Hull, 22 April 1936, in *Territorial Papers of the United States,* 22–23; Clarence Carter to W. K. Boyd, 15 May 1937, box 14, Boyd Papers.

51. Norman Yetman, ed., *Voices from Slavery* (New York: Holt, Rinehart, and Winston, 1970); Benjamin Botkin, ed., *Lay My Burden Down: A Folk History of Slavery* (Chicago: University of Chicago Press, 1945). More generally, see Jerrold Hirsch, *Portrait of America: A Cultural History of the Federal Writers' Project* (Chapel Hill: University of North Carolina Press, 2003); Jerre Mangione, *The Dream and the Deal: The Federal Writers' Project, 1935–1943* (Boston: Little, Brown, 1972).

52. Kenneth Stampp, "Rebels and Sambos: The Search for the Negro's Personality in Slavery," *Journal of Southern History,* 37 (August 1971), 367–69.

53. George P. Rawick, ed., *The American Slave: A Composite Autobiography,* 17 vols. (Westport, CT: Greenwood Press, 1972).

54. John B. Cade, "Out of the Mouths of Ex-Slaves," *Journal of Negro History,* 20 (July 1935), 294–337, quotation at 295.

55. *DAS,* 1951 ed., 769; Charles S. Johnson conducted similar interviews at Fisk University. See Charles S. Johnson, *Shadow of the Plantation* (Chicago: University of Chicago Press, 1934); Mangione, *The Dream and the Deal,* 257.

56. Norman Yetman, "The Background of the Slave Narrative Collection," *American Quarterly,* 19 (Fall 1967), esp. 542–43.

57. Benjamin A. Botkin, "Folklore as a Neglected Source of Social History," in Caroline F. Ware, ed., *The Cultural Approach to History* (New York: Columbia University Press, 1940), 312.

58. Frederick Gutheim, "America in Guide Books," *SRL,* 14 June 1941, 5.

59. Robert Cantwell quoted in Mangione, *The Dream and the Deal,* 353.

60. Gutheim, "America in Guide Books," 5, quotation at 4; Hirsch, *Portrait of America,* 95–96.

61. *DAS,* 1951 ed., 977.

62. Ray Allen Billington to Editor, *NYT,* 21 July 1937, enclosure in Bert Loewenberg to Arthur M. Schlesinger, 23 July 1937, box 12, Schlesinger Papers; Schlesinger to W. L. Woodring, 21 June 1937, ibid.; Schlesinger to George H. Blakeslee, 20 May 1937, ibid.

63. Samuel F. Bemis to Herschel Landru, 22 June 1934, series I, box 38, file 493, Samuel Flagg Bemis Papers, Yale University Library.

64. William B. Hesseltine and Louis Kaplan, "Doctors of Philosophy in History: A Statistical Study," *AHR,* 47 (July 1942), 775.

65. Harold Ickes to Arthur M. Schlesinger, 12 November 1937, box 12, Schlesinger Papers; Schlesinger to Ickes, 4 November 1937, ibid.; Louis Howe to John D. Hicks, 25 June 1934, box 13, Hicks Papers; Thomas P. Martin to Hicks, 2 November 1934, ibid.

66. W. K. Boyd to John Franklin Jameson, 27 July 1934, box 13, Boyd Papers; Robinson to Franklin D. Roosevelt, 20 June 1934, box 7, file 53, Edgar E. Robinson Papers, Department of Special Collections, Stanford University Libraries; Thomas P. Martin to Hicks, 2 November 1934, box 13, Hicks Papers.

67. Thomas P. Martin to Hicks, 2 November 1934, box 13, Hicks Papers. While Martin's comments betrayed malice born of thwarted ambition, his complaint about regional bias did have some substance. William Kenneth Boyd used prior contacts with R. D. W. Connor in North Carolina to recommend for the archives such students as Dr. Nelson Blake, who had been teaching in the Durham schools after gaining a doctorate from Duke University. See Boyd to Jameson, 27 July 1934, box 13, Boyd Papers; Boyd to Connor, 20 April 1935, ibid.

68. Joseph C. Robert to Boyd, 11 January 1933, box 13, Boyd Papers.

69. Culver Smith to Boyd, 21 November 1933, ibid.

70. Elbert Cox to Boyd, 5 September 1933, ibid.; William D. McCain to Boyd, 22 June 1935, ibid.; A. P. Stauffer to Schlesinger, 10 September 1936, box 12, Schlesinger Papers.

71. Robert to Boyd, 19 January 1934, box 13, Boyd Papers.

72. Eugene D. Owen to Boyd, 27 February 1934, box 13, Boyd Papers. See also Douglas Adair to Schlesinger, 8 February 1938, box 12, Schlesinger Papers; *DAS*, 1951 ed., 3.

73. Ned Meaney to Schlesinger, 7 August 1937, box 12, Schlesinger Papers.

74. A. P. Stauffer to Schlesinger, n.d. [1937], ibid.

75. Herschel Landru to Bemis, 20 November 1933, series I, box 38, file 493, Bemis Papers.

76. Landru to Bemis, 8 June 1934 and 3 December 1934, ibid.

77. Bemis to Landru, 22 June 1934, ibid.

78. Kidder, "Historical Records Survey," 144.

79. Smiley, "W.P.A. Historical Records Survey," 21, 25–26, quotation at 24.

80. Blegen, "Historical Work under the New Deal," 195–206.

81. Arthur M. Schlesinger, *The New Deal in Action, 1933–1939* (New York: Macmillan, 1940), 32.

82. Schlesinger to Senator David I. Walsh, 23 February 1937, box 12, Schlesinger Papers.

83. Schlesinger to Archibald MacLeish, 23 September 1941, box 130, file "War History Commission," AHA Papers.

84. Binkley, "Strategic Objectives in Archival Policy," 168.

Chapter Eleven

1. Arthur M. Schlesinger, "War and Peace in American History," *NR*, 21 September 1942, 337.

2. John Franklin Jameson, "Historical Scholars in War-Time," in Morey D. Rothberg and Jacqueline Goggin, eds., *John Franklin Jameson and the Development of Humanistic Schol-*

arship in America, vol. 1, *Selected Essays* (Athens: University of Georgia Press, 1993), 328, 329.

3. William T. Hutchinson, "The American Historian in Wartime," *MVHR*, 29 (September 1942), 185.

4. Arthur M. Schlesinger to Archibald MacLeish, 23 September 1941, box 130, file "War History Commission," AHA Papers, LC. See also "Plans for the Historiography of the United States in World War II," *AHR*, 49 (January 1944), 244; William C. Binkley, "Two World Wars and American Historical Scholarship," *MVHR*, 33 (June 1946), 17.

5. "Plans for the Historiography of the United States in World War II," 243.

6. Binkley, "Two World Wars," 18.

7. Franklin D. Roosevelt to Harold Smith, 4 March 1942, box 16, Arthur M. Schlesinger Papers, Harvard University Archives.

8. "Report and Recommendations of the Committee of the American Historical Association on the Historian and the Federal Government" [1952], box 444, file "Committee on the Historian and the Federal Government," AHA Papers.

9. "Plans for the Historiography of the United States in World War II," 245.

10. "Minutes of Meeting of the Committee on Records of War Administration," 9 November 1942, box 16, Schlesinger Papers.

11. Arthur M. Schlesinger to Merle Curti, 1 April 1943, box 17, Schlesinger Papers. See also Binkley, "Two World Wars," 20; Shepard B. Clough, "Clio and Mars: The Study of World War II in America," *Political Science Quarterly*, 60 (September 1945), 425–36.

12. Cf. William J. Breen, "Why Is There No World War II 'Civil Series' in the United States? The Struggle between Social Scientists and Historians over the Objective of an Official History of the Homefront Mobilization, 1941–1947," paper presented to Australian and New Zealand American Studies Association Biennial Conference, Geelong, Vic., July 2002.

13. Binkley, "Two World Wars," 24, 25.

14. Deborah Dash Moore, foreword to Caroline F. Ware, *Greenwich Village, 1920–1930: A Comment on American Civilization in the Post-war Years* (Berkeley and Los Angeles: University of California Press, 1994), x–xxi; Ellen Fitzpatrick, "Caroline F. Ware and the Cultural Approach to History," *American Quarterly*, 43 (June 1991), 185–89; *DAS*, 1951 ed., 986.

15. *DAS*, 1951 ed., 864; J. Carlyle Sitterson, *Sugar Country: The Cane Sugar Industry in the South, 1753–1950* (Lexington: University of Kentucky Press, 1953).

16. Schlesinger to Curti, 5 May 1943, box 17, Schlesinger Papers.

17. Irving Bernstein to Schlesinger, 5 June 1942, box 16, Schlesinger Papers; Schlesinger to Bernstein, 9 June 1942, ibid.

18. Arthur M. Schlesinger Jr., *A Life in the Twentieth Century: Innocent Beginnings, 1917–1950* (Boston: Houghton Mifflin, 2000), 284.

19. Henry May to Arthur M. Schlesinger, 5 May 1942, box 16, Schlesinger Papers; May to Schlesinger, 12 July 1942, ibid.

20. Blake McKelvey to Schlesinger, 5 February 1942, ibid.

21. Schlesinger, *A Life in the Twentieth Century*, 290; see also Arthur M. Schlesinger to Curti, 5 May 1943, box 17, Schlesinger Papers.

22. Robin W. Winks, *Cloak and Gown: Scholars in the Secret War, 1939–1961* (New York: William Morrow and Co., 1987), 495.

23. *DAS*, 1951 ed., 168.

24. Ray S. Cline, *Secrets, Spies, and Scholars: Blueprint of the Essential CIA* (Washington, DC: Acropolis, 1976); William L. Langer, *In and Out of the Ivory Tower: The Autobiography of William L. Langer* (New York: Watson, 1977); Richard W. Leopold, "Sarell Everett Gleason," *Massachusetts Historical Society Proceedings*, 86 (1974), 90–94.

25. Obituary, *AHR*, 65 (April 1960), 799; Winks, *Cloak and Gown*, 73, 115, 496.

26. Frederic L. Paxson, *American Democracy and the World War*, 3 vols. (Boston: Houghton Mifflin, 1936–48); Carol Reardon, *Soldiers and Scholars: The U.S. Army and the Uses of Military History, 1865–1920* (Lawrence: University Press of Kansas, 1990), 192–93, 198–99.

27. Newton D. Baker cited by Reardon, *Soldiers and Scholars*, 198; Forrest C. Pogue and Holly C. Shulman, "Forrest C. Pogue and the Birth of Public History in the Army," *Pubic Historian*, 15 (Winter 1993), 44; Binkley, "Two World Wars," 21.

28. Quotations in Benjamin F. Cooling, "History Programs in the Department of Defense," *Public Historian*, 12 (Fall 1990), 48–49.

29. Ibid., 23.

30. *DAS*, 1951 ed., 657; Clanton Williams, "The Army Air Force Historical Program," series II, box 44, file 582, Samuel Flagg Bemis Papers, Manuscripts and Archives, Yale University Library.

31. John D. Millett (major, chief of the General Reports Section, Control Division) to Arthur M. Schlesinger, 22 March 1943 (quotation), box 17, Schlesinger Papers; Col. Clarence B. Lober (chief of the Historical Branch) to Schlesinger, 23 March 1943, ibid.; Schlesinger to Lober, 30 March 1943, ibid.

32. Kent Greenfield to Howard K. Beale, 12 January 1953, box 444, file "Committee on the Historian and the Federal Government," AHA Papers.

33. William B. McClintock, "Clio Mobilizes: Naval Reserve Historians during the Second World War," *Public Historian*, 13 (Winter 1991), 35, 28.

34. David M. Potter, "C. Vann Woodward," in Marcus Cunliffe and Robin Winks, eds., *Pastmasters: Some Essays on American Historians* (New York: Harper and Row, 1969), 384.

35. Ibid., 384–85; C. Vann Woodward, *The Battle for Leyte Gulf* (New York: Macmillan, 1947).

36. Kent Greenfield, *The Historian and the Army* (New Brunswick, NJ: Rutgers University Press, 1954), 6–7; Cooling, "History Programs in the Department of Defense," 50; *DAS*, 1951 ed., 355; Kent Greenfield, ed., *United States Army in World War II*, 79 vols. to date (Washington: Historical Division/Office of the Chief of Military History, 1947–2004).

37. Frank Craven and James Lee Cate, eds., *The Army Air Forces in World War II*, 7 vols. (Chicago: University of Chicago Press, 1948–58); Williams, "Army Air Force Historical Program," 6–7; Kent Roberts Greenfield, "Notes on the Army History Program," Historical Division, Special Staff, United States Army, Washington, [1948], box 7, file "U.S Army Historical Division," W. Stull Holt Papers, Department of Special Collections, University of Washington Libraries.

38. W. J. Paul to Richard L. Watson, 27 May 1947, Army Air Force Historical File,

Richard L. Watson Jr. Papers, uncatalogued, 1946–51, Duke University Library; David Schoem to Watson, 18 June 1948, ibid.; Frank Futrell to Watson, 16 July 1951, ibid.; *Durham Morning Herald,* 15 August 1948, ibid.

39. Arthur M. Schlesinger to C. Andrews, 29 October 1942, box 16, Schlesinger Papers.

40. Samuel Eliot Morison, *Vistas of History* (New York: Knopf, 1964), 33; Gregory M. Pfitzer, *Samuel Eliot Morison's Historical World: In Quest of a New Parkman* (Boston: Northeastern University Press, 1991), 279–81.

41. Morison, *Vistas of History,* 34.

42. Williams, "Army Air Force Historical Program."

43. Ernest J. King quoted in McClintock, "Clio Mobilizes," 39, 41.

44. Hicks to Dear Bill [Hesseltine], 7 July 1943, box 10, John D. Hicks Papers, Bancroft Library, University of California, Berkeley. See also Hicks to Alphonse Fiore, 11 June 1943, ibid.

45. Hicks to Dear Bill [Hesseltine], 7 July 1943, box 10, Hicks Papers; Wallace Davies to Thomas Bailey, 27 May 1945, box 3, file 9, Thomas Bailey Papers, Department of Special Collections, Stanford University Libraries; oral history conducted in 1996 by Ann Lage: *Kenneth M. Stampp, Historian of Slavery, the Civil War, and Reconstruction, University of California, Berkeley, 1946–1983* (Berkeley: Regional Oral History Office, Bancroft Library, University of California, 1998), 96.

46. Gabriel circular letters, 26 and 31 January 1942, series I, box 6, file 104, Ralph Gabriel Papers, Manuscripts and Archives, Yale University Library; Gabriel to Post Commander, Windsor Locks A.F.B., 6 February 1942, ibid.

47. Gabriel to R. A. Griffin, 26 January 1942, ibid.; "Army Orientation Course—Meeting of January 21, 1942," ibid.

48. Ned Rehkopf to Bemis, 15 January 1940, series II, box 44, file 581, Bemis Papers.

49. Edward M. Earle to Gabriel, 2 January 1942, series I, box 6, file 102, Gabriel Papers; Earle, "American Security: Its Changing Conditions," *Annals of the American Academy of Political and Social Science,* November 1941, copy in Gabriel to Earle, 30 January 1942, ibid.

50. R. A. Griffin to Gabriel, 12 December 1941, series I, box 6, file 104, ibid.

51. Griffin to Gabriel, 2 December 1941, ibid.

52. Griffin to Gabriel, 16 January 1942, ibid.

53. G. S. McCullough to Hicks, 2 December 1942, box 10, Hicks Papers.

54. H. J. Knoll to Thomas Bailey, 15 April 1942, box 2, file 26, Bailey Papers.

55. Richard A. Meyerhoff to Bailey, 10 January 1942, ibid.; Meyerhoff to Bailey, 21 February 1942, file 28, ibid.; H. J. Knoll to Bailey, 15 April 1942, file 26, ibid.

56. Bailey, "Our National Effort, 1939–1941," Bureau of Public Relations, War Dept. Orientation Course, lecture 14, box 2, file 28, ibid.

57. Schlesinger, "War and Peace in American History," 337, 339. Bailey echoed these remarks: Bailey, "Our National Effort, 1939–1941."

58. R. A. Griffin to Gabriel, 30 December 1941, series I, box 6, file 103, Gabriel Papers; Gabriel to Ross Nixon, 30 January 1942, box 6, file 110, ibid.; Nixon to Gabriel, 9 January 1942, box 6, file 110, ibid.

59. Gabriel to J. R. Cadwell, 31 January 1942, series I, box 6, file 99, ibid.; Griffin to Gabriel, 30 December 1941, box 6, file 103, ibid.

60. John M. Gaus to Gabriel, 9 September 1941, series I, box 6, file 104, ibid.; Betty W. Mezines to Gabriel, 28 April 1948, box 10, file 107, ibid.

61. Hicks to Alphonse Fiore, 11 June 1943, box 10, Hicks Papers.

62. Alan Cobb to Hicks, 22 December 1942, ibid.; John D. Hicks, *The Federal Union: A History of the United States to 1865* (Boston: Houghton Mifflin, 1937).

63. Confidential, Colonel Spaulding's report to the executive committee of the AHA, 2 September 1943, p. 4, box 122, file "Historical Service Board, 1943," AHA Papers.

64. Merle Curti to Guy Stanton Ford, 30 August 1943, box 122, file "Historical Service Board, 1943," AHA Papers; Charles Beard to Ford, 28 September 1943, ibid.; Ford to Beard, 16 September 1943, ibid.; "Minutes of the Meeting of the Council of the American Historical Association, . . . December 28, 1943," *AHR*, 49 (April 1944), 588–89.

65. Confidential, Colonel Spaulding's report; Henry L. Stimson to Ford, 8 September 1943, box 122, file "Historical Service Board, 1943," AHA Papers.

66. Merle Curti, "The Responsibility of the Teacher in Times of Crisis," *SE*, 5 (April 1941), 251, 253.

67. Ann Lage, *Stampp*, 92.

68. Beard to Guy Stanton Ford, 13 September 1943, box 122, file "Historical Service Board, 1943," AHA Papers.

69. Beard quoted in Ellen Nore, *Charles Beard: An Intellectual Biography* (Carbondale: Southern Illinois University Press, 1983), 198.

70. Binkley, "Two World Wars," 26.

71. J. F. Wellemeyer Jr., "Survey of United States Historians, 1952, and a Forecast," *AHR*, 61 (January 1956), 344–45.

72. Morison, *Vistas of History*, 30, 31.

73. Pogue and Shulman, "Pogue," 28. Ironically, military history was taught at Duke by Theodore Ropp, who had not been in the military. See Theodore Ropp, *War in the Modern World*, new ed. with introduction by Alex Roland (1959; Baltimore: Johns Hopkins University Press, 2000).

74. Kent Greenfield to Howard Beale, 12 January 1953, box 444, file "Committee on the Historian and the Federal Government," AHA Papers.

75. Greenfield, *The Historian and the Army*, 7.

76. C. Vann Woodward, *Thinking Back: The Perils of Writing History* (Baton Rouge: Louisiana State University Press, 1986), 46, 47.

77. Potter, "C. Vann Woodward," 385.

78. John M. Blum et al., *The National Experience: A History of the United States* (New York: Harcourt, Brace, and World, 1963).

79. Arthur Mann, "The Progressive Tradition," in John Higham, ed., *The Reconstruction of American History* (New York: Harper and Row, 1962), 158.

80. Thomas Bailey, *A Diplomatic History of the American People*, 5th ed. (New York: Appleton-Century-Crofts, 1955); William L. Langer and Everett S. Gleason, *The Challenge to Isolation, 1937–1940* (New York: Harper for Council on Foreign Relations, 1952); Samuel Flagg Bemis, *The United States as a World Power: A Diplomatic History, 1900–1950* (New York: Holt, 1950); Samuel Flagg Bemis, "American Foreign Policy and the Blessings of Liberty,"

AHR, 67 (January 1962), 291–305; Richard L. Watson Jr., *The Development of National Power: The United States, 1900–1919* (Boston: Houghton Mifflin, 1976); Arthur M. Schlesinger Jr., *The Crisis of the Old Order, 1919–1933*, vol. 1 of *The Age of Roosevelt* (Boston: Houghton Mifflin, 1957); Arthur M. Schlesinger Jr., *The Coming of the New Deal*, vol. 2 of *The Age of Roosevelt* (Boston: Houghton Mifflin, 1958).

81. Samuel Eliot Morison, "Faith of a Historian," *AHR*, 56 (January 1951), 273, 267.

82. Howard R. Lamar, "The New York Meeting, 1951," *AHR*, 57 (April 1952), 802.

83. R. W. Winnacker to Conyers Read, 27 February 1951, box 444, black file on historians and federal government, AHA Papers.

84. Morison, "Faith of a Historian," 271.

85. Ibid., 273. These conservative influences could make a considerable impression. Henry May related that former OSS official Raymond Sontag talked in class at Berkeley about "the menace of Marxist materialism, with a most powerful influence on the students." May to Henry Nash Smith, 21 June [1946], box 4, file 19, Henry Nash Smith Papers, Bancroft Library, University of California, Berkeley.

86. Peter Novick, *That Noble Dream: The "Objectivity Question" and the American Historical Profession* (New York: Cambridge University Press, 1988), 318–19.

87. Thomas Bailey, "The Political Significance of the United States in the World (the Long War against Communism)," an address before the Commonwealth Club of California, 21 July 1950, box 86, file 14, Bailey Papers.

88. Henry Steele Commager, *Freedom and Order: A Commentary on the American Political Scene* (New York: G. Braziller, 1966), 82, 83; Michael Wreszin, "Arthur Schlesinger, Jr., Scholar-Activist in Cold War America, 1946–1956," *Salmagundi*, 63–64 (Spring–Summer 1984), 255–85; Thomas Cox to John D. Hicks, 19 April 1948, box 14, Hicks Papers; Hicks to Mr. and Mrs. DeWitt Wallace (editors, *Readers' Digest*), 20 April 1948, ibid.; enclosure, "The Roots of American Radicalism" (delivered 16 April 1948), ibid.

89. Raymond Sontag, "Training Historians for Government Service," paper presented to the AHA Annual Convention, 1952, box 444, file "American Historical Association—Committee on the Historian and the Federal Government," AHA Papers; Sidney Painter, "The Washington Meeting, 1952," *AHR*, 58 (April 1953), 761–62.

90. Lamar, "New York Meeting," 795.

91. David Owen, "The Boston Meeting, 1949," *AHR*, 55 (April 1950), 757. See also *Annual Report of the American Historical Association for the Year 1949*, vol. 1 (Washington, DC: Government Printing Office, [1950]), 7.

92. "Report and Recommendations of the Committee of the American Historical Association on the Historian and the Federal Government," 9.

93. [Charles Roland], "Memorandum on Opportunities for Historians in the Federal Government," in ibid., appendix, 22.

94. Sontag's comments reported in Painter, "Washington Meeting," 762.

95. *Annual Report of the American Historical Association for the Year 1949* (Washington, DC: Government Printing Office, [1950]), 1:7; *Annual Report of the American Historical Association for the Year 1951*, vol. 1 (Washington, DC: Government Printing Office, [1952]), 55.

96. "Report and Recommendations of the Committee of the American Historical Association on the Historian and the Federal Government," 2.

97. *Annual Report of the American Historical Association for the Year 1951*, 1:56, 59.

98. Guy Stanton Ford, "The Year's Business, 1952," *AHR*, 58 (April 1953), 775.

99. Richard Newhall (b. 1888) was professor of European history at Williams College. Boyd C. Shafer, "The Year's Business, 1953," *AHR*, 59 (April 1954), 811; Boyd Shafer, "The Year's Business, 1955," *AHR*, 62 (April 1957), 786–87; *Annual Report of the American Historical Association for the Year 1955*, vol. 1, *Proceedings* (Washington, DC: Government Printing Office, [1956]), 31–32.

100. Harry Truman to Samuel Eliot Morison, 22 December 1950, box 170, file "Committee on Historians and the Federal Government, 1950–51," AHA Papers.

101. Ibid.; Committee on Historians and the Federal Government, Seventh Meeting, 10 April 1951, box 170, file "Committee on Historians and the Federal Government, 1950–51," AHA Papers.

102. Morison to Harry Truman, 2 January 1951, box 170, file "Committee on Historians and the Federal Government, 1950–51," AHA Papers; Committee on Historians and the Federal Government, Sixth Meeting, 9 January 1951, ibid.

103. Albert B. Corey to Guy Stanton Ford, 29 May 1953, box 179, file "Archivist of the United States," AHA Papers; Theodore C. Blegen to Edward F. Mansur, 26 May 1953, ibid.; Donald C. MacKay to Maxwell Rabb, 19 May 1953, ibid.

104. R. W. Winnacker to Conyers Read, 27 February 1951, box 444, black file on historians and federal government, AHA Papers.

105. Paul Scheips, "Memorandum on the 1952 Report of the Committee of the American Historical Association on the Historian and the Federal Government," box 176, file "Historian and the Federal Government," AHA Papers. See also Paul Scheips, "The Historian and the Nature of History: Some Reflections for Air Force Historians," *Military Affairs*, 16 (Fall 1952), 123–31.

106. "Report and Recommendations of the Committee of the American Historical Association on the Historian and the Federal Government," 7.

107. Donald M. Dozer, "Memorandum on Historical Studies in the Department of State," 12 August 1953, box 176, file "Committee on the Historian and the Federal Government," AHA Papers. See also "Historical News and Comments," *MVHR*, 29 (June 1942), 138–39.

108. "Report and Recommendations of the Committee of the American Historical Association on the Historian and the Federal Government," 7.

109. *Washington Post*, 29 December 1952.

110. "Who's to Write the History of the War?" *Saturday Evening Post*, 220 (4 October 1947), 172, quoted in Nore, *Charles Beard*, 205.

111. Howard K. Beale, "The Professional Historian: His Theory and His Practice," *Pacific Historical Review*, 22 (August 1953), 244, 245.

112. Novick, *That Noble Dream*, 512–21; Ronald Grele, "Whose Public? Whose History? What Is the Goal of a Public Historian?" *Public Historian*, 3 (Winter 1981), 40–48; Terence O'Donnell, "Pitfalls along the Path of Public History," in Susan Benson, Stephen Brier, and Roy Rosenzweig, eds., *Presenting the Past: Essays on History and the Public* (Philadelphia: Temple University Press, 1986), 239–44.

113. Painter, "Washington Meeting," 762.

114. *Annual Report of the American Historical Association for the Year 1951*, 1:56; Greenfield, *The Historian and the Army*, 7.

115. Richard G. Hewlett and Jo Anne McCormick Quatannens, "Richard G. Hewlett: Federal Historian," *Public Historian*, 19 (Winter 1997), 53–54.

116. Roger R. Trask, "Small Federal History Offices in the Nation's Capital," *Public Historian*, 13 (Winter 1991), 48.

117. Scheips, "Memorandum on the 1952 Report."

118. Frank H. Colley, "Memorandum for Kent Roberts Greenfield," 5 June 1950, box 444, untitled black file on historians in federal government, AHA Papers; Kent Greenfield to Richard Humphrey, 9 June 1952, ibid.

119. "Report and Recommendations of the Committee of the American Historical Association on the Historian and the Federal Government," 20.

120. *Annual Report of the American Historical Association for the Year 1955*, 1:31. It was then announced that the procedures were to be changed to the (at least partial) satisfaction of the AHA from 1956.

121. Oron J. Hale, "The Washington Meeting, 1955," *AHR*, 61 (April 1956), 757.

122. *Annual Report of the American Historical Association for the Year 1955*, 1:31. The MVHA was also affected. See Thomas D. Clark, "Our Roots Flourished in the Valley," *JAH*, 65 (June 1978), 95.

123. Scheips, "Memorandum on the 1952 Report."

124. See chap. 12 below.

125. Boyd C. Shafer, "The Year's Business, 1954," *AHR*, 60 (April 1955), 757. See also Merle Curti, "Intellectuals and Other People," *AHR*, 60 (January 1955), 280.

126. Stephen T. Leonard, introduction to Leon Fink, Stephen T. Leonard, and Donald M. Reid, eds., *Intellectuals and Public Life: Between Radicalism and Reform* (Ithaca: Cornell University Press, 1996), 10–12.

127. See, e.g., Edward Shils, *The Intellectuals and the Powers* (Chicago: University of Chicago Press, 1972); Talcott Parsons, "'The Intellectual': A Social Role Category," in Philip Rieff, ed., *On Intellectuals: Theoretical Studies/Case Studies* (New York: Doubleday, 1969), 3–26.

128. Merle Curti, "The Democratic Theme in American Literature" [1952], in Merle Curti, *Probing the Past* (New York: Harper and Brothers, 1955), 30; cf. Conyers Read, "The Social Responsibilities of the Historian," *AHR*, 55 (January 1950), 275–85.

129. Curti, "Intellectuals and Other People," 280.

130. Jacques Barzun, *The House of Intellect* (1959; repr., London: Mercury Books, 1962), 145–46. Benda's views were little understood in the United States. See Samuel Eliot Morison, letter to editor, *Saturday Review*, 15 June 1968, 19, cited in Ray Nichols, *Treason, Tradition, and the Intellectual: Julien Benda and Political Discourse* (Lawrence: Regents Press of Kansas, 1978), 199 n. 47, 200; Thomas Reeves, *John F. Kennedy: A Question of Character* (London: Bloomsbury, 1991), 228.

131. Barzun, *House of Intellect*, 151, 156, quotation at 159n.

132. Ian Tyrrell, *The Absent Marx: Class Analysis and Liberal History in Twentieth-Century America* (Westport, CT: Greenwood Press, 1986), 73; Novick, *That Noble Dream*, 332–36;

Richard Hofstadter to J. R. Pole, 9 February 1968, box 7, Richard Hofstadter Papers, Rare Books and Manuscripts, Butler Library, Columbia University.

133. Oscar Handlin, *Truth in History* (Cambridge: Belknap Press, Harvard University Press, 1979), 415; Oscar Handlin, review of *Basic History of the United States*, by Charles Beard and Mary Beard, *Partisan Review*, 11 (Fall 1944), 466–68.

134. See below, epilogue; Thomas Bender, *New York Intellect: A History of Intellectual Life in New York City, from 1750 to the Beginnings of Our Own Time* (New York: Alfred A. Knopf, 1987), 316–17.

135. William C. Johnstone to Thomas Bailey, 8 August 1945, box 3, file 12, Bailey Papers; G. Bernard Noble to Bailey, 29 December 1958, box 5, file 8, ibid.; Thomas Bailey, *Diplomatic History of the American People* (New York: F. S. Crofts and Co., 1940).

136. Carlton Savage to Bemis, 25 September 1961, series I, box 38, file 488, Bemis Papers.

137. Bemis to Savage, 30 September 1961, 30 November 1961, series I, box 38, file 488, Bemis Papers; Savage to Bemis, 13 March 1962, ibid.; Savage to Bemis, 2 November 1962, file 489, ibid.

138. Bemis to Henry Cabot Lodge, 20 May 1958, series I, box 25, file 311, ibid.

139. Bemis, "American Foreign Policy and the Blessings of Liberty," 292.

140. John R. Alden, "The Washington Meeting, 1961," *AHR*, 67 (April 1962), 854, 874.

141. Hugh Davis Graham, "The Stunted Career of Policy History: A Critique and an Agenda," *Public Historian*, 15 (Spring 1993), 26–27; Julian E. Zelizer, "Clio's Lost Tribe: Public Policy History since 1978," *Journal of Policy History*, 12, no. 3 (2000), 370; Howard Zinn, *Postwar America, 1945–1971* (Indianapolis: Bobbs-Merrill, 1973), 3–36.

Chapter Twelve

1. *Proceedings of the Nineteenth Annual Conference of Historical Societies, Columbus, Ohio, December 29, 1923* (n.p.: Conference of Historical Societies, 1924), 11.

2. The isolation of state and local historians in the United States is noted by the State Historical Society of Wisconsin in "Different Directions (1914–1941)," *Exchange*, The Office of Local History at the Wisconsin Historical Society, 38, no. 3 (1996), http://www.wisconsinhistory.org/localhistory/articles/different_directions.asp (accessed 29 September 2004).

3. John Higham, *History: The Development of Historical Studies in the United States* (Englewood Cliffs, NJ: Prentice Hall, 1965), 27.

4. Henry E. Bourne, "The Work of American Historical Societies," *Annual Report of the American Historical Association for the Year 1904* (Washington, DC: Government Printing Office, 1905), 117; Lucy Salmon, "A Plan for Affiliated Historical Societies," box 94, file 762, John Franklin Jameson Papers, LC.

5. *Annual Report of the American Historical Association for the Year 1898* (Washington, DC: Government Printing Office, 1899), 567–72; *Annual Report of the American Historical Association for the Year 1899*, vol. 1 (Washington, DC: Government Printing Office, 1900), 24, 25.

6. John Franklin Jameson to G. B. Adams, 13 January 1896, box 471, Historical Manuscripts Commission file, AHA Papers, LC.

7. See, e.g., Nils Olsen to Jameson, 10 August 1910, box 126, file 1491, Jameson Papers; Jameson to Olsen, 24 August 1910, ibid.; memo to Olsen, 2 August 1910, ibid.

8. "The Meeting of the American Historical Association at Baltimore," *AHR*, 11 (April 1906), 505; Jameson to Joseph Schafer, 25 March 1926, box 126, file 1492, Jameson Papers.

9. "The Meeting of the American Historical Association at Baltimore," 505.

10. Jameson to A. W. H. Eaton, 22 December 1911, box 94, file 762, Jameson Papers.

11. Ibid.

12. Jameson to Nathaniel Paine, 18 October 1906, box 113, file 1155, ibid.

13. Bonnie Gene Smith, "Gender and the Practices of Scientific History: The Seminar and Archival Research in the Nineteenth Century," *AHR*, 100 (October 1995), 1150–77; Joan Scott, *Gender and the Politics of History* (New York: Columbia University Press, 1988), chap. 9; Jacqueline Goggin, "Challenging Sexual Discrimination in the Historical Profession," *AHR*, 97 (June 1992), 769–802.

14. Cited by Dixon Ryan Fox, "Local Historical Societies in the United States," *Canadian Historical Review,* 13 (September 1932), 263.

15. Louise Kellogg received her doctorate from the University of Wisconsin in 1901 and had been one of Frederick Jackson Turner's students. William C. Haygood, "Louise Phelps Kellogg," *NAW,* 2:321–22.

16. Albert Bushnell Hart, "The Historical Opportunity in America," *AHR,* 4 (October 1898), 19.

17. John Franklin Jameson to Samuel Eliot Morison, 5 January 1926, box 114, file 1175, Jameson Papers; John Franklin Jameson, "The Functions of State and Local Historical Societies with Respect to Research and Publication," in Morey D. Rothberg and Jacqueline Goggin, eds., *John Franklin Jameson and the Development of Humanistic Scholarship in America* (Athens: University of Georgia Press, 1993), 259–60.

18. Solon Buck, "The Progress and Possibilities of Mississippi Valley History," *MVHR,* 10 (June 1923), 6.

19. St. George L. Sioussat, "Historical Activities in the Old Southwest," *MVHR,* 1 (December 1914), 400–401; John H. Stetson Jr., "Florida as a Field for Historical Research," in "Proceedings of the Eighteenth Annual Conference of Historical Societies," *Annual Report of the American Historical Association for the Year 1922,* vol. 1 (Washington, DC: Government Printing Office, 1926), 197; David Van Tassel, "The American Historical Association and the South, 1884–1913," *Journal of Southern History,* 23 (November 1957), 465–82.

20. David W. Blight, *Race and Reunion: The Civil War in American Memory* (Cambridge: Belknap Press, Harvard University Press, 2001), 295–96.

21. Gaines Foster, *Ghosts of the Confederacy: Defeat, the Lost Cause, and the Emergence of the New South, 1865 to 1913* (New York: Oxford University Press, 1987), 186.

22. "The Meeting of the American Historical Association at New York," *AHR,* 15 (April 1910), 489; W. E. B. Du Bois, "Reconstruction and Its Benefits," *AHR,* 15 (April 1910), 781–99; Peter Novick, *That Noble Dream: The "Objectivity Question" and the American Historical Profession* (New York: Cambridge University Press, 1988), 77.

23. M. P. Campbell (Oklahoma Historical Society custodian) to Jameson, 17 May 1912, box 94, file 762, Jameson Papers.

24. Jeanne E. Wier to Jameson, 27 April 1922, ibid.

25. Jameson to Frederick Jackson Turner, 19 February 1916, box 132, file 1653, Jameson Papers; Jameson to Samuel Eliot Morison, 5 January 1926, box 114, file 1175, ibid.; John Franklin Jameson, "The Meeting of the American Historical Association at New Haven," *AHR*, 28 (April 1923), 425.

26. James Trustlow Adams to Jameson, 5 March 1918, box 45, file 20, Jameson Papers.

27. "The Meeting of the American Historical Association at New York," 488.

28. Alexander Lawton to Jameson, 13 October 1927, box 53, file 80, Jameson Papers.

29. M. P. Campbell to Jameson, 17 May 1912, box 94, file 762, ibid.

30. Preface to *Collections and Researches Made by the Michigan Pioneer and Historical Society*, vol. 22 (Lansing, MI: Robert Smith and Co., 1894), iii.

31. Amanda Laugesen, "Disciplining History," paper presented to the Australian and New Zealand American Studies Association Conference, Australian National University, Canberra, 15 April 1998.

32. L. Belle Hamlin to Jameson, 1 November 1912, box 94, file 762, Jameson Papers.

33. Jameson to A. W. H. Eaton, 22 December 1911, ibid.

34. Clarence Burton to Jameson, 23 October 1911, box 113, file 1143, ibid.

35. Jameson to Burton, 26 January 1909, ibid.

36. Jameson to Clarence Burton, 15 November 1906, box 66, re letter of 13 November 1906, ibid.; Burton to Jameson, 22 November 1905, box 113, file 1143, ibid.

37. Burton to Waldo Leland, 27 December 1904, box 113, file 1143, ibid.

38. Ray Allen Billington, "Tempest in Clio's Teapot: The American Historical Association Rebellion of 1915," *AHR*, 78 (April 1973), 348–69, quotation at 357.

39. John Franklin Jameson, "The Meeting of the American Historical Association at Cincinnati," *AHR*, 22 (April 1917), 514; Augustus M. Shearer memo to council, Conference of Historical Societies Correspondence file, n.d. [1916–17], box 471, AHA Papers; *Annual Report of the American Historical Association for 1915* (Washington, DC: Government Printing Office, 1917), 238–39.

40. *Proceedings of the Nineteenth Annual Conference of Historical Societies*, 11.

41. Jameson to John Swarbrick, 18 May 1928, box 94, file 762, Jameson Papers.

42. Sioussat, "Historical Activities in the Old Southwest," 400–401. On the rise of patriotic societies see John Bodnar, ed., *Bonds of Affection: Americans Define Their Patriotism* (Princeton: Princeton University Press, 1996).

43. "Proceedings of the Meeting of Patriotic Societies of Connecticut," in *Annual Report of the American Historical Association for the Year 1922*, 1:209–32.

44. "The Meeting of the American Historical Association at Buffalo and Ithaca," *AHR*, 17 (April 1912), 467–68; "The Meeting of the American Historical Association at Cincinnati," 514; John Franklin Jameson, "The Meeting of the American Historical Association at Philadelphia," *AHR*, 23 (April 1918), 509. The report of the December 1916 annual meeting noted "the fine spirit of patriotism animating them [the patriotic societies]"; "The Meeting of the American Historical Association at Cincinnati," 515. For the AHA's Committee on Hereditary Societies, see John Franklin Jameson, "The Meeting of the American Historical Association at Washington," *AHR*, 26 (April 1921), 438.

45. "Proceedings of the Meeting of Patriotic Societies of Connecticut," 209–32.

46. Bethany Andreasen, "Treason or Truth: The New York City Textbook Controversy, 1920–1923," *New York History,* 66 (October 1985), 397–419; Jonathan Zimmerman, "'Each "Race" Could Have Its Heroes Sung': Ethnicity and the History Wars in the 1920s," *JAH,* 87 (June 2000), 92–111.

47. John Franklin Jameson, "The Meeting of the American Historical Association at Columbus," *AHR,* 29 (April 1924), 428; Bessie Louise Pierce, *Public Opinion and the Teaching of History in the United States* (New York: Alfred A. Knopf, 1926); Samuel Eliot Morison to Jameson, 14 June 1926, box 114, file 1175, Jameson Papers.

48. Jameson to Milo Quaife, 12 April 1916, box 136, Wisconsin State Historical Society file, Jameson Papers; Quaife to Jameson, 8 April 1916, ibid.; Albion Small to Jameson, 31 October 1919, and attached letters and documents, file 80, ibid.; Jameson to A. R. Newsome, 15 November 1927, ibid.; Newsome to Jameson, 14 and 18 November 1927, box 53, file 80, ibid. See also box 251, file "Allied Activities," AHA Papers.

49. Jameson to Clarence W. Alvord, 24 February 1908, box 47, file 38, Jameson Papers.

50. Jameson to Alvord, 24 May 1908, ibid.

51. "The Meeting of the American Historical Association at Chicago," *AHR,* 11 (April 1905), 493.

52. Augustus Shearer to AHA Executive, n.d. [c. 1916–17], box 471, Conference of Historical Societies Correspondence file, AHA Papers.

53. See Mississippi Valley Historical Association Papers, Special Collections and Archives, Indiana University—Purdue University Library, Indianapolis. E.g., Clarence Paine to Charles Aldrich (curator, Historical Department, Iowa), 23 July 1906, box 24, file "1906 Correspondence."

54. Cf. Novick, *That Noble Dream,* 183.

55. Jameson to Clarence W. Alvord, 24 February 1908, box 47, file 38, Jameson Papers; Jameson to Alvord, 14 July 1908, ibid.

56. Alvord to Jameson, 5 February 1908, box 113, file 1155, ibid.

57. Solon Buck, "Clarence Walworth Alvord, Historian," *MVHR,* 15 (December 1928), 314.

58. James L. Sellers, "Before We Were Members—The MVHA," *MVHR,* 40 (June 1953), 8.

59. Jameson to Clarence Alvord, 10 November 1916, box 113, file 1155, AHA Papers.

60. *MVHR,* vol. 6 (1919–20), had local reports in three of four issues, and vol. 7 (September 1920) concluded with A. C. Cole, "Historical Activities in the Old Northwest," 127–41.

61. Clara Paine to John D. Hicks, 14 July 1936 and 14 October 1936, box 13, John D. Hicks Papers, Bancroft Library, University of California, Berkeley.

62. Hicks to Avery Craven [draft], n.d., in reply to Craven to Hicks, 9 July 1936, box 13, Hicks Papers.

63. Thomas D. Clark, "Our Roots Flourished in the Valley," *JAH,* 65 (June 1978), 99, 100. Only after Paine's resignation in 1952 was serious debate over the change of name to the Organization of American Historians feasible, but the *MVHR* did not become the *Journal of American History* till 1964.

64. *DAS*, 1951 ed., 758.

65. "Notes and News," *AHR*, 18 (July 1913), 880.

66. John Bodnar, *Remaking America: Public Memory, Commemoration, and Patriotism in the Twentieth Century* (Princeton: Princeton University Press, 1992), 175–79.

67. Michael Kammen, *Mystic Chords of Memory: The Transformation of Tradition in American Culture* (New York: Knopf, 1991), 332, 474–77; Theodore Blegen, *Grass Roots History* (Minneapolis: University of Minnesota Press, 1947).

68. Julian Boyd, "State and Local Historical Societies in the United States," *AHR*, 40 (October 1934), 36–37.

69. C. C. Crittenden, "The North Carolina Historical Commission," in *Proceedings of the Conference of State and Local Historical Societies, Held at Chicago, Illinois, December 28, 1938* (n.p., n.d.), 18, 19.

70. Ibid., 18.

71. Novick, *That Noble Dream*, chap. 9.

72. Crittenden, "North Carolina Historical Commission," 20, 16.

73. In 1937 academics such as Schlesinger and Nichols sought with Social Science Research Council funds to stimulate a new interdisciplinary approach to regional history within the academy. See "Proceedings, Conference on Comparative Local History," 24 September 1937, box 6, file "Comparative Local History," Solon Buck Papers, LC.

74. [The Editors], "Educating Clio," *AHR*, 45 (April 1940), 516; Ellen Fitzpatrick, *History's Memory: Writing America's Past, 1880–1980* (Cambridge: Harvard University Press, 2002), esp. 186–87.

75. "Educating Clio," 516, 517; Constance McLaughlin Green, "The Value of Local History," in Caroline F. Ware, ed., *The Cultural Approach to History* (New York: Columbia University Press, 1940), 275–86.

76. *DAS*, 1951 ed., 139; Lester J. Cappon to Arthur M. Schlesinger, 23 January 1930, box 4, Arthur M. Schlesinger Papers, Harvard University Archives.

77. Lester J. Cappon, "Two Decades of Historical Activity in Virginia," *Journal of Southern History*, 6 (May 1940), 198, 192.

78. Cappon, "Two Decades of Historical Activity in Virginia"; Crittenden, "North Carolina Historical Commission," 15–21.

79. Alvin P. Stauffer and Charles W. Porter, "The National Park Service Program of Conservation of Areas and Structures of National Historical Significance," *MVHR*, 30 (June 1943), 25–48; Charles B. Hosmer Jr., *Preservation Comes of Age: From Williamsburg to the National Trust, 1926–1949*, 2 vols. (Charlottesville: University Press of Virginia, for Preservation Press, National Trust for Historic Preservation in the United States, 1981), esp. 2:884–88; Charles B. Hosmer Jr., "Verne E. Chatelain and the Development of the Branch of History of the National Park Service," *Public Historian*, 16 (Winter 1994), 25–38; Bodnar, *Remaking America*, 175–79; Harlean James, *Romance of the National Parks* (1939; repr., New York: Arno Press, 1972), 229–32.

80. C. C. Crittenden, "The Need for a Strong Federation of American and Canadian Historical Organizations," 25 April 1940, p. 3, box 117, Conference of Historical Societies file, AHA Papers; Theodore Blegen, "Some Aspects of Historical Work under the New Deal," *MVHR*, 21 (September 1934), 199–200.

81. William F. Birdsall, "Archivists, Librarians, and Issues during the Pioneering Era of the American Archival Movement," *Journal of Library History,* 14 (Fall 1979), 457–79.

82. Julian P. Boyd to Conyers Read, 6 December 1935, box 98, Conference of Historical Societies file, AHA Papers.

83. C. C. Crittenden circular letter, 12 December 1939, box 116, ibid.

84. Crittenden, "Need for a Strong Federation of American and Canadian Historical Organizations"; Boyd to Read, 6 December 1935, box 98, Conference of Historical Societies file, AHA Papers.

85. Read to Christopher Coleman, 10 September 1935, box 102, Conference of Historical Societies file, AHA Papers; "Report of the Conference of Historical Societies, 1 September 1934–31 August 1935," box 98, ibid.

86. Boyd to Read, 6 December 1935, box 98, Conference of Historical Societies file, ibid.

87. "Proceedings of the Policy Committee of the Conference of Historical Societies," Washington, DC, Monday, 3 June 1940, p. 6, box 117, Conference of Historical Societies file, ibid.

88. *State and Local History News,* 2, no. 2 (n.d., c. 1943), in box 133, AHA Papers.

89. Mary Cunningham to Clifford Lord, 22 November 1946, box 1, file 9, SHSW-COS, Madison, WI; quotation from Clifford Lord to Mary Cunningham, 10 March 1947, and attached flyer, Sylvester K. Stevens to "Dear Friend," on *American Heritage,* ibid.

90. Michael Kennedy, "The Historical Society Magazine: Does It Have a Future?" *History News,* 16, no. 3 (January 1961), 37.

91. A. Gilbert Wright to Clifford Lord, 15 June 1954, box 2, file 3, SHSW-COS; *Florida State Museum, a Pictorial Record, 1953* (Gainesville: University of Florida, 1953); Clifford Lord to Howard H. Peckham, 23 March 1951, box 2, file 6, SHSW-COS.

92. Kammen, *Mystic Chords,* 573–81; James G. Bradsher, "Taking America's Heritage to the People: The Freedom Train Story," *Prologue: Journal of the National Archives,* 17 (Winter 1985), 229–45.

93. Clifford Lord, ed., *Ideas in Conflict: A Colloquium on Certain Problems in Historical Society Work in the United States and Canada* (Harrisburg, PA: AASLH, 1958), 3.

94. Sylvester K. Stevens, Clifford Lord, and Albert B. Corey, "Making our Heritage Live," *Bulletins of the American Association for State and Local History,* 2, no. 5 (November 1951), 147, quotation at 129.

95. Crittenden, "North Carolina Historical Commission," 18.

96. Conyers Read, "The Social Responsibilities of the Historian," *AHR,* 55 (January 1950), 275–85; Samuel Eliot Morison, "Faith of a Historian," *AHR,* 56 (January 1951), 273.

97. Walter Muir Whitehill, *Independent Historical Societies: An Inquiry into Their Research and Publication Functions and Their Financial Future* (Boston: Athenaeum, 1962), 515.

98. Roy Rosenzweig, "Marketing the Past: American Heritage and Popular History in the United States," in Susan P. Benson, Stephen Brier, and Roy Rosenzweig, eds., *Presenting the Past: Essays on History and the Public* (Philadelphia: Temple University Press, 1986), 21–30.

99. Clifford Lord to Lancaster Pollard, Oregon Historical Society, 25 May 1954, box 4, file 3, SHSW-COS.

100. David D. Van Tassel and James A. Tinsley, "Historical Organizations as Aids to

History," in William B. Hesseltine and Donald R. McNeil, eds., *In Support of Clio: Essays in Memory of Herbert A. Kellar* (Madison: State Historical Society of Wisconsin, 1958), 138.

101. Lord to Pollard, 25 May 1954, box 4, file 3, SHSW-COS.

102. *History News,* 13 (March 1957), 35–38, quotation at 37.

103. John Franklin Jameson to Samuel Eliot Morison, 5 January 1926, box 114, Jameson Papers; Morison to Jameson, 21 December 1925, ibid.

104. State Historical Society of Wisconsin, "Different Directions (1914–1941)," at n. 10.

105. Lewis Beeson to Clifford Lord, 1 December 1952, box 2, file 12, SHSW-COS.

106. Louis Hacker, Comments, in Lord, *Ideas in Conflict,* 155.

107. S. K. Stevens, Comments, in ibid., 70.

108. Whitehill, *Independent Historical Societies,* 520.

109. See "J.P.L.," review of *The Old Northwest: The Beginning of Our Colonial System,* by Dr. B. A. Hinsdale (Boston: Silver Burdett, 1898), *Iowa Historical Record,* 15 (October 1899), 557.

110. Reuben Gold Thwaites, ed., *Wisconsin Historical Collections of the State Historical Society of Wisconsin,* vol 15. (Madison: Democrat Printing Co., 1900), viii.

111. "The Society and the State," *Wisconsin Magazine of History,* 8 (September 1924), 119. See also "News and Comment," *Minnesota History Bulletin,* 1 (November 1915), 236–37; George E. Vincent, "The Social Memory," *Minnesota History Bulletin,* 1 (February 1916), 250; "News and Comment," *Minnesota History Bulletin,* 1 (August 1916), 407; Lester B. Shippee, review of *The Illinois Country, 1673–1818,* vol. 1 of *The Centennial History of Illinois,* ed. Clarence W. Alvord, 5 vols. (Springfield: Illinois Centennial Commission, 1918–20), *Minnesota History Bulletin,* 4 (February–May 1921), 50.

112. Milo Quaife, "The Wider Field," *Wisconsin Magazine of History,* 2, no. 3 (1918–19), 387; Louise Houghton, *Our Debt to the Red Man: The French-Indians in the Development of the United States* (Boston: Stratford Co., 1918); Thomas Teakle, *The Spirit Lake Massacre* (Iowa City: State Historical Society of Iowa, 1918).

113. Joseph Schafer to Grace Edgington (editor, *Old Oregon*), 9 December 1920, box 3, file 6, Joseph Schafer Papers, SHSW.

114. Edward Potts Cheyney, *The European Background of American History, 1300–1600,* American Nation: A History, vol. 1 (1904; repr., New York: Collier Books, 1961), 7.

115. W. J. Harte, "Local History: An Exeter Experiment," *History,* 8 (April 1923), 21.

116. Reba N. Sofer, *"Discipline and Power": The University, History, and the Making of an English Elite, 1870–1930* (Stanford: Stanford University Press, 1994); Rosemary Jann, "From Amateur to Professional: The Case of the Oxbridge Historians," *Journal of British Studies,* 22 (Spring 1983), 122–47.

117. Raphael Samuel, *People's History and Socialist Theory* (London: Routledge and Kegan Paul, 1981); John Braeman, "Charles A. Beard: The English Experience," *Journal of American Studies,* 15 (August 1981), 177, 185–86; Harlan B. Phillips, "Charles Beard, Walter Vrooman, and the Founding of Ruskin Hall," *South Atlantic Quarterly,* 50 (April 1951), 186–91.

118. Edward Royal, "Local History in Context: Twenty Years of the Conference of Regional and Local Historians (CORAL)," *Local Historian,* 28 (August 1998), 178, 179.

119. Ibid., 177.

120. Jameson, "Functions of State and Local Historical Societies," 256–57.

121. Marc Bloch, *The Île-de-France: The Country around Paris,* trans. J. E. Anderson (London: Routledge and Kegan Paul, 1971), 62; Richard M. Andrews, "Some Implications of the *Annales* School and Its Methods for a Revision of Historical Writing about the United States," *Review,* 1 (Winter–Spring 1978), 165–80; Marc Bloch, *The Historian's Craft,* trans. R. R. Palmer (New York: Alfred A. Knopf, 1953); Peter Burke, *The French Historical Revolution: The Annales School, 1929–1989* (Stanford: Stanford University Press, 1990); Stuart Clark, ed., *The Annales School,* 4 vols. (London: Routledge, 1999).

122. Bloch, *The Île-de-France,* 50.

123. Ibid., 48, 52–53.

124. Ibid., 106.

125. Ibid., 120, 123.

126. Andrews, "Some Implications of the *Annales* School," 165–80; Frederick Jackson Turner, *The Significance of Sections in American History* (1932; repr., Gloucester, MA: Peter Smith, 1950).

127. Christophe Prochasson, "Is There a Crisis in History in France?" *Perspectives,* May 1998, 9.

Epilogue

1. Merle Curti to Schlesinger, 27 April 1958, P-11 C (Cr–Cu), file 4, Arthur M. Schlesinger Jr. Papers, John F. Kennedy Library, Boston.

2. On Schlesinger, see Michael Wreszin, "Arthur Schlesinger, Jr., Scholar-Activist in Cold War America, 1946–1956," *Salmagundi,* 63–64 (Spring–Summer 1984), 255–85.

3. Neil Jumonville, *Henry Steele Commager: Midcentury Liberalism and the History of the Present* (Chapel Hill: University of North Carolina Press, 1999), esp. 102–21.

4. C. Vann Woodward, *Thinking Back: The Perils of Writing History* (Baton Rouge: Louisiana State University Press, 1986), 88–89.

5. Merrill Jensen, *The New Nation: A History of the United States during the Confederation, 1781–1789* (New York: Knopf, 1950).

6. Merle Curti, "Intellectuals and Other People," *AHR,* 60 (January 1955), 280.

7. Richard Gillam, "Richard Hofstadter, C. Wright Mills and 'The Critical Ideal,'" *American Scholar* 47 (Winter 1978), 79; Richard Wade to Arthur M. Schlesinger Jr., 22 January 1957, box P-25, file "Richard Wade, 1951–1960," Arthur M. Schlesinger Jr. Papers; Wade to Schlesinger, 11 November 1959, ibid.

8. Cited in *Saturday Review,* 16 July 1955, 13.

9. Daniel Bell, "Modernity and Mass Society: On the Varieties of Cultural Experience," in Arthur M. Schlesinger Jr. and Morton White, eds., *Paths of American Thought* (Boston: Houghton Mifflin, 1963), 424. It is no accident that during this period Richard Hofstadter wrote, with C. De Witt Hardy, *The Development and Scope of Higher Education in the United States* (New York: Columbia University Press, 1952), one of a series sponsored by the Commission on Financing Higher Education, begun in 1949.

10. *PW,* 2 January 1950, 249.

11. Dixon Wecter, "What Can University Presses Teach Professors?" *PW,* 10 July 1948, 115; "Means, Extremes, Percentages, and Averages of University Presses," *PW,* 21 May 1949, 2049.

12. Eric Goldman to W. Stull Holt, 29 September 1954, box 19, file 6, Eric F. Goldman Papers, LC; William L. Shirer to Goldman, 2 February 1970, box 29, file 5, ibid.; quotations from Goldman to Shirer, 9 February 1970, ibid.

13. "Looking Forward," *Saturday Review,* 4 April 1953, 26.

14. Martin Tucker, "Vintage from the Campus Presses," *Saturday Review,* 21 May 1960, 23.

15. "Pick of the Paperbacks," *Saturday Review,* 4 May 1957, 34. E.g., Richard Hofstadter's *Social Darwinism in American Thought,* rev. ed. (Boston: Beacon Press, 1955), originally appeared in 1944 through the University of Pennsylvania Press but later sold 200,000 copies as a paperback.

16. "Pick of the Paperbacks," 34.

17. "University Press Survey: Reports from the Campuses," *Saturday Review,* 16 July 1955, 13.

18. "Pick of the Paperbacks," 34.

19. David M. Potter, "C. Vann Woodward," in Marcus Cunliffe and Robin Winks, eds., *Pastmasters: Some Essays on American Historians* (New York: Harper and Row, 1969), 397–98; Woodward, *Thinking Back,* 93.

20. Oscar Handlin, "Comments on Mass and Popular Culture," *Daedalus,* 89 (Spring 1960), 325–32; Oscar Handlin, *Truth in History* (Cambridge: Belknap Press, Harvard University Press, 1979), 413.

21. Richard Hofstadter, *Anti-intellectualism in American Life* (New York: Knopf, 1962); Neil Jumonville, *Critical Crossings: The New York Intellectuals in Postwar America* (Berkeley and Los Angeles: University of California Press, 1991), 222.

22. Arthur Schlesinger Jr., "The Highbrow in American Politics," *Partisan Review,* 20 (March–April 1953), 165.

23. Arthur M. Schlesinger Jr., "Probing the American Experience" [1958], reprinted in Arthur M. Schlesinger Jr., *The Politics of Hope* (London: Eyre and Spottiswoode, 1964), 52, 49.

24. Daniel Joseph Singal, "Beyond Consensus: Richard Hofstadter and American Historiography," *AHR,* 89 (October 1984), 983.

25. D. W. Brogan, "Fifty Years of Dreams, Protests, and Achievements," *NYTBR,* 16 October 1955, 7; David Freeman Hawke, "Richard Hofstadter, Interview," *History,* 3 (1960), 136; Michael Kazin, "Hofstadter Lives: Political Culture and Temperament in the Work of an American Historian," *Reviews in American History,* 27, no. 2 (1999), 333–34; John D. Hicks, review of *The Age of Reform,* by Richard Hofstadter, *Saturday Review,* 22 October 1955, 12. For surveys of Hofstadter's work, see Stanley Elkins and Eric McKitrick, "Richard Hofstadter: A Progress," in Stanley Elkins and Eric McKitrick, eds., *The Hofstadter Aegis: A Memorial* (New York: Vintage, 1973), 300–367; Arthur M. Schlesinger Jr., "Richard Hofstadter," in Cunliffe and Winks, *Pastmasters,* 278–315.

26. Hofstadter to J. R. Pole, 9 February 1967 and 9 February 1968, box 7, Richard Hofstadter Papers, Rare Books and Manuscripts, Butler Library, Columbia University.

27. Alfred Kazin, "Richard Hofstadter, 1916–1970," *American Scholar,* 40, no. 3 (1971), 397–401.

28. Daniel Walker Howe and Peter Elliott Finn, "Richard Hofstadter: The Ironies of an American Historian," *Pacific Historical Review,* 43 (February 1974), 16. On Hofstadter's early career, see Susan Stout Baker, *Radical Beginnings: Richard Hofstadter in the 1930s* (Westport, CT: Greenwood, 1985), 89–91.

29. Richard Hofstadter, *The American Political Tradition and the Men Who Made It* (New York: Knopf, 1948); Richard Hofstadter, *The Age of Reform: From Bryan to F.D.R.* (New York: Knopf, 1955).

30. Richard Hofstadter, "A Note on Intellect and Power," *American Scholar,* 30 (Autumn 1961), 596.

31. Leon Fink, *Progressive Intellectuals and the Dilemmas of Democratic Commitment* (Cambridge: Harvard University Press, 1997), 280.

32. Richard Hofstadter, "History and the Social Sciences," in Fritz Stern, ed., *The Varieties of History: From Voltaire to the Present* (New York: Meridian, 1956), 360. See also Hofstadter, "Note on Intellect and Power," 588–98.

33. Hofstadter to Goldman, 11 March 1964, Domestic Affairs, Richard Hofstadter, 1964, box 56, file 12, Goldman Papers.

34. Richard Hofstadter, *The Progressive Historians: Turner, Beard, Parrington* (New York: Knopf, 1968), 464.

35. Richard Hofstadter, "Two Cultures: Adversary and/or Responsible," *Public Interest,* no. 6 (Winter 1967), 72–74.

36. Goldman's specialist works include *Charles J. Bonaparte, Patrician Reformer: His Earlier Career* (Baltimore: Johns Hopkins University Press, 1943) and *John Bach McMaster, American Historian* (Philadelphia: University of Pennsylvania Press, 1943).

37. Eric F. Goldman, "Historians and the Ivory Tower," *Social Frontier,* 2 (June 1936), 278–80.

38. Eric F. Goldman, Erling Hunt, and Frederic C. Lane, eds., *The World's History* (New York: Harcourt, Brace, and Co., 1947).

39. Goldman to Eleanor Riger, 23 December 1959, and the letters in box 34, files 10–12, on *The Open Mind,* Goldman Papers; Peter M. Affe to Goldman, 14 March 1963, box 34, file 9, ibid.

40. Eric F. Goldman, *The Tragedy of Lyndon Johnson* (New York: Alfred A. Knopf, 1969), 133, 134, 159. Goldman is briefly treated in Tevi Troy, *Intellectuals and the American Presidency: Philosophers, Jesters, or Technicians?* (Lanham, MD: Rowman and Littlefield, 2002), 54–57.

41. Peter Novick, *That Noble Dream: The "Objectivity Question" and the American Historical Profession* (New York: Cambridge University Press, 1988), 304n; Walter Rundell to W. Stull Holt, 24 April 1964, box 8, American Historical Association, Correspondence, April 1963–August 1964, W. Stull Holt Papers, Department of Special Collections, University of Washington Libraries.

42. Frederick Jackson Turner, "The Significance of History" [1891], reprinted in John Mack Faragher, *Rereading Frederick Jackson Turner* (New York: Henry Holt, 1994), 25.

43. Goldman to A. Neville, 26 March 1969, box 26, file 1, Goldman Papers; letter to the

editor, *NR,* 6 (March 1969), by Neville attached to Neville to Goldman, 17 March 1969, ibid.

44. Goldman to Holt, 11 May 1970, box 19, file 6, Goldman Papers; Holt to Goldman, 8 April 1970, ibid.; Goldman to Holt, 5 February 1972, ibid.

45. Robin W. Winks, *Cloak and Gown: Scholars in the Secret War, 1939–1961* (New York: William Morrow and Co., 1987), 472, 473.

46. Holt to Goldman, 6 June 1980, box 19, file 6, Goldman Papers.

47. Ellen Fitzpatrick, *History's Memory: Writing America's Past, 1880–1980* (Cambridge: Harvard University Press, 2002), chap. 5.

48. James Weinstein and David Eakins, eds., *For a New America: Essays in History and Politics from "Studies on the Left," 1959–1967* (New York: Random House, 1970).

49. Gabriel Kolko, *The Triumph of Conservatism: A Reinterpretation of American History, 1900–1916* (New York: Free Press, 1963); James Weinstein, *The Corporate Ideal in the Liberal State, 1900–1918* (Boston: Beacon Press, 1968).

50. Jesse Lemisch, *On Active Service in War and Peace: Politics and Ideology in the American Historical Profession* (Toronto: New Hogstown Press, 1975), 110.

51. Howard Zinn, "The Politics of History in the Era of the Cold War," in Noam Chomsky et al., *The Cold War and the University: Toward an Intellectual History of the Postwar Years* (New York: The New Press, 1997), 57, 61.

52. Irwin Unger, "The New Left and American Historiography: Some Recent Trends in United States Historiography," *AHR,* 72 (July 1967), 1237–63; David Donald, review of *Towards a New Past: Dissenting Essays in American History,* ed. Barton J. Bernstein (New York: Vintage Books, 1969), *AHR,* 74 (December 1968), 533; Handlin, *Truth in History,* 103, 393, 403–15.

53. Staughton Lynd, "Intellectuals, the University and the Movement," in "Voices from the Past," *JAH,* 76 (September 1989), 484–85. Lemisch responded that intellectual work was itself of political significance.

54. Jonathan Wiener, "Radical Historians and the Crisis in American History, 1959–1980," *JAH,* 76 (September 1989), 422.

55. Maldwyn Jones, "Oscar Handlin," in Cunliffe and Winks, *Pastmasters,* 270.

56. Lemisch, *On Active Service in War and Peace.*

57. Jesse Lemisch, "The American Revolution Seen from the Bottom Up," in Bernstein, *Towards a New Past,* 4–6, 29; Jesse Lemisch, "Present-Mindedness Revisited," paper presented to the AHA Convention, Washington, DC, 1969, later revised and published as *On Active Service in War and Peace;* "Interview with Mike Wallace," *Radical History Review,* no. 79 (Winter 2001), 64.

58. Mari Jo Buhle, Ann G. Gordon, and Nancy Schrom, "Women in American Society: An Historical Contribution," *Radical America,* 5 (July–August 1971), 3–66.

59. Unger, "The New Left and American Historiography," 1263; Donald, review of *Towards a New Past,* 533; Handlin, *Truth in History,* 103, 393, 403–15; Ian Tyrrell, *The Absent Marx: Class Analysis and Liberal History in Twentieth-Century America* (Westport, CT: Greenwood Press, 1986), 126, 145–46.

60. Robert H. Zieger, "Workers and Scholars: Recent Trends in American Labor Historiography," *Labor History,* 13 (Spring 1972), 265, 257, 263; James Green, "Engaging in

People's History: The Massachusetts History Workshop," in Susan P. Benson, Stephen Brier, and Roy Rosenzweig, eds., *Presenting the Past: Essays on History and the Public* (Philadelphia: Temple University Press, 1986), 342, 347–48.

61. "Interview with Mike Wallace," 64. See the issues of *Radical History Review,* 1975–79, and Benson, Brier, and Rosenzweig, *Presenting the Past.*

62. Green, "Engaging in People's History," 345.

63. Fitzpatrick, *History's Memory,* epilogue.

64. For the continuity, see Rebecca Conrad, *Benjamin Shambaugh and the Intellectual Foundations of Public History* (Iowa City: University of Iowa Press, 2002).

65. See box 13, file "Committee on Historians and the Media, 1976–1978," Papers of the Organization of American Historians, Special Collections and Archives, Indiana University—Purdue University Library, Indianapolis.

66. Boyd Shafer to Alvin Eurich, 8 January 1960, box 669, file "Committee on TV, 1960," AHA Papers, LC.

67. Paul Ward, "Motion Pictures and the Study of History: The Possibilities of a Radical Change in Attitude and Practices," p. 2, box 701, file "Feature Film Correspondence," AHA Papers.

68. William H. McNeill, "The Historian and Historical Films," pp. 11–12, paper presented to the AHA Convention, Toronto, 28 December 1967, p. 12, box 703, file "Film Project, General Correspondence," AHA Papers. See also Henry Steele Commager, *The Commonwealth of Learning* (New York: Harper and Row, 1968), 252–67.

69. Robert Sklar, *Movie-Made America: A Cultural History of American Movies* (New York: Random House, 1975); Thomas Cripps, *Slow Fade to Black: The Negro in American Film, 1900–1942* (New York: Oxford University Press, 1977).

70. Peter C. Rollins, ed., *Hollywood as Historian: American Film in a Cultural Context* (Lexington: University of Kentucky, 1983), 258.

71. Hazel Whitman Hertzberg, "The Teaching of History," in Michael Kammen, ed., *The Past before Us: Contemporary Historical Writing in the United States* (Ithaca: Cornell University Press, 1980), 487–88, 494.

72. Naomi R. Lamoreaux, "Economic History and the Cliometric Revolution," in Anthony Molho and Gordon S. Wood, eds., *Imagined Histories: Americans Interpret the Past* (Princeton: Princeton University Press, 1998), 71–75.

73. Samuel Eliot Morison, "Faith of a Historian," *AHR,* 56 (January 1951), 272–73.

74. Allan Nevins, "Recent Progress of American Social History," *Journal of Economic and Business History,* 1 (May 1929), reprinted in Ray Allen Billington, comp., *Allan Nevins on History* (New York: Charles Scribner's Sons, 1975), 117–20.

75. One sees this in the legacy, e.g., of David Thelen, editor of the *Journal of American History* from 1985 to 1999.

INDEX

American Economic History Association, 31

American exceptionalism, 67, 69, 70, 136, 160

American Heritage, 66–67, 69, 71, 73, 244; and state and local history movement, 66, 226, 227–28

American Historical Association, 4; agricultural history, 166–67; amateur history, 49, 210, 213; and Beard, 115, 162; and College Entrance Examination Board, 124–25; and Commission on the Social Studies, 77, 121–22, 123–24, 124–25; conventions, 32, 79, 223–24; courts political allies after 2000, 261n.42; and curriculum internationalizing, 136; and federal government, 199–203, 244; and mass audience, 89, 94–95, 97; and Mississippi Valley Historical Association, 171, 219–20, 221, 252; and National Archives, 177–78, 182; National Board for Historical Service, 163; and National Education Association, 116; and New Deal measures, 184; and *New York Times* campaign, 133–34; Pamphlets on Teaching, 137; and park service work, 173, 174; and patriotic groups, 131, 217–18, 319n.44; and preservation/local history, 171; and radio, 90, 93–94, 104; rejects magazine of history, 44, 63–64, 65, 66; relativist controversy in, 53; and school curriculum, 119, 120, 128; and school teachers, 120, 137, 142–43; schools influence, 116–17; Society of American Historians and, 68; and specialization, 26, 28, 34, 38–39; and state and local history, 208, 209, 210, 211, 214, 216–17, 221, 222, 223, 224–25; and teacher educators, 147; Teaching Division, 251; and *Territorial Papers,* 178, 179; and war history, 186, 197; women's history in, 29; and world history, 148; World War II pamphlet series, 194–95. *See also* American Historical Association committees; Commission on the Social Studies; Radio Committee

American Historical Association, committees: Ad Hoc Committee on the Historian and the Federal Government, 199–200, 202–3, 205; Committee of Eight, 117; Committee of Five, 117; Committee of Seven, 117; Committee of Ten, 116–17, 143; Committee on American History in Schools and Colleges (Wesley committee), 134–35, 143; Committee on Hereditary Societies, 217; Committee on History and Education for Citizenship (Schafer committee), 118–19, 120; Committee on Historical Source Materials, 176, 184; Committee on Teaching, 120, 121, 148; Committee on the Historian and the Federal Government, 203, 244; The History Inquiry (Dawson committee), 120. *See also* Commission on the Social Studies; Radio Committee

American Historical Review, 17, 245; amateurs and, 215, 218; condemned by Nevins, 65; lack of film coverage, 87; and *Mississippi Valley Historical Review,* 28; reviewing fiction, 53

American history: advanced placement, 138; college curriculum, 136–37; compulsory in schools, 138–39, 140–41, 142; hegemonic position, 139–40; internationalizing, 136–37; national focus, 148, 149; and western civilization idea, 13

American History, An (Curti et al.), 36

American History in Schools and Colleges (Wesley), 134

American Humor (Rourke), 51

American Jewish Historical Society, 29

American Legion, 19, 69, 104, 115

American Library Association, 177, 220

American Nation (series), 47, 54

American Negro Slavery (Phillips), 165

American Pageant Association, 58, 60

American Story (radio program), 103

American studies, 37, 136–37

Anderson, Howard, 139, 146

Andrews, Charles McLean, 26, 27, 33, 39, 57, 59, 78; *Colonial Folkways,* 59

Angell, James R., 100, 102

Angle, Paul, 220

Annales, 233, 234, 235

Annals of American Sport (Krout), 59

Anthony Adverse (H. Allen), 48

anti-Communism, 115, 116, 198–99, 314n.85,

Fine, Benjamin, 111

Finn, Chester E., Jr., 112; *What Do Our 17-Year-Olds Know?*, 112

Fish, Carl, 57

Fitzgerald, John C., 155

Fitzpatrick, Ellen, 6

Flickinger, Floyd, 175

Fogel, Robert W., 166

Foley, Rev. M. J. 131

folklore, 180

Fonda, Henry, 106

Ford, Guy Stanton, 53, 103, 121, 134; and historians' war activities, 162, 163, 186, 190, 194; on specialization, 34, 36

Ford, Henry, 172

Ford, Worthington C., 215

Ford Foundation, 103

Forman, Henry, 77

Fort Duquesne, 175

Fox, Dixon Ryan, 61; on amateur history, 54; local history and, 208, 209, 218; on motion pictures, 78, 79, 81; and Pageant of America, 59; and radio, 91, 104, 105; on school history, 122; A History of American Life, 34–35, 60, 62

Fox, Richard W., 15–16

Fox Film Corporation, 82, 83

Fox-Genovese, Elizabeth, 15

fragmentation. *See* specialization

France, history in, 23–24, 233–35

Franklin, John Hope, 140, 141, 238

Fraser, Hugh Russell, 133

Freedom's Ferment (Tyler), 51

Freedom Train, 226

Freeman, Douglas, 50, 66

Fremont: Pathmarker of the West (Nevins), 85

Frisch, Michael, 17

Gabriel, Ralph, 56; American studies and, 37, 136; on audiovisual aids, 87; and Chronicles of America Photoplays, 79; and Pageant of America, 58–60; radio and, 94; as textbook writer, 145; war work, 192, 193; WORKS: *The Course of American Democratic Thought*, 194; *Exploring American History*, 145; *Main Currents in American History*, 194

Gambrill, J. Montgomery, 120, 146

Gans, Herbert, 22

Gates, Paul W., 168

Gateway to History, The (Nevins), 35

genealogy, 29, 212, 215, 224, 228, 230, 254

Genovese, Eugene, 11–12, 13, 15

geography, 21–22

George Washington Bicentennial Commission, 94

Ginn and Co., 140

Gipson, Lawrence Henry, 60

Glasgow, Robert, 57, 78

Glazer, Sydney, 91

Gleason, S. Everett, 188, 197, 202; *The World Crisis and American Foreign Policy*, 189

Goldman, Eric F., 237, 238, 239, 243–45; *The Crucial Decade*, 243; *Rendezvous with Destiny*, 239, 243; *The Tragedy of Lyndon Johnson*, 244, 245; *The World's History*, 244

Gone with the Wind (Mitchell), 48, 83

Gottschalk, Louis, 76, 83

Graham, Hugh, 156

Gramsci, Antonio, 6

Granbery, John C., 33–34

Grand Traverse Historical Society, 229

Gray, Lewis C., 165; *History of Agriculture in the Southern United States to 1860*, 165–66

Green, Constance McLaughlin, 199, 200, 224

Greene, Evarts B., 26, 57, 121, 163

Greene, Felix, 97

Greenfield, Kent R., 191, 196, 198, 199, 200, 202–3

Griffith, D. W., 76

Grover, Wayne C., 201

Growth of the American Republic, The (Morison and Commager), 56, 144–45

Guide to the Archives of the Government of the United States in Washington (Leland and Van Tyne), 177

guidebooks, historic, 180–81

Hacker, Louis M., 33, 229

Hamer, Philip, 307n.31

Hamerow, Theodore, 16

Hamlin, L. Belle, 216

Handlin, Oscar, 205, 237, 239, 247; *Truth in History*, 247

history-making. *See* useful history concept
historymobiles, 226
Hobsbawm, Eric, 98, 286n.86
Hofstadter, Richard, 147, 164, 205, 324n.9;
  public intellectual, 239, 240, 241–44;
  WORKS: *The Age of Reform*, 241; *The Amer-*
  ican Political Tradition and the Men Who
  Made It, 241; *The Progressive Historians*,
  242; *Social Darwinism in American*
  Thought, 325n.15
Holbrook, Stewart, 69
Holt, W. Stull, 113, 147, 149, 245, 266n.73
Houghton Mifflin Co., 194
Houghton, Louise, 231; *Our Debt to the Red*
  Man, 231
House, Edward M., 163
Howland, Hewitt, 49
Huber, Richard M., 37
Hughes, H. Stuart, 189
Hughes, Robert, 13–14
Hunt, Erling, 123, 125, 244
Hylan, John F., 131

Ickes, Harold, 172, 181
In Defence of History (Richard Evans), 17
Independent Historical Societies (Whitehill),
  229
Indiana University, 137
Industrial Worker, The (N. Ware), 30
Inquiry, The, 163–64, 185
Iowa Applied History Series, 159
Irish World and American Liberator, 131

Jackson, Barbara, 113
Jackson, Kenneth T., 2, 14, 112, 113
Jackson, W. Turrentine, 175
Jacoby, Russell, 16; *The Last Intellectuals*, 16
James, Marquis, 49, 66, 71, 104
Jameson, John Franklin: on amateurs, 52,
  218, 228, 270n.67; and archives, 177,
  182; compared to Marc Bloch, 233, 234;
  on general history, 34, 93; *Guide to the*
  Archives of the Government of the United
  States in Washington, 177; and *Mississippi*
  Valley Historical Review, 220; on "Negro
  history," 28; and patriotic societies, 218;
  and realist literature, 55; on schools
  committee, 121; and specialization, 27–
  29; and the state, 155; and state and local

history, 210–12, 214, 215, 216, 217, 228;
  war work, 162, 163, 185
Jeffersonian Heritage, The (Malone), 103
Jensen, Merrill, 238
jeremiad, 2–3, 254; comparisons, 23–24; de-
  bunked, 15; distinctions within, 12; ex-
  aggerated, 21; fears in 1950s, 39; in
  France, 235; and professionalization,
  16–17; in public history, 155; and read-
  ing audience, 43–45; recurrent, 252;
  and schools, 112–13, 139; and specializa-
  tion, 14
Johnson, Allen, 57, 59, 215
Johnson, Charles S., 308n.55
Johnson, Henry, 82, 119, 121, 146
Johnson, Lyndon, 244
Jones, Howard Mumford, 35
Jones, Maldwyn, 247
Josephson, Harold, 164
Josephson, Matthew, 50
Journal of American History, 17, 23, 245,
  320n.63
Journal of American History (National Histori-
  cal Society), 218
Journal of Southern History, 32, 174–75
Journal of the National Education Association,
  33
journalism, 49–52
Joyce, Patrick, 17
Judd, Charles H., 34

Kammen, Michael, 5, 6, 18, 71, 154, 155;
  Mystic Chords of Memory, 5
Kaplan, Louis, 35, 181
Keith Foundation, 99
Kellar, Herbert, 29, 30, 138, 167, 176, 184
Kelley, Robert, 23, 154
Kellogg, Louise, 172, 212, 318n.15
Kemble, John H., 192, 196
Kemper, John T., 190
Kennedy, David, 112
Kennedy, John F., 3, 206, 237, 238, 244, 245
Kepner, Tyler, 123, 125, 126, 140
Kersey, Vierling, 123
King, Ernest J., 192
Kirk, Russell, 14
Kirkendall, Richard, 251, 287n.5
Knowlton, Daniel, 80, 118, 146
Knox, Dudley, 189, 190, 191

American, 28; area, 28–29, 31–32; chronological, 31–32; church history, 28, 262n.13; comparisons, 22–24; criticisms differentiated, 33–35; defenses of, 35–37; ethnic history, 29; and historical practice, 31, 33–34, 38; Historical Society and, 8; in History Book Club, 68, 70; in literary studies, 35; and Progressive history, 8, 29–30; reading audience, 46; and relativism, 33; and schools, 113, 137; Scientific History welcomes, 27–29; social sciences and, 30; and state and local history, 209; and teaching, 137; thematic, 30–32; types, 25–26; university presses and, 239–40

Spirit Lake Massacre, The (Teakle), 231

sports history, 59

St. Augustine Restoration Program, 174

Stampp, Kenneth, 56, 192, 195, 238, 239

Stanford University, Institute of American History, 135–36, 137, 144

state, and historians, 5, 149; as audience, 7; in Cold War period, 199, 205–6, 244–45; historical analysis, 253; international comparisons, 155–56; in New Deal, 179, 181–84; and New Left, 246, 247, 248; and public history, 155–58; since 1970s, 249; structures in U.S., 209; in World War I, 162–63; in World War II, 185–86, 193, 194–95

state and local history, 157; academics and, 206–7, 223–24; and American Historical Association, 214–15, 216–17, 218–19, 224–26; as audience, 7; divided, 212–14, 218–19; gender issue, 212; international comparisons, 225–26, 232–35; isolation of, 317n.2; in Midwest, 213, 214; in Mississippi Valley, 211; and Mississippi Valley Historical Association, 219–20; national approach, 229; and New Deal, 175; in New England, 214; in Oklahoma, 223; patriotic/hereditary societies, 217–18; popularization movement, 209, 222–23, 226–29; preservation work, 172; professionalism in, 209, 210–12, 221–24, 228, 229, 230, 252; radio and, 91, 101; Scientific History practice and, 230–32; in South, 213, 214, 222, 224; and *Territorial Papers*, 179; in

Virginia, 224. *See also* American Association for State and Local History

State and Local History News, 226

State Historical Society of Iowa, 91, 159

State Historical Society of Wisconsin, 172, 221, 231

Stauffer, Alvin P., 174, 175, 183

Stavrianos, L. S., 148

Stephenson, Nathaniel, 78, 80, 81, 94, 278n.20

Sterns, Peter, 155

Stevens, Sylvester, 227

Stevenson, Adlai, 238

Still, Bayard, 190

Stine, O. C., 166, 167

Story behind the Headlines, The: beginnings, 93, 98–101; and *Cavalcade of America,* 104–7; decline of, 102–4; program content, 100, 101–2; as war work, 101–2

Strange Career of Jim Crow, The (C. Vann Woodward), 238, 240

Strassel, Kimberley, 21

Strayer, Joseph, 134, 148

Stryker, Sheldon, 22

Studies on the Left, 246

Sullivan, Mark, 49; *Our Times,* 49

Sulzberger, Iphigene Ochs, 112

Sumner, Helen, 159

Survey of Federal Records, 307n.31

synthesis: calls for, 34; combats specialization, 15–16; cooperative publications, 34–35; interdisciplinary, 36–37; as Progressive issue, 253; public culture concept, 15; textbooks as, 36

Tarr, Joel, 155

Taylor, Henry C., 165, 166

teacher educators, 121, 125, 143, 146–47

teaching: and films, 82, 85, 86; and radio, 91–92; and specialization, 38–39; university, 144, 147–48

Teakle, Thomas, 231; *The Spirit Lake Massacre,* 231

Teggart, Frederick, 26

television: as audience, 7; cable, 251; *Cavalcade of America* on, 104; Columbus documentary, 14; historians and, 87, 238, 244, 249, 250, 251; history on, 2, 3; impact in 1950s, 71; as mass media chal-

Made in the USA
Lexington, KY
02 June 2017